THE IMPACT OF JESUS OF NAZARETH

Historical, Theological, and Pastoral Perspectives

VOLUME 1
HISTORICAL
AND THEOLOGICAL
STUDIES

SCD Press
2020

CGAR SERIES, NO 1

The Impact of Jesus of Nazareth:
Historical, Theological, And Pastoral Perspectives

Volume 1 : Historical and Theological Studies
CGAR Series, No 1
Edited by Peter G. Bolt and James R. Harrison

© SCD Press and Contributors 2020

SCD Press
PO Box 1882
Macquarie Park NSW 2113
scdpress@scd.edu.au

ISBN-13: 978-1-925730-13-5 (Paperback)
ISBN-13: 978-1-925730-14-2 (E-book)

Cover design and typesetting by Lankshear Design.

THE IMPACT OF JESUS OF NAZARETH

Historical, Theological, and Pastoral Perspectives

VOLUME 1
HISTORICAL
AND THEOLOGICAL
STUDIES

SCD Press
2020

CGAR SERIES, NO 1

CGAR Series:

1. Peter G. Bolt & James R. Harrison (eds.), *The Impact of Jesus of Nazareth: Historical, Theological, and Pastoral Perspectives.* Vol. 1: *Historical and Theological Studies* (Macquarie Park, NSW: SCD Press, 2020).

2. Peter G. Bolt & James R. Harrison (eds.), *The Impact of Jesus of Nazareth: Historical, Theological, and Pastoral Perspectives.* Vol. 2: *Social and Pastoral Studies* (Macquarie Park, NSW: SCD Press, forthcoming).

CONTRIBUTORS

Darrell L. Bock is Senior Research Professor of New Testament Studies at Dallas Theological Seminary in Dallas, Texas. He also serves as Executive Director of Cultural Engagement for the Seminary's Center for Christian Leadership. His special fields of study involve hermeneutics, the use of the Old Testament in the New, Luke-Acts, the historical Jesus, Gospel studies and the integration of theology and culture. He has served on the board of Chosen People Ministries for over a decade and also serves on the board at Wheaton College. He is a graduate of the University of Texas (B.A.), Dallas Theological Seminary (Th.M.), and the University of Aberdeen (Ph.D.). He has had four annual stints of postdoctoral study at the University of Tübingen, the second through fourth as an Alexander von Humboldt scholar (1989-90, 1995-96, 2004-05, 2010-2011). He also serves as elder emeritus at Trinity Fellowship Church in Richardson, Texas, is a writer for *Christianity Today*, served as President of the Evangelical Theological Society for the year 2000-2001, and has authored over forty books, including a New York Times Best Seller in non-fiction and award winning commentaries on Luke and Ephesians. He is married to Sally and has three married children (two daughters and a son), three grandsons and a granddaughter.

Peter G. Bolt is the Academic Director of the Sydney College of Divinity, and the Director of the SCD Centre for Gospels & Acts Research and the Editor of *Journal of Gospels and Acts Research*. A graduate of Moore College, Australian College of Theology, Macquarie University, and King's College London, he is a New Testament scholar with research interests in the Gospels and Acts, Biblical Theology, magic and demonology, eschatology, the earliest Christian missionary movement, and the intersection between the New Testament and the Graeco-Roman world. He has published *Jesus' Defeat of Death. Persuading Mark's Early Readers* (Cambridge, 2003, 2008); *The Cross from a Distance. Atonement in Mark's Gospel* (IVP, 2004); (with Sharon Beekmann), *Silencing Satan: A Handbook of Biblical Demonology* (Wipf & Stock, 2011); and the popular-level *Living With* *the Underworld* (Matthias Media, 2007); and *A Light Shining in Our Darkness. Reading Matthew Today* (Acorn Press, 2014).

Chris Booth is an Australian Army Chaplain to the 3rd Combat Engineer Regiment, Townsville, Queensland. He holds a BA in Politics and History from the Royal Military College, Duntroon. Upon graduation, he served as an officer in the Ordnance Corps of the Australian Army, deployed for a time in Afghanistan. After deciding to become a Chaplain, he gained a BD from Moore College, Sydney, and served as Assistant Minister at Guildford Anglican Church, before taking up his position in Townsville.

Alan Cadwallader is Research Professor at the Centre for Public and Contextual Theology. He has published extensively on the site of ancient Colossae and is currently completing an Earth Bible commentary on the Gospel of Mark. His latest publication is *The Politics of the Revised Version*.

Aaron Chidgzey is is the Director of Online Learning at Vose Seminary in Perth, as well as lecturing in systematic theology, New Testament, and church history. His research interests particularly revolve around the theological implications of Jesus' resurrection, Wolfhart Pannenberg, and N.T. Wright, having recently completed his Ph.D. at Murdoch University.

John A. Davies is Principal Emeritus of Christ College, Sydney, and a Research Associate of the Sydney College of Divinity. He is the author of *A Royal Priesthood* (2004), *A Study Commentary on 1 Kings* (2012), *Unless Someone Shows Me* (2015), *Lift Up Your Heads* (2018) and *Heaven Ain't Goin' There: A Down-to-Earth Look at Eternal Life* (2019).

James R. Harrison studied Ancient History at Macquarie University and graduated from the doctoral program in 1997. Professor Harrison, FAHA, is the Research Director at the Sydney College of Divinity. His recent monographs include *Paul and the Imperial Authorities at Thessalonica and Rome* (Mohr Siebeck, 2011), *Paul and the Ancient Celebrity Circuit* (Mohr Siebeck, 2019), and *Reading Romans with Roman Eyes* (Lexington/Fortress, 2020). He is also the chief editor of *New Documents Illustrating the History of Early Christianity Vols. 11-15* (forthcoming), co-editor with L. L. Welborn of *The First Urban Churches Vols. 1-6* (SBL, 2015-2020; Vols. 7-9 forthcoming 2021-2023), and is editor of the Cascade collection of E. A. Judge, *The Conflict of Cultures: The Legacy of Paul's Thought Today* (Cascade, 2019).

Benjamin Ho completed his BD at Moore College, Sydney in 2008. His final year project examined the theme of unbelief in John's Gospel. Ben is currently the Senior Pastor at St Lucia Evangelical Church having been part of the church for 30 years and pastoring it for 11.

Dr Lyn M. Kidson is a lecturer in New Testament at Alphacrucis College, specialising in the Pastoral Epistles. Her PhD dissertation will be available in 2020 through Mohr Siebeck under the title, *Persuading Shipwrecked Men: Rhetorical Strategies in 1 Timothy 1* (WUNT series). She has published a number of book chapters and articles on a range of topics including early Christianity and numismatics.

Francis J. Moloney, SDB, AM, FAHA, joined the Salesians of Don Bosco in 1959 and was ordained a Priest in 1970. He has studied at Melbourne University, the Salesian Pontifical University, the Pontifical Biblical Institute, both in Rome, and at the University of Oxford (D. Phil.: 1976). Foundation Professor of Theology at Australian Catholic University (1994–1999), Dean and Professor of New Testament at the Catholic University of America (1999–2005), he is a Member or the Order of Australia (AM), and a Fellow of the Australian Academy of the Humanities (FAHA). The author of many books and shorter studies, he is currently a Senior Professorial Fellow at the Catholic Theological College in Melbourne, Australia, part of the ecumenical University of Divinity.

Willis Salier, Principal, Youthworks College, Sydney. Bill has had a long term interest in the Fourth Gospel stemming from his PhD, *The Rhetorical Impact of the semeia in the Gospel of John* (Mohr Siebeck, 2004). This interest has been expressed in a series of thematic studies in John exploring the temple, the obedience of the Son, Satan, and the relationship of the Imperial cult to the presentation of Jesus. He has branched out into the Johannine epistles, teaching at a Masters level. More recently his research interests have been in the area of spiritual formation in theological education.

Chris Seglenieks teaches New Testament and Greek at the Bible College of South Australia. He has published several articles on faith and the Gospel of John, and his book *Johannine Belief and Graeco-Roman Devotion* will be published with Mohr Siebeck in 2020.

Debra Snoddy BATh (Hons) MFSS MTh STL PhD STD lectures in Biblical Studies at Catholic Institute of Sydney in Strathfield, NSW. She previously lectured in Ireland at Carlow College, Carlow, and All Hallows College, Dublin. Her doctoral work at Catholic University of Louvain, Belgium, was in the Gospel of John. Debra is a member of the Research Group for the Study of the Johannine and Pauline Literature at the Faculty of Theology of KULeuven, Belgium as well as the European Biblical Association and the Australian Catholic Biblical Association. Publications include the co-authoring of *Parish Pastoral Councils: A Formation Manual* (Dublin: Veritas, 2010) as well as articles and book chapters for national and international publications.

Robert Tilley lectures in Biblical Studies at the Catholic Institute of Sydney. His most recent publication is 'Crisis? What Crisis? Gospel Criticism and the Ideological use of an Illiterate Jesus Movement' in the *Journal of Gospels and Acts Research* vol.3, 2019. He is currently working on a research project on the impact of usury on biblical exegesis in the Late Second Temple Period.

Wendy Turnour is currently undertaking doctoral studies at the Sydney College of Divinity. She has a background in Social Work, and voluntary work while parenting four children together with her husband, Matthew. Since 2005, she has served as a Pastor at Whitehill Church of Christ, Ipswich.

CONTENTS

1. Peter Bolt, *Introduction* 1

Historical and Theological Studies

2. Darrell Bock, *What Got Jesus into Trouble? Understanding the Significance of Jesus' Ministry by Looking at Its Jewish Context: Part One— The Irritant Events* 9

3. John Davies, *Nonverbal Responses to Jesus in the Gospels* 39

4. Aaron Chidgzey, *Transcending Categories: The Impact of the Resurrection of Jesus of Nazareth* 57

5. Peter Bolt, *Synoptic Comparison & Oral History: A South Pacific Analogy* 85

6. James Harrison, *The Historical Jesus as Social Critic: A Comparison of 'Q' Traditions (Matt 5:43-48; Lk 6:27-36)* 107

7. Robert Tilley, *Usury and the Interpretation of the Sacred Text* 149

Matthew

8. Wendy Turnour, *The Hermeneutical Significance of the 'Double Love Commandments' in Matthew's Gospel* 181

9. Chris Booth, *The Now and Not Yet of Seeing Jesus of Nazareth. Reading Matthew's Gospel as Narrative* 217

Mark

10. Alan Cadwallader, *Sometimes One Word Makes a World of Difference: A Return to the Origins of Mark's Gospel (Mark 1:38)*. 233

John

11. Francis J. Moloney, *The Fourth Gospel and the Beginnings of Jesus' Ministry* 267

12. Lyn Kidson, *The Woman at the Well, Jesus, and Prejudice in Samaria (John 4:3–43)* 289

13. Debra Snoddy, *Johannine Altruism: A Biblical Tonic for the Randian Plague*............................ 307

14. Chris Seglenieks, *The Johannine Messiah and the Isaianic Servant: Identity and Response*......................... 325

15. Willis (Bill) H. Salier & Benjamin Ho, *John: The Gospel of Unbelief* 347

CHAPTER 1

Introduction

Peter Bolt

Despite his relatively short life and his tragic death, Jesus of Nazareth made a profound impact upon the first-century Graeco-Roman world. Almost immediately after he died, the 'good news' about him was first announced, only to spread like a tidal wave across that world, before eventually transforming it almost entirely. As that impact continued, the new-found freedoms discovered in the risen Son (cf. John 8:36) and proclaimed to Jew and Gentile alike (e.g. Luke 4:18; Gal 2:4; 5:13), took concrete shape in the freedoms at the core of Western Civilization. Wherever his heritage is celebrated and remembered, Jesus of Nazareth continues to make an impact.

Writing from a variety of perspectives, the essays in *The Impact of Jesus*, volumes 1 and 2, explore the impact of Jesus of Nazareth on his own and subsequent times. Volume 1 collects historical and theological essays.

In the first part of a study to be completed in volume 2, Darrell Bock works through the nature of Jesus' ministry to show what initially created the skeptical approach to him taken by the leaders of his day. Arguing that the narrative-line of the Gospels has a core historical credibility, Bock assembles a cluster of 'minor irritants' about Jesus, that combined to provoke his opponents to the skeptical reaction that eventually spelled his demise.

John Davies examines the Gospels for non-verbal responses to Jesus, whether gestures, indications of emotion, or interpersonal space, and whether positive or negatively evoked. Jesus exuded authority, but he appealed to some and threaten others. Together with people's verbal expressions, the Gospels record nonverbal responses which highlight the impact Jesus had on the crowds, on his followers, and on his opponents. These expressions of suspicion, astonishment, gratitude, adoration, mockery, and the like, are suggestive of eyewitness testimony. But in any case, the Gospel writers use them as part of their depiction of the character of Jesus' messianic identity and through their impact, readers are invited to consider their own response to him.

The resurrection of Jesus is understandably a hotly contested issue. After surveying the general trends within scholarship on the resurrection, Aaron Chidgzey argues that most interpretations emphasize either continuous or discontinuous elements, at the expense of the other. That is, either the historical, literal, and material, or the eschatological (supra-historical), metaphorical, or immaterial elements of the resurrection are highlighted. Jewish eschatological notions of resurrection rarely referred to a post-mortem re-embodiment of individual bodies, interacted in a mutually-conditioning fashion with the broader eschatological motifs of redemption of relationship, the re-creation of the present created order, and the dispensation of divine justice. The New Testament similarly portrays Jesus' resurrection: as the inauguration of the new eschatological age – the unification of heaven and earth. As such, Jesus' resurrection cannot be reduced to a mere re-embodiment, and thus cannot be restricted to emphasizing either its continuous or discontinuous elements, but must incorporate both, transcending and unifying both categories. As their early hearers recognized, the earliest Christians proclaimed the remarkable message that 'in Jesus, the resurrection of the dead' (Acts 4:2).

In view of the well-established practice of synoptic comparison of written Gospels, with the assumption of underlying reports circulating orally, Peter Bolt's essay provides an analogy from the history of the South Pacific. The essay examines three independent written reports of a killing spree that took place on Rarotonga in August 1814, with a view to discerning the oral testimony that lay behind them. Each has its own bias, and each has a different relationship to eyewitness reports. Nevertheless, it remains possible to gain an historical understanding of what happened, through discerning the underlying sources to draw a coherent picture.

James Harrison and Robert Tilley, each in their own way, explore Jesus' interaction with prevailing understandings and systems of economics. As a social critic of the Graeco-Roman reciprocity system, Jesus proposed instead a communal model of the servant-benefactor who even has the enemy in view (Harrison). As an inheritor of the Jewish Law, he countered the usury of a system of individual status and financial gain with a 'heavenly usury' which is both communal and God-honouring (Tilley). Both essays have lessons that reach beyond the first century, that impact not only on the use of money, but also —as hinted at, somewhat tantalisingly, by Tilley—the reading of the Bible in the modern world.

Two essays deal with Matthew's Gospel. Wendy Turnour argues that Jesus' double love command (love of God and neighbour), provide a hermeneutical key to the theological reading of the Gospel. This key opens the door to a God-centred, relational and communal reading of Jesus' life, death, and resurrection, with major implications for the contemporary praxis of Christian discipleship. Adopting a reader-response stance, Chris Booth provides close readings of Matthew's Transfiguration and Resurrection narratives, with a special focus on Matthew's use of vision, also in the service of understanding Matthew's goal of making disciples, both then and now.

In a sharply focused but wide-ranging essay, Alan Cadwallader isolates one Markan *hapax legomenon*, κωμόπολις, and explores its potential contribution to larger questions. When the scribal textual tradition is examined the traditions associated with the west appear ignorant of the word. Its use in Josephus and earlier ancient literature not only clarifies its meaning, but also reinforces its use in the east. The Byzantine use of the term is an appropriation from earlier days. The meaning of the word arising from the survey not only illuminates Mark 1:38, but, being eastern, it provides evidence relevant to the question of the Gospel's provenance.

The volume closes with five essays on the Gospel of John. After decades of studying John, Francis Moloney re-opens the question of its value as a historical source for Jesus of Nazareth. Most who have been involved in the three quests for the historical Jesus have dismissed the Fourth Gospel as a possible source for the authentic words and works of Jesus. Taking as a point of departure C.H. Dodd's argument that the Gospel of John draws on independent traditions often closely related to those of the Synoptics, Moloney explores whether the Gospel of John might provide a better framework for some episodes in Jesus' story. Since this is acknowledged for the end of this ministry, the question is explored for its beginning. Through an examination of the Johannine material on John the Baptist, the vocation of the earliest disciples, and Jesus' action in the temple, potentially genuine historical reminiscences are uncovered and a framework for the beginning of Jesus' ministry is suggested.

In another wide-ranging essay, Lyn Kidson seeks to illuminate the social situation of the Samaritan woman who met Jesus by the well. It is commonly assumed that John's Gospel portrays her as a sinner, or at least as compromised by a relationship with a man described as 'not your husband'. This assumption echoes ancient prejudices, for both Romans and Jews characterised women who did not fit neatly into the traditional family scheme as sexually promiscuous. After investigating the possibilities in regard to the woman's multiple marriages in the context of Roman Palestine, as well as various impediments that lay in the way of her marrying, the story becomes one of poverty and prejudice in regards to gender, race, and social dislocation.

Debra Snoddy sharply contrasts the particular brand of individualism proposed by Ayn Rand, whose 'virtue in selfishness' philosophy despised the notion of altruism, with the kind of altruism evident in John's portrayal of Jesus of Nazareth. A proper kind of altruism involves a disinterested (unselfish) empathy, and, for John, this is anchored in the *agápē* love that defines Christian life and teaching. This is 'love centred in moral preference based on a divine imperative', and it promotes an active engagement with the world. This is the love of Christ for us, and the love which binds disciples to God and opens God's children up to the indwelling of the Father, Son and Holy Spirit. Far from being destructive of our humanity (as Rand would have it), this altruism based on the divine love permits us 'to be fully human in an increasingly inhuman world'.

Recognising that the Gospel of John draws upon a rich Old

Testament background to portray the identity of Jesus, Chris Seglenieks argues that the connections between the Gospel and the Passover have been overplayed. Instead, the book of Isaiah is critical for understanding Jesus' identity, for it shows Jesus is not only the Servant of God, but that he is himself divine. The Isaianic background is also significant for understanding the response to Jesus John aims to evoke (John 20:31). The God of Isaiah called for belief and witness, and so too does the Johannine Jesus.

John's Gospel is clearly concerned with encouraging belief that leads to life, but Willis (Bill) Salier and Benjamin Ho argue that this purpose is supported by a corresponding theme of unbelief. Through an examination of key words and characters, especially the composite characters of 'the Jews' and 'the world', the authors expose John's presentation of the phenomenon of unbelief in response to Jesus' ministry. Exploring the character, manner, motivation, and consequences of unbelief reveals how it serves John's overall positive presentation of Jesus as the Christ, the Son of God, so that belief in his name might lead to life.

While the historical side of these essays grounds the discussion in the impact Jesus made in the first-century, their theological reflections point us towards the remarkable impact for people of subsequent ages, whether actual or potential.

HISTORICAL AND THEOLOGICAL STUDIES

CHAPTER 2

What Got Jesus into Trouble? Understanding the Significance of Jesus' Ministry by Looking at Its Jewish Context: Part One—The Irritant Events

Darrell L. Bock

Abstract

The following study of Jesus comes in two parts. Part one will work through the nature of Jesus' ministry to show what initially created the skeptical approach leaders took to him. The second (in volume 2) will focus on events at his ministry's close and examine what led to his death. These final events build on the emergence of a skeptical reaction to Jesus that the first set of events created. They show the 'narrative' line the Gospels present about Jesus. We argue that narrative line has a core historical credibility.

Understanding the life of Jesus generally takes two tacks. One emphasizes a focus moving unit by unit and applying criteria of authenticity, standards which are much discussed.[1] One thinks of John Meier's Herculean and still incomplete, multi-decade effort. Another, more recent approach has been to focus on the coherence of an overall, synthetic understanding of the Jesus story. N. T. Wright's project may be the most well-known example of the latter, although the work of Ben

---

1   A critique of this approach is Keith & LeDonne, *Jesus, Criteria, and the Demise of Authenticity*. See Bock & Komoszewski, *Jesus, Skepticism and the Problem of History*.

Meyer also fits here.[2] Is there a way to try and fuse these two approaches? Could such a fusion protect against weaknesses of each of the two tacks? That is what I shall try to sketch in these short essays. In doing so I will also look for what might be called a 'middle' Jesus, a Jesus who represents a transition from roots in Judaism to what emerged later in the early church of the disciples as reflected in our earliest Christian sources.[3] Perhaps such a 'middle' Jesus helps to clear the way across Lessing's famous, supposedly uncrossable ditch, a historical Jesus who makes sense of the Christ of faith.

A key to appreciating the survey we are about to undertake is to see Jesus' ministry as a connected unit. This is what I mean by a narrative read of the Jesus account. Actions in one area also reflect and refract off of activity in another.

One of the weaknesses of the unit by unit approach is that it severs these links. Such critics take the Jesus story and cut it up into pieces of individual traditional units, one of the negative results of form critical assumptions about the tradition. This atomistic investigation attempts to 'divide and conquer' by suggesting that a given piece of evidence can only be pushed to say so much about Jesus. By disconnecting the single strand of action from others, the full impact of all Jesus did and how it correlates can be lost, as pieces and actions become isolated from one another, largely lacking any context. We argue here for a more synthetic understanding of what Jesus did and said. We hope to show the benefit of fitting the pieces together. In doing so, however, we shall not assume the historicity of the material but will try to argue for its historical likelihood before putting it to use. For this step we shall appeal to the criteria, as well as to other factors tied to the first century background. We shall keep a special eye on evidence of transition or continuum with

---

2   Meyer, *Aims of Jesus*; Wright, *Jesus and the Victory of God*.
3   This description acknowledges the application of such a description to Judaism by Gabriele Boccaccini in his overview of the history of Jewish thought, *Middle Judaism*. For him the description represents the move from ancient Judaism to rabbinic Judaism in the same period of intense change. This essay also owes a debt to the work of seeking a continuum approach to Jesus. See Holmén, *Jesus from Judaism to Christianity*.

Judaism, where Jesus appears as a transitional figure in a development moving from Second Temple Judaism into a new sect of Judaism possessing its own distinctive elements. Is it possible that a 'middle' Jesus reflects an authentic figure of transition?

I hope to consider many factors that contributed to official irritation with Jesus that sets the backdrop for his ultimate fate on the cross. Is there evidence that such irritants also share this 'middle' Jesus picture? Might such a 'middle' position suggest that these irritants are authentic, at least in the gist of what they represent? In addition, did such factors combine to lead to full-fledged opposition against Jesus? Did these irritants culminate in Jesus being brought before Pilate sometime in the early thirties? Some of these factors serve as minor irritants that produced initial discomfort and suspicion that evolved into full blown skepticism about him. Others, particularly a series of events in the last portion of his ministry, were seen as challenges that could not be ignored, reflecting major disagreements and incidents. Those latter events will be the focus of part two of this study. We focus initially on events that had a public dimension to them, in most cases involving those who could help to decide how Jesus should be regarded. Any sequence of these events is not so much in view as their presence by the time we get to the end of Jesus' career. They set the stage for the final events in his ministry regardless of their sequential order.

1. Getting into Trouble: Minor Irritants Leading to Opposition

Minor Irritant 1: Association with Tax Collectors and Sinners.

The first cause of tension comes from Jesus' welcome of tax collectors and sinners. The opening up to the fringe of society stood in contrast to the kind of separatism of the Qumran community of the Dead Sea, as well as the emphasis on moral purity and issues of cleanliness tied to the Pharisees. It may even eventually have stepped on the more elitist, social orientation of the Sadducees, although it is not clear they were engaged with Jesus at the earlier points in his work and they would have supported the collection of taxes unlike many other Jews.

The issue of a distinction between the righteous and sinners is built into the core of Jewish thinking about faith, purity, and sin. Even access to the Temple was restricted to those who were clean and in some cases without defect. E. P. Sanders argues for this element of Jesus' work as an irritant in his *Jesus and Judaism*.[4] Numerous texts from various source levels point to this feature of Jesus' ministry (Mk. = Mark 2:13–17= Matthew 9:9–13=Luke 5:27–32; Mark 7:24–30=Matthew 15:21–28; L = Luke 18:13; 19:7; 7:36–50; 10:29–37; Luke 19:1–10; Q = Matthew 11:19=Luke 7:34). The collection of texts shows the theme is multiply-attested or have a deep layer of memory to use a term Sean Winter introduced to me at the SCD Historical Jesus Conference in Sydney, Australia, in 2017. This theme appears repeatedly in more than one layer of the Gospel tradition. It also is in multiple forms as parables, sayings, and narratives are involved. All of this points to authenticity at a historical level. Boring adds the note in support for authenticity that the detail about the location of the tax collector booth in Capernaum also points to an early tradition, before this Galilean region came under the authority of Philip in 39 C.E.[5] No account makes the point more vividly in terms of Jesus' motivation than the anointing by the sinful woman in Luke 7:36–50. The reaction of the hosting Pharisee to the woman's seemingly offensive action speaks to a difference in perspective between Jesus' host and the teacher who accepts the publicly shocking action. Jesus is suggesting that God is open to accepting a wide array of people, if they will turn to him and respond to his grace, which is the point of the parable he tells within the scene (7:41–47). The pronouncement of Mark 2:17 coheres with this understanding. Jesus, like a physician, had come to deal especially with the spiritually sick, to bring them to a place of healing.

Some see concern about proper rules regarding purity in this Mark 2:17 scene, much like what appears in Mark 7:1–23.[6] Klauwens goes

---

4   Sanders, *Jesus and Judaism*, 204–207.
5   Boring, *Mark*, 80 n. 26.
6   Klawans, 'Moral and Ritual Purity', 281, who notes that Mark 2:17, like Mark 7, is not a strict contrast, but a prioritized emphasis. Boring, *Mark*, 82, notes the purity view as one of two options here. Jesus is seen as walking into a situation of likely impurity. The other option is that such people were simply seen as sinners and as unconcerned about God and his standards, as well as his people. The remarks about Jesus' teaching apply no matter which option is taken. Such people were seen as unacceptable to God, or at least unwelcome in their current state.

on to argue the ambiguity in the statement of Mark 7 is for its possible historicity. The same ambiguity applies to Mark 2, especially as it includes a reference to the Pharisees as 'righteous and healthy' who in the later church were seen as opponents and unrighteous. There is a transitional feel to this text's portrayal of Pharisees and scribes. Klawans next notes that at Qumran there was not a clear distinction between moral and ritual purity as we often see in the rabbis, probably because of the loss of the temple. At Qumran, he argues that ritual purity was often associated with sin; rather than being distinct from it because it was associated with cleanliness for worship, a category alongside and between sin and personal righteousness. He appeals to Rule of the Community 2:25–3:6; 4:9–11; 5:13–14, 18–19; 6:24–26; 8:16–18, and 4Q512 (Purification Liturgy) 29–32, lines 8–10. Klawans makes the case that for the rabbis, the heirs of Pharisaism, there was a distinction, but that they regarded both ritual and ethical purity as equally important. Judaism was not unified. Jesus fits into this backdrop but with his own take. His position expresses itself with some ambiguity with regard to the position of those questioning him (at least initially where he calls the Pharisees righteous). Yet his remarks also operate in a manner distinct from how the early church expressed itself on vices and the unrighteous (1 Cor. 6:9–11; Eph. 5:5–6). In some contexts, Jesus highlights the vice that is unrighteousness; the early church pointed to groups that were unrighteous.

What does this event show? It shows someone making a judgment about who is acceptable to God and who is able to enter into his blessing, an acceptance that does not require any stop at the temple or any offer of sacrifices. This is the remark of a prophet at the least, if not one bearing more authority. A. J. Levine says it this way as she discusses the way similar texts like the Good Samaritan or the Tax Collector and the Pharisee work. These passages had a sting to them before there was two thousand years of good public relations for tax collectors and Samaritans:

> When the parable is heard with first-century Jewish ears, however, the response is by no means so simple. The idea that a tax collector would receive approval over a Pharisee should,

instead, shock. To see the tax collector as justified is tantamount to a member of the local population claiming that an agent of a foreign, invading government, an agent whose job it is to take money from the local population and funnel it to the capital of the invading empire, is the one to be admired and to serve as a moral exemplar.[7]

Jesus is indicating who can belong to God's community in surprising ways as he explains how the righteousness that transforms is received. His claim is that such righteousness can come to anyone, but not on the basis of our own strength, effort or social role. Rather it comes in grateful response to an invitation, received as God's grace. So grace leads to righteousness, not righteousness to grace. Jesus as one called to heal and preach the gospel of the kingdom defines who can have access to God's grace on the basis of his own teaching, authority, and ultimately, his person. This claim of authority over righteousness and forgiveness was an irritant to the Jewish leadership as their reaction in the similarly directed scene of Luke 7:48–50 shows. The woman was not asked to make individual restitution in order to receive forgiveness, but Jesus offered her forgiveness directly. That direct approach brought initial reaction against him.

This was different from many strands of Judaism that required restitution and repentance. The principle of paying back an extra 'fifth' came from Leviticus 6:1–5. Baba Qamma 9.6 in the Mishnah makes the point:

> [If the thief] paid him back the principal but did not pay the added fifth, [if the victim] forgave him the value of the principal but did not forgive him the value of the added fifth, [if] he forgave him for this and for that, except for something less a perutah out of the principal, he need not take it back to him.

---

[7] Levine, *The Misunderstood Jew*, 38. Her later defense of the prayer of the Pharisee as being Luke's anti-Jewish construction is not a likely explanation for this text. She claims that the Pharisee's prayer is a 'there I go but for the grace of God' prayer. However, this fails to see the prayer's distortion of the praise psalm form where one thanks God for what the deity has done, not for what one has done for God.

> [If] he [the thief] gave him back the added fifth and did not hand over the principal. [If the victim] forgave him the added fifth but did not forgive him the principal, forgave him for this and for that, except for an amount of the principal that added up to a perutah, then he has to go after him [to make restitution, wherever he may be].

In the same work, Baba Metzia 4.8 says, 'He who steals from his fellow that which is worth a perutah and takes a [false] oath to him [when he wishes to confess and effect restitution] adds a fifth'. The first passage shows that forgiveness of the 'fifth' does not nullify the need to make financial restitution of the principle. The second shows that to lie about the promise of restitution is grounds to add to the restitution required.

Jesus' direct declaration might well have raised the question over who has the right to fiddle with God's Law. Now one may object that these Mishnaic texts have to do with how people treat other people, but the point is that this principle was grounded in making restitution for any act of wrongdoing. Restitution was the principle on which sacrifice was built, where sin cost and an act of restitution was required before God. Later this restitution, the church will claim, is what Jesus paid (Rom. 3:21–31; Heb. 8–10).

In addition, in Judaism, how one treats others is tied to how one responds to God. Many strands of Judaism saw a relationship between how one relates to God and to others as the Ten Words shows in its two sections and as the description of Elijah as a prophet of restoration indicates (Mal. 4:5–6). The Jewish religious leaders perceived Jesus as reconfiguring such a priority, a cause of potential irritation to those who wanted to be sure a distinction would remain between the righteous and sinners.[8]

Minor Irritant 2: Forgiveness of Sins

Two texts are important with regard to Jesus' claim to forgive sins. They connect to the previous category of how Jesus treated sinners as well.

---

8   The text does not show what Jesus thinks of sacrifice here. The mere direct act would be the irritant.

In both Mark 2:1–12 and par. and in Luke 7:36–50, Jesus forgives sins. This concept is mildly multiply-attested in terms of authenticity with its appearance in a tradition reflected in Mark and one that Luke alone uses. In both places the instant reaction is the same by the Jewish theologians present. They object, 'Who can forgive sins but God?'

The best we can tell there are only two potential parallels to this kind of an act in Judaism. One is in 2 Sam. 12:13, where Nathan as a prophet declares to David, 'The Lord has taken away your sin'. The second is a text found at Qumran known as 4QPrNab (=4Q242) 1.4. In this work known as the *Prayer of Nabonidus*, an exorcist is said to have forgiven sin. No rabbinic texts make such an association. Forgiveness is seen as God's business. Nathan merely announces what God has done with a direct mention of God that Jesus' statement lacks. This is also in contrast to such claims in the early church where forgiveness in the name of Jesus or variations on such ideas appear. The *Nabonidus* text is fragmentary and possesses two approaches to its unusual content. First, it may simply summarize the impact of what the exorcist helps to facilitate on the basis of a principle explicitly expressed later in the Jewish Talmud of the fifth century B.C.E, 'No one gets up from his sickbed until all his sins are forgiven'. (*Nedarim* 41[a]). On the second view, the text shows the exorcist's powerful, more direct authority. In this case, it is an exceptional text for a strictly Jewish context. What is also important to note is that this text is a report of the result of the exorcist's act either way it is read. By contrast, Jesus declares sins forgiven directly. This is not a narrator's note. Now Jesus does say, 'your sins are forgiven' with a passive verb, suggesting God does the forgiving, since this remark is often read as a 'divine' passive. However, in Mark 2:10 Jesus says far more than this when he says, 'That you might know that the Son of Man has authority on earth to forgive sins, I say to you get up and walk'. The lack of explicit mention of God and the 'team' authority ministry this implies in directly declaring a forgiveness God permits would have been an irritant to Jewish sensibilities about God's unique glory and authority over sin. There is more than an interpretive dispute here; the issue is authority.

In this event Jesus links an act that cannot be seen (forgiveness) with an act that can and that requires God's work (healing a paralytic). God is said to act in response to Jesus' initiative in a text where the authority Jesus claims is his own as Son of Man. This is precisely the reverse of what one would expect in terms of the declaration of authority to forgive. Yes, God has given authority to forgive sins, but such authority now comes through the Son of Man. This is Jesus' favorite name for himself, a position Jesus will ultimately associate with the imagery of judgment and ruling authority tied to Daniel 7.[9] So this theme presents Jesus has having authority to forgive sin, an authority closely linking him to God and the divine work. Such authority coheres with the remarks Jesus makes about who can associate with God, our first irritant category.

Minor Irritant 3: Sabbath Incidents and Healings

Yet another area of authority that touches on the law is Jesus' healing activity tied to the Sabbath, as well as Jesus' defense of the disciples' Sabbath activity. Once again the collection of texts is impressive in terms of distribution (Mark: Mark 2:23–3:6=Matt 12:1–14=Luke 6:1–11; L: Luke 13:10–17; 14:1–6; John: John 5:1–18; 7:22–23). Some question these events arguing that there was no set Sabbath policy in Judaism and that the idea that some followed Jesus around to see what he would do is ludicrous.[10] The point about no set Jewish policy is correct, but Eugene Boring also properly notes that in the passage the view is 'unless there is a life threatening situation, Sabbath laws should be observed'. The Essenes at Qumran were more strict than others, not even permitting help to an animal in trouble on the Sabbath (Cairo Geniza, CD 11:13–14 = 4Q270 [=4QD^d] Frag. 6, col. v, 17–18—'Let no beast be helped to give birth on the Sabbath day; and if it fall into a cistern or into a pit, let it not be lifted out on the Sabbath'), whereas

---

9   The debate over the authenticity of the Son of Man expression is almost endless. I have defended its authenticity in my *Jesus according to Scripture*, 601–605, updated in my and Ben Simpson's *Jesus, God-Man*, 92–91. Of course for those who reject such healings or miracles, this scene and the saying linkage is a creation of the church. It is interesting, however, that Josephus in reporting about Jesus recognizes he did unusual works (*Ant*. 18.61–64) and the idea that Jesus performed such works is about as multiply attested a theme as one can find in the Gospels. For an assessment of this aspect of Jesus' ministry, Twelftree, *Jesus The Miracle Worker*.

10 Sanders, *Jesus and Judaism*, 264–267. For the variety of Jewish views on Sabbath labor, Boring, *Mark*, 94 n. 39, who notes how moderate later rabbinic teaching became, even allowing for the treatment of a sore throat lest it become more serious (*m. Yoma* 8.6, cited below).

the Pharisees and Sadducees allowed such help except on a feast day (*m. Shabbat* 18.3).[11] This text reads:

> They do not deliver the young of cattle on the festival, but they help out. And they do deliver the young of a woman on the Sabbath. They call a midwife for her from a distant place, and they violate the Sabbath on her [the woman in childbirth's] account. And they tie the umbilical cord. R. Yose says, "Also: They cut it. And all things required for circumcision do they perform on the Sabbath".[12]

However, the key point is that on some things there was agreement, such as the fact that Sabbath rest was required when life was not at risk. So, for example, reads *m Yoma* 8:6, 'And any matter of doubt as to danger to life overrides the prohibitions of the Sabbath, where if there is a matter of life and death, then the Sabbath can be overridden'. Otherwise, one would assume there is no override. The fact that there was no life or death situation in these Sabbath healings or events meant that they could wait for another day (Luke 13:14). In sum, these texts show that (1) differing views about how God saw this action stands behind Jesus and his claims and (2) Jesus has an authoritative take on Torah versus his opponents, especially given that Jesus restores the one healed. This assumption of Jesus' act is that this takes place with God's help and approval, for would God really help a Sabbath sinner perform such a deed? His opponents challenge such work, even if it comes about because of issues tied to the Sabbath; but the question about the act raised by the assumption lingers in the background.

It is important to note that these texts record a variety of events that take place on the Sabbath. Each act raised such an objection. These scenes include more than one healing, as well as the plucking grain on the Sabbath incident (as already noted: Mark: Mark 2:23–3:6=

---

11 We have followed the translation of the Cairo Geniza text from Dupont-Sommer, *The Essene Writings of Qumran*, 153. The Qumran fragment is found in Parry & Tov, *Dead Sea Scroll Reader*, 156–157. This version reads, '[Let no one deliver the young of an animal on the Sabbath day;] and if it falls into a pit or a ditch let him not [raise it on the Sabbath]'. A few lines later one is also not supposed to pull up a human with a ladder, rope or utensil (lines 19–20).

12 Citations of the *Mishnah* are from Neusner's version.

Matt 12:1–14=Luke 6:1–11; L: Luke 13:10–17; 14:1–6; John: John 5:1–18; 7:22–23). The incident in John 5 is the most developed with claims that Jesus defended himself on the basis that he and the Father were working on the Sabbath (vv. 17–18). This is precisely what the ultimate theological significance was. Either Jesus was healing through God's enablement on the Sabbath or Jesus' power came from elsewhere, as opponents raised the alternative option of Beelzebul's authority in Luke 11:15. The leadership clearly understood the implication of Jesus' action here. The power came from some transcendent source. The question was which one. Jesus claimed a tie to God. The more Jesus repeated the act, the more it would intensify the irritation.

One should not miss another significance of this act. Who has the authority to determine what is appropriate on the Sabbath, a day sanctified by one of the Ten Words (= Ten Commandments) and around which the creation story itself is built (Exod 20:8–11; seven days of Creation followed by God's rest in Gen 1, esp. Exod 20:11)? In addition, Deuteronomy 5 argues that Sabbath observance as part of the Ten Words is related to covenant and to honoring God's deliverance through the Exodus. Who has authority over the sacred calendar, not to mention the core of the law as summarized in the key commandments? Jesus does not appeal to a tradition here; he simply raises issues from Scripture and then acts directly, appealing to his own authority. Again, in the end, more than interpretation is in view.

Here is where the 'divide and conquer' approach of more skeptical critics does its 'denarratizing' work as it severs the connection and integration of healing, association, acceptance, forgiveness, and repeated healings on the day of rest and reflection with its inherent deep challenge of a currently widespread Sabbath theology. As Witherington has argued, these acts show that the category of teacher or prophet is inadequate to explain who Jesus is nor do those categories reflect the real scope of his actions. Either he is a lawbreaker or one who sits adjudicating the law with an individual, not a traditional, authority to declare its scope.[13] It is no accident then, nor is it insignificant that Jesus claims that 'the Son of Man is Lord of the Sabbath' (Mark 2:28).

---

13 Witherington, *The Christology of Jesus*, 69.

The one who represents humanity has been given ruling authority. He even has authority over the Sabbath. Much in the same manner as Jesus claimed to be able to forgive sin, so he claims to have authority over the divine calendar. Although many like to challenge the portrait in John's Gospel, this particular event runs down the same conceptual track as the Synoptics when it comes to articulating the roots and significance of Jesus' Sabbath authority.[14]

Let's consider an important challenge to the historicity of such scenes. Some have explained such a scene by an appeal to the retrojecting of Passion concerns into an account Mark is said to have stylized for such polemical reasons.[15] Boring argues that what we have here is an attempt to raise the issue of blasphemy earlier than it really arose and to root later conflict into an earlier timeframe. The text for him is symbolic of what became an issue later. I do not find persuasive such a suggestion when one analyzes the five reasons Boring gives, as I shall do shortly. This opposition of history and symbol is an 'either-or' standard to something that can reflect a 'both-and view' of Jesus and his ministry. Something moved the church to reject the traditions surrounding the Sabbath as the last day of the week. It is more than a move in a Gentile direction, as Gentiles could be related to Judaism and the Jesus movement without such a move in time being necessary. The retention of the details of such Sabbath disputes about actions on a Jewish Sabbath day does not seem to be an issue in the early church. In the church, the day had changed already. Something set up that move and it appears to be more than just a choice about celebrating the day of resurrection because how the day was handled is also in view. This event involves a dispute that occupies the 'middle' Jesus position of a time when the community following Jesus was still quite Jewish and struggling over Jewish things about that day.

It is important, however, to make specific arguments about the weaknesses of seeing a retrojection here and not only claim the possibility of authenticity. Let's consider the five points of Boring's case for retrojection. The five alleged points of contact with the Passion in

---

14 On a defense of work in John's Gospel being relevant to historical Jesus work, see Anderson, 'The John, Jesus, and History Project'. Also Charlesworth, 'The Historical Jesus in the Fourth Gospel'.
15 Boring, *Mark*, 96.

such scenes do not necessarily point to a retrojection. (1) His claim that the scene in Mark 3:1–6 assumes a political charge reads too much into the mention of the Herodians in v. 6 alongside the Pharisees. In Jesus' challenges there would be both a political destabilizing dimension to his work because of its social implications as well as religious concerns. A religion changing views on how the Sabbath was observed would create public tension Herod would have to keep his eye on. (2) That 'blasphemy' is the charge in each case (Passion and here) fails to see that Jesus' act of blasphemy in offering forgiveness is an implied theological deduction (Mark 2:1–10) more than a directly insulting word that impinges upon God's uniqueness as appears in Mark 14:62–64 where Jesus claims the Son of Man sits at God's side. This is why we have applied the description of an irritant to Jesus' claim to forgive. (3) The mixture of wrath and grief in both reflects emotions tied to conflict with people one might hope would have been more responsive. Such emotional mixtures do not belong exclusively to either time frame of Jesus' ministry or the Passion. (4) The fact that terms of destroying Jesus and plotting to do so overlap between Mark 3:6, 11:18, and the Passion scene are also reflections of conflict and resolution acts that are often tied to the world of emerging, escalating, or expanding opposition. (5) The ethical issues of doing good or doing harm in the polemics of the conflict does not merely 'proleptically portray what is at stake as the Jerusalem religious and political leaders make their decision in response to Jesus', it also coheres with the irritations Jesus' actions and teachings introduced into the debate that arose between the leadership and Jesus. Those debates did not emerge out of a religious vacuum. Surely, when pressed, Jesus defended such acts on religious, ethical lines. Such events are too widely attested in being attached to him to evolve out of thin air after the fact. Something beyond mere concern for Gentiles created these new views, something loosening the moorings of how Sabbath was seen would seem required to have proceeded the move later tied to a Gentile context. This is a 'middle' Jesus event. A consideration of Boring's points shows the conclusion of retrojection does not follow and is more problematic in explaining the sociological dynamics required for such a challenging theological move. It looks like such a move far more likely took place in stages rather than all at once.

This portrait about Jesus' attitude toward the Sabbath is coherent and does run along the historical continuum, given that the church did not observe the Sabbath on the same day as Judaism did, at least perhaps from the time of the mid-fifties for some Christians, if the gathering for the church collection takes place on the first day of each week as the letter to Corinth suggests (1 Cor. 16:1–2). In contrast, Jesus both affirms the Sabbath as sacred while also questioning how acts of compassion fit into that sacred day, a claim that does not fit normal Jewish views.[16] However, the key difference between the Sabbath controversies involving Jesus and the early church is that 'working on the Sabbath' does not appear as an early church dispute, only the day being special seems to be the issue (Rom 14; Col. 2). So the issues Jesus raised appear to be unique to his time and distinct from early church concerns. Again, Jesus appears to be in the 'middle' of a transition.

Authority Pictured 1: Exorcisms

John's Gospel has no exorcisms, but the category is widely attested in the Synoptics (M: Mark 1:21–28=Luke 4:31–37; Mark 5:1–20=Matt 8:26–39=Luke 8:26–39; Mark 7:24–30=Matt. 15:21–28; Mark 9:14–29=Matt.17:14–20=Luke 9:37–43; Mark 3:22 [one of a few Mark only texts]; Mark 9:38–40=Luke 9:49–50; summaries include Q: Matt 12:24=Luke 11:15; L: Luke 13:32). The key text, however, is Matthew 12:24–28=Luke 11:14–20, which is from Q. This is one of the few events that Q presents. This text also cuts against the normal grain of Q in that it points in a christological direction, something that speaks for the passage's authenticity in that a christologically driven passage adheres to a Q tradition that normally does not exploit such themes.[17]

---

16 Again Boring, *Mark*, 95, is correct to note that Jesus does not 'break' the Sabbath, as he claims no violation and there is a Christological point to such scenes. However, Jesus does 'break' the Sabbath in the more traditionally grounded view of his opponents who do not recognize his authority. We are dealing with the challenge of competing 'preunderstandings' about the Sabbath here from within a Jewish worldview. The evidence of gathering on Sunday is not unanimous on the Sabbath, as the Ebionites and Nazareans are said to still gather on the Sabbath and 1 Corinthians is not clear. However, according to Eusebius, *Ecclesiastical History* Book 3, 27, 5; Epiphanius, *Heresies* 29, the Jewish Christian groups did continue to gather on the Sabbath.

17 By saying this, I do not commit myself to Q as a document or as the reflection of a single community. My point is only that such material, whether oral or written in origin, is out of character with the normal material Matthew and Luke share together.

The dispute here is about the source of Jesus' actions. Are they from God or from Beelzebul, from above or below?

This final passage from Matthew 12 and Luke 11 comes in a deviation from normal form for a miracle account, a literary deviation that shows the text's importance. Usually a miracle story gives much detail about the circumstances of the healing and summarizes the reaction. This miracle reverses the normal form, spending only one verse on the healing and the rest of the time on the reaction. This unique manner of presenting the miracle is important because the controversy reflects a summary about Jesus' miraculous activity as tied to the source of Jesus' authority. Given the religious context and the acceptance that something happened, only two options are possible.[18] Either Jesus works with the power of God and divine kingdom authority or his authority is from the devil.

It is significant to note that the one category not contemplated here is that nothing has taken place. The first century Jewish historian Josephus in his testimony about Jesus observes that the Jews acknowledged Jesus performed unusual works (*Ant.* 18.61–64). This recognition runs for centuries through the Jewish reaction to Jesus. The later Jewish suggestion that Jesus was a magician appears in *b Sanhedrin* 43ª (=Sanh 6:1 JII C–D in Neusner's versification). This magician charge accepts the unusual nature of his works while challenging its source. The Talmudic text, censored from many versions of the Talmud reads,

> On the eve of the Passover Yeshu was hanged. For forty days before the execution took place, a herald went forth and cried, 'He is going forth to be stoned because he has practiced sorcery and enticed Israel to apostasy. Any one who can say anything in his favor, let him come forward and plead on his behalf'. But since nothing was brought forward in his favor he was hanged on the eve of the Passover! Ulla retorted: Do you suppose that he was one for whom a defense could be made? Was he not

---

18 Of course, a naturalist option exists that somehow all of these events have some form of naturalist explanation or are simple fabrications, but the fact the opponents also seem to accept what has taken place without going to such a claim makes it hard to see this as a likely option. The Jewish tradition argued Jesus was a magician or sorcerer, showing they accepted something was going on that needed an appeal to a transcendent level of activity of some sort. See the following discussion.

a Mesith [enticer], concerning whom Scripture says, Neither shall you spare, neither shall you conceal him (Deut. 13:9)?

To call someone an enticer is to charge them with sorcery and is to put them in connection with the authority of evil forces (Matt. 9:34; 10:25; 12:24, 27).[19] Justin Martyr in the mid-second century notes this is a Jewish charge when he says in his *Dialogues* 69.7, 'they said it [his miracle power] was a display of magic art, for they even dared to say he was a magician and a deceiver of the people'. So by the end of the first century, it is affirmed from a widely attested array of sources that Jesus was recognized as having performed unusual deeds, an affirmation that later sources on both sides of the debate also affirm.

The passage in Q has Jesus explain his authority this way, 'If I cast out demons by the finger (Lk)/Spirit (Matt) of God, then the kingdom of God has come upon you'. Jesus presented his acts as tied to the kingdom rooted in the authority and power he bore.[20] Others saw the power but saw its source as destructive. Jesus' power comes from beyond, either for good or for ill. The polemic of positive or negative ethical import shows itself here, just as it did in the Sabbath debate. Again one can speak of coherence.

Of course, this category is not so unprecedented. Many figures were said to be able to perform exorcisms. By the time of Jesus, Solomon in particular was associated with such power as Josephus notes in *Antiquities* 8.42–49. This text defends the powers of a figure named Eleazar and reads:

> Now the sagacity and wisdom which God had bestowed upon Solomon was so great, that he exceeded the ancients, insomuch that he was no way inferior to the Egyptians, who are said to have been beyond all men in understanding; nay, indeed, it is evident that their sagacity was very much inferior to that of the king's. He also excelled and distinguished himself in wisdom above those who were most eminent among

---

19 On this association of Jesus with the devil, sorcery or false prophecy, see Stanton, 'Jesus of Nazareth: A Magician', 166–71.
20 For a vigorous defense of the authenticity of this particular saying, see Dunn, 'Matthew 12:28 / Luke 11:20'.

the Hebrews at that time for shrewdness: those I mean were Ethan, and Heman, and Chalcol, and Darda, the sons of Mahol. He also composed books of odes and songs, a thousand and five; of parables and similitudes, three thousand; for he spoke a parable upon every sort of tree, from the hyssop to the cedar; and in like manner also about beasts, about all sorts of living creatures, whether upon the earth, or in the seas, or in the air; for he was not unacquainted with any of their natures, nor omitted inquiries about them, but described them all like a philosopher, and demonstrated his exquisite knowledge of their several properties. God also enabled him to learn that skill which expels demons, which is a science useful and sanative to men. He composed such incantations also by which distempers are alleviated. And he left behind him the manner of using exorcisms, by which they drive away demons, so that they never return, and this method of cure is of great force unto this day; for I have seen a certain man of my own country whose name was Eleazar, releasing people that were demoniacal in the presence of Vespasian, and his sons, and his captains, and the whole multitude of his soldiers. The manner of the cure was this:—He put a ring that had a root of one of those sorts mentioned by Solomon to the nostrils of the demoniac, after which he drew out the demon through his nostrils; and when the man fell down immediately, he abjured him to return into him no more, making still mention of Solomon, and reciting the incantations which he composed. And when Eleazar would persuade and demonstrate to the spectators that he had such a power, he set a little way off a cup or basin full of water, and commanded the demon, as he went out of the man, to overturn it, and thereby to let the spectators know that he had left the man; and when this was done, the skill and wisdom of Solomon was shown very manifestly; for which reason it is, that all men may know the vastness of Solomon's abilities, and how he was beloved of God, and that the extraordinary virtues of every kind with which this king was endowed may not be unknown to any people under the sun; for this reason, I say, it is that we have proceeded to speak so largely of these matters.

This text shows that it was not unusual to tie exorcism to the activity of humans. However, one point about this text on Eleazar in comparison with Jesus should not be missed. Exorcists like Eleazar relied on formulae and incantations, as well as acts to invoke their exorcisms in ways Jesus did not.

The careful study of the context of Jesus' miracles by Eric Eve makes this distinction of approach clear.[21] Eve makes an important distinction between different kinds of healer-exorcists that in turn is dependent on work by Werner Kahl.[22] There are those who are (1) 'bearers of numinous power' (BNP), (2) those who are 'petitioners of numinous power' (PNP) and (3) those who are 'mediators of numinous power' (MNP). Mediators use formulae or some other means to as an aid in their work. Petitioners simply pray for the healing. Bearers of numinous power act directly with no intermediary elements. They 'incorporate healing power in themselves'.[23] What is crucial to see is that Jesus is a bearer of such power, while Eleazar is a mediator of such power. Eve notes a parallel in Greco-Roman works with a later figure Apollonius of Tyana (He is a first-century figure written about 150 years later). Otherwise Eve says that Jesus is, 'virtually unique in being an immanent BNP'.[24] In his conclusion, Eve sees that Jesus is unique in the surviving Jewish literature of his time in being portrayed as performing a large number of healings and exorcisms. Eve notes that,

> Kahl is correct that he [Jesus] is virtually unique in Jewish literature in being portrayed as an immanent BNP in these acts of power, with two provisos. First, some Jewish texts can appear to make human figures act as immanent BNPs where the context suggests they are really only mediators of God's numinous power. Secondly, whatever may be true of individual miracles stories, the Gospels show some tendency to indicate it is God's

---

21 Eve, *The Jewish Context of Jesus' Miracles*, esp. 15–16.
22 Kahl, *New Testament Miracle Stories*.
23 Kahl, *Miracle Stories*, 76.
24 Eve, *Jewish Context*, 16.

power at work in Jesus, not merely his own (e.g., Mt. 12:28/ Lk. 11:20; Lk 5:17). If Jesus is a BNP, it is because he is a bearer of God's Spirit, which is the source of Jesus' power. Indeed, if God were not in some sense behind Jesus' acts of power, they would not count as miracles.[25]

Now Eve's conclusion is solid, but his provisos need probing. Yes, Jesus was tied to the kingdom and the Spirit. God is behind his work. Jesus made these connections (L: Luke 4:16–18; Q: Matt 12:28=Luke 11:20). Yes, narrative can simplify events, and these narratives do ultimately point to God's work. The questions this essay is raising and that comes to us again and again as we add to these categories of authority include: (1) How did Jesus understand the nature and scope of his role? (2) Why does he express his actions by not only mentioning God but including himself? In other words, how do we explain the kind of authority Jesus claims *for himself without backing off its potential offense* in relationship to sin, Sabbath and law, unless there is a very tight linkage between Jesus and God? The very ambiguity of how these texts express this connection, while insisting on it, and the uniqueness of the way they present Jesus' acts may suggest that Eve's provisos risk qualifying the Gospels' portrait of Jesus too much, making them appear more like the parallels than perhaps they are.

That the Gospels' only real point is that God is really at work in Jesus may well be a variation of the 'divide and conquer' approach by looking only at miracles as bearing on the question of the source of Jesus' actions. This essay prefers to argue that what we see in this set of exorcism texts is a claim that adds yet another element that reflects Jesus' 'irritating' claims of *his own* authority. With this element in place, miracles as a whole also need to be considered, while noting that many figures in Scripture performed miracles so the issue is not the performance of miracles *per se*, but their scope, role, and connection to the person of Jesus, along with how the gospels have Jesus frame his miracles as pointing to a new era. In other words, these miracles are not just random acts of deliverance and power, but point to a special time and someone

---

25 Eve, *Jewish Context*, 378–379.

more. If God is behind these acts, then he is behind this framing as well. That is why John the evangelist called such miracles 'signs.' They were signs testifying to a promise and a person.

Jewish texts confirm a kingdom-defeat of Satan association. In the *Testament of Moses* 10:1–2, the significance of the devil's defeat is stated this way, 'Then his kingdom will appear throughout the whole creation. Then the devil will have an end. Yea, sorrow will be led away with him. Then will be filled the hands of the messenger, who is in the highest place appointed. Yea, he will at once avenge them of their enemies'.[26] This juxtaposition of an avenging victory and the defeat of Satan reflects the picture of total victory of the Old Testament with a little more detail (Isa. 65–66). However, there is a difference with Jesus and this Jewish portrait. The victory over Satan for Jesus comes in stages, one represented by his ministry, the other after Jesus has suffered and then been vindicated. In Judaism, this was a once for all expectation, a package deal. In Christianity after Jesus, this demarcation was made even clearer in the movement to a second, delayed coming (Acts 3:19–23; 1 Thess. 4:16–17). Again, Jesus occupies a 'middle' position.

Jesus' enemy is not a particular race or the nations, but sin. This cosmological element of his work is also a fresh element Jesus emphasized and sought to reveal as now present in a new way that pointed to a new era, an era he called the inbreaking of God's promised kingdom, but here the early church simply took up this emphasis rather than developing it.

Minor Irritant 4: Purity in Association with Other Legal Practices

The issue of purity involves mainly one set of texts (Mk: Mark 7:1–23 =Matt 15:1–20). These are the only Gospel texts where the question of what is 'common' or 'profane' (κοινός [i.e., unclean]) comes up. What is disputed is the disciples' failure to keep 'the tradition of the elders'. They fail to wash their hands to prevent uncleanness in their handling of food.[27] The objection leads Jesus into the larger category of legal practices in general.

Thus, the uniqueness of this dispute should probably not be separated

---

26 Translation of the Pseudepigrapha are from Charlesworth, *Old Testament Pseudepigrapha*. This text can be found in 1:931–932.
27 For discussion of the Jewish practice here, see Booth, *Jesus and the Laws of Purity*, 155–187.

too greatly from other 'legal practice' texts over halakah. Other 'legal practice' texts address Jesus' practice in relationship to fasting or point to Jesus' critique of the religious practices of the Jewish leaders (L: Luke 5:33–39; Q?: Luke 11:37–54=Matt. 23, unless one sees these as distinct scenes in which case M and L are present).[28] So even though the specific 'common' question is not multiply attested, it does fit into a larger theme of Jesus and discussions about the law that is multiply attested.

These texts do not so much challenge purity practices as reprioritize them, making true piety a reflection of more than one's ability to follow detailed legal practices, something that various strands of Judaism also saw as important, given the prophetic tradition that made it clear that sacrifices alone are not what God requires but sacrifices offered from a genuine heart (Isaiah 58). This class of texts shows Jesus making a serious challenge to a major stand of Jewish legal or halakic tradition that are reflected in Pharisaism and practices like those of the Essenes or Enochic Judaism.[29] Jesus' response and actions showed a kind of indifference to the efforts to prop up support of the law through the development of tradition. His more tradition sensitive opponents like

---

28 The relationship of Luke 11 to Matthew 23 is complex. It may be the same tradition, but the settings are distinct enough that one cannot be sure. At the least, this is Q tradition. At the most, it may represent two distinct controversies, one from M and the other from L. Either way, this means this more general category is also multiply attested. For the category of 'legal practices' as a whole is from Mark, Q, and L, if not Mark, M and L.

29 Here one can appeal to the argument of Meyer, *The Aims of Jesus*, 137–153 on eschatological Torah, where he makes the case that Jesus' most vigorous challenge was against the *halaka* or the tradition that was becoming attached to the Law and that Jesus treated such rulings as the 'tradition of men' versus the 'commands of God' (Mark 7:8). Meyer goes on to say (150–151), 'The ritual order received neither the accent nor development in the proclamation of Jesus. On the contrary, his central themes of eschatological consummation repeatedly cross the grain of ritual tradition and so violated religious sensibilities (Mark 2:15 parr., 19–21 parr., 23–28 parr., 3:4 parr., 7:1–23 par., 10:3–9 parr.; Matt 8:21f. par.; 11:16–19 par.; 17:24–26 Luke 15:1f.; 19:5–7; John 2:19 [=Mark 14:58 par.; 15:29 par.])'. I would add that it was so hard for many in this period to sort out the law from the tradition because the two were often perceived as indistinguishable. Such practice was seen as an expression of faithfully living before God as one who embraced the practice of the Law that made a Jew distinct from the practices of the non-monotheists that surrounded them in the larger culture. For those who see Jesus directly challenging the law and rejecting it through an emphasis on Mark 7:19, it is important to remember two things. (1) The early Jewish-Christian church appears to have been careful to keep the law, if the early chapters of Acts and Matthew are a worthy guide, and tended to discuss only how Gentiles relate to that law in Acts. (2) Mark 7:19, if original to Mark as is likely, is a remark by Mark as the narrator, not a remark of Jesus, so that what is present is an implication of what Jesus said that was probably crystallized much later. What this means is that Jesus' statements and actions relative to purity and practice look to challenge not so much the law as the tradition that surrounds it. Again it is a 'middle' Jesus who is in view.

the Pharisees read his approach as indifference to the law at best and unfaithfulness to it at worst. The other side of this dialectic about legal practices is that Jesus claims an authority over how to understand the law that pointed to his own authority, especially when he did not appeal to Scripture or to any other authorities but to his own logic or personal position in making the case.

In Matthew, Jesus replies in kind to the charges of law breaking made against him, by noting that the tradition of the Pharisees and scribes breaks the ethical side of the law by violating the command to honor mother and father. He then goes on to assert that it is not what goes into a person that defiles but what comes out of the mouth. When the disciples note that the Pharisees were offended by his statements, Jesus drives the point home: 'Every plant that *my* heavenly Father has not planted will be rooted up'. Then he calls the Pharisees blind guides. Jesus' final remark on the topic is that what comes out of the mouth and out of the heart is what defiles, 'but to eat with unwashed hands does not defile'. It was this seeming indifference to practice that would have been shocking.

Mark goes a similar route, even describing the custom for his Gentile audience in 7:3–4. When asked, Jesus challenges his opponents for their hypocrisy with regard to honoring mother and father. Then he tells the crowd that defilement does not involve what comes from outside but what comes out of a person. Mark stresses that impurity comes from what emerges from the heart. He alone also adds the implication of Jesus' remarks (although the result Mark underscores was not immediately recognized as an implication at the time of Jesus' remarks): Jesus 'declared all foods clean'. This very note shows that what Jesus said here ended up eventually yielding a radical reconfiguring in the early church that had not yet taken place in the time of Jesus' ministry or even in the earliest church, if Acts is of any help. Again we see a 'middle' Jesus.

All of this tradition about handwashing reflected a scrupulous Jewish concern to be faithful to Leviticus 15, where being made unclean by a discharge required a washing. Although the body was still considered unclean for a time after the washing, a rinsing by 'living water' rendered the hands clean. The Jewish tradition sought to explain and guarantee that no violations of cleanness took place. Thus it expanded the teachings of Leviticus 15. The entirety of this expansion took centuries to develop and codify, ending in the collection of the *Mishnah* in c. AD 180 and the production of an elaborate commentary of it called the *Talmud* in the fifth century. This is a direction Jesus did not go in pursuing issues of the law and legal practices.

What Jesus responds to, then, is mostly the tradition treating uncleanliness, not the Torah *per se*. Jesus' response makes it clear that he rejected the use of oral law in this way. However, when Jesus goes on to elaborate his response, he does comment on matters of 'defiling' that Torah does treat. Here he opts for a focus on the ethical dimensions of the law in terms of personal, relational behavior. Both the rebuke that confronts the Jewish leaders on how parents are dishonored and the emphasis on defiling coming from the heart show this ethical, relational priority as the law interacts in one's relationships. In force, this is little different from the 'do good versus do harm' argument we saw earlier concerning Sabbath practices. There is a coherence to the logic applied here. When Mark adds the narrative comment that the effect of Jesus' remarks was to make all foods clean (Mark 7:19), the import is that Jesus, by the emphasis he gave, has reconfigured how the law is seen. He read it as less about issues of form and surface stipulation and more about questions pointing to the heart, an appeal to 'eschatological Torah' that Meyer suggests is present, at the least for the Gentile believers who are Mark's key audience. Reading Matthew gives one the same sense, but with a lesser degree of contrast. The emphasis on the interpersonal relationships is still there, but the explicit statement of foods being declared clean is lacking.[30] Nonetheless, it appears the practice of the early church ended up far down the road from what Jesus says here by making his remarks into a kind of prioritized paradigm for the topic.

Jesus' comments are not merely those of a prophet commenting on the law, nor are they the work of a scribe interpreting the law. Rather, the point is that Jesus, in light of his authority, has the right to comment

---

30 There is a complex issue of how Jewish Christians saw and related to the Law wrapped up in this observation. Matthew is written with Jewish concerns especially in mind. His lack of this implication may well reflect the difference in audience and in application at an ethnic level. Such differences reflect the other side of the continuum that sees Jesus in the 'middle'. For some there is enough connection that Law is still in play. For others, the direction of Jesus' teaching has implications for the Law, at least in terms of some practices and some audiences.

and even prioritize on matters tied to purity. There is no 'thus says the Lord' in Jesus' answers, but the clear statement of what the standard is. As already noted, Ben Meyer speaks of an 'eschatological ethic' at work here as the arrival of the new age brings a fresh look at the law and its priorities. A standard of righteousness is being more effectively worked out in conjunction with the promise of the new era.[31] Jesus' remark in defense of his lack of fasting—that new wine requires new wineskins—makes the point explicitly (Mark 2:22=Matt. 9:17=Luke 5:38). It is important that this statement is retained even in a more Jewish oriented Gospel like Matthew. This kind of prioritizing and the authority to declare some kind of distinction in the application of the law also must point to an authority bearing revealer, when the revealer does not point explicitly to God's revelation as the basis for the judgment. As Meyer states, 'Since the Mosaic code was conceived to have been divinely revealed, any code claiming to supersede it had somehow to include the claim to be equally revealed—indeed, to belong to a superior revelation.'[32] I might want to question the judgment that the claim is of a superior revelation here, since Jesus does appear to have embraced Moses and Torah. However, what is key about the observation is that the response represents the arrival of a new era, which is what makes the 'newness' eschatological. In other words, Jesus is not teaching that Moses is inferior, but that God is introducing a fresh emphasis as he calls people to righteousness, something the new dynamics of the eschaton makes possible, something even set up by the prophets in their remarks about the priority of mercy over sacrifice. The law as promise has set up the arrival of promise. The presence of the eschaton seems to be tied to the acts and presence of Jesus. Once again personal authority is central as these links are made and highlighted.

So this consistent exercise of interpretive authority over the law also has implications for the revelator. Who could emphasize and reveal

---

31 Meyer, *The Aims of Jesus*, 138–139. He goes on to say, 'Jesus was not a rabbi but a prophet and, like John, "more than a prophet". He was the unique revealer of the full final measure of God's will' (151). What is harder to determine is whether the new Torah is intended as a new standard or as what the goal was of God's standard all along. The very ambiguity of Jesus' response to the question posed this way and the variety of responses his teaching seems to have provoked also adds to the likelihood we are dealing with Jesus as a bridge figure in this area.
32 Meyer, *The Aims of Jesus*, 152.

the scope of the law and practice that God gave through Moses? It is someone through whom God was introducing a time that transcended that of Moses and who transcended Moses himself. Here, Jesus did not claim to go up to the mountain to get the revelation of God as Moses had. Rather, he spoke directly of what '*my* Father' would do and what divinity requires. Thus, these acts inherently present a claim of inherent authority and divine insight. This is yet another colorful tint in the self portrait of authority Jesus' actions painted, stones that were tossed one by one serving as irritants and threats to what Judaism must be according to his opponents.

Jesus' handling of other issues tied to the law work in a similar manner and thus coheres to what we have seen, but perhaps not with the edge of these already treated legal practice texts. He prioritizes the commandments so that loving God and neighbor are the two on which the law is summarized (Mark 12:28–34=Matt. 22:35–40=Luke 10:25–28). Rabbi Hillel is said in later sources to have taught something like this declaring, 'What seems to you to be hurtful, do not do to your neighbor; that is the whole Torah. All the rest is commentary' (*b. Shabbat* 31ᵃ). On this point, Jesus is not so distinctive.

Perhaps the most revealing texts in this regard are what are called the 'antitheses', which interestingly enough come right after Jesus declares that no one should teach anyone to ignore the least of the commandments of the law while also noting that not one dot or iota of the law will pass away until all is accomplished (Matt. 5:17–48).[33] The juxtaposition of this fulfill the law saying with Jesus' exposition of the antitheses must mean that to understand the jot and tittle saying, one must read the exposition of these six contrasts.

These contrasts are revealing. Sometimes it is argued that Jesus is merely rejecting oral law in his 'you have heard it said, but I say to you' remarks. Appeal is made to Matthew 5:17–20 to justify this distinction. This argument is not entirely satisfying, given that the contrasts appear right after the affirmation of the law. The juxtaposition must indicate

---

33 Whether 'antitheses' is the best name for 5:20–48 is debatable if one is only thinking of the Torah. What is clear is that Jesus is challenging how the law was being applied and sets up six contrasts to how it was being read and how elements of it were being emphasized or prioritized at the time.

that what Jesus means is explained by how Jesus handles the topics that follow his declaration. Jesus' contrasts intensify each command, pressing it in terms of its internal intent. So the issue is not just murder but also anger that leads to murder. The issue is not just adultery but also lust that leads to adultery. The issue is not thinking through how one can get out of marriage, but taking one's vow seriously in order to keep it, recognizing also that God is involved in bringing a couple together. The issue is not how an oath is worded, but the integrity that makes oath taking unnecessary. The issue is not eye-for-eye retribution, but a kind of non-retaliation that keeps the spiral of violence from spinning out of control. Note how this contrast simply cites Exod. 21:24 or Lev. 24:20. There is no oral law being appealed to here. It is the law that is being elaborated and intensified in this contrast. Jesus is prioritizing how to see Torah. This last example is particularly instructive, showing Jesus' emphasis on the law's relational dimension, pointing to a fresh hub for law, so that relationships do not break down. Absence of retribution again is the point in Jesus' stepping back from the call to hate one's enemy. The standard may not be what is 'fair' or 'equal', but what goes beyond the call of normal duty to reverse the cycle that causes relationships to be destroyed. The outcome is that the standard of righteousness that Jesus' reading of the law calls for exceeds that of the scribes and Pharisees. This righteousness operates at a relational and internal heart standard greater than that which the world or the Jewish leadership lives by and reflects God's character in the process. It reads the law not in terms of conformity to standards of external measurement or mere stipulations, but from the inside in terms of heart motivation. It takes the law and focuses it on its theological-ethical-relational roots.

It is also in this light that Jesus' remarks about coming to fulfill the law in Matt. 5:17–20 must be read. Here, Jesus is not discussing a casuistic reading of legal detail and scribal ruling, but a reading that looks at the law's scope and intended goal to enhance relationships and reflect God's gracious character and righteousness.

All of this raises the question of who has the authority to expound the inner intent of the law in this manner, discerning what is to be kept and what is less important, as well as revealing when certain legal limitations apply and when they do not. Once again, Jesus makes no appeal to outside authorities. The authority comes in his personal declaration. In this, Jesus is unlike Judaism or anything one sees in the Old Testament. Jesus speaks with a 'but I say to you'.[34] A quotation from Witherington pulls all the strands of this section together: 'All of this suggests that Jesus did not see himself as a Galilean Hasid ["holy man"] or another prophet, even one like Elijah. He saw himself in a higher or more authoritative category than either of these types familiar to Jewish believers'.[35]

This summary is well stated and correctly surfaces the question of what kind of person Jesus saw himself to be that he could arrogate to himself such authority, including the array of authority we have already traced that got him into so much hot water. Jesus had no doubt that he could serve as the revelator of God, speaking and revealing the divine way and will as he taught of the eschaton's approach. He and the Father were one when it came to understanding what Law and divine will required.

Jesus' response in John 5 to the 'breaking' of the Sabbath proceeds in exactly this way. Once again John's Gospel is shown to be parallel in its conception to what the Synoptics reveal, even though the form of expression differs and is stated more explicitly. Jesus' attitude to the law set a direction that later was taken up in the early church's insistence that circumcision was not required for Gentile believers even though it had been so central a sign in the law. It took a while for this emphasis to make itself clear to the early church, as Acts 10–15 testifies. In the meantime, two other points are clear from Jesus' teaching: (1) compassion and accountable character are what the law was designed to help form and serve; (2) Jesus' reading of the law shows his authority over it. If I may paraphrase, it shows that the Son of Man is not simply Lord of the Sabbath; he is Lord over the reading of the law. In this, Jesus reveals not only his authority, but also his wisdom as the interpreter of the law par excellence.

We have surveyed issues tied to the law and Israel, but nothing was more sacred to Judaism than the most holy space Israel had, the temple

---

34 When Paul faces a similar kind of judgment about issues tied to marriage in 1 Corinthians 7, the apostle's consciously making a distinction from what the Lord teaches and speaking by appealing to wisdom shows the difference in approach in the early church.
35 Witherington, *Christology of Jesus*, 65.

and its representation of the presence of God located in Jerusalem. The sense of God being in the midst of His people was more visibly manifest here than in any other spot on the globe. We will turn in part two to events in Jerusalem next and ask about Jesus' Temple act as well as other activity associated with it. In doing so, we still are operating in the context of Jewish law and rite, a context that Jesus is working to impact.

What we have observed about Jesus' handling of associations, forgiveness, Sabbath, purity, and legal practices is that Jesus is a 'middle' figure between Judaism as it otherwise was and what came to emerge in the early church of his disciples. All these controversies took place in public. The manner of the challenges also seem to have a coherent connection to them in terms of raising kingdom associations already present in key strands of first century Judaism. At the same time, Jesus also challenged some practices and attitudes associated with extant Jewish views. The synthetic reading of Jesus as part of a historical continuum moving from Judaism to the practice of the early church has a cohesion to it that makes cultural sense for a first century Judaism finding its way in the Greco-Roman world. These challenges irritated Jesus' opponents. They were seen as giving away too much and as reflecting an unfaithfulness to the God who had revealed the Torah. However, Jesus' practice of ministering in the hinterlands of Galilee, the Decapolis, and the Jordan did not elevate his work to a threat level that required radical action against him. They did suggest a need only to keep a keen eye on developments. All of that changed when Jesus entered Jerusalem for the last time and went quite public. These earlier irritants set the stage for his reception by those who held power and contributed to their skeptical reaction to similar kinds of acts that came later. These irritants set the stage for raising tensions to a confrontation level in Jesus' last week in the most sacred of national spaces, Jerusalem and her temple. When such claims and acts invaded Israel's religious hub and confronted some of Israel's most sacred locales and liturgy along with her top public pleaders, these irritants set a perceptual backdrop, an official preunderstanding about Jesus that likely had filtered to the religious leaders of Jerusalem and that then escalated the trouble to new heights when he finally acted out such authoritative claims in Jerusalem. The combination got Jesus killed. Jesus' invasion of sacred space combined with earlier perceived irreverent acts produced major incidents and forced a reaction that could no longer be ignored. The combination resulted in his opponents' decision to act. The portrait has cultural coherence, but with a twist if one looks carefully at the 'middle' position Jesus occupies between Jewish and later Christian practice. But that is a story for part two of our study.[36]

---

36 See Bolt & Harrison, *Impact of Jesus*, Volume 2.

Bibliography

Anderson, Paul N. 'The John, Jesus, and History Project and a Fourth Quest for Jesus', Darrell L. Bock & J. Ed Komoszewski (eds.), *Jesus, Skepticism and the Problem of History* (Grand Rapids: Zondervan Academic, 2019), 222–268.

Boccaccini, Gabriele *Middle Judaism: Jewish Thought 300 B.C.E. to 200 C.E.* (Minneapolis: Fortress Press, 1991).

Bock, Darrell L. *Jesus according to Scripture* (Grand Rapids: Baker, 2002).

Bock, Darrell L., & J. Ed Komoszewski (eds.) *Jesus, Skepticism and the Problem of History: Criteria and Context in the Study of Christian Origins* (Grand Rapids: Zondervan Academic, 2019).

Bock, Darrell L., & Ben Simpson *Jesus, God-Man* (Grand Rapids: Baker, 2016).

Booth, Roger *Jesus and the Laws of Purity: Tradition History and Legal History in Mark 7* (JSNTSup 13; Sheffield: JSOT, 1986).

Boring, M. Eugene *Mark: A Commentary* (The New Testament Library; Louisville: Westminster/John Knox, 2006).

Charlesworth, James H. *Old Testament Pseudepigrapha* (2 vols.; New York: Doubleday, 1983).

———, 'The Historical Jesus in the Fourth Gospel', *Journal for the Study of the Historical Jesus* 8 (2010), 3–46.

Dunn, J. D. G. 'Matthew 12:28 / Luke 11:20—A Word of Jesus?', in W. H. Gloer (ed.), *Eschatology and the New Testament: Essays in Honor of George Raymond Beasley-Murray* (Peabody: Hendrickson, 1988), 24–49.

Dupont-Sommer, A. *The Essene Writings of Qumran* (Gloucester: Peter Smith, 1973).

Eve, E. *The Jewish Context of Jesus' Miracles* (JSNTMS 231; Sheffield: Sheffield Academic Press, 2002).

Holmén, Tom (ed.) *Jesus from Judaism to Christianity: Continuum Approaches to the Historical Jesus* (London: T&T Clark, 2007).

Kahl, W. *New Testament Miracle Stories in Their Religious-Historical Setting: A Religionsgeschichtliche Comparison from a Structuralist Perspective* (Forshungen zur Religion und Literatur des Alten und Neuen Testaments 163; Göttingen: Vandenhoeck & Ruprecht, 1994).

Keith, Chris, & Anthony LeDonne (eds.) *Jesus, Criteria, and the Demise of Authenticity* (London: T&T Clark, 2012).

Klawans, Jonathan 'Moral and Ritual Purity', in Amy-Jill Levine, Dale C. Allison, Jr., & John Dominic Crossan (eds.), *The Historical Jesus in Context* (Princeton Readings in Religion; Princeton: Princeton University Press, 2006), 266–84.

Levine, A. J. *The Misunderstood Jew: The Church and the Scandal of the Jewish Jesus* (New York: HarperSanFrancisco, 2006).

Meyer, Ben *The Aims of Jesus* (London: SCM, 1979).

Parry, Donald W., & Emmanuel Tov (eds.) *The Dead Sea Scroll Reader. Part 1: Texts Concerned with Religious Law* (Leiden: Brill, 2004).

Sanders, E. P. *Jesus and Judaism* (Philadelphia: Fortress, 1985).

Stanton, Graham 'Jesus of Nazareth: A Magician and a False Prophet Who Deceived God's People?', in Joel B. Green & Max Turner (eds.), *Jesus of Nazareth Lord and Christ: Essays on the Historical Jesus and New Testament Christology* (Grand Rapids: Eerdmans, 1994), 164–180.

Twelftree, Graham *Jesus The Miracle Worker: A Historical and Theological Study* (Downers Grove, IL: InterVarsity Academic, 2009).

Witherington, B. *The Christology of Jesus* (Philadelphia: Fortress, 1990).

Wright, N. T. *Jesus and the Victory of God* (Philadelphia: Fortress, 1996).

CHAPTER 3

Nonverbal Responses to Jesus in the Gospels

John A. Davies

Abstract

The canonical Gospels record a range of nonverbal responses (gestures, indications of emotion, proxemics) to the ministry of Jesus. Jesus exuded authority: appealing to some, threatening to others. Together with people's verbal expressions, their recorded nonverbal responses, positive or negative, serve to highlight the impact Jesus had on the crowds, on his followers, and on his opponents. The Gospel writers make use of these expressions of suspicion, astonishment, gratitude, adoration, and mockery to depict something of the character of Jesus' messianic identity and thereby invite us to consider our own response to him.

1. Introduction

One of the ways a person's impact on others is gauged is by the body language of those with whom they interact. This article considers some of the accounts of the varying nonverbal responses to Jesus as recorded in the canonical Gospels.[1] Nonverbal communication includes the use

---

1 Some of the material in this chapter is drawn from my book *Lift up Your Heads*. Used by permission of Wipf and Stock, www.wipfandstock.com.

of facial expression, gesture, stance, and the like, either in conjunction with or apart from speech. Of course literary accounts of nonverbal communication, such as we have in the Gospels, are highly selective and stylised. The medium of words on a page can never fully describe the subtlety of expression of which nonverbal communication is capable. How firm is a touch? How long does a gaze last? How far away is 'at a distance'? Yet the Gospel writers have left an account of the impact Jesus had on those around him in part by describing their bodily postures and movements, and if the arguments of scholars like Richard Bauckham are to be accepted, these accounts have their basis in eyewitness testimony.[2] Though briefly sketched, and with due allowance for literary convention, these recollections of how people responded to Jesus serve to further the literary-theological purposes of the Gospel writers. Though readers may often overlook these references, focusing on the dialogue, the intimations of nonverbal response add something to what the writers want the readers to consider as to how they respond to Jesus.

2. Jesus Made an Impression

The first point to make about the impact Jesus had on others is that one simply could not ignore him. Crowds flocked to him. There are 144 references to crowds (ὄχλοι) in the Gospels, the vast majority relating to the popular following Jesus attracted wherever he went. People went to considerable lengths to see and hear him, following him to remote places without thought of provision of food (Matt. 14:14–15), running to him when this may have been considered undignified (Mark 5:6; 9:15; 10:17), climbing a tree to get a better view (Luke 19:2–4), or travelling a considerable distance (Jerusalem to Galilee) for the purpose of gathering evidence against him because of the threat he was perceived to pose (Matt. 15:1; Mark 3:22; 7:1). Jesus had what we might call presence. His words and actions commanded the attention of those with whom he came into contact.

While those who heard Jesus did not always appreciate or even comprehend his message, something compelled them to take him seriously.

---

2   Bauckham, *Jesus and the Eyewitnesses*.

At the outset of his public ministry, when Jesus read from the scroll of Isaiah in the synagogue at Nazareth, Luke recounts that 'the eyes of all in the synagogue were fixed on him' (Luke 4:20), and that was before his bombshell declaration, 'Today this scripture has been fulfilled in your hearing' (v. 21).[3] The word ἀτενίζω suggests paying close attention, not infrequently with a sense of wonderment, and in Second Temple and early Christian texts is particularly the word used of gazing into heaven or at supernatural phenomena; for example, 'I am not worthy to look up, to gaze into heaven because of my many sins' (Pr. Man. 9); 'Through him [Jesus Christ] let us gaze steadfastly toward the heights of the heavens' (*1 Clem.* 36:2).[4] The same word is used for the disciples' gazing into heaven at Jesus' ascension (Acts 1:10) and Stephen, just prior to his stoning in Acts 7:55, 'filled with the Holy Spirit, gazed into heaven and saw the glory of God and Jesus standing at the right hand of God'. So perhaps Luke in describing the scene in the Nazareth synagogue is already hinting that, right at the outset of Jesus' ministry, to gaze on Jesus takes on something of an apocalyptic character.

Luke amplifies his mention of the synagogue congregation's nonverbal response: 'All spoke well of him and were amazed at the gracious words that came from his mouth' (Luke 4:22).[5] There is in fact an overwhelming reaction of amazement or astonishment exhibited by Jesus' followers and opponents alike (θαυμάζω, θαμβέω, ἐκπλήσσω, ἐξίστημι, ἔκστασις λαμβάνει: Matt. 7:28; 8:27; 9:33; 12:23; 13:54; 15:31; 21:20; 22:22, 33; Mark 1:22, 27; 2:12; 5:20, 42; 6:2; 10:32; 11:18; 15:5; Luke 2:47, 48; 4:22, 32, 36; 5:9, 26; 8:25; 9:43; 11:14; 20:26; 24:12; John 4:27; 7:15, 21). Sometimes people are even 'greatly amazed' or 'exceedingly astounded', with various superlative expressions (Matt. 19:25; 27:14; Mark 5:42; 6:51; 7:37; 9:15; 10:26; 12:17; Luke 5:26). There are over forty recorded instances of astonished reactions at what people see and hear of Jesus.[6] While such expressions are dependent on context for understanding the emotion, and there might at times be an element

---

3   All Scripture quotations are from the NRSV.
4   Cf. Strelan, 'The Ascension', 227.
5   Jeremias argues for a negative reading of the amazement: Jeremias, *Jesus' Promise*, 44–46; but cf. Nolland, 'Impressed Unbelievers'.
6   See Nolland, 'Impressed Unbelievers'; Dwyer, *Motif*.

of disquiet or shock (Matt. 19:25; 27:14; Mark 10:22, 26, 32; 15:5; Luke 2:48), generally this wonder approaches the sense of admiration. At times it could be a step in the direction of faith.[7] Note the substitution of προσεκύνησαν 'worshipped' in Matthew 14:33 for ἐθαύμασαν 'marvelled' in the contextually similar Matthew 8:27 (cf. Wis. 8:11; Sir. 7:29). While undoubtedly the narratives are shaped for the purpose of highlighting for the reader the significance of the events, it is difficult to account for the proliferation of such references if they did not in some way 'describe the historical and psychological impression made by Jesus on the crowd'.[8] There may be in these references an echo (with a twist from negative to positive nuance) of the reaction to the Isaianic Servant (Isa. 52:14) whose observers were 'astonished', i.e., appalled (LXX ἐκστήσονται), at his appearance. How is astonishment registered? According to Charles Darwin, who made a close study of emotional expressions, it is largely instinctive rather than cultural, shown in such things as raised eyebrows and wide open eyes, dropped jaw and open mouth, a fixed stare, and perhaps raised hands.[9] A passage from *The Iliad* graphically illustrates for us the prototypical nonverbal character of astonishment:

> Achilles was astounded when he saw King Priam, and so were all his men. They looked at each other in amazement, as people do in a rich noble's hall, when a foreigner who has murdered a man in his own country and is seeking refuge abroad bursts in on them like one possessed (*Iliad* 24, lines 480–84).[10]

Frequently the astonishment at Jesus comes to expression in words (though the expressions for amazement suggest at least a momentary hiatus before the speech), for example, '[T]he crowds were amazed and said, "Never has anything like this been seen in Israel"' (Matt. 9:33; cf. Matt. 8:27; 12:23; 13:54; 19:25; 21:20; Mark 1:27; 6:2; 7:37; 10:26;

---

7 Bertram, 'θαῦμα', 38.
8 Bertram, 'θαῦμα', 37. Bertram comes to a different conclusion on the authenticity of the Gospel accounts of amazement.
9 Darwin, *Expression*, 278–308. For a more contemporary discussion, see Campos et al., 'What Is Shared'.
10 From the translation by Rieu.

Luke 2:48; 4:22; 5:26; 8:25; John 7:15).[11] Some of the amazement is in response to Jesus' demonstrations of power (δυνάμεις), or signs (σημεῖα), or, from the crowd's perspective, 'strange things' (παράδοξα; Luke 5:26), such as restoring the sight of the blind, making the lame walk, or stilling a storm (Matt. 8:27; 12:23; 15:31; 21:20; Mark 2:12; 5:20; Luke 5:9; 8:25; 11:14; John 7:21). These are outworkings of the messianic expectations of such passages as Isaiah 35:5–6:

> Then the eyes of the blind shall be opened, and the ears of the deaf unstopped; then the lame shall leap like a deer, and the tongue of the speechless sing for joy. For waters shall break forth in the wilderness, and streams in the desert (cf. Matt. 11:5).

Some of Jesus' actions appear to display divine characteristics. Jesus' mastery over the elements calls to mind a psalmist's words: 'O LORD God of hosts, who is as mighty as you, O LORD? Your faithfulness surrounds you. You rule the raging of the sea; when its waves rise, you still them' (Ps. 89:8–9). At other times the reader simply imagines the astonishment on the faces of Jesus' observers and hearers, and perhaps other unspecified gestures, as people are reduced to silence at Jesus' argumentation. Sometimes the silence is implicit as Jesus has the last word or people simply walk away, as happened following Jesus' response to the attempt of the Pharisees and Herodians to ensnare him with a loaded question about paying taxes to the emperor: 'When they heard this, they were amazed; and they left him and went away' (Matt. 22:22; cf. Mark 12:17). At other times the evangelists remark upon people's silence (φιμόω, σιωπάω), as at Jesus' rejoinder to the Pharisees about sabbath healings: 'Then he said to them, "Is it lawful to do good or to do harm on the sabbath, to save life or to kill?" But they were silent' (Mark 3:4; cf. Matt. 22:34; Luke 20:26). The disciples are scandalised and speechless at Jesus' countercultural act of having a private conversation with a woman at a well (John 4:27).

---

11 The noted Australian linguist Nick Enfield observes (from a study across twelve languages) that 'there is a standard one-second time window for responding in conversation': Enfield, *How We Talk*, 1. The average response time in normal turn-taking is in fact only 200 milliseconds, so any gap much longer than this is interpreted as hesitation (for whatever reason); cf. Sacks, Schegloff, and Jefferson, 'A Simplest Systematics'. So entrenched is the avoidance of the awkward silence that there are now emojis for filling the gaps in a texting conversation; see Danisi, *Semiotics*, 19–20.

A similar notion to silencing is 'putting to shame' (καταισχύνω). When a synagogue leader challenged Jesus regarding his healing on the sabbath, Jesus' response was such that 'all his opponents were put to shame; and the entire crowd was rejoicing at all the wonderful things that he was doing' (Luke 13:17). Did the faces of those who were shamed turn red, we wonder (cf. LXX 2 Sam. 19:5; Ps. 34:5; Isa. 3:15; Jer. 7:19 where the Greek reflects the Hebrew idiom by locating shame in the face), or did they perhaps lay their hands to their mouths (cf. LXX Mic. 7:16)? In the case of Pilate, his amazement is at the fact that at his trial Jesus remained silent, offering no defence: 'But he gave him no answer, not even to a single charge, so that the governor was greatly amazed' (Matt. 27:14; cf. Mark 15:5; possibly echoing Isa. 53:7 and Isa. 52:15).

Jesus' public teaching, both its manner and its content, are constant cause for astonishment. He exhibited wisdom, learning, and grace in excess of that which his apparently limited education might lead people to expect (Matt. 13:54; Mark 6:2; Luke 4:22, John 7:15), even from his youth (Luke 2:47). As with his miracles, this often rendered his listeners speechless with amazement (Matt. 7:28; 22:33; Mark 1:22, 27; 11:18). A cause for much of the recorded amazement in the Gospels is the tone of authority (ἐξουσία) with which Jesus spoke or acted. His mode of teaching was not like that practised by the scribes, the Jewish legal authorities, of citing a succession of revered rabbis (Mark 1:22; Luke 4:32). Jesus taught on his own authority, even pitting it against Moses, or at least what was understood as Mosaic teaching: 'You have heard that it was said ... but I say to you' (Matt. 5:38–39, 43–44). Jesus had a reputation for wisdom and authority in all he said and did (Matt. 7:29; 9:6–8; 11:19; 12:42; 13:54; 21:23–27; 28:18; Mark 2:10; 6:2; 11:27–33; Luke 2:40, 52; 5:24; 7:35; 11:31; 20:1–8; cf. Isa. 9:6–7). One is perhaps reminded of the personified Wisdom who proclaims: 'Likewise in the beloved city he gave me rest, and in Jerusalem was my power [ἐξουσία]' (Sir. 24:11; cf. Sir. 45:17).

While there were notable exceptions (Matt. 9:30–31; 19:21–22; Mark 1:44–45; 10:21–22), it was therefore normal for people to respond without question to Jesus' directives: to a man with a withered hand, 'come and stand here' and 'stretch out your hand' (Luke 6:8, 10; cf. Matt. 12:13; Mark 3:5); to a paralysed man, 'take your bed and go home' (Matt. 9:6-7; cf. John 5:8-9); to those in attendance at a wedding, 'fill the jars with water' (John 2:7); to Peter on a boat as Jesus walked on the water, 'come' (Matt. 14:28-29); to a donkey owner, 'the Lord needs them' (Matt. 21:3); to Simon, an experienced fisherman, 'let down your nets' (Luke 5;4-9; cf. John 21:6). The compliance extended beyond the bounds of normal human voluntary behaviour and even to natural forces: to a man with a skin disease, 'be made clean' (Matt. 8:3); to a blind beggar, 'receive your sight' (Luke 18:42-43); to the ears of a deaf man, 'be opened' (Mark 7:32-35); to the dead daughter of a synagogue leader, 'little girl, get up' (Mark 5:41-42; cf. Luke 8:54-55); to Lazarus in the tomb, 'come out' (John 11:43); to the raging storm, 'Be still' (Mark 4:39). Unclean spirits or demons also complied with Jesus' directives to 'go' or 'come out' of those they had possessed (Matt. 8:16, 28-32; Mark 1:25-27; 5:2-13; 9:25-27; Luke 4:35-36; 8:26-33; 9:42), again prompting amazement on the part of those who witnessed these events (Mark 1:27; Luke 4:36; 9:43; 11:14). These episodes exhibit the same fiat-fulfilment formula used in the OT for divine commands (e.g., Gen. 1:3). They may also be seen as exhibiting the authority of God's appointed king seen in such passages as Psalm 2 and Isaiah 9:6-7.

Closely associated with amazement is the emotion of fear or awe (φόβος, φοβέομαι, τρέμω). God had promised his people that he would instil fear and amazement into the hearts of the nations (Exod. 23:27; cf. 1 Sam. 17:11; 28:5; Isa. 60:5; Ezek. 2:6; 26:16; Mic. 7:17; Hab. 3:2; Wis. 5:2). We see this being fulfilled in the ministry of Jesus, for example, in the response of those who witnessed the healing of the paralysed man, along with the forgiveness of his sins: 'Amazement seized all of them, and they glorified God and were filled with awe, saying, "We have seen strange things today"' (Luke 5:26; cf. Matt. 9:8; Mark 10:32). The disciples were overcome with awe in the presence of Jesus as he walked on water or calmed the storm (Mark 4:41; 6:51; Luke 8:25; John 6:19). This fear or awe (φόβος) is the same word used throughout Scripture for the appropriate response to the rule of God or his appointed king (e.g. LXX Exod. 20:20; 2 Sam. 23:3; 1 Chr. 14:17; 2 Chr. 19:7; Ps. 2:11; 22:23; 119:120; Mal. 2:5). It might be possible to hide one's fear to some extent (though in no Gospel incidents is this said to be the case), but generally some physiological manifestation of the fear is evident. In at least one case, the woman who had suffered from haemorrhages for twelve years, the fear is expressed as trembling (Mark 5:33). It would be wrong to assume that 'fear and trembling' is always simply a literary expression for an inner emotion, for we read, for example, in Ezra 10:9 of a dual causation—emotional and environmental—for the people's trembling: 'All the people sat in the open square before the house of God, trembling because of this matter and because of the heavy rain'.

Fear may also cause people to drop to the ground. The woman who had suffered from haemorrhages not only trembled but fell to the ground with fear (Mark 5:33). The soldiers who came to arrest Jesus were temporarily overawed by his presence or his self-revelatory response, 'I am he' (with its possible overtones of divine identity; cf. Exod. 6:2) so that 'they stepped back and fell to the ground' (John 18:6). The sight of Jesus being transfigured produced a response of fear from his disciples as they 'fell to the ground and were overcome by fear' (Matt. 17:6). In these responses, we are perhaps to see a blend of fear in the sense of alarm, and fear in the sense of reverence.

There is also at times a note of joy and rejoicing (χαίρω, χαρά) in response to Jesus. 'The entire crowd was rejoicing at all the wonderful things that he was doing' (Luke 13:17; cf. Luke 19:37). The word χαίρω introduces the LXX rendering of the prophet Zechariah's summons to the people of God at the arrival of their anticipated king:

> Rejoice greatly, O daughter Zion! Shout aloud, O daughter Jerusalem! Lo, your king comes to you; triumphant and victorious is he, humble and riding on a donkey, on a colt, the foal of a donkey (Zech 9:9).

This scene is of course acted out in the exuberant welcome extended to Jesus by the crowds on Palm Sunday, where the holding of palm branches suggested a victory celebration (Matt. 21:8–9; John 12:13; cf. 1 Macc. 13:51). This joy comes to its fullest realisation in the reaction of the disciples to Jesus' rising from the dead: 'After he said this, he showed them his hands and his side. Then the disciples rejoiced when they saw the Lord' (John 20:20; cf. Ps. 119:74; Isa. 35:2; 66:14; Matt. 28:8; Luke 24:41). This joy echoes the anticipated joy of Israel's return from exile: 'So the ransomed of the Lord shall return, and come to Zion with singing; everlasting joy shall be upon their heads; they shall obtain joy and gladness, and sorrow and sighing shall flee away' (Isa. 51:11; cf. Isa. 9:3; 24:14; 29:19; 35:2, 10; 51:3).

3. Acts of Obeisance toward Jesus

The Gospel reader notes the frequency of accounts of acts of obeisance directed at Jesus. Prostration, or falling down at the feet of one who is highly revered or in a position of power and authority, was a widespread gesture in ancient Western Asia (and in the Greek world prostration before the statues of deities). It served several purposes. One was to demonstrate a high level of respect, marking and reinforcing a social distinction between inferior and superior. The OT abounds in references to people bowing, kneeling, falling on their faces, and the like, in displays of profound respect or reverence. David, for example, prostrated himself three times before Jonathan, the royal heir (1 Sam. 20:41).

Falling down before another also serves as a gesture accompanying an entreaty or supplication, or as a demonstration of gratitude, as with the woman who suffered from haemorrhages (Mark 5:33; Luke 8:47). Supplication may involve grasping the feet or knees of the one entreated. In supplication, one places oneself in the position of a lowly servant in order to curry favour, and the deferential language of master/slave may be used.[12]

Jesus accepted physical displays on the part of those demonstrating profound honour, love, and gratitude, or those with an earnest plea for him to take action. Several verbs and phrases are used for the action: πίπτω ('fall'), προσπίπτω ('fall down'), γονυπετέω ('kneel down'), τίθημι τὰ γόνατα ('place the knees'), ἀσπάζομαι ('greet'), and προσκυνέω. προσκυνέω is used fifteen times in the Gospels with reference to responses to Jesus, variously rendered 'bow', 'kneel', 'pay homage', or 'worship', and it is not always easy to tell the extent of physical movement involved. But parallel expressions such as 'fall to one's knees', 'fall on one's face', 'fall at someone's feet', suggest that often, at least, more than simply a perfunctory nod or an inner attitude of respect is

---

12 See Bridge, 'The "Slave"'.

involved. Even the word normally translated 'greet' (ἀσπάζομαι) does not refer simply to a verbal exchange but to gestures—an embrace of social equals, or more elaborate shows of deference to social superiors—which could be time-consuming, and hence to be avoided when the urgency of gospel proclamation takes priority (Luke 10:4).[13]

Jesus' earthly life from cradle to grave and beyond it was bookended by displays of obeisance toward him. While English translations might not be clear, Matthew has the magi present their gifts to Jesus from a prostrate position, using both πίπτω 'fall' and προσκυνέω: 'they knelt down and paid him homage' (Matt. 2:11). Ancient images depict such processional tribute scenes, with those behind carrying gifts, while those nearest the enthroned monarch have dropped to the ground, and Matthew likely has something analogous to such a court scene in mind, echoing Isaiah 60:5–6:

> Then you shall see and be radiant; your heart shall thrill and rejoice, because the abundance of the sea shall be brought to you, the wealth of the nations shall come to you. A multitude of camels shall cover you, the young camels of Midian and Ephah; all those from Sheba shall come. They shall bring gold and frankincense, and shall proclaim the praise of the LORD.[14]

In his final pericope, Matthew records that the disciples worship the risen Lord as he declares his universal authority (Matt. 28:17), again with προσκυνέω.[15] In between, we have a succession of individuals responding to Jesus with gestures of devotion or supplication. Just to stick with Matthew for the moment, we have the man with a skin condition in search of healing and social acceptance (Matt. 8:2), the synagogue leader whose daughter has died (Matt. 9:18), the disciples in the boat as they respond to Jesus' appearance on the water (Matt. 14:33; cf. Ps. 77:19; Isa. 43:16), a Canaanite woman seeking help for her daughter (Matt. 15:25), the father of a man with epilepsy (Matt. 17:14), the mother of James and John (Matt. 20:20), and the disciples encountering

---

13 See Windisch, 'ἀσπάζομαι', 498.
14 Pritchard, *The Ancient Near East in Pictures*, #45, #46, #47. See Brown, *Birth*, 165–201.
15 See Bauckham, *Jesus and the God of Israel*, 25, 179.

the risen Jesus (Matt. 28:9). In all, Matthew uses the expression ten times with reference to responses to Jesus, and I concur with Bauckham that 'Matthew uses *proskunein* in a semi-technical way for the obeisance that is due to Jesus'.[16] It is even possible to detect in Matthew's wording of the bringing to Jesus of those in need of healing an echo of the offering of tribute: 'They put them at his feet' (Matt. 15:30).[17]

The woman who anointed Jesus' feet at a banquet performs the most elaborate display of honour in the Gospels (Luke 7:36-38). Approaching Jesus from behind (because of the seating arrangement at a banquet), she placed herself at his feet, and with tears streaming down, anointed Jesus with an expensive bottle of perfume, bathed his feet in her tears, dried them with her hair (respectable women did not let their hair down in public), and carried on kissing Jesus' feet in a very unselfconscious display of humility and gratitude (Luke 7:36-38; cf. John 11:2; 12:3).[18]

The kneeling of the Roman soldiers at the cross was of course an aspect of the mockery to which Jesus was subjected (Matt. 27:29; Mark 15:19), part of the humiliation and suffering which the messiah had to undergo on Jesus' own understanding of his mission (Matt. 20:19; Mark 10:34; Luke 18:32).

Though our English translations sometimes prefer the word 'worship' as a translation of προσκυνέω, I am not suggesting that each or even any of those who fell down before Jesus did so with the understanding that they were worshipping deity. But perhaps the Gospel writers from their vantage point of hindsight have included their instances of obeisance with a hint that these can be viewed as early demonstrations of that which the church came to regard as the worship rightfully due to Jesus as God. The actions of Peter in falling down at Jesus' knees and saying, 'Go away from me, Lord, for I am a sinful man!' (Luke 5:8) or of Peter, James, and John at the transfiguration, when they 'fell to the ground [lit.: on their face] and were overcome by fear' (Matt. 17:6)

---

16 Bauckham, *Jesus and the God of Israel*, 131; cf. Hurtado, *How on Earth?*, 158-59. Some mss also have ἐθαύμασαν for ἐφοβήθησαν at Matt. 9:8.
17 Hagner, *Matthew 14-28*, 445. Cf. the posture of the king of Heracleopolis 'on his belly' as he brought tribute to the pharaoh: *The Victory Stela of King Piye*, 55-56 (*Context of Scripture*, 2:46).
18 Bailey, *Through Peasant Eyes*, 8.

must surely come close to this. As the Apostle Paul would express it, 'at the name of Jesus every knee should bend, in heaven and on earth and under the earth' (Phil. 2:10), an echo of the prostration before God to which the psalmists summon his people, for example, 'O come, let us worship and bow down, let us kneel before the LORD, our Maker!' (Ps. 95:6; cf. Ps. 99:5; 132:7; Isa. 45:23).

Another gesture of honour is when the crowds 'went ahead' of Jesus, as well as behind him, at his entry to Jerusalem (Matt. 21:9; Mark 11:9). En route they spread their outer garments on the ground in front of Jesus, consistent with this being portrayed as a royal processional entry (Matt. 21:8; cf. 2 Kgs 9:13).

4. Negative Gestures toward Jesus

Not all of the attention paid to Jesus was admiring, of course. The crowds could be fickle, and ultimately Jesus faced rejection by the mob who preferred to release an insurrectionist (Matt. 27:21; Luke 23:18). Disbelief could be expressed as laughter, as when Jesus said that the daughter of the synagogue leader was not dead, but sleeping (Matt. 9:24; Mark 5:40; Luke 8:53). There were those who jealously 'eyed' Jesus (παρατηρέω) in order to find fault, for example at his healing on the sabbath of the man with the withered hand (Mark 3:2; Luke 6:7; cf. Luke 14:1; 20:20). In time, religious and political opposition to Jesus hardened as his agenda seemed at odds with the interests of those of other groups. Mockery of Jesus by his opponents could be both verbal and nonverbal. We have already noted the mock obeisance of the soldiers. Matthew and Mark also record that those who witnessed Jesus' crucifixion shook their heads at him in derision (Matt. 27:39; Mark 15:29). This of course is an echo of Psalm 22 (the psalm which is alluded to elsewhere in the crucifixion scene in the Gospels): 'All who see me mock at me; they make mouths at me, they shake their heads' (Ps. 22:7). Head wagging could be a gesture of pity: Job's friends shake their heads in sympathy with his sufferings (Job 2:11), and Jeremiah laments the condition of the land under God's judgement: 'All who pass by it are horrified and shake their heads' (Jer. 18:16). In the case of the response to Jesus' crucifixion, as in the psalm, it is of course a cruel mock pity, the reaction of the wicked to the suffering of the righteous.

To cover one's face is a gesture of shame. On one reading of Peter's remorse in the courtyard of the high priest (Mark 14:72), he 'covered [ἐπιβάλλω, i.e. his head or face] and wept', perhaps indicating that he pulled his garment or his arm over his head, in a manner depicted in Egyptian art to indicate shame, but we cannot be certain of the meaning of the verb here (cf. NRSV 'he broke down and wept').[19] To cover the face of another is then to subject them to shame or humiliation. Jesus' face was covered at one point in his trial. As well as setting the scene for a demand for a 'prophecy' as to who struck him, the covering of Jesus' face was then itself part of the shame he endured (Mark 14:65; Luke 22:64).

Jesus' opponents regarded his self-referential statements and actions as tantamount to blasphemy—dishonouring the God of Israel—which probably no ordinary messianic claimant would necessarily be considered guilty of (Matt. 9:3; 26:63–66; Mark 2:7; 14:61–65; Luke 5:21; 22:66–71; John 10:31–39; 19:7).[20] The high priest tore his garments (which presumably he did not do every week) to dramatise his outrage at Jesus' blasphemy (Matt. 26:65; Mark 14:63; cf. 2 Kgs 18:37; 19:1, 4, 6, 22 LXX; Acts 14:14; *m. San.* 7:5). The humiliation of Jesus also involved mock regal salutation, spitting, and slapping his face (Matt. 26:67; 27:29–30; Mark 14:65; 15:18–19; John 18:22; 19:3) in accordance with Jesus' own predictions of the messianic sufferings that awaited him (Mark 10:34; Luke 18:32).21 Isaiah spoke of one who declares, 'I gave my back to those who struck me, and my cheeks to those who pulled out the beard; I did not hide my face from insult and spitting' (Isa. 50:6; cf. Num. 12:14; Deut. 25:9; Job 30:9–10; Mic. 5:1). The irony of slapping Jesus and asking him to prophesy will not be lost on the reader familiar with the account in 1 Kings 22:24 of the false prophet Zedekiah humiliating the prophet of the LORD, Micaiah, as he slapped him on the cheek. All of these actions at the passion are consistent with

---

19 For other suggestions, see Evans, *Mark 8:27–16:20*, 466–67; Brown, *Death*, vol. 1, 609–10.
20 See Brown, *Death*, vol. 1, 530–47; Twelftree, 'Blasphemy', 77; Theobald, "'Ihr habt der Blasphemie gehört!'".
21 Brown, *Death*, 568–86, 868–77.

the notion that Jesus, with his allusion to Daniel 7:13 and Psalm 110:2, was understood to be claiming in some way to share in God's glory and authority and, in Mark's version, perhaps even subtly to appropriate the divine name with his response 'I am' (Matt. 26:64; Mark 14:62). Even the placement by the soldiers of the two criminals on either side of Jesus (Matt. 27:38; Mark 15:27; Luke 23:33) can be seen as a deliberate aspect of the regal mockery (cf. Isa. 53:12): this 'king' has known criminals in attendance upon him.

5. Proxemics in Relation to Jesus

Proxemics—a study of the way people position themselves in terms of closeness or distance from one another in different situations—can be instructive. People of all social backgrounds responded to Jesus in terms of close physical dealings. A Pharisee felt comfortable inviting Jesus to a meal (Luke 7:36), while social outcasts like 'tax collectors and sinners' were also happy to take a seat at the dinner table in Jesus' home, much to the consternation of the Pharisees (Matt. 9:10–13). So to a fault (as some saw it: v. 11), Jesus was very sociable, not in the least aloof.

To follow a leader is a prominent motif of Scripture. Elijah challenged the people of Israel: 'How long will you go limping with two different opinions? If the LORD is God, follow him; but if Baal, then follow him' (1 Kgs 18:21). Military leaders physically led their troops into battle. Prophets and teachers went ahead of their disciples when out walking. So to be a follower of such a prophet or teacher was not simply metaphorical (1 Sam 13:7, 15; 25:27; 1 Kgs 1:35, 40; 19:20; 20:19; Acts 5:36). Jesus calls some fishermen and immediately they leave their nets and follow him (Matt. 4:20), and the Gospels abound in references to Jesus summoning and people following him (e.g. Matt. 4:19–20, 22, 25; 8:1, 10, 22, 23; 9:9; 10:38; 12:15; 14:13; 16:24; 19:2, 21, 27, 28, 29; 20:34; John 1:37–38, 40, 43; 6:2; 8:12; 10:27; 12:26; 21:19), and this had both literal and metaphorical significance. Mark particularly makes it explicit that on the journey to Jerusalem (the way to the cross), Jesus led the way while his disciples came behind (Mark 10:32; cf. Matt. 9:10).

Physical touching is a form of identification with others and Jesus was often said to touch people in acts of blessing or healing. Despite his disciples' protest, when children were brought to him, 'he took them up in his arms, laid his hands on them, and blessed them' (Mark 10:16; cf. Matt. 8:15; 9:29; 17:7; 19:13–15; 20:34; Mark 6:5; 7:33; 8:23–25; Luke 4:40; 13:13; 18:15; 22:51). Nor was Jesus averse to touching that which was considered ritually unclean, such as a man with a skin disease: 'He stretched out his hand and touched him, saying, "I do choose. Be made clean"' (Matt. 8:3; cf. Mark 1:41; Luke 5:13). Jesus made a point of touching the funeral bier of a young man, stopping those who were carrying it in their tracks (Luke 7:14). This willingness on Jesus' part to have physical contact with those in need no doubt gave encouragement to them to reach out to Jesus: 'All who had diseases pressed upon him to touch him' (Mark 3:10; cf. Mark 6:56; Luke 6:19). The sick who came to Jesus for healing 'begged him that they might touch even the fringe of his cloak' (Matt. 14:36; Mark 6:56). The accounts of the woman who suffered from haemorrhages (Matt. 9:20–22; Mark 5:25–34; Luke 8:43–48) make much of the woman's touching Jesus. On that occasion Jesus' question as to who it was who touched him seems prompted by a desire that the woman make a public acknowledgement of her identification with Jesus in this way, and it is on this basis that she is assured of 'salvation' (Mark 5:33–34).[22] Jesus' post-resurrection words to Mary, 'Do not hold on to me' (John 20:17) imply that she is in fact holding him, perhaps clinging to his feet in adoration and affection (cf. Matt. 28:9). While a number of interpretations of Jesus' words are possible, Jesus perhaps simply means that Mary is not to linger, as he gives her a task to do: to tell his disciples that he is in the process of 'ascending' to the Father.

The proxemics of Jesus' disciples in relation to him in the passion and crucifixion scenes are also described. Jesus enters the garden with the eleven, but soon leaves all but his inner circle of Peter, James, and John. He then leaves these three, going on further to pray by himself. Three times he returns to find the disciples sleeping (Matt. 26:36–46; Mark 14:32–42; cf. Luke 22:40–46). While Jesus undergoes this agonised time of testing, the disciples are passive and weak, and soon abandon

---

22 For an insightful treatment of this pericope, see Gosbell, 'The woman'.

their master altogether. Jesus must experience this 'cup' alone. Peter 'was following him at a distance' as Jesus was led to trial at the high priest's residence (Matt. 26:58; Mark 14:54; Luke 22:54). Similarly all three synoptic Gospels make mention of the women who kept their distance as Jesus breathed his last (Matt. 27:55; Mark 15:40; Luke 23:49). The distance of Jesus' followers is consistent with Jesus' own understanding of the abandonment the messiah must endure (see Ps. 38:12; Zech 13:7; Matt. 26:31; John 16:32).

6. Conclusion

Much more could be said, but from the above we can see that Jesus provoked a wide range of nonverbal responses from those who encountered him—amazement, fear, jealousy, abandonment, adoration, mockery. The Gospel writers appear to have selected and shaped their accounts to highlight those aspects of the effect Jesus had on people that served each writer's purpose. In part, this purpose was to show that the impact Jesus made was in line with messianic expectations, at least as Jesus clarified and redefined these. By their actions as well as their words, many showed that they expected Jesus to bring salvation to them and to the nation, while others reacted negatively with regard to those expectations. Perhaps also the seeds of a high Christology, where Jesus is understood to be in some way identified with Israel's God, are to be seen in the way the Gospel writers portray the impact of Jesus. Their portrayals might also prompt readers to ponder our own responses to the way Jesus continues to impact each of us.

Bibliography

Bailey, Kenneth E. *Through Peasant Eyes: More Lucan Parables, Their Culture and Style* (Grand Rapids: Eerdmans, 1980).

Bauckham, Richard *Jesus and the Eyewitnesses: The Gospels as Eyewitness Testimony* (Grand Rapids: Eerdmans, 2006).

Bauckham, Richard *Jesus and the God of Israel: God Crucified and Other Studies on the New Testament's Christology of Divine Identity* (Grand Rapids: Eerdmans, 2008).

Bertram, Georg 'θαῦμα κτλ.', TDNT vol. 3, 27–41.

Bridge, Edward J. 'The "Slave" Is the "Master": Jacob's Servile Language to Esau in Genesis 33.1–17', *JSOT* 39 (2014), 263–78.

Brown, Raymond E. *The Birth of the Messiah: A Commentary on the Infancy Narratives in Matthew and Luke* (London: Geoffrey Chapman, 1977).

Brown, Raymond E. *The Death of the Messiah from Gethsemane to the Grave: A Commentary on the Passion Narrative in the Four Gospels* (2 vols.; The Anchor Bible Reference Library; New York: Doubleday, 1964).

Campos, B., M. N. Shiota, D. Keltner, G. C. Gonzaga, & J. L. Goetz 'What Is Shared, What is Different? Core Relational Themes and Expressive Displays of Eight Positive Emotions', *Cognition and Emotion* 27 (2013), 37–52.

Danisi, Marcel *The Semiotics of Emoji* (London: Bloomsbury, 2017).

Darwin, Charles *The Expression of the Emotions in Man and Animals* (New York: D. Appleton & Company, 1872).

Davies, John A. *Lift up Your Heads: Nonverbal Communication and Related Body Imagery in the Bible* (Eugene: Pickwick Publications, 2018).

Dwyer, Timothy *The Motif of Wonder in the Gospel of Mark* (JSNTSup 128; Sheffield: Sheffield Academic, 1996).

Enfield, N.J. *How We Talk: The Inner Workings of Conversation* (New York: Basic Books, 2017).

Evans, Craig A. *Mark 8:27–16:20* (WBC; Nashville: Thomas Nelson, 2001).

Gosbell, Louise — 'The Woman with the "Flow of Blood" (Mark 5:25–34) and Disability in the Ancient World', *Journal of Gospels and Acts Research* 2 (2018), 22–43.

Hagner, Donald A. — *Matthew 14–28* (WBC; Dallas: Word, 1995).

Hallo, W.W. — *The Context of Scripture. 2. Monumental Inscriptions from the Biblical World* (Leiden: E.J. Brill, 2003).

Homer. — *The Iliad* (E. V. Rieu, transl.; Harmondsworth: Penguin, 1950).

Hurtado, Larry W. — *How on Earth Did Jesus Become a God? Historical Questions about Earliest Devotion to Jesus* (Grand Rapids: Eerdmans, 2005).

Jeremias, Joachim — *Jesus' Promise to the Nations* (SBT 24; London: SCM, 1958).

Nolland, John — 'Impressed Unbelievers as Witnesses to Christ (Luke 4:22a)', *JBL* 98 (1979), 219–29.

Pritchard, J.B. — *The Ancient Near East in Pictures: Relating to the Old Testament* (Princeton: Princeton University Press, ²1969 [original: 1954]).

Sacks, Harvey, Emanuel A. Schegloff, & Gail Jefferson — 'A Simplest Systematics for the Organization of Turn Taking for Conversation', in J. Schenkeim (ed.), *Studies in the Organization of Conversational Interaction* (London: Academic Press, 1978), 7–55.

Strelan, Rick — 'The Ascension as a Cultic Experience in Acts', in D.K. Bryan & D.W. Pao (eds.), *Ascent into Heaven in Luke–Acts: New Explorations of Luke's Narrative Hinge* (Minneapolis: Fortress, 2016), 213–32.

Theobald, Michael — '"Ihr habt der Blasphemie gehört!" (Mk 14:64): Warum der Hohe Rat in Jerusalem auf den Tod Jesu hinwirkte', *Novum Testamentum* 58 (2016), 233–58.

Twelftree, G.H. — 'Blasphemy', in J.B. Green & S. McKnight (eds.), *Dictionary of Jesus and the Gospels* (Downers Grove: InterVarsity, 1992), 75–77.

Windisch, H. — 'ἀσπάζομαι', in *TDNT* vol. 1, 496–502.

CHAPTER 4

Transcending Categories: The Impact of the Resurrection of Jesus of Nazareth

Aaron Chidgzey

Abstract

This article examines the general trends within scholarship on the resurrection, arguing that most interpretations emphasize either the continuous or discontinuous elements of the resurrection at the expense of the other. That is, either the historical, literal, and material, or the eschatological (supra-historical), metaphorical, or immaterial elements of the resurrection are highlighted. This article argues that both the continuous and discontinuous must be equally accounted for. An analysis of the Jewish eschatological notion of resurrection reveals that 'resurrection' rarely referred to a post-mortem re-embodiment of individual bodies, but interacted, in a mutually-conditioning function, with the broader eschatological motifs of redemption of relationship, the re-creation of the present created order, and the dispensation of divine justice. This is similarly present in the New Testament portrayals of Jesus' resurrection, which is depicted as the inauguration of the new eschatological age—the unification of heaven and earth. As such, Jesus' resurrection cannot be reduced to little more than a re-animated body, and thus cannot be restricted to emphasizing either its continuous or discontinuous elements, but must incorporate both, transcending and unifying these categories.

1. Introduction: Defining the Categories

The claim that Jesus rose from the dead is a significantly polarizing theological issue, especially since the Enlightenment era, with interpretations generally falling into two camps. The first stresses the continuity of the risen Jesus with the pre-crucifixion Jesus, emphasizing an *historical*, *material*, or *literal* interpretation of the claim. The second stresses the discontinuity, emphasizing a *supra-historical*, *immaterial*, or *metaphorical* interpretation. Though the vast majority of scholarship can, by and large, be separated into one of these two camps, I contend that this is theological reductionism, a remnant perhaps of a lingering pervasive foundationalist epistemology. I believe a better interpretation of the resurrection is one which equally incorporates both aspects, upholding them in a dialectic tension. In this essay I argue that the theological notion of resurrection should not be reduced to little more than the re-animation of an individual body, for it encompasses within itself a broad spectrum of eschatological hope, especially the hope for cosmic re-creation, redemption of relationship, and the dispensation of divine judgment. As such, there is both continuity and discontinuity with present reality; Jesus' resurrection is the personification of these eschatological hopes and so had considerable impact upon contingent history and temporal reality, marking the inauguration of the new eschatological age, namely the new heavens and earth.

This first section sets the scene, discussing how the majority of scholarship has continually restricted the interpretation Jesus' resurrection to one category at the expense of the other. Either the continuous elements of Jesus' resurrection have been emphasized and so ignores the discontinuous, or vice versa, rather than attempting to hold the two in tension. The second section then re-evaluates the notion of resurrection in Jewish eschatology prior to its adoption by the early Christian communities. This framework through which Jesus' post-mortem fate was interpreted is not a homogenized, universal 'doctrine', but a malleable image utilized to envisage, not a post-mortem individual existence, but a variety of eschatological motifs. The third section then turns its attention to the New Testament portrayals of Jesus' resurrection where the eschatological motifs connected to resurrection in Jewish eschatology are repeated, reframed around the events of Easter. Jesus' resurrection may indeed include his body (though it is impossible to discern a concrete picture of what that might have looked like), but it had to do with far more than that, and so both continuity and discontinuity must be upheld.

1.1 Continuity: Historical, Material, Literal

Prior to the Enlightenment and the dawn of rationalistic criticism and historical empiricism the majority position was a literal, historical reading of the resurrection. That is, the continuity of Jesus' resurrection with his pre-crucifixion body was a virtually ubiquitous presupposition. Some transformation of Jesus' body is certainly asserted, but woefully limited. Clement's Second Letter to the Corinthians in the early to mid-second century explicitly claims, 'Let none of you say that this flesh will not be judged or rise again. [...] For just as you were called in the flesh, you will come in the flesh,'[1] Justin Martyr confidently proclaimed, 'We look forward to receiving again our own bodies,'[2] and for Tertullian, 'Nothing rises again but what has already been'.[3]

Augustine so strongly interpreted the resurrected body as one that bears considerable continuity with the present (or, in Jesus' case, the pre-crucifixion body) that he was concerned with trimmed hair and nails. The risen body, he argued, shall be composed 'of the matter of which it was originally composed', which includes hair and nails, but not the trimmings on the barber's floor. Neither are deformities or obesity present in the resurrected body, except of course for the wicked, who will retain their deformities.[4] Later, Thomas Aquinas shared these concerns, maintaining that the resurrected body will be the 'selfsame body' and shall be resurrected 'identically' and so discussed to great length the problem of hair and nails, as well as blood, whether the risen shall rise the same age as when they die, and if the risen body shall be the same size.[5]

This strong stress upon a historical and literal resurrection continued through Anselm—righteous man 'will be restored in the body in

---

1   2 Clem. 9.1, 4.
2   1 Apol. xviii, 4.
3   *On Resurrection*, 53.9–11, 26.
4   *Enchiridion*, xxiii, 84–93.
5   Aquinas, *The Summa Theologica*, III. Suppl., Q. 79, art. 1–2.

which he lives in this life'[6]—to the Reformation. Martin Luther takes the rather uninspiring position that the resurrected body shall not eat, drink, digest, bear children, keep house, or govern, even though 'everyone's body will remain as it was created'.[7] Similarly, Ulrich Zwingli maintained that Jesus' risen body 'is identical with that which was crucified', and that it 'is impossible to deny that the flesh and blood which was put to death for us ascended up into heaven'.[8]

The forcefulness of Zwingli's hyperbole is matched only by Charles Spurgeon's claim that 'the resurrection of Jesus Christ from the dead is one of the best attested facts on record', and 'we cannot and we dare not doubt that Jesus rose from the dead'.[9] Indeed, for Spurgeon it was unimaginable that a Christian might believe that the resurrected body be anything other than 'the very flesh in which he now walks the earth',[10] an interpretation that was emerging during this time of the burgeoning Enlightenment.

We shall return to these other interpretations momentarily, but this emphasis upon the continuity of the resurrected body has been upheld in recent scholarship. Perhaps the most notable and lengthy defences of a historical and bodily resurrection are those presented by Wolfhart Pannenberg and N. T. Wright. Pannenberg's Christology 'from below' —the methodological insistence that the historian or theologian 'get behind' the text to discover the *human* Jesus of Nazareth before working up to the *divine* Christ of Faith—led him to maintain the historicity and the historical accessibility of the resurrection. This developed in his later work toward a methodology somewhere between 'from below' and 'from above' but he retained a strong emphasis upon historical research. If the resurrection cannot be considered public knowledge, it cannot then be universal and so, therefore, cannot be divine revelation.[11] Wright's extensive study on the resurrection similarly stresses the need for historical Jesus research and that the resurrection must be historically accessible. Jesus' risen body was 'robustly physical', but

---

6   Quoted in Davis and Evans (eds.), *Anselm of Canterbury*, 317.
7   Luther, '1 Corinthians', 171.
8   Zwingli, 'On the Lord's Supper', 232.
9   Spurgeon, 'The Resurrection of the Dead', 108.
10 Spurgeon, 'The Resurrection of the Dead', 98.
11 Pannenberg, *Jesus—God and Man*, 17–18, 83–104.

introduces what he calls 'transphysicality' (transformed physicality) to explain this body.[12] Though both seem closer than most scholarship in drawing the continuous and discontinuous elements of the resurrection into a unified whole, neither do so adequately, resorting to a depiction of resurrection that is primarily and essentially historical and physical.

The Baptist theologian Stanley Grenz argues for the validity of both the empty tomb and appearance traditions. For the former, he insists that it is unlikely that the tomb would be mistaken, that the disciples stole the body, or that the Jewish authorities moved the body. For the latter, it is unlikely that the appearances were either fabrications or hallucinations, because so many people were witnesses to the risen Jesus.[13] William Lane Craig and Gary Habermas maintain this position, employing several rigid tests to determine the best explanation for the historical data, which they contend is a physical, historical resurrection. Craig includes the tests of explanatory scope, explanatory power, plausibility, less ad hoc, and the outstripping of rival theories. A traditional interpretation of the resurrection, he concludes, fulfils each of these tests.[14] For Habermas, naturalistic explanations fail to explain away the resurrection, and the best understanding is of a bodily resurrection.[15]

Norman Geisler continues this interpretation, believing that Jesus returned 'in the same material body of flesh and bones that had been crucified' and the resurrection 'has overwhelming historical reliability'.[16] Bruce Milne echoes Grenz, Craig, and Habermas by claiming that the empty tomb, appearances, and transformation of the disciples is adequate evidence, and that this evidence 'is as irrefutable as [...] the bricks and mortar of the nearest church building'.[17] Finally, Michael Licona's 'new historiographical approach' amounts to little more than a reframing of a strong positivistic methodology, including a reaffirmation of many of the criteria of authenticity, which have come under heavy scrutiny in recent scholarship.[18] His 2004 collaboration with Habermas

---

12 Wright, *The Resurrection of the Son of God*, 477–78.
13 Grenz, *Theology for the Community of God*, 256–60.
14 Craig, *Assessing the New Testament Evidence for the Historicity of the Resurrection of Jesus*, 418.
15 Habermas, 'Affirmative Statement', 20–25.
16 Geisler, *When Skeptics Ask*, 128–29, 259.
17 Milne, *Know the Truth*, 182.
18 Licona, *The Resurrection of Jesus*.

argued that Matthew, Mark, and Luke 'portray a bodily resurrection of Jesus in the plainest of terms'.[19]

The two most significant problems with an interpretation of the resurrection of Jesus which emphasizes the continuity of the resurrected body with the pre-crucifixion body (one that is thoroughly historical, physical/material, and a literal interpretation of the New Testament portrayal of resurrection) at the expense of its discontinuity are as follows. First, the resurrection is reduced to a mere event within contingent history unlike any other event. When treated as such, with the employment of ordinary historical methods, this event is stripped of any of its miraculous characteristics. As shall be examined below, this event is a profoundly—and extremely significant—*eschatological* event, and as such is distinct, in some way, to every other historical event. Second, the notion of resurrection in first-century Jewish eschatology, and in the New Testament's depiction, is one which depicts radical transformation, to the extent that the language of 'physicality' and 'materiality' are inappropriate. I shall return to this. For now, it is important to note that these interpretations of the resurrection which emphasize the historical, material, and literal elements of the claim that Jesus rose from the dead essentially portray only one half of the equation, neglecting the elements of discontinuity.

1.2 Discontinuity: Metaphor and Suprahistory

On the other hand, there are those who fall into the opposing camp, whose interpretation of the resurrection stresses the discontinuity of the risen body. The resurrection is interpreted in terms of the categories of metaphor and suprahistory. As with those above, only one half of the equation is depicted, stressing the discontinuity at the expense of the continuity. It should be noted that though these three categories often represent distinct interpretive traditions, they frequently overlap.

The first to be observed here is a metaphorical interpretation. David Hume, Gotthold Lessing, and David Strauss are responsible for inspiring some of the strictest critical methodologies, whose legacy remains pervasive. For Hume, the correlation between cause and effect can in

---

19   Habermas and Licona, *The Case for the Resurrection of Jesus*, 157.

no way be demonstrated, but rather simply *expected*, based on repeated experience. We do not experience resurrections today, so cannot affirm that they ever occurred.[20] Lessing argued that contingent and accidental historical events cannot determine universal and necessary truths of reason. There is, thus, a gap between historical and rational truth, the 'ugly great ditch'. Miracles, which constitute a necessary truth of reason, are therefore historically inaccessible.[21]

Strauss claimed, on the basis of these arguments, that miracle accounts cannot be considered historically factual and so the New Testament accounts must be 'demythologized'. That is, they must be stripped of mythological elements—language expressing spiritual ideas which the primitive community failed to comprehend—in order to ascertain the bare fact of what really happened. Resurrection was mythological language expressing an intense emotional memory; 'resurrection' was the interpretation of this memory.[22] This critical tradition is expressed most explicitly by Ernst Troeltsch, who maintained the homogeneity of history, that events remain universally similar, and so the principal of analogy must be applied universally. Resurrections, he insists, do not occur today, and so can only be explained as the significant impact Jesus had upon his disciples.[23]

Paul Tillich and Willi Marxsen similarly interpret the resurrection metaphorically. Tillich asserts that resurrection is not something that happened in the distant past, but is something that continually happens. Resurrection is the realization of Jesus as Christ in the minds of his followers; 'Resurrection is not an event that might happen in some remote future, but is the power of the New Being to create life out of death'.[24] For Marxsen, the resurrection eludes historical research on account of its nature as miracle, but the tradition arose as 'an inference derived from personal faith'. The birth of faith in the disciples, expressed as the resurrection of Jesus, is the *real* miracle. Resurrection happened to the disciples, not Jesus.[25]

---

20 Hume, *Enquiries Concerning Human Understanding and Concerning the Principals of Morals.*
21 Lessing, 'On the Proof of Spirit and Power', 249–50.
22 Strauss, 'Reimarus and his Apology', 52–55.
23 Troeltsch, *The Christian Faith*, 75–96; Troeltsch, *The Absoluteness of Christianity*, 106–12.
24 Tillich, *The New Being*, 24.
25 Marxsen, *The Resurrection of Jesus of Nazareth*, 128–40.

For John Dominic Crossan, resurrection is Jesus' ongoing presence and the tradition had primarily to do with power relationships within the early Christian communities.[26] James Dunn maintains that the resurrection is Jesus' exaltation,[27] as does Gerd Lüdemann who, reflecting Strauss, maintains that the appearances of the risen Jesus were hallucination caused by extreme emotion.[28] The key observation of this discussion of metaphorical interpretations is the assumption that the resurrection is so discontinuous with Jesus' pre-crucifixion body that it cannot be interpreted literally or historically, let alone materially, and so must be metaphor.

A similar approach is one which views the resurrection primarily as kerygma. It may or may not have occurred within temporal reality, but the significance for historical research is the *message* of the narratives of Jesus, not the definitive *bruta facta*. Käsemann, responding to his mentor Bultmann (who shall be addressed below), insists that the Gospels were fundamentally theology expressed as historical narrative. He doesn't explicitly address the historicity of the resurrection but affirms that the disciples and then the early church recognized Jesus as the risen Lord, and that this event described as resurrection was the impetus for recognizing Jesus as Lord.[29] Bornkamm also claims that the determination of the brute facts of 'what happened' is largely futile. The resurrection is beyond historical scrutiny and so cannot be conclusively established.[30] Hans Frei points the interpreter toward—and no further—the narrative itself. Rather than ascertaining absolute historical facts, the interpreter looks to the story, to the message of Christ's living presence. Arguments surrounding the literal or metaphorical, bodily or historical nature of the event is a distraction and provide nothing to our faith.[31]

Others, particularly emerging as a response to the first 'Quest for the Historical Jesus' in the early to mid-twentieth century following the methodological critique of Schweitzer, argued for a 'suprahistorical' interpretation. That is, the resurrection of Jesus is of such eschatological

---

26 Crossan, *The Historical Jesus*, 395–96; Crossan, *Jesus*, 158.
27 Dunn, 'How are the Dead Raised?', 5–18; Dunn, *Jesus Remembered*, 826–78.
28 Lüdemann, 'Opening Statements', 40–45.
29 Käsemann, *Essays on New Testament Themes*, 23.
30 Bornkamm, *Jesus of Nazareth*, 14.
31 Frei, *The Eclipse of Biblical Narrative*, 87, 316.

character that it transcends history and cannot thus be examined historically. This was especially introduced by Rudolf Bultmann, who claimed that the central concern of the evangelists was not presenting historical 'fact' but with leading individuals to an encounter with Christ in the present. The resurrection was—and is—the subjective experience and elevation of Jesus to Lord in the minds of his followers. It is something that is realized existentially in believers.[32] Bultmann's emphasis upon the existential experience of the living Jesus is later reflected in Jürgen Moltmann's 'Theology of Hope', claiming that Christian hope is 'resurrection hope', for God has revealed the future of creation in the event of Jesus' resurrection, enabling and equipping faith in the present.[33] It cannot be put under the microscope of historical criticism for it occurred within eschatological history and is therefore inaccessible.[34]

This suprahistorical interpretation was then profoundly reinforced by Karl Barth. For Barth, Jesus did indeed rise from the dead in a bodily sense—both his humanity and divinity were resurrected. However, it transcends ordinary human experience, functioning as the *eternalization* of Jesus, who is given immortality so that he is available *pro nobis*, for all times.[35] He famously claimed that 'In the resurrection the new world of the Holy Spirit touches the old world of the flesh, but touches it as a tangent touches a circle, that is, without touching it'.[36]

The perspective that the resurrection transcends ordinary human experience and so escapes the reach of historical inquiry is continued in the work of those who focus their interpretation upon the *exaltation* and *glorification* of Jesus, such as Karl Rahner, who argued that this event is simultaneously the cause and result of the faith of the disciples, a mutually conditional relationship between faith in, and experience of, Jesus' glorification.[37] According to Joachim Jeremias, resurrection was understood in Jewish literature as the arrival of the new eschatological creation; Jesus' post-mortem fate was thus interpreted eschatologically,

---

32 Bultmann, *Jesus Christ and Mythology*, 14, 150.
33 Moltmann, *Theology of Hope*, 16–21.
34 Moltmann, *The Way of Jesus Christ*, 213–24.
35 Barth, *Church Dogmatics*, vol. 4.1, 283–357.
36 Barth, *The Epistle to the Romans*, 30.
37 Rahner, *Foundations of Christian Faith*, 267–77.

accordingly as his entry into glory.[38] For Edward Schillebeeckx, the empty tomb was a narratological tool, a later tradition inspired by the event of Jesus' exaltation (rather than the empty tomb inspiring belief in the resurrection).[39] Similarly, Luke Timothy Johnson alleges that the resurrection eludes historical reconstruction, elevating 'Jesus beyond the merely human; he is no longer defined by time and space'.[40]

Those presenting a suprahistorical interpretation of Jesus' resurrection have stressed the eschatological character of Jesus' post-mortem fate to such an extent that it is disqualified as an event within temporal history. Rather, it is within *eschatological history*, in the 'new world of the Holy Spirit', totally inaccessible by human cognition and entirely disparate to human experience.

The central debilitating problem for these interpretations which focus upon the discontinuity of Jesus' risen nature with his pre-crucifixion body, or the discontinuity of this event with ordinary reality and experience, is the failure to acknowledge the redemption of history and of creation itself. To reduce the claim that Jesus rose from the dead to mere metaphor or to separate the event from ordinary reality invariably results in a resurrection which ultimately has nothing to do with the created order. This, I believe, is a serious misunderstanding of what the notion of resurrection meant in Second Temple Jewish and early Christian eschatology, which—as shall be demonstrated in the following sections—envisaged the redemption and renewal of the present creation at the end of (and which does not entail an absolute separation from) history. If it were an event which redeemed present, temporal reality, then it must in some sense be *a part of* and *within* contingent and ordinary history. Of course, we must be careful not to pivot into the other interpretive camp which ignored the fact that this event is, nevertheless, *not* an ordinary historical event. Jesus' resurrection cannot be reduced to one of these two opposing categories, but must uphold both in tension, for this event *transcends* these categories, unifying them without compromising either.

---

38 Jeremias, *New Testament Theology*, 308–10.
39 Schillebeeckx, *Jesus*, 73–76.
40 Johnson, *The Real Jesus*, 136.

2. Jewish Eschatology: Revisiting the Categories

In the above I argued that scholarship on the resurrection can generally be divided into those who argue for a resurrection that bears considerable *continuity* with ordinary reality and those who argue for a resurrection that bears considerable *discontinuity* with ordinary reality. The central problem with this dichotomy, I contend, is that a correct understanding of the notion of resurrection in Jewish eschatology which formed the framework through which Jesus' post-mortem fate was interpreted precludes the possibility of such a division. Rather, the notion of resurrection was of such malleability and interacted with such a diversity of eschatological expectations that discerning a universal or homogenized doctrine is impossible and encompasses within itself the hope for both renewal and radical transformation. In other words, the notion of resurrection embodied both the continuous and discontinuous expectations; the scholarship analysed in section one failed to incorporate both. This section revisits the notion of resurrection in Jewish eschatology,[41] demonstrating the mutually conditioning and inseparable relationship between resurrection and several other eschatological categories, especially the hope for the relational redemption, the transformation of the cosmos, and the dispensation of divine judgment. Section three then demonstrates how this is evident within the New Testament corpus.

2.1 Resurrection and Redemption

The key theme connected to resurrection throughout the Hebrew Bible is the redemption of relationship. Specifically, resurrection was an illustration of Israel's return to her God, Yhwh; in her disobedience, Israel became dead, but through covenantal obedience would return to life. There are very few explicit instances of resurrection in the Hebrew Bible (Hos. 6.2; Ezek. 37.1–14; Isa. 26.19; Dan. 12.1–3), and its scarcity

---

41 It is important to note that this research is not restricted to a specific era or category, such as Second Temple, Apocalyptic, etc. as my interest lies in the overall development of the notion of resurrection, from its inception to its eventual framing of Jesus' post-mortem fate. However, it should be noted that the purpose of the research is to understand, primarily, the framework within which the early Christians understood the Christ event and so does not include Jewish eschatology beyond the second century CE.

indicates how peripheral this notion was. It becomes more prominent in later apocalyptic literature but, as shall be seen below, there is a great deal of diversity regarding how it was understood and presented.

Perhaps the earliest explicit mention to resurrection is Hosea 6.2: 'On the third day he will raise us up'.[42] Wright argues that the presence of the three day motif, which was taken up in the Gospels and Paul in reference to Jesus' resurrection, indicates that Hosea's resurrection should be interpreted as a belief in a post-mortem individual and physical return from death. He purports that this 'passage has a claim to be the earliest explicit statement that YHWH will give his people a new bodily life the other side of death'.[43] This, I believe, is unlikely. It is very probable that this is one of the earliest resurrection passages, but it is far less explicit and bodily than Wright assumes. The context, after all, is preoccupied with the return of Israel to obedience to YHWH and so the passage is better understood as a metaphorical reference to a hope in national revival.[44]

Following this comes the tale of the Valley of Dry Bones in Ezekiel 37.1–14. Again, the concern here is with the re-creation of God's covenantal people rather than post-mortem existence; for Ezekiel, the relationship between Israel and her God has died and God will give it new life. Cut off from the life giver, the Israelites are metaphorically dead, and as the bodies are restored so is the relationship. This reinforced by the presence of the covenantal formula elsewhere in Ezekiel: 'They shall be my people, and I will be their God' (11.20; 14.11; 37.23, 27; 34.24; 36.28). This restoration is represented in the re-establishment of a united nation (37.15–28), the renewal of the monarchy (34.23–24; 37.22, 24–25), and the construction of a new temple (chs. 40–42). As in Hosea, the imagery of resurrection is analogical, representing the redemption of relationship.

The third prominent resurrection passage in the Hebrew Bible is Isaiah 26.19, which has very often been interpreted as envisaging a post-mortem resurrection of individual bodies, many scholars insisting

---

42 Scriptural quotes in this essay are taken from the nrsv translation.
43 Wright, *The Resurrection of God*, 118–19.
44 This is the most common interpretation among commentators. Cf. Chase, 'The Genesis of Resurrection Hope', 470; Collins, *Apocalypticism in the Dead Sea Scrolls*, 111.

that 25.8 and 26.14, 20–21 indicates physicality.[45] Matthew McAffee, for example, argues that 'those long dead' (lit. 'the shades') in 26.19b is directly responding to Ugaritic ancestral worship of Rapa'uma (Shades), presenting bodily resurrection as the superior hope.[46] The parallels to Ugaritic religion is compelling, but I am unconvinced that this is a reference to a post-mortem return to life of individual bodies, but rather, as in Hosea and Ezekiel, the imagery of resurrection is utilized as a metaphor for national restoration. The image of resurrection in 26.19 is directly followed by the image of Israel as a woman in labour and the earth itself giving birth (26.17–19). In light of 26.13–15, resurrection here refers to the restoration of the covenantal relationship.

Finally, Daniel 12.1–3 should also be interpreted analogically. Here it becomes evident how resurrection became connected to the broader eschatological motifs of re-creation, justice and national restoration, cast onto a cosmic landscape. There is probably here an expectation of a post-mortem return to life, however there is much more to it, and it is certainly not a resurrection of physical bodies.[47] There is some ambivalence here; those who are resurrected come from 'the dust of the earth', implying corporeality, but the faithful 'shall shine like the brightness of the sky, [...] like the stars forever and ever'. This is further complicated by the claim that 'many'—and not all—will be raised, some to life and some to shame. What is clearer, however, is that Daniel's concern throughout the book—written during persecution under Antiochus Epiphanes—is justice for his oppressed people. Echoing Isaiah, resurrection is here the hope for a grander restoration.

The most explicit references to the notion of resurrection in the Hebrew Bible have larger concerns than the resurrection of individual physical bodies. Of course, hope for a post-mortem return to life was likely present in Jewish eschatology, but it was neither particularly common nor developed, and its use in the Hebrew scriptures has

---

45 Cf. Russell, *The Method and Message of Jewish Apocalyptic*, 368; Nickelsburg, *Resurrection, Immortality, and Eternal Life*, 31–32; Martin-Achard, *From Death to Life*, 130–31; Hasel, 'Resurrection in the Theology of Old Testament Apocalyptic', 275; Cook, 'Apocalyptic Prophecy', 28.
46 McAffee, 'Rephaim, Whisperers, and the Dead', 77–94.
47 I particularly take issue with Wright's statement that this passage 'does indeed speak of bodily resurrection [...] in a concrete sense' and 'unquestionably refers to physical resurrection' (Wright, *Resurrection of the Son of God*, 109, 322).

predominately to do with God's power and desire to restore covenantal relationship.

2.2 Resurrection and Transformation

Where some of the earliest resurrection references were metaphorically speaking of the renewal of Israel's covenantal relationship with Yhwh, as the eschatological notion developed it interacted significantly with other eschatological categories. Resurrection became increasingly focused upon a radical transformation, not just of bodies but of the entire cosmos. Here it becomes clear that creation itself is redeemed, not replaced, but changed significantly.

Prior to the vision of the Dry Bones, Ezekiel 36 depicts a restoration of the people of Israel, a theme which continues, as seen above, into the next chapter where resurrection explicitly comes to the fore. However, in chapter 36, this restoration is described in terms of re-creation. The language echoes Genesis 2–3, especially with the population multiplying and becoming fruitful (Ezek. 36.10–11) and the land becoming like the Garden of Eden (36.35). Similarly, in chapter 37, the dry bones coming back to life reflects the creation of humanity. This creation motif frames the narrative of 2 Maccabees 7, where seven brothers and their mother are being persecuted, tortured and executed for refusing to disobey their covenantal obligations and eat pork. To strengthen her sons' resolve to God's Law, she declares,

> The creator of the world who shaped the beginning of humankind and devised the origin of all things, will in his mercy give life and breath back to you again. [...] I beg you, my child, to look at the heaven and the earth and see everything that is in them, and recognize that God did not make them out of things that existed. (2 Macc. 7.23, 28)

Resurrection is connected to creation, and God's ability to create *ex nihilo*. The seven days of Genesis 1 are evoked in 4 Ezra 7.31–32—'And after seven days the world, which is not yet awake, shall be roused, [...] and the earth shall give up those who are asleep in it'. Curiously, the earth itself awakes, not just those within it; 'resurrection' again carries cosmic overtones.

For the author of 1 Enoch, resurrection is itself transformative, functioning as entrance into God's sanctuary (1 En. 22), a sanctuary which, as described in ch. 25, contains a paradisiacal tree which revitalizes and maintains this renewed existence. In a later chapter, creation is renewed, with mountains dancing, hills leaping, and the earth rejoicing (1 En. 51.1–5). In the *Messianic Apocalypse,* this renewed creation is depicted as a vast cosmic landscape, where the righteous inhabit the heavens and the wicked are confined to the 'valley of death' (4Q521 fr. 7). Similarly, Daniel depicts the resurrected faithful as shining like the stars forever and ever, indicating, again, a radical transformation that goes well beyond mere bodies (Dan. 12.1–3). This connects to the instances in Jewish apocalyptic where resurrection is depicted as an exalted heavenly existence. Here Daniel implies a non-corporeal resurrection, reflected in 2 Baruch 50.2–3 and 1 Enoch 104.2–6.

Casey Elledge has recently and helpfully categorized two distinct beliefs: some understandings of resurrection and re-creation envision a celestial experience (e.g. *Epistle of Enoch,* 4 Ezra, 2 Baruch, the *Messianic Apocalypse,* and Daniel), while others locate this new existence on a transformed, renewed earth (e.g. *Book of Watchers,* 2 Maccabees, *Pseudo-Ezekiel,* and Pseudo-Philo's *Biblical Antiquities*).[48] Evidently, there is no uniform understanding of what the resurrected creation shall look like, reinforcing my argument that the notion of 'resurrection' was not restricted to bodies. This is further reflected in the ambiguity regarding the description of this transformed reality. There is great diversity within apocalyptic literature, from a physical, corporeal existence, to an immaterial one. However, the descriptions were rarely concrete or precise; the essential expectation was for a thoroughgoing transformation of a redeemed and renewed creation.

Of course, not all accepted resurrection, seen most particularly in the Sadducees, as well as the Corinthian Christians (hence Paul's long argument in 1 Cor. 15). Indeed, a Hellenized belief in an immortal soul was not uncommon (cf. Jub. 23.31; 1 En. 91–104; *Assumption of Moses* 10.9; *Jewish War* 2.154–58). Wright has attempted to downplay the significance of the doctrine of immortality in Jewish apocalyptic, claiming

---

48 Elledge, *Resurrection of the Dead,* 37–42.

that the Hellenistic language is merely translation of a Jewish, physical and material understanding.[49] This is unconvincing, as he has not sufficiently acknowledged the sheer diversity of Jewish understandings of the afterlife. Furthermore, his assertion that *Wisdom of Solomon* teaches an immortality that involves a renewed bodily life seems to ignore the Platonic overtones of the book, especially where it states, 'A perishable body weighs down the soul, and this earthly tent burdens the thoughtful mind' (Ws. 9.15).

2.3 Resurrection and Justice

Finally, the notion regularly interacts with the eschatological hope for judgment. This should be evident based on what has already been discussed, particularly the redemption of Israel's relationship with Yhwh, but there are several instances where this is especially explicit. The hope for resurrection developed significantly during times of persecution, when the threat of exile was looming or when the nation was submitting to oppressive Hellenistic rule. Resurrection became a solution to the problem of theodicy, especially for the martyred faithful, and a transformed creation was envisaged wherein the righteous could dwell in redeemed relationship with Yhwh. As Elledge notes, in *Messianic Apocalypse* 4Q521 frs. 2 and 4, Psalms of Solomon 3.11–12, and 4 Ezra 7.31–34, resurrection hope is 'the central expression of God's righteous judgment and mercy for the Jewish people'.[50] Throughout the *Testament of the Twelve Patriarchs,* 4 Ezra, 2 Baruch, and *Wisdom of Solomon,* resurrection emphasizes the righting of the created order.

For the authors of Daniel and 2 Maccabees, the martyrdom of the pious leaders was theologically problematic, and the submission to foreign rule was a threat to the covenantal promises. Chapters 7 through 11 of Daniel assure the reader that this persecution will end—but what justice is there for those who have been murdered? In Daniel 12, justice is provided to those already dead by way of resurrection; justice is given to those treated unjustly. The final utterances of the brothers and their mother in 2 Maccabees 7 demonstrate hope for divine vindication. The

---

49 Wright, *Resurrection of the Son of God,* 324.
50 Elledge, *Resurrection of the Dead,* 84.

second brother declares, 'The King of the universe will raise us up to an everlasting renewal of life, because we have died for his laws' (7.9), the second willingly offers his tongue and hands claiming that he will receive them back (7.10–11), and the fourth confidently declares that their torturer shall receive no resurrection (7.14).

The hope for resurrection developed in conjunction with the hope that God would bring judgment, reward for the righteous and punishment for the wicked. Resurrection, as an eschatological expectation, was inseparable from the theological and sociological hope for justice; 'Resurrection and divine justice came to be so intimately interconnected that they offered mutual [...] corroboration'.[51] The point here is that it was never restricted to the return to life of individual bodies, but interacted—at an essential level—with the other eschatological hopes in a mutually-conditioning function. The notion of resurrection implied the radical transformation and re-creation of present reality, which itself was an act of divine judgment and within which justice prevails, and which enabled unhindered relationship between YHWH and his creation.

Reducing resurrection to the hope for a post-mortem re-embodied existence ignores the malleability of the imagery of resurrection in Jewish eschatology and its mutually conditioning relationship with the other eschatological expectations. When this is taken seriously, it becomes evident that this notion cannot be restricted to bearing either continuity or discontinuity with present created reality, but both, and hence does not fall into either of the categories of material or immaterial, historical or suprahistorical, literal or metaphorical. In this sense, resurrection transcends and unifies these categories as both redemption and transformation of the created order. This is the framework through which Jesus' post-mortem fate was interpreted, and as we shall see in the following section, when discussing Jesus' post-mortem fate, the New Testament authors were concerned with far larger eschatological issues than his personal re-embodiment.

---

51 Elledge, *Resurrection of the Dead*, 82.

3. Heaven and Earth: Unifying the Categories

The majority of scholarship on Jesus' resurrection has emphasized one category over the other, at the expense of the other. That is, interpretations have emphasized either the *continuity* of the resurrection with the pre-crucifixion Jesus (an event which occurred to Jesus' physical body within the ordinary contingency of time and space) or the *discontinuity* of the resurrection with the pre-crucifixion Jesus (an event which was either of such an eschatological character that it transcends ordinary history, or of such an extraordinary character that it must be myth and metaphor). I contend that this dichotomy is a misinterpretation of the eschatological framework through which Jesus' post-mortem fate was interpreted. Rather, a closer inspection of the use of the notion of resurrection in Jewish eschatology (between Hosea and second-century apocalyptic literature) reveals that the notion was inseparably connected to the broader eschatological motifs of redemption of relationship, transformation of the entire created order, and the dispensation of judgment. This demonstrates, first, that 'resurrection' rarely referred to the post-mortem existence of individual bodies, and, second, the hope for both restoration *and* radical transformation indicates that there is *both* continuity and discontinuity. This is reflected in the New Testament portrayals of Jesus' resurrection: The risen Jesus is presented as the *personification* of the broader eschatological hopes, bearing a dialectic tension between continuity and discontinuity with ordinary reality *within himself.*

3.1 The Risen Jesus as the Personification of Eschatological Hope

A first-time reader of the New Testament might be quick to notice the strangeness of the descriptions of Jesus' resurrected nature. The Easter narratives of the Gospels are littered with ambiguous accounts of Jesus' post-resurrection body and his interactions with others. Jesus' body was touchable and bore the wounds of his crucifixion (Matt. 28.9; Luke 24.39–40; John 20.20, 27), he could eat (Luke 24.43), had breath (John 20.22), and was not a 'ghost' (Luke 24.39). The evangelists have gone to great lengths to ensure that the risen Jesus is the *same* Jesus as before, with the same body. However, this body is *not* the same. Jesus could 'suddenly' appear among them, despite locked doors (Matt. 28.9;

Luke 24.36; John 20.19, 26), was not immediately recognized (Luke 24.16; John 20.14–15; 21.4, 12), would vanish (Luke 24.31), some of the witnesses doubted, despite their joy and worship (Matt. 28.18; Luke 24.41), was carried into heaven (Luke 24.51; Acts 1.9–10), and his appearance bears similarities with theophanies, causing fear and providing reassurance (Matt. 28.10; Luke 24.36–37; John 20.19).

This ambiguity is similarly present in Paul's great resurrection chapter of 1 Corinthians 15. It seems exceedingly difficult for Paul to find a suitable analogy to describe the nature of the risen Jesus, employing multiple illustrations—a seed to a plant (15.37), the many different types of bodies (15.38–41), perishability to imperishability (15.42), dishonour to glory, weakness to power (15.43), natural to spiritual (15.44), the man of dust and the man from heaven (15.45–49)—in the attempt to incorporate both continuity and discontinuity. As the plant is the same as the seed (continuity) and yet entirely different (discontinuity), so Jesus' risen nature is the same as his pre-crucifixion nature and yet entirely different.

Paul's σῶμα πνευματικόν is not comparable to present physicality (in v. 50 he states that flesh and blood cannot inherit the kingdom of God). However, neither is it an immaterial existence, for it is still body. The resurrection is not a discarding of the created order, but a re-affirmation. Yet this re-affirmation includes considerable change. Wright's claim that the body remains 'robustly physical'[52] is wholly inadequate, failing to encompass the extent of this transformation. After all, Paul is not describing a new type of *physicality,* but a new type of *body*.[53] I do not believe this to be splitting hairs, for the point for Paul, as in the Gospels, is that in Jesus' post-mortem fate the eschatological hopes had been fulfilled; hence, the description of the risen Jesus is as the personification of the expectations for justice, redeemed relationship, and transformation.

This interaction with the broader themes extends to the inauguration of the new eschatological age, which arrived in and through Jesus, and his exaltation and glorification. Each of the synoptics stresses that the empty tomb was discovered at dawn on the first day of the week.

---

52 Wright, *Resurrection of the Son of God*, 478.
53 Cf. Smith, 'N.T. Wright's Understanding of the Nature of Jesus' Risen Body', 41.

Mark includes almost gratuitous detail in this regard, especially considering the brevity of his Easter narrative (16.1–8), noting that the women discovered the tomb 'very early on the first day of the week, when the sun had risen' (16.2). The reference to the sun here recalls Jesus' death (15.33) and its rising symbolizes Jesus' return from death. Curiously, there is no reference to Jesus' body, indicating that Mark's use of the empty tomb was not an attempt at defending a physical event. These elements demonstrate that the resurrection was the dawning of a new eschatological age.

This is all the more explicit in Matthew, where several apocalyptic elements have been incorporated, including the presence of angels, reflecting traditional theophanies, the saints rising from their tombs, and the earthquake. Similarly, Paul suggests this in Romans 4.25 in the assertion that Jesus was raised for our justification. What is of particular interest here is how Jesus' resurrection is the means for our vindication. One might quite easily connect his resurrection to his own vindication, but that this extends to his followers only makes sense when resurrection is connected to the broader eschatological hope for the inauguration of a new eschatological age, with the dispensation of judgment and the renewal of creation.

For Luke, the significance of this event was Jesus' exaltation: Jesus receives the new titles of Messiah and Lord (Luke 24.26, 34, 46); the author claims that what happened was the fulfilment of ancient promise (24.6, 27); and Jesus ascends into heaven (24.50–53). This continues through Acts, reflected in the common resurrection formula: the Jews crucified Jesus; God raised him from the dead (Acts 2.23–24; 3.15; 4.10; 5.30; 10.39–40; 13.29–30). Reflecting the hope for justice in Jewish apocalyptic (particularly, as we saw, in Daniel and 2 Maccabees), the fate of Jesus is reversed; the crucified one becomes the Lord of all. So Paul also describes Jesus' post-mortem fate in Romans 1.3–4 and Philippians 2.6–11 (both likely pre-Pauline liturgical formulas). In the former, Jesus is exalted to Son of God, and the reference to the line of David and the use of the technical ἀναστάσεως νεκρῶν carries significant eschatological overtones. That is, Jesus' elevation indicates a new, eschatological age. In the latter, there is no mention at all of resurrection, but speaks primarily of Jesus' vindication and exaltation. Paul refers to the resurrection in this very letter (Phil. 3.10–11), indicating that resurrection was presupposed in his adoption of this hymn. Jesus' resurrection was envisaged as his exaltation and elevation to a new position of authority.

Finally, Jesus' resurrection is connected to cosmic re-creation. In 1 Corinthians 15.39–41, 45–49, Paul again uses an array of images to connect Jesus' post-mortem fate with the Jewish eschatological hope for the renewal of creation. He speaks of animals, the heavenly and earthly, the sun, moon, and stars, and the 'first man', Adam, who was from the dust, framing the resurrection by the creation motif, echoing the Genesis creation accounts. This reflects the texts which envisage an antediluvian and paradisiacal reality (Hos. 2.18; Isa. 11.6–8; 65.25; Ezek. 34.25–27; 1 En. 25.3–7; 61.12; 2 En. 8.1–8; 30.1; 42.4; T. Levi 18.10–11; Jub. 2.7; 4 Ezra 3.6; 6.26; 2 Bar. 4.3). Furthermore, John's account (20.1–29) envisages the renewal of creation, also echoing the Genesis creation accounts in setting the resurrection within a garden (19.41), reinforced by Mary mistaking Jesus for a gardener (20.15). Moreover, Jesus breathes the spirit upon the disciples (20.22) alluding to God breathing the breath of life into Adam, and it occurs on the first day of the week, repeated twice (20.1, 19).[54]

Evidently, the New Testament portrayals of Jesus' resurrection connote significant eschatological themes reflecting the hopes of the earlier Jewish eschatology. The strangeness and ambiguity of the description of the risen Jesus signifies that this act was one of new creation, not *ex nihilo* but *ex vetere*,[55] not out of nothing but out of the old. It is the *same* but radically *different*. There is both continuity and discontinuity, and both must be maintained. The new eschatological age has dawned with Jesus as Lord of this re-created cosmos. This is all encompassed within the resurrection itself.

3.2 The Risen Jesus as the Unification of Heaven and Earth

In my estimation, the best analogy for describing what is encapsulated within the risen Jesus is the eschatological image of the new heavens and earth, which appears in Isaiah 65.17, 2 Peter 3.13, and Revelation

---

54 Cf. Brown, 'Creation's Renewal in the Gospel of John', 275–90.
55 I have borrowed this from Emerson, 'Does God Own a Death Star?', 291.

21.1. Importantly, these passages do not depict an entirely new act of creation analogous to the original act of creation. What is anticipated in this image is not a destruction of the present world to be replaced by a new instance of *creatio ex nihilo*. Rather, what is depicted is a *unification* of heaven and earth. Earth has not been discarded but transformed as it is united with the heavenly realm. Hence, both categories of continuity (earth) and discontinuity (heaven) are present and united in this image of the eschatological future, the future that is personified in the risen Jesus.

The context of the Isaiah passage is postexilic optimism envisaging a time opposite to the 'former troubles' of the preceding verse. Hence, the act of new creation is one of salvation; the earth itself is saved. The word 'new' in this instance refers to the renewal of the present, similar to 2 Corinthians 5.17, where those in Christ are not discarded but transformed into a new creation. Rather than annihilation, a peaceful reality is depicted, where redemption extends beyond humanity.

At first glance, 2 Peter 3.12–13 might appear to be the most explicit biblical account of the total destruction of the earth by fire. However, it is not, instead being much closer to Isaiah in depicting renewal rather than annihilation. This is evident in two respects. First, the comparison with the Noahic Flood (2 Pet. 3.5–6) is telling; the purpose of the Flood was renewal (Gen. 6.7–21) and of which there were survivors (Gen. 9.1–29). If the author of 2 Peter intended to depict total destruction, the Flood was not a good illustration. Second, the imagery of fire was commonly used in reference to judgment and refinement (e.g. Ps. 12.6; Isa. 48.10; Zech. 13.9; Mal. 3.2; 1 Cor. 3.13; 1 Pet. 1.7; 4.12; Rev. 3.18). Furthermore, the verb παρελεύσονται in reference to the heavens 'passing away' (1 Pet. 3.10) primarily signifies movement, either of time or of someone passing by, rather than annihilation (e.g. Sir. 42.20; 1 Macc. 5.48; Matt. 5.18; 8.28; 14.15; 24.35; 26.39; Mark 6.48; 13.31; Luke 16.17; Acts 27.9; 2 Cor. 5.17). Consequently, Peter's use of the imagery of the new heavens and earth suggests global renewal; reality is transformed into a new creation following purification.

The most overtly apocalyptic reference is Revelation 21.1. The first five verses of this chapter bear remarkable similarity with Isaiah 65.17–25, indicating the author's reliance upon Isaianic eschatology. We can thus assume that the author of Revelation similarly anticipated cosmic renewal and similarly stressed the renewal of relationship. The author adopts the covenantal language of Leviticus 26.12 and Ezekiel 14.11 in Revelation 21.3, presenting an unprecedented intimacy, with God wiping away every tear. This is the goal of eschatological transformation: intimate relationship with God. The vision of the new Jerusalem—a reference to the people themselves—which never actually touches earth but functions as a threshold between heaven and earth, indicating the unification of these two realms.

The point that I am trying to make here is that a common hope for the *eschaton* was a renewal of the present creation that was nevertheless a radical transformation which enabled unhindered relationship with God and within which justice was pervasive. In other words, the future eschatological reality was characterised by both continuity and discontinuity with present reality. This is a characteristic shared by the depictions of the risen Jesus.

4. Conclusion: Transcending the Categories

I have argued in this essay that the majority of scholarship has misinterpreted the claim that Jesus rose from the dead, that interpretations tend to either emphasize either the continuity or discontinuity of the risen Jesus, and usually at the expense of the other, and that a better understanding of the notion of resurrection in Jewish eschatology reveals that Jesus' resurrection refers primarily to the fulfilment of a broad spectrum of eschatological hope, especially the motifs of re-creation, redemption of relationship, and the dispensation of divine justice. Through this event, the new eschatological age has dawned—the unification of heaven and earth—which includes the re-affirmation of the created order and its radical transformation.

An illustration from the natural world might clarify this. Hydrogen and oxygen are separate elements, completely different when apart from one another. However, when unified, a *new* substance is formed: Water. Water (H_2O) is made up of both hydrogen and oxygen but is no longer either. Yet, hydrogen and oxygen are still indispensable for water to be water. Indeed, it is literally defined by both elements. Their unification creates an entirely new substance, but it is a new substance that comes from, and is made up of, the old. This is the same for Jesus' resurrection, which is the personification of the unification of heaven and earth. The continuous elements—historical, material, literal—are unified with the discontinuous—eschatological, immaterial, metaphorical—creating something new that nevertheless incorporates the old. The new eschatological age, which dawned in the resurrection of Jesus of Nazareth, is an act of new creation that is the redemption and perfection of the present created order.

Bibliography

Aquinas, Thomas — *The Summa Theologica*. Vol. 2. (Fathers of the English Dominican Province, transls.; Chicago: Encyclopaedia Britannica, 1952).

Barth, Karl — *The Epistle to the Romans* (Edwyn C. Hoskyns, transl; Oxford: Oxford University Press, 1933).

———. *Church Dogmatics* (G. W. Bromiley & T. F. Torrance, eds.; H. Knight, G. W. Bromiley, J. K. S. Reid & R. H. Fuller, trnsls.; Massachusetts: Hendrickson, 1960).

Bornkamm, Günther — *Jesus of Nazareth* (Irene & Fraser McLuskey, & James M. Robinson, trnsls.; London: Hodder and Stoughton, 1960).

Brown, Jeannine — 'Creation's Renewal in the Gospel of John', *CBQ* 72.1 (2010), 275–90.

Bultmann, Rudolf — *Jesus Christ and Mythology* (New York: Charles Scribners Sons, 1958).

Chase, Mitchell L. — 'The Genesis of Resurrection Hope: Exploring Its Early Presence and Deep Roots', *JETS* 57.3 (2014), 467–80.

Collins, John C. — *Apocalypticism in the Dead Sea Scrolls* (London: Routledge, 1997).

Cook, Stephen L. — 'Apocalyptic Prophecy', in John J. Collins (ed.), *The Oxford Handbook of Apocalyptic Literature* (Oxford: Oxford University Press, 2014), 19–35.

Copan, Paul, & Ronald K. Tacelli (eds.)   *Jesus' Resurrection: Fact or Figment?* (Downers Grove: InterVarsity Press, 2000).

Craig, William Lane   *Assessing the New Testament Evidence for the Historicity of the Resurrection of Jesus* (New York: Edwin Mellen, 1989).

Crossan, John Dominic   *The Historical Jesus: The Life of a Mediterranean Jewish Peasant* (New York: HarperCollins, 1991).

_____.   *Christianity in the Making.* Vol. 1: *Jesus: A Revolutionary Biography* (New York: HarperCollins, 1994).

Davis, Brian & G. R. Evans (eds.)   *Anselm of Canterbury: The Major Works* (Oxford: Oxford University Press, 2008).

Dunn, James D. G.   '"How are the Dead Raised? With What Body do they Come?": Reflections on 1 Corinthians 15', *SwJT* 45.1 (2002), 4–18.

_____.   *Christianity in the Making.* Vol. 1: *Jesus Remembered* (Grand Rapids: Eerdmans, 2003).

Elledge, C. D.   *Resurrection of the Dead in Early Judaism 200 BCE – CE 200* (Oxford: Oxford University Press, 2017).

Emerson, Matthew Y.   'Does God Own a Death Star? The Destruction of the Cosmos in 2 Peter 3:1–3', *SwJT* 57.2 (2015), 281–93.

Frei, Hans   *The Eclipse of Biblical Narrative: A Study in Eighteenth and Nineteenth Century Hermeneutics* (London: Yale University Press, 1974).

Geisler, Norman L.   *When Skeptics Ask: A Handbook of Christian Evidences* (Grand Rapids: Baker, Revised edition, 2013).

Grenz, Stanley J.   *Theology for the Community of God* (Grand Rapids: Eerdmans, 2000).

Habermas, Gary R., & Michael R. Licona   *The Case for the Resurrection of Jesus* (Grand Rapids: Kregel, 2004).

Habermas, Gary R.   'Affirmative Statement', in Terry L. Miethe (ed.), *Did Jesus Rise from the Dead? The Resurrection Debate* (New York: Harper & Row, 1987), 15–32.

Hasel, Gerhard F.   'Resurrection in the Theology of Old Testament Apocalyptic', *ZAW* 92.2 (1980), 267–84.

Hume, David   *Enquiry Concerning Human Understanding* (Eric Steinberg, ed.; Indianapolis: Hackett, 2nd edition 1977).

Jeremias, Joachim — *New Testament Theology* (John Bowden, transl.; London: SCM, 1971).

Johnson, Luke Timothy — *The Real Jesus: The Misguided Quest for the Historical Jesus and the Truth of the Traditional Gospels* (New York: HarperCollins, 1996).

Käsemann, Ernst — *Essays on New Testament Themes* (W. J. Montague, transl.; London: SCM, 1964).

Lessing, Gotthold Ephraim — 'On the Proof of Spirit and Power', in Alister E. McGrath (ed.), *The Christian Theology Reader* (West Sussex: Wiley-Blackwell, 4th edition 2011), 249–50.

Licona, Michael R. — *The Resurrection of Jesus: A New Historiographical Approach* (Downers Grove: InterVarsity Press, 2010).

Lüdemann, Gerd — 'Opening Statements', in Paul Copan & Ronald K. Tacelli (eds.), *Jesus' Resurrection: Fact or Figment?* (Downers Grove: InterVarsity Press, 2000), 40–45.

Luther, Martin — '1 Corinthians', in *Luther's Works, Vol. 28: Commentaries on 1 Corinthians 7, 1 Corinthians 15, Lectures on 1 Timothy* (Hilton C. Oswald, ed.; Martin H. Bertram, trans.; Saint Louis: Concordia, 1973), 57–213.

Martin-Achard, Robert — *From Death to Life: A Study of the Development of the Doctrine of the Resurrection in the Old Testament* (John Penney Smith, transl.; Edinburgh: Oliver and Boyd, 1960).

Marxsen, Willi — *The Resurrection of Jesus of Nazareth* (Margaret Kohl, transl.; London: SCM, 1970).

McAffee, Matthew — 'Rephaim, Whisperers, and the Dead in Isaiah 26:13–19: A Ugaritic Parallel', *Atlanta* 135.1 (2016), 77–94.

Miethe, Terry L. (ed.) — *Did Jesus Rise from the Dead? The Resurrection Debate* (New York: Harper & Row, 1987).

Milne, Bruce — *Know the Truth: A Handbook of Christian Belief* (Nottingham: InterVarsity Press, 3rd edition 2009).

Moltmann, Jürgen — *Theology of Hope: On the Ground and the Implications of a Christian Eschatology* (James W. Leitch, transl.; London: SCM, 1967).

—— *The Way of Jesus Christ* (Margaret Kohl, transl.; London: SCM, 1990).

Nickelsburg, George W.   *Resurrection, Immortality, and Eternal Life in Intertestamental Judaism and Early Christianity* (Cambridge: Harvard University Press, Expanded edition 2006).

Pannenberg, Wolfhart   *Jesus – God and Man* (Lewis L. Wilkins & Duane A. Priebe, trnsls.; London: SCM, 2002).

Rahner, Karl   *Foundations of Christian Faith* (William V. Dych, transl.; London: Darton, Longman & Todd, 1978).

Russell, D. S.   *The Method and Message of Jewish Apocalyptic* (Philadelphia: Westminster, 1964).

Schillebeeckx, Edward   *Jesus: An Experiment in Christology* (Hubert Hoskins, transl.; London: William Collins, 1979).

Smith, Joseph J.   'N.T. Wright's Understanding of the Nature of Jesus' Risen Body', *HeyJ* 57.1 (2016), 29–73.

Spurgeon, Charles H.   'The Resurrection of the Dead', in *The New Street Pulpit* (London: Passmore & Alabaster, 1856), 2.97–112.

Strauss, David   'Reimarus and his Apology', in *Fragments* (Charles H. Talbert, ed.; Ralph S. Fraser, ed.; London: SCM, 1971), 44–57.

Tillich, Paul   *The New Being* (London: SCM, 1959).

Troeltsch, Ernst   *The Absoluteness of Christianity* (David Reid, transl.; London: SCM, 1972).

———.   *The Christian Faith* (Garrett E. Paul, transl.; Minneapolis: Fortress, 1991).

Wright, N. T.   *The Resurrection of the Son of God* (Minneapolis: Fortress, 2003).

Zwingli, Ulrich   'On the Lord's Supper', in *Zwingli and Bullinger* (LCL 14; G. W. Bromiley, transl.; London: SCM, 1953), 176–238.

CHAPTER 5

Synoptic Comparison & Oral History: A South Pacific Analogy

Peter G. Bolt

Abstract

This article examines three written reports of an event that took place on Rarotonga in August 1814 in order to discern the oral testimony lying behind them, drawing some lessons for synoptic studies of the Gospels.

1. Synoptic Comparison and Pacific Oral History

1.1 Orientation[1]

Synoptic comparison has long been a staple part of the historical study of the Gospels, as has the assumption of an oral phase between the events of Jesus Christ and the written accounts, during which what was remembered was not read, but spoken. This is the period of oral history.[2]

---

1 An earlier version of this essay was read at the SCD Centre for Gospels and Acts Research on 25/7/17.
2 Eddy, 'Orality and Oral Transmission', 646. Technically the term 'oral tradition' should be reserved for content that is passed by word of mouth over several generations. Given the brevity of the time between the events and the New Testament documents, what we are dealing with, more correctly, is 'oral history'.

In the Pacific, indigenous oral history has survived in sufficient strength to resist, and even do battle with, the arrival and attempted dominance of European documentary culture.[3] The presence of European (or at least English) influence in the Pacific for a mere 250 years on the one hand, and the existence of a living oral culture amongst the peoples of the Pacific on the other, provides a potential fund of untapped case studies for better understanding how oral history passes into written form and, once it has done, how it can be detected. This, in turn, could aid the better understanding of what is exactly the same process in regard to the Gospels.

As a preliminary sounding, this article examines one such case study, and draws attention to just two of the many lessons that could be drawn from this analogy of value to Jesus Research: 1. The connection of written accounts with oral sources with their own 'bias'; and 2. Detecting the eyewitnesses of the underlying events. It focuses on a known event in South Pacific history, which—rather surprisingly given its character—played a key role in the impact of Jesus on Rarotonga, and the subsequent spread of the gospel of Jesus Christ throughout the Pacific (see below, 4.1).

1.2 The event in summary

The basic components of the event are relatively easy to narrate. In 1814, after a group of Sydney speculators hastily formed the Rarotongan Sandalwood Company, with some secrecy they sent the schooner, the *Cumberland*, to the island of Rarotonga in the hope of gaining lucrative cargoes of sandalwood for the China market.[4] Captained by Philip Goodenough and with the young William Charles Wentworth on board as supercargo protecting the Company's interests, the *Cumberland* arrived at Rarotonga, probably in the last week of May,

---

3 The relationship between the documentary history favoured by Europeans, and the living indigenous oral history is a long-standing and still current discussion in the South Pacific, having already been tested in the Cook Islands Land Courts at the turn of the twentieth century (see Campbell, 'History in Prehistory'), and in New Zealand's Waitangi Tribunal set up in 1975 and still in operation (Williams, 'Reparations and the Waitangi Tribunal'; see further, Waitangi Tribunal).

4 She sailed on 20 January 1814, *SG* 22/1/1814. A later report puts her departure on 18th (*SG* 22/10/1814).

1814.[5] They tried to land in the Southeastern district of the island, Ngatangiia (near today's Muri beach), but were frightened off by the locals' overly-enthusiastic greeting—since they had never seen white men before.[6] They sailed to the North, where they spent a week of friendly relations with the locals of a different social grouping to those in the Southeast.[7] While there, a Tahitian and a New Zealander from the ship demonstrated the fire power of the white man's guns by killing several from the Arorangi people, whose homelands were on the West

5   Maude & Crocombe, 'Rarotongan Sandalwood', 37, guess 'She should have arrived at Walker's Island during March', but other indications confuse the portrait.
    Kloosterman, 'Discoverers', 48, notes in the literature a great deal of confusion even about the year in which the *Cumberland* arrived, with suggested dates out by from between 4 to 7 years: 1818; 1820; 1821. There is, however, no major confusion in the primary references, whether the white man's documentary evidence or the island's oral history. The *Cumberland* left Sydney on 18 or 20 of January 1814 (*SG* 22/1 and 22/10/1814), and Wentworth gave an account of the visit to 'Larotonga' as soon as they returned, *SG* 22/10/1814. Even if by 1856 island memory on the west was vague for Gill ('about 1820')—, in 1827 it was more precise for Williams when, drawing on the reports of (at least) two eyewitnesses, he wrote in *SG* 22/3/1827 of 'a vessel leaving your colony 14 or 15 years ago'. Informed by the Gazette report, reprinted in the Naval Chronicle for 1816, Pitman referred to the 'skirmish about seven years before the introduction of the Gospel into this land', evidently dating the latter to the arrival on Papeiha on Aitutaki in 1821; Pitman to Ellis, 10/8/1839.
    At the other end, we know that Croker was killed on 12 August (SG 22/10/1814), but the ship remained on Rarotonga until the 18th, missing by a week Siddons, who arrived in the *Campbell Macquarie* on 25th; *SG* 11/3/1815. After calling at Aitutaki, the *Cumberland* arrived in Sydney on 20/10/1814.
    It seems that Gill and Maretu draw independently on oral tradition to give further rather precise chronological indications. After first unsuccessfully landing at Ngati-Tangii, she went to Avarua 'for nearly a week', before returning to Ngati-Tangii harbour for 'three months'; Gill, *Gems*, 6–7; Maretu, *Cannibals*, 42 [2].
    Kloosterman, 'Discoverers', 48, suggests she arrived in May. On May 23, 1814 the *Seringapatam* came close to Rarotonga, and the next day some natives, who came out in their canoes, came aboard, who 'seemed to have no knowledge whatever of ever seeing a Ship or any White Person'; Seringatapam, Journal. Rather than the *Cumberland* being hidden from view (so Maude & Crocombe, 'Rarotongan Sandalwood', 57, the *Seringatapam*'s lack of awareness of her indicates she had not yet arrived. This would clearly show the 3 months to be precise.
6   Even though no white man had stepped on their shore, the Rarotongans had heard of these fabled creatures from Tahitian visitors who spoke of the 'Kookes' (those with Captain Cook, 1769; Cook was also on Mangaia on 29/3/1777), and the LMS missionaries who followed him, arriving on Tahiti in 1799 'to teach them about the great God Jehovah, and his son Jesus Christ'; Gill, *Gems*, 6. Part of their excitement at the *Cumberland*'s arrival was the expectation that they, too, had been visited by the 'Kookes'.
7   By 1814, Rarotonga had three districts ruled by three ariki, 'high chiefs': Takitumu in the east, under the joint *ariki*, Pa and Kainuku; Puaikura (or Arorangi) in the west, under Tinomana; and Te Au o Tonga (or Avarua) in the north, under Makea; Maude & Crocombe, 'Rarotongan Sandalwood', 38–39.

of the island, with whom those in the north were in conflict at the time. This shocked everybody, including the *Cumberland*'s northern hosts, and everybody wanted the foreigners to leave.[8]

Still without a cargo, Captain Goodenough sailed the *Cumberland* back to the Southeast, where they had attempted their first landing. Once moored in that much better harbour and with the local Ngatangiia now willing to help, the ship soon learned that there was not a stick of sandalwood on the island. Supercargo Wentworth agreed to take instead a shipload of *nono* wood, which was used to make a yellow dye, and sixty locals were hired to help the crew cut the trees and load the ship.

After three months at this task, a quick succession of events left several Rarotongans and about half of those on the *Cumberland* dead and, after being killed, some of the Europeans were eaten.

Without suggesting any causal links at this stage, the sequence went something like this. Just before August 12th, the day of the killings, Goodenough and Wentworth learned that some locals, who were unhappy about the *Cumberland*'s impositions, had formed a conspiracy, aided by Tupe, a New Zealander. Even though he had come with the ship, Tupe had proposed a scheme for killing the white men.[9] During the night before the 12th, probably already preparing for a hasty departure, the ship sent a shore party led by the Tahitian, Te Ara, back to the north, to steal the coconuts they had seen in the storehouse of Makea Ariki—the high chief who had given them hospitality during the week after their first arrival. Makea Ariki cried out and Rupe, one of his relatives and a fierce warrior, pursued the shore party, killed them, and later returned to eat them. He then sought out the New Zealander, Veretini, also from the ship but living on shore because he had married

---

8 Gill, *Gems*, 7–8.
9 Maretu talks of Tupe in another context, but nevertheless in relation to the same events, *Cannibals*, Ch. 2, p.41 [494–495]: 'It was an act of revenge which caused Tute [probably Tupe] to be eaten. It was defiance of lawful authority. He continually took his women on board the ship, stole pigs and food. He even went as far as stealing coconuts from the storehouse of Makea Senior [i.e. Tinirau] at Araitetonga. That high chief cried out and thus roused Rupe's desire for vengeance. He attacked and killed the offender. The high chiefs ordered Tute's body to be buried, but the avengers [i.e. Rupe] came at night, stole it, took it away and ate it. Those who wanted revenge ate him'.

a local woman, who also happened to be related to Rupe. Having found Veretini at his home, Rupe killed him too.

Overlapping with this sequence of events, in a dawn raid on the 12th, two men from the *Cumberland* went to the house of the New Zealand conspirator, Tupe, who had also married a local and was living onshore, where they called him outside and shot him. Amongst all this killing, Goodenough's ship-board mistress, Ann Butcher, who had previously been taken on shore by a Rarotongan, was also killed and later eaten—thereby achieving the fame of becoming the second of only two European women who met that fate in the South Pacific.[10]

That evening another shore party landed, apparently intent on further killing. The Rarotongan women and children were sent to the mountains for six days. The two local chiefs, Pa and Kurunauku, made peace with 'the two officers', Goodenough and Wentworth, and the loading of the ship was finished, the workers paid, and the *Cumberland* was made ready to leave. As she was leaving, the women and children arrived back from the mountains and a Rarotongan man, Kapautu, and two young women were kidnapped and taken on board, one of them being Rupe the warrior's 18 year old daughter, Tepaeru [Tapairu].[11] In an emotional scene, Rupe made a desperate attempt to stop this happening, but—rather strangely given the ferocity he had shown in his

---

10 The first was Mrs Elizabeth Broughton, who, at the end of 1809, was amongst the victims when the people of Whangaroa took revenge on the *Boyd* for Captain Thomson's abuse of their young chief George Te Ara; see Bolt, 'The Boyd Set-Back' and 'George Te Ara'. Some years later, an account of Ann Butcher's death was related to LMS missionary Pitman; see Pitman to Ellis, 10/8/1839.

11 From Tepaeru's grave plaque, Avarua CICC: 'highly esteemed daughter of Rupe Toa Te Aia O Makea (aka Tauira-ariki-o-Makea) the warlord and noted warrior of the Chiefly Makea Tribe of Te-Au-o-Tonga and his wife Ngamata a Taramai-te-tonga', and grand-daughter of Makea Pini Ariki. 'Historical records indicate that on 12 August 1814, the 18 year old Tepaeru-ariki was kidnapped along with her niece Mata Kavau [...] and a seaman, Kupauta, by the mischievous crew of the "Cumberland" under the command of an atrocious Captain Philip Goodenough who wanted revenge for the killing of some of his crew by Rupe'. The plaque mistakenly places the kidnapping on the same day as the killings (see next note). It also reveals the reason why Kapauta was taken with the girls: as a seaman, he was useful to supplement the *Cumberland*'s now depleted crew.

In her edition of Maretu, Crocombe reveals that 'Mata Kavaau, was the daughter of the chief Kainuku Tamoko of Avana' (*Cannibals*, 46 n.49). Thus one girl was related to the chief from the north (and, according to Crocombe, a classificatory sister of 'Makea Tinirau, the high chief of the Avarua district'), the other to the chief from the southeast. It does not seem to be random that such 'royalty' were either taken by the white men, or permitted to be taken by the Rarotongans.

killing spree on the 12th—he failed, and Tepaeru sailed off with the other two captives on board the ship.[12]

1.3 An Exercise in Method

Although it is possible to provide a coherent account of the exact sequence of events and their causal connection, this essay does not intend to do so.[13] Instead, it focuses upon method. To get to a satisfying explanation of this series of events on Rarotonga, the historian must engage in a Synoptic comparison of surviving written sources and discern through their previous oral history to ascertain what really happened. This event therefore provides a real-life methodological analogy for those working with the Gospels and it therefore yields some lessons for Jesus Research.

2. The Sources

As for Jesus and Socrates, the historian's difficulty in understanding this event does not arise from the absence of sources, but from their multiplicity.[14] The August 1814 clashes on Rarotonga have left three major written accounts, as well as several supporting sources, both documentary and oral. The three main written accounts, two in English and one in Rarotongan, are independent of one another, and they appear to draw on largely independent oral sources, thus giving an opportunity to view the same set of events from several different points of view. For they very clearly each have their own 'slant'.

---

12 This would have been on the 19th or 20th August. Croker was killed on the 12 August, but the ship didn't leave then (contra Kloosterman, 'Discoverers', 48). After six days in the mountains, the people returned and she left 'soon after'; see Maretu, *Cannibals*, 45 [8].

13 I hope to subsequently publish, 'What Really Happened in Rarotonga in August 1814?'.

14 'The problem of the identity of the historical Socrates parallels that of discussion of the historical Jesus at all times, the picture of the one influencing that of the other, from Justin Martyr's "a Christian before Christ" to Baur's determination to insert "or" between their names'; Perkins, 'Introduction', 11; 'Because [Socrates] wrote nothing down, our only access to him and his teaching is through the surviving accounts by his three contemporaries, Aristophanes, Plato, and Xenophon. Hence emerges the so-called problem of Socrates: the historical-philosophical problem of ascertaining who the "historical" Socrates really was, and what he actually taught. To this problem around which has accrued a scholarly literature of oceanic proportions, it is usually conceded there can be no definite solution, and that the person today "looking for the historical truth about Socrates, finds himself in a swamp of myth, archaic interpretation, and emotional need"'; Ziolkowski, 'From *Clouds* to *Corsair*', 198, citing Levi, 'The Idea of Socrates', 94.

2.1 W.C. Wentworth (& P. Goodenough), *Sydney Gazette* 22/10/1814

The earliest written account can be labelled contemporary, for it was published in the *Sydney Gazette* two days after the *Cumberland* arrived back in Sydney (Thursday 20 October 1814), and just ten weeks after the event. The story almost certainly provides Wentworth's account of events.

This account is strongly biased in favour of the Europeans and an evaluation of all the sources suggests that it is a deliberately selective telling of the event to cover up what really happened. Because of his strong connections with South Seas Islanders, Rev. Samuel Marsden soon heard a different version of events from the Islanders among the crew of the *Cumberland* and pressed for a public inquiry, which failed as soon as it began.[15]

Since the *Gazette* noted that the European victims had been eaten, Sydney's general reading public would have been immediately prejudiced against a version of events that may have suggested that the white representatives of the civilized world may have had some culpability.[16] Since the white man at the centre of the problem was the twenty-four year old William Charles Wentworth,[17] one of the three heroes who had crossed the Blue Mountains the year before, and who would go on to take a prominent role in NSW politics, there was probably little chance NSW society would have been swayed to the version Marsden had heard—even if his attempted official inquiry had let the evidence be aired.[18]

The first written account was therefore European, culturally and geographically distant, and deliberately biased towards cover-up.

---

15 See Bolt, 'The Failure of the Philanthropic Society'.
16 Locally, Sydney was still reeling from the killing and eating of the crew of the *Boyd* in the Bay of Islands in November 1809; see further Bolt, 'The Boyd Set-Back'. As well as providing the richest account of the *Cumberland* incident on Rarotonga, Maretu left an account of South Seas cannibalism from an insider's perspective; see Maretu, *Cannibals*, 33–42; for another version of the same events, see Pitman to Ellis, 10/8/1839.
17 The massacre occurred shortly before his twenty-fourth birthday. On the voyage to NSW, his father, surgeon D'Arcy Wentworth, had an affair with 17 year old convict Catherine Crowley, and when they arrived in Sydney on 29 June 1790, Catherine was heavily pregnant. On 1 August, they were sent to Norfolk Island on the *Surprize* and William was born before they arrived, despite later claims that he was born in 1794; Tink, *William Charles Wentworth*, 5–6, 7, 8.
18 Marsden to Pratt, 26/10/1815: 'At the meeting many objections were started against examining into any of the transactions of the *Cumberland* while she was amongst the islands'.

2.2 William Gill, 1856

The next account was published in 1856, forty-two years after the events, by the Rev. William Gill, who was a London Missionary Society missionary on Rarotonga from 1839 to 1852.[19] Although his presence in LMS circles and on Rarotonga potentially gave him access to Rarotongan accounts of the events, he was stationed on the West of the island, amongst the Arorangi people, whereas in 1814 the events took place in the Eastern and Northern districts.

As for bias, Gill was an English missionary, outraged on behalf of his Rarotongan flock at the behaviour of his fellow countrymen. He appears to retell the account in order to draw the negative lesson that the excesses of those on the *Cumberland* led to the Rarotongans deciding that white men were more wicked than themselves, and therefore never wanting anything to do with them thereafter—perhaps to the detriment of his own missionary endeavours!

2.3 Maretu, 1871 and 1873

The third and latest account appears to write up the event with exactly the opposite message to tell. Writing in the early 1870s (almost 60 years after the event),[20] Maretu was a Rarotongan, who had grown up and lived and worked amongst the Eastern/Northern people, but also in LMS circles.[21] Despite being the latest source, being a party to oral

---

19 See Gill, *Gems*. After returning from Rarotonga to serve 'for nearly twelve years [as] minister of Rectory-place Chapel, Woolwich', Gill died on 14/8/1878, in his 66th year, at his residence in Blackheath, England; see *SMH* 14/10/1878.

20 Maretu, *Cannibals*, 42–46. As well as recording a detailed account of the *Cumberland*'s visit in 1871, Maretu also touched on the same events in his account of cannibalism recorded in 1873; see bibliography for details.

21 See Crocombe's 'Maretu's life, work and context', Maretu, *Cannibals*, 1–28, and Maretu's own 'reminiscences on the introduction of Christianity', 198–202. See the Editor's note, 'The Coming of Goodenough's Ship to Rarotonga', 191–192: 'Amongst Dr. Wyatt Gill's papers is the following, which, perhaps, is copied from a tombstone:—

"Maretu. A missionary from Nga-Tangiia, who died 25th January, 1880. He was admitted into the church on 31st August, 1833, and he then took up the work of God. He assisted the Rev. Mr. Pitman in teaching the Gospel at Nga-Tangiia; and it was he who built up the church at Mangaia Island and at Manihiki Island. Subsequently he became guardian of the church at Nga-Tangiia in Rarotonga. He was engaged for 47 years in the work of God'".

Pitman to Ellis, 10/8/1839, also gives an account of Maretu's conversion and subsequent persuasive Christian influence.

accounts of the events, probably from boyhood into adult life, ensured that Maretu's written account is far richer in detail than the other two.

As a Rarotongan, Maretu was appalled at past practices of his people (including their cannibalism), and glad for the coming of the Christian gospel to the island, despite the chaos occurring at the same time as its arrival. Although the *Cumberland* visitors do not come out unscathed by his recounting, the Rarotongan Christian convert and missionary views the events of 1814 as illustrative of the heathen past of his people, as well as a rather strange 'opening of Providence',[22] in that the ship not only first brought the gospel to the island, but the disastrous events of 12 August 1814 even paved the way for the rapid conversion of the island after 1823.

To sum up this point. Each source has a different relationship to the events in terms of time-line, and cultural and personal distance. Each also has a clear bias: one negative (as a cover up against potential legal troubles); and two positive (as promotions of the missionary cause). But this is not at all problematic for getting at the facts. Even the cover-up tells a version of the truth. It simply leaves out certain key events in the sequence and slants the account by manipulating the reader to see events in a certain prejudicial way.

The similarity with the Gospels is clear, with each Gospel account being different from each other in terms of the time-lapse from the events and in cultural and personal connection to Jesus, and each having a definite bias, or *Tendenz*, or, more neutrally: persuasive purpose. However, each of these aspects, even the bias, is a natural part of life and not something to be awfulised, feared or rejected, but simply something that the historian needs to recognize in order to bring it into consideration.

3. Two Translational Issues

This section of the essay presents two issues arising from the translation of Maretu. The first illustrates how an improper translation can confuse later interpreters of a text, who do not, or cannot, work with its original language.

---

22 This is not Maretu's term, but it expresses the sentiments of the missionary world-view in the Pacific; see Falloon, 'Openings'.

3.1 *Papaa*

When the *Cumberland* first attempted to land, the natives had never seen a white man. But by the time Gill wrote in 1856, and certainly by the time Stephen Savage translated Maretu in 1911, white Europeans had been visiting the island, and—since 1827—living on the island, for decades.[23] When Gill and Savage heard the word *papaa* it meant European, or, as Gill heard it used of him, 'white man'. This was how Gill rendered it in his account, how Savage translated it in his version of Maretu, and, for the most part, even Crocombe followed suit in her 1983 translation. However, pointing out that *papaa* actually means 'foreigner', when Crocombe rendered the word in this way at significant points in the account, events were clarified considerably.

For when the sources for the 1814 events are read carefully, some of the foreigners to Rarotonga were not *European* foreigners. Two were Lascars from India, called 'black men' by Maretu; three were New Zealand Māori; and four were Tahitians. At points, whereas Gill and Savage, rendering *papaa* 'European' or 'white man', obscured details of the account, Crocombe's translation, by using 'foreigner', at last permitted English readers to see that, although the whites were by no means squeaky clean, the troubles leading to the day of the killings began with the foreigners from Tahiti and New Zealand.

Without developing the point at all, this not only illustrates the interdependence of oral and written communication, but also demonstrates that oral culture doesn't stop when something is written down. For the community reading and interpreting the written text has its own ongoing oral culture, and the written text (such as a translation, or a particular interpretation) can then shape the subsequent oral tradition within that 'interpretive community' in such a way that it affects the reading of the text, for better and for worse.

---

23 'In 1823 John Williams [... of LMS] arrived, initiating the missionary era'. 'Two Raiatean converts, Papeiha and Rio, were set ashore in 1823 as native teachers, though not as consecrated missionaries. A permanent European presence was not established until 1827 when Charles Pitman with his wife Elizabeth established a mission station at Ngatangiia. The next year Aaron Buzacott and his family did likewise at Avarua. Papeiha then ran the Arorangi station (Rio having disgraced himself committing the "common sin" of fornication)'; Campbell, 'History in Prehistory', 225.

3.2 Names and their variants

The second translational issue concerns names and their variants.

Human action is always located in time and place. For Wentworth and the visitors, local names (whether of place or persons) were irrelevant, for the *Cumberland* crew was simply in a foreign place amongst people they deemed primitive natives. Even Gill's account, being written from the West about events in the South East, has a certain distance to it. But in contrast, Maretu's account is rich in persons and places, named because the places are still part of his island and the persons are amongst the recent ancestry of his own contemporaries.

In regard to place names, these not only provide local colour to the account, anchoring it in the real world, but some, such as references to where people were buried, act as 'memory sites' for the events being narrated, and as such, they add further authenticity.[24] In addition, occasionally a reference to a location reveals the author's point of view, such as when Maretu uses the word 'here'.[25]

Similarly, when the Gospels mention specific locations, this not only provides local colour, but anchors the events in Jesus' real world, and so the geographical and topographical features should be given due weight in interpreting the Gospels accounts. At times the language is extremely specific, revealing the point of view of someone who understood the terrain extremely well, such as when Luke narrates Jesus moving through the residential section of Jericho (19:1, διήρχετο), passing by the Herodian palaces at the foothills (cf. the allusion to Archelaus in 19:12), before climbing up the steep ascent towards Jerusalem (v.28, ἀναβαίνων), reaching the region of Bethphage and Bethany (v.29), and then past the summit of the Mount of Olives, then the place where the road begins to descend (v.37, πρὸς τῇ καταβάσει), before he approaches and catches a glimpse of the city (v.41, ὡς ἤγγισεν ἰδὼν τὴν πόλιν).[26]

Names—as such, but especially in their variation—act both as a mark of the written document's authenticity to the underlying oral

---

24 Even Gill knows some, such as when the New Zealander, 'Tumu' [i.e. Tupe] was shot and buried in 'Matapare'; *Gems*, 8.
25 Maretu, *Cannibals*, 42 [2] 'Vaikokopu harbour *here* at Ngatangiia'; 46 [10] 'a woman from *here*'; 46 [11], 'the ship's stay *here*' (my italics).
26 For Luke's 'local colour', see Hengel, 'Luke the Historian' and Pixner, 'Luke and Jerusalem'.

testimony and also as an aid to memory in oral culture. True to the island culture so intensely interested in genealogy, Maretu precisely lists sixteen persons from the *Cumberland,* providing the Rarotongan names that many of them had been given by the locals during their three month stay. On occasion he also refers to the nicknames or pet names they had also acquired, even providing an account of how they acquired them (e.g. Rangi for Veretini). The sources show the same phenomena displayed amongst the names in the New Testament: variations in spelling of names for the same person (Simon/Simeon; Cleopas/Clopas); nick names applied (Simon/Peter; Boanerges for the Zebedees); different names used in different social settings or cultural contexts (Peter/Cephas; Saul/Paul); formal and informal names (Silas/Silvanus); and sometimes a similar difficulty in deciding whether the one name refers to one person, or to two with the same name (Mary).[27]

To sum up this point, the manner in which the sources utilize names of persons and places conveys the impression that the writing is an authentic record of the underlying human realities.

But, in addition, names also provide a clue to the eyewitness source of the writer's information.

4. Detecting the Eyewitnesses

Richard Bauckham has recently revived discussion about the role of the eyewitnesses who gave the oral reports that lie behind the written Gospels. As one rule of thumb to detect these crucial sources, he suggests that we follow the lead of the characters who are named in the Gospels, on the principal they must have been known to the Gospels' original intended audience(s) and so the mention of their name could alert the audience, among other things, to their corroborative potential.[28]

From what we know of South Pacific oral history, this is completely logical, given that personal names act as memory devices in oral

---

27 For a discussion of the usage of Palestinian Jewish names, see Bauckham, *Jesus and the Eyewitnesses,* Ch. 2.
28 Bauckham, *Jesus and the Eyewitnesses,* Ch.3, but this is the theme of the whole book.

tradition.[29] The accounts from this Rarotongan event provide a good test case for this rule of thumb.

The Rarotongan sources contain a number of such named characters. But before we get to them, it is also worth noting that some people are named not because they are eyewitnesses to the story, but because they *are* the story—as is true also in the Gospels, most obviously in the case of Jesus.

As mentioned above, Maretu lists sixteen of those on the *Cumberland*, many by their Rarotongan name.[30] But these named characters were not his eyewitnesses, since by the time he wrote they had all long gone. Some, but not all, were named because they were participants in the events to be recounted. Given the significance of genealogical relationships for Pacific oral history, it is as if Maretu needed to list the *Cumberland* 'family', before he proceeded to report what happened with them.

On the other hand,—and again, as is obvious in the Gospels with, for example, the crowds who follow Jesus or who hear him teaching, or who get themselves healed—there are many people who could, and maybe even did, act as eyewitnesses, but they remain unnamed and part of an undifferentiated mass. For example, the sixty men who worked with the crew gathering *nono* every day for three months would have had their stories to tell. One thing they did tell was how, after being on board ship and learning of the murders on shore, they became frightened that they would be killed by the whites in revenge. They also told of their relief that they were kept safe. But Maretu did not single out a specific eyewitness behind these reports. There was no need to, for they were all telling basically the same story.

And again, what of the other crewmen on the *Cumberland*? What did they know? Or the many women in the account, who probably also held many secrets not told, but which were probably very important to events. There are the Tahitian wives of Te Are and Tomi, one of them,

---

29 Cf. Sharrad, 'Making Beginnings', 128, where Johnny 'asserts Puka Puka culture by providing an explanation of names as memory devices'.
30 Maretu's sixteen differs from Gill's count (see below). Other mistakes or vagaries in Gill's account (e.g. the ship coming 'about 1820'; 'Tumu', not Tupe; not realising the *Cumberland* returned to the place it first attempted landing; that the Ngatangiia incited the shooting of the Arorangi), compared with the precision with which Maretu recounts events, including providing many of the names of the crew, favours Maretu's list being closer to reality.

as we learn elsewhere, a Christian believer and a keen evangelist.[31] And what of the New Zealand woman that was killed? Despite being a complete mystery to the story, she may well have been a key player.[32]

However, although there were others involved who potentially had a story to tell, the persons named by the accounts probably represent the sources behind them. I will give three examples, one from Gill and two from Maretu, and all female.

4.1 Tepaeru

Gill's account reads as if it was drawn from a range of sources, but they, too, like him, were rather distant in time, geography, and tribal culture from those who were intimately involved with the events first-hand. For the Rarotongans, he speaks mostly at the level of people groups (even 'parties'), rather than individuals. And even for the 1814 visitors, although he gives a precise number (probably wrong), stating there were, besides the captain, 19 Englishman, two New Zealanders, and one New Zealand woman, he named only one of them later in his account, and when he did so, he probably got the name wrong. For he told of 'Tumu' the New Zealander (a mistake for Tupe) being shot as an example because of his conspiracy. He also knew that, besides Tupe, four other 'white men' (i.e. foreigners) and the New Zealand woman

---

31 As Maretu reported the island memory: 'The knowledge that was learned from that ship, actually from Veretini and Teara [Te Ara], was of a new god called Tiova [Jehovah] and Tititarai [Jesus Christ], who was almighty in the heavens as well as on the earth'; Maretu, *Cannibals*, 42 [2]. These two were joined by one of the Tahitian women, Maude & Crocombe, 'Rarotongan Sandalwood', 53, citing Maretu, 'On Rarotongan history', 1. According to LMS Missionary John Williams, her evangelistic efforts 'excited so much interest, that the king, Makea, called one of his children "Tehovah" (Jehovah), and another "Teeteetry" (Jesus Christ). An uncle of the king, whom we hope is at this time a truly good man, erected an altar to Jehovah and Jesus Christ, and to it persons afflicted with all manner of diseases were brought to be healed; and so great was the reputation which this *marae* obtained, that the power of Jehovah and Jesus Christ became great in the estimation of the people'; Williams, *Narrative*, 28.

32 Just as Ann Butcher was Goodenough's consort, I suspect the unnamed New Zealand woman may have been Wentworth's. The two women were therefore killed as a direct affront to the 'two captains', as they were called, and after the Ngatangiia chiefs struck a secret deal with them, the two women put on the ship as it left were 'replacements' to satisfy *utu*. See Bolt, 'What Really Happened on Rarotonga'.

were also killed, but he gave no names.³³

On the other hand, as he closed his account with the departure of the *Cumberland*, he gave a moving account of a young chieftainess, Tepaeru, who was taken on board, despite the best attempts of her father to save her from this fate worse than death and her being dragged from his arms, as the ship sailed away—without apparently knowing that her father was Rupe, the warrior who went on the killing spree, which, in fact, Gill doesn't even mention! This final paragraph is the most detailed of any paragraph in Gill's account, and it is the most emotionally textured. It is only here that we get the impression that he knew his source, that he had heard it in her own words, and that he had felt the emotion behind her words. In fact, he was so moved by her account of events that he finished off with a denunciation of the wickedness of the white men who would do such things.

In fact, the young chieftainess, Tepaeru, is the only Rarotongan named in Gill's whole account. We know from other sources, including Maretu, that after leaving the island the *Cumberland* dropped her and her niece Mata Kaavu off on Aitutaki. They were still there in 1821, when the Tahitian evangelist Papeiha was landed on that island by LMS missionary John Williams and they were both converted. In 1823 they went with Papeiha back to Rarotonga, to assist him in securing the dramatic conversion of Rarotonga in about eighteen months.³⁴ We also know that Tepaeru lived on the island until she died in 1881 at the ripe old age of 85,³⁵ one of the heroes of the LMS. In other words, when Gill names Tepaeru, he is naming perhaps his only eyewitness. She had participated in the events of 1814, even if only at the end of the events—and then as a traumatized eighteen-year-old who was more a victim of, than a participant in, the main action.

---

33 Gill's mention of the New Zealand woman is probably evidence of Tepaeru's version of events finding its way into his account, alongside the female point of view being evident in several other details, such as, 'pigs, property, and women were hidden in the mountains'; 'allowed the women to come again about the beach'. The *Sydney Gazette* ignores the New Zealand woman who was killed probably because she was (illegally, in violation of a recent Government Order) picked up at the Bay of Islands on the voyage outwards, and probably because she was Wentworth's consort and her mention could open him up for trouble.
34 Maretu, *Cannibals*, 198. Although his name is variously spelt (Pepeia, Peia, Papehia), Crocombe standardises to 'Papeiha' following the early records and his own signature, see p.55 n.79.
35 Tepaeru Grave Plaque, Avarua CICC graveyard.

Our next two examples come from Maretu's account.

As in the Gospel accounts, Maretu's tale names various minor characters who play no real part in the events. These seem to be most likely analogous to Bauckham's named characters, who act as eyewitnesses and are still known in that capacity by the intended audience. This is confirmed by the fact that the passages in which they are named are rich in detail and high in emotional texture and, as with Gill, there are signs in the accounts that the emotional telling of the event made an impact on Maretu himself and so affected his writing. Two of the clearest examples are the accounts of the killing of Veretini and of Tupe.

4.2 Terangiuira: The killing of Veretini

This scene is filled with close detail. The exact location of the house: 'Teikamoeava's house at Kaireva in the Avana district'; the exact location of Veretini when Rupe came: 'found Veretini asleep in the doorway'; and his state: 'he was intoxicated from imbibing too much kava'; and his companions: 'beside him were two women picking lice from his hair' (so, as the scene is described, he has his body inside the hut, but his head and shoulders are in the doorway, with the two women on either side, picking lice and, presumably, throwing their carcases out of the doorway).

A detailed description of the killing is provided from close quarters: Rupe called 'Eh, Rangi'—using a pet, familiar name; narrated from a hearer's perspective; Veretini turned his face to Rangi—presumably arching backwards to look over his head to the outside of the hut; Rupe slashed the neck, severing his head from his body; then Rupe rolled the body into the house—again, the description given from the perspective of someone inside.

This scene gives us the perspective of the two women. Although clearly known, initially they are not named, but by the end of the account one is named. As his death is described, Maretu rather randomly gives Veretini's physical and moral description: he was a big man, a good man, a warrior. His face was tattooed. A son-in-law of Rupe had given Veretini the pet name Rangi, which Rupe now used to take him off guard and end his life. In this description, we can hear the voice of someone who was intimately connected to both Veretini and Rupe—and someone who felt betrayed. For the description of his death ends with the appalling and emotionally charged note, 'but Rupe had no sympathy for his niece Terangiuira, who was Veretini's wife'. This appears to be a report from Maretu's eyewitness for this scene.

She could also then bear witness to Rupe's killing of John Croker and the escape of Wentworth that happened just outside her door—again told with a high degree of detail, but this time without the rich emotion, due to Terangiuira having little connection to Wentworth or Croker. His death was just more horror on her doorstep.

4.3 Tupe's wife: The killing of Tupe

Like Veretini, his fellow New Zealander Tupe lived onshore having married a Rarotongan woman (NB: 'from here'). Maretu tells us that he lived with 'one of Pa's sons'—Pa being one of the two ariki [high chiefs] who were over this district. Crocombe's translation adds the detail from her wider knowledge drawn from the living oral history on the island, that this son's name was Veia.[36]

Tupe was responsible for teaching the Rarotongans a scheme to kill the visitors. Whereas Gill only knew that somehow the ship found out about the conspiracy, Maretu named another character, Kurikuri, as the man who informed them. He also knew that this man was a classificatory father of Pa, so no doubt got the information from Pa's son, with whom Tupe and wife were residing. Maretu also knows that Kurikuri informed not just anyone, but 'the two officers', that is, Goodenough and Wentworth.

As the account continues, it is detailed and, as with the Veretini account, it reads as a report given by someone inside the house at the time of the event: two of the foreigners (on my theory, probably Goodenough and Wentworth themselves) arrive; at dawn; reach the house (note the detail of its location: at Turangi); they call out to him and he awoke (incidental detail) and he goes outside (all from the perspective of someone inside with him); and 'instantly they shot and killed him', expressing the shock of an observer of this sudden killing; and then a brief statement is added which reads like an epitaph: 'thus that man from New

---

36 Maretu, *Cannibals*, 46 [10].

Zealand died'. What lies behind this oddity? It is unnecessary, unless it is simply the record of a reflective poignant comment from someone connected to him. It expresses something like, 'the great warrior from New Zealand died in a dawn ambush, shot as he woke up from his sleep. What a way to end'. Although this report may have come from Tupe's host, Veia, it is more likely to be that of Tupe's wife, who had been lying at his side just before he was murdered.

Earlier in his account Maretu told what amounts to the 'official version' of events on Rarotonga, probably derived from Pa and Kanauku, that Rupe's killing spree was an act of vengeance for the theft of the coconuts from Makea Ariki, the Northern chief. But Maretu ended his account with this detail-rich, emotionally full, description of Tupe's murder by the white men. And then, despite having previously narrated the official version and with no embarrassment about introducing an alternative version, he then declares that, 'this [i.e. the conspiracy with Tupe's help, and his consequent murder] was the event which began the troubles of that day'.[37]

How intriguing! Maretu is quite clearly suggesting that the key to the events on August 12th, 1814, is not to be found in the 'official version' about the theft of the coconuts, but in the two men from the *Cumberland* murdering the New Zealander, Tupe, for his part in the conspiracy to get rid of the ship from the island. Little wonder the white men distorted their report in the *Sydney Gazette* and then stifled Marsden's inquiry.

Conclusion

Although the analogy of written sources in the living oral culture of the South Pacific may contain yet more lessons for Gospels study, in

---

37 Maretu, *Cannibals,* 46 [9], completely ignores the kidnapping, simply stating that the ship departed 'taking with her the chieftainess Tepaeru, Mata Kavaau and a man named Kupauta'. This is intriguing, not only in comparison to Gill's account, but also because she was a niece of Maretu's father (p.198), and readily available to act as one of Maretu's sources. If Maretu was aware that this (staged) kidnapping occurred because a deal had been done behind the scenes to assuage the two white captains by replacing their murdered consorts (as is my theory; see Bolt, 'What Really Happened?'), perhaps it was a story best left untold and, given the agreement, the girls were simply taken on board, despite any play-acting Rupe may have engaged in.

terms of the two that this study has itemised, an examination of the sources relating to the 1814 visit to Rarotonga of the *Cumberland* indicates that, 1. biased sources do not preclude the recovery of the underlying events; and 2. Bauckham's rule of thumb appears to be a good one, for those minor characters who are named, in the midst of a narrative rich in detail and emotional texture, are most likely the source of the account.

Bibliography

Abbreviations: CICC = Cook Islands Christian Church; LMS = London Missionary Society; *SG* = *Sydney Gazette*; *SMH* = *Sydney Morning Herald*; SOAS = School of Oriental and African Studies, University of London.

Primary Sources & Realia:

Maretu	*Cannibals and Converts. Radical Change in the Cook Islands* (M.T. Crocombe, trans. & ed.; Suva, Fiji: Institute of Pacific Studies, University of the South Pacific, 1983).
Maretu, 1873.	'Extracts from the Papers of the late Rev. W. Wyatt Gill, LL.D. No. 14. 'E tuatua no te Kai-tangata i Rarotonga [A Word about Cannibalism at Rarotonga]', translated by Stephen Savage. *Journal of the Polynesian Society*, 20.4 (80) (1911), text: 196–201; translation: 201–209. Archive.org. See now Maretu, *Cannibals*, pp. 33–42.
Maretu, 1871	MS. On Rarotongan History, 1871. Polynesian Society, Wellington.
Maretu	'Ko te Taeanga mai o te pai o Kurunaki ki Rarotonga nei, i ta mataiti 1820'. [The Coming of Goodenough's Ship to Rarotonga in 1820 (sic)], in: *Journal of the Polynesian Society*, 20.4(80)(1911), text: 189–191, translation: 191–196 (Gill's Extracts, no.13). See now Maretu, *Cannibals*, pp. 42–46.
Marsden, S., to J. Pratt, 26/10/1815	(www.marsdenarchive.otago.ac.nz/MS_0055_035).

Pitman, C., to W. Ellis, 10/8/1839. (SOAS: London Missionary Society Correspondence: South Seas, Box 12. London, L.M.S. archives).

Seringapatam — *Journal of the ship Seringapatam from the island Nooevah towards Port Jackson, 6 May to June 22, 1814.* Anonymous MS. Written on the back of two charts, Nos. 8 and 9 of Arrowsmith's Chart of the Pacific Ocean in 9 sheets (Mitchell: MS X980/7).

Tepaeru's grave plaque, Avarua CICC.

Williams, J. — *A Narrative of Missionary Enterprises in the South Sea Islands with remarks upon the natural history of the islands, origin, languages, traditions and usages of the inhabitants* (London: J. Snow, 1837). https://babel.hathitrust.org. OR https://archive.org/stream/narrativeofmissi00willuoft.

Secondary Sources:

Bauckham, R. — *Jesus and the Eyewitnesses. The Gospels as Eyewitness Testimony* (Grand Rapids: Eerdmans, 22017 [2006]).

Bolt, P.G. — 'What Really Happened in Rarotonga in August 1814?' (forthcoming).

Bolt, P.G. — '"Let Our Anger Cease". George Te Ara as a Case Study of the Encounter between Human Trauma and Gospel Healing', D.G. Smith & R.A. Fringer (eds.), *Wesleyan Perspectives on Human Flourishing* (Eugene: Wipf & Stock [Pickwick], 2020 [in press]).

Bolt, P.G. — 'The Failure of the Philanthropic Society', in P.G. Bolt & M. Falloon (eds.), *Freedom to Libel? Samuel Marsden v. Philo Free. Australia's First Libel Case* (Epping, NSW: Bolt Publishing Services, 2017), 130–194.

Bolt, P.G. — 'The *Boyd* Set-Back to Marsden's Mission: The View from New South Wales', in P.G. Bolt & D.B. Pettett (eds.), *Launching Marsden's Mission. The Beginnings of the Church Missionary Society in New Zealand, viewed from New South Wales* (London: The Latimer Trust, 2014), 61–78.

Campbell, M. — 'History in Prehistory. The Oral Traditions of the Rarotongan Land Court Records', *Journal of Pacific History* 37.2 (2002), 221–238.

Crocombe, M.T.   'Maretu's Life, Work, and Context', *Cannibals and Converts: Radical Change in the Cook Islands* (Marjorie Tuainekore Crocombe, transl., ed., annot.; Suva, Fiji: Institute of Pacific Studies University of South Pacific, 1983; repr. 1987, 1993, 2001), 1–30. https://books.google.com.au/books?id=N-jCFqMMu5YwC&pg=PA45&lpg=PA45&dq. Numbers in [square brackets] indicate the pagination of Maretu's manuscript.

Eddy, P.R.   'Orality and Oral Transmission', in J.B. Green, J.K. Brown, & N. Perrin (eds.), *Dictionary of Jesus and the Gospels* (Nottingham & Downers Grove: IVP, 22013), 641–650.

Falloon, M.   '"Openings of Providence": The Shaping of Marsden's Missionary Vision for New Zealand', in P.G. Bolt & D.B. Pettett (eds.), *Launching Marsden's Mission. The Beginnings of the Church Missionary Society in New Zealand, viewed from New South Wales* (London: The Latimer Trust, 2014), 129–138.

Gill, William   *Gems from the Coral Islands; or, Incidents of Contrast Between Savage and Christian Life of the South Sea Islanders.* Vol. 2: *Eastern Polynesia* (London: Ward & Co, 1856).

Hengel, M.   'Luke the Historian and the Geography of Palestine in the Acts of the Apostles', *Between Jesus and Paul. Studies in the Earliest History of Christianity* (Eugene: Wipf & Stock, 2003 [German: 1983; ET: 1983]), 97–128.

Kloosterman, A.M.J.   'Discoverers of The Cook Islands and the Names They Gave', *Cook Islands Library and Museum Bulletin* 1 (Second Revised and Augmented Edition, 1976). https://viewer.waireto.victoria.ac.nz/client/viewer/IE681078/rep/REP681324/FL681326?dps_dvs=1579249551253~568.

Levi, A.W.   'The Idea of Socrates: The Philosophic Hero in the Nineteenth Century', *Journal of the History of Ideas* 17 (1956), 89–107.

Maude, H., & M. Crocombe 'Rarotongan Sandalwood. The Visit of Goodenough to Rarotonga in 1814', *Journal of the Polynesian Society*, 71.1 (1962), 32–56. www.jstor.org/stable/20703963. Originally presented as a paper at the Tenth Pacific Science Congress of the Pacific Science Association, University of Hawaii, 21 Aug to 6 Sept 1961. Also found at http://hercolano2.blogspot.com.au/2010/08/rarotongan-sandalwood-visit-of.html?m=1.

Perkins, R.L. 'Introduction', in R.L. Perkins (ed.), *International Kierkegaard Commentary. The Concept of Irony* (Macon, GA: Mercer University Press, 2001), 1–16.

Pixner, B. 'Luke and Jerusalem', *Paths of the Messiah and Sites of the Early Church from Galilee to Jerusalem* (R. Riesner, ed.; K. Myrick, S. & M. Randall, transls.; San Francisco: Ignatius, 2010 [German: 1991]), 423–432.

Sharrad, P. 'Making Beginnings: Johnny Frisbie and Pacific Literature', *New Literary History 25.1* (1994), 121–136.

Tink, A. *William Charles Wentworth. Australia's Greatest Native Son* (Crows Nest, NSW: Allen & Unwin, 2009).

Waitangi Tribunal www.waitangitribunal.govt.nz.

Williams, J.V. [Chief Judge] 'Reparations and the Waitangi Tribunal. Paper to "Moving Forward" Conference, 15–16 August 2001', www.humanrights.gov.au/reparations-and-waitangi-tribunal (access: 23/9/17).

Ziolkowski, E. 'From *Clouds* to *Corsair*: Kierkegaard, Aristophanes, and the Problem of Socrates', in R.L. Perkins, *International Kierkegaard Commentary. The Concept of Irony* (Macon, GA: Mercer University Press, 2001), 193–234.

CHAPTER 6

The Historical Jesus as 'Social Critic': An Investigation Of Luke 6:27–36

James R. Harrison

Abstract

The time is opportune for a re-appraisal of the complex issues raised by Luke 6:31–35. After examining select sources illustrating the Graeco-Roman reciprocity system, the article addresses several questions. How far has Luke adapted Jesus' teaching in Luke 6:27–36 for his Hellenistic audience? What evidence is there that the historical Jesus critiqued Hellenistic reciprocity? How far does Jesus modify the traditional understanding of reciprocity in regard to divine beneficence and the return of favour? What alternative models of beneficence does Jesus promote? It concludes that Jesus critiqued the ancient reciprocity system, subjecting its operations to his messianic appraisal, in order to establish a community of servant-benefactors—drawn in many cases (though not exclusively) from the marginalised subgroups of society—who would act beneficently as much towards their enemies as to their friends.

1. Jesus and the Graeco-Roman Reciprocity System

In antiquity reciprocity was fundamental to relationships involving beneficence. It created networks of obligation that spanned the divine and human world.¹ Modern sociological studies have afforded New Testament scholars insight into the way that the ethos of reciprocity shaped a range of relationships in the Gospels.² However, as useful as this approach is, there has been insufficient analysis of the ancient evidence regarding reciprocity rituals in the ministry of the historical Jesus. Few scholars have explored the extent to which the documentary and literary evidence throws light on Jesus' critique of the reciprocity system in Luke 6:27–36, especially as articulated in vv. 31–36.³ Does this pericope represent Luke's own redaction of Q traditions—whether oral or written—or are we dealing here with an independent historical tradition regarding Jesus as a social critic, notwithstanding its Lucan redaction?⁴ Moreover, we run the risk of simplifying the complexity

---

1   This essay, slightly reduced, was originally published with the *Journal of Gospels and Acts Research* 2 (2018), 53–74 and is reproduced here with permission. On reciprocity in the ancient world, see Gill, *et. al., Reciprocity*; Briones, *Paul's Financial Policy*, 26–41. For a helpful coverage of what exchange theorists have said regarding reciprocity in the sociological and psychological literature from the 1900's, see Molm, 'The Structure of Reciprocity'. I will adopt the general definition of reciprocity provided by Seaford, 'Introduction', 1: 'Reciprocity is the principal and practice of voluntary requital, of benefit for benefit (positive reciprocity) or harm for harm (negative reciprocity)'.
2   Moxnes, *Economy*; Moxnes, 'Patron–Client Relations'; Malina & Rohrbaugh, *Social–Science Commentary*, 325. For assessments of 'reciprocity' studies in New Testament, see de Silva, 'Patronage and Reciprocity'; MacGillivray, 'Re-Evaluating Patronage'.
3   See Van Unnik, 'Die Motivierung'; Theissen, 'Nonviolence'; Betz, *Sermon on the Mount*, 590–614; Kirk, '"Love Your Enemies"'; Marshall, *Jesus, Patrons, and Benefactors*, 193–247. For other studies on reciprocity in Luke–Acts, see Capper, 'Reciprocity'; Knowles, 'Reciprocity'; Bertschmann, 'Hosting Jesus'.
4   Lührmann, 'Liebet eure Feinde', 413–15, has argued that the Sermon on the Mount and the Sermon on the Plain have significant parallels throughout and that the order of the subject matter is the same in each Gospel. Similarly, Piper, *Wisdom in the Q Tradition*, 193, cf. 77–82. On this basis many scholars, including Arnal, *Jesus and the Village Scribes*, 168, conclude that Q was a written document. Theissen, *Social Reality*, 141 n. 52, argues more cautiously. He suggests that Luke and Matthew reproduce 'a common tradition, probably a written source, even though it is impossible to see all the divergences between Matthew and Luke as editorial changes'. However, Piper, 'Love Your Enemies', 49–51, has warned against assuming that there existed a definitive form of Q upon which Luke and Matthew relied. Piper moves in the right direction in acknowledging the speculative nature of much Q scholarship, but he does not sufficiently reckon with the possibility that Jesus taught some of these materials (e.g. Matt 5:43–48; Luke 6:27–36), adapted to different contexts (e.g. 6:32–36), on two or more different occasions. See our discussion in §3.1 below. For excellent discussion of the critical options, see Bock, *Luke. Volume: 1:1–9:50*, 553–56. On the reliability of the oral forms behind the Gospels, see Gerhardsson, *Memory and Manuscript*; Wansbrough, *Jesus and the Oral Gospel*; Keener, *Matthew*, 27–29. Whether Q was just an oral source rote memorized in Christian communities, or a single source written in either Greek *or* Aramaic and derived from a *specific* Christian community, or—in a more chaotic model of Q—tradition handed down from *different* Christian communities and written on wax tablets in Greek *and* Aramaic, will be bypassed here.

of ancient reciprocity rituals when we view them through a sociological lens.⁵ In neglecting the ancient evidence, we overlook contemporary critiques of the benefaction system that provide a useful backdrop against which we can assess Jesus' criticism of the reciprocity system.

By the first-century BC, the Graeco-Roman reciprocity system had taken firm hold in Palestine and its conventions were well known to the Judaean elite, in its Herodian and imperial expression.⁶ According to Josephus, Herod the Great—a client of Augustus and a benefactor of international repute in his own right⁷—established and maintained bonds of reciprocity throughout his reign (*AJ* 15.18, 310–316; *BJ* 1.457–458).⁸ Inscriptions from the Athenian Acropolis (*OGIS* 414, 427) and agora (*SEG* 12 [1955] 150) eulogise Herod for his beneficence to the city (εὐεργεσία) and emphasise his status as a friend of both the Romans (Φιλορωμαῖος) and the Emperor (Φιλοκαῖσαρ).⁹ The Herodian dynasty was able to count on the return of favour from its clients, as the presence of a Herodian faction at the time of Jesus testifies (Mark 3:6; Matt 22:16; Matt 16:16).¹⁰ The Herods were adept at appealing to the reciprocity system in their interactions with the imperial rulers. Philo's rendering of Herod Agrippa's letter to Gaius Caligula regarding the erection of his statue in the Temple is a case in point. The letter illustrates how a dependent might invoke loyalty to his patron as tool of persuasion

---

5   See Harrison, *Paul's Language of Grace*, 17–23.
6   For recent discussions of reciprocity and gift giving in ancient Israel and Second Temple Judaism, see Rajak, 'Benefactors'; Stansell, 'The Gift'; Matthews, 'The Unwanted Gift'; Joubert, *Paul as Benefactor*, 93–99; Harrison, *Paul's Language of Grace*, 97–166; Marshall, *Jesus, Patrons, and Benefactors*, 24–124; Schwartz, *Were Jews a Mediterranean Society?*; Novick, 'Charity and Reciprocity'; Wilfred, *Poverty, Charity and the Image of the Poor*, 255–59.
7   Two inscriptions, one from Jerusalem (*IEJ* 20 [1970], 97–98), the other from Ashdod (*ZPE* 105 [1995], 81–84), refer to Herod the Great as respectively 'Benefactor (εὐ[εργέτης])' and 'Friend of Caesar (φιλοκ[αίσαρος])' and 'pious (εὐσέβειας) and Friend of Caesar (φιλοκαίσαρος)'. For discussion, see Richardson, *Herod*, 204. On the benefaction of the Herodian dynasty, see Marshall, *Jesus, Patrons, and Benefactors*, 125–73.
8   On Herod the Great as benefactor, see Richardson, *Herod*, 93–94, 127, 174–77, 272–73.
9   For discussion, see Richardson, *Herod*, 207–08.
10 The fact that Herod Antipas, like his father, cultivated and maintained client–patron relations with Greek cities overseas is evident from two inscriptions that honour Herod Antipas as 'guest and friend' (Cos: *OGIS* 416; cf. Luke 23:12) and which praise him 'on account of [his] piety and good' (Delos: *OGIS* 417). For discussion, see Richardson, *Herod*, 208–09.

in order to pressure him to change his policy.[11] The Roman Prefects were also dependent upon their imperial patrons and were vulnerable to threats of the withdrawal of Caesar's friendship, as the prefecture of Pilate amply demonstrates (John 19:12; Josephus, *BJ* 18.85–89; Philo, *Leg.* 299–305).[12]

While later Jewish writers were critical of the imperial reciprocity system,[13] the presence of a Phoenician honorific inscription from Greece—rendered in Semitic apart from the concluding reference in Greek to the Sidonian Council—confirms the presence of Hellenistic reciprocity rituals in the wider Semitic world. The Sidonian assembly awards Shama'baal, superintendent of the temple at Sidon and its buildings, a gold crown and erects an inscribed stele in his honour. Traditional reciprocity rituals are enunciated in the decision of the Sidonian assembly:

> —to crown Shama'baal son of MGN, who (had been) a superintendent of the community in charge of the buildings in the temple court and did all that was required of him by way of service;—that the men who are our superintendents in charge of the temple should write this decision on a chiseled stele, and should set it up in the portico of the temple before the eyes of men;—(and) that the community should be named as guarantor. For this stele the citizens of Sidon shall draw 20 drachmae sterling from the temple treasury. So may the Sidonians know

---

11 Philo, *Leg.* 276–329, esp. 285–289, 294–298, 323–326. The boundaries that the imperial rulers could erect between themselves and their overly enthusiastic Jewish clients when occasion warranted is well illustrated by Claudius' letter to the Alexandrians (10th November AD 41: *CPJ* 2.153).
12 For Josephus' presentation of the operations of the imperial reciprocity system, see Harrison, *Paul's Language of Grace*, 138–40.
13 SibOr 8:52–55 (ad 185) speaks of Hadrian's benefactions and conquests thus: 'there will be a grey-haired prince with the name of a nearby sea, inspecting the world with polluted foot, giving gifts. Having abundant gold, he will also gather more silver from his enemies, and strip and undo them'. Collins discounts the possibility that this is another case of Christian interpolation in the Sibylline Oracles; 'The Sibylline Oracles, Book 8', 416: 'Jewish authorship of the remainder of the first section of the Sibylline Oracles 8 is supported by the animosity towards Hadrian in verses 50–59'. For criticism of Hadrian in the rabbinic literature, see *Tanh.*, Bereshit, §7, f.10b–11a (translated Montefiore & Loewe, *Rabbinic Anthology*, §13). See also SibOr 12.1–299 for an extended diatribe against the Roman imperial rulers. Notwithstanding the negative attitude to the imperial rulers in the Sibylline Oracles, SibOr 11:269–271 highlights the piety of the Roman people towards Julius Caesar at his funeral because of his friendship towards them.

that the community knows how to requite the men who have rendered service before the community.¹⁴

Similarly, while many Jewish inscriptions from Diaspora synagogues retain distinctive features that differentiate them to some extent from their eastern Mediterranean counterparts, there are inscriptions that operate according to traditional Greek models of reciprocity. For example, in a third-century AD decree from Phocaea, Tation is accorded conventional honours in the standard eulogistic vocabulary:

> Tation, daughter (or wife) of Straton, son of E(m)pedon, having erected the assembly hall and the enclosure of the open courtyard with her own funds (ἐκ τῶ[ν ἰδ]ίων), gave them as a gift (ἐξαρίσατο) to the Jews. The synagogue of the Jews honoured (ἐ[τείμη]σεν) Tation, daughter (or wife) of Straton, son of E(m)pedon, with a golden crown (χρυσῷ στεφάνῳ) and the privilege of sitting in the seat of honour (προεδρίᾳ).¹⁵

In the Gospels, however, Jesus is portrayed as one who criticised the rule of the Hellenistic and Roman Benefactor-Kings (Luke 22:25), along with their affluent Herodian clients in palaces (Matt 11:7–8; cf. Luke 13:32).¹⁶ He castigated the synagogal benefactors for seeking public honours in recompense of their acts of generosity (Matt 6:2–4; contra, Luke 7:4–8). This (largely) negative attitude of Jesus towards the Jewish and Gentile representatives of the Graeco-Roman benefaction system was extended to its underlying social dynamic. Jesus, as depicted by Luke in 6:32–36, jettisoned the entire modus operandi of the reciprocity system, thereby setting himself against one of the most fundamental social

---

14 For a translation of the inscription (Piraeus: III. cent. BC or 96 BC), see Gibson, *Syrian Semitic Inscriptions* III. §41, 148–151. I am indebted to Dr. J.A. Davies for drawing this inscription to my attention. For discussion of the Greek model upon which the Syrian inscription is based, see Harrison, *Language of Grace*, 37–43.
15 Lifshitz, *Donateurs et Foundateurs*, §13. Translated by Brooten, *Women Leaders,* Appendix §3. For discussion, *ibid.*, 143–44. For other examples, see ibid., §6. For two inscriptions from Delos (150–50 BC) in which Samaritans honour their benefactors with the traditional coronal honours, see Llewelyn, *New Documents* 8. §12 (pp.148–151).
16 For the historicity of the Matt 11:7 *logion*, see Theissen, *Gospels in Context*, 26–42.

conventions of antiquity.[17] But how do we account for (what seems to be) Jesus' ringing endorsement of reciprocity conventions in Luke 6:31?

Modern scholars have made much of v. 31 in discussion of the Lucan pericope, asserting that reciprocity was a key value in Jesus' exposition of his in-breaking Kingdom. Several examples will suffice. First, Theissen proposes that the charismatic movement of Jesus would reverse the social aggression that they encountered in their itinerant wanderings by means of the Q 'love your enemies' command. Although the Golden Rule (Luke 6:31) is a fundamental expression of human reciprocity, Luke interprets love for the enemy as the new hope and goal for social relationships.[18]

Second, R.A. Horsley divests Luke 6:27–36 of its purported anti-Roman polemic. He posits that the Jesus movement restored peasant practices of reciprocal generosity—and over against Theissen's 'itinerancy' thesis—in the *settled* context of households, villages and towns.[19]

Third, J.L. Reed has argued that Jesus rejected monetisation (e.g. Luke 12:33–34; 12:13–21; 15:8–9; 16:31; Matt 23:16–17) in favour of the ideal of reciprocity (Luke 6:27–35; 9:57–61). Reed believes that reciprocity found its expression not so much at the level of family and

---

[17] After the Second Jewish Revolt, a rabbinic tradition (b Shabbat 33^b; cf. 'Abodah Zarah 2^b) cynically exposes the self-centered motives that animated the gift-giving rituals of imperial and local Roman benefactors in the empire: 'How splendid are the works of this people', declared Rabbi Judah; 'they have built marketplaces, baths, and bridges'. ... But Rabbi Simeon bar Yohai answered, 'Everything they have made they have made only for themselves—marketplaces, for whores; baths, to wallow in; bridges, to levy tolls'. Cited in Elliott, 'Paul and the Politics of Empire', 32. More generally, see de Lange, 'Jewish Attitudes'; Alexander, 'The Family of Caesar'. However, we must not assume that such negative attitudes to Roman benefactors, including the ruler, were universal in post-ad. 70 Judaism. One rabbinic commentator on Deuteronomy 32:9 (Midrash Ha-Gaddol Deuteronomy 32:9: see §1.3.10 in Maas, *Readings in Late Antiquity*) speaks of the importance of choosing the imperial benefactor as a patron instead of his underlings because of his superior power: 'Some made of the governor their patron, some of the duke, some of the chief of the army. There was one clever fellow there. He said: All these people are under the authority of the king, and cannot prevent him from doing whatever he may wish to do. But he can prevent them from doing what they wish to. I shall choose as my patron none other than the king who can prevent all others from doing anything he objects to'.

[18] Theissen, 'Nonviolence', 121–25; Theissen, *First Followers*, 98–99. Vaage, *Galilean Upstarts*, 121–27, considers Luke 6:27–35 to be general instruction on how to manage social conflict in antiquity, without any specific context.

[19] Horsley, *Jesus and the Spiral of Violence*, 255–75; Horsley, *Sociology*, 125–26. Similarly, Freyne, 'The Geography, Politics, and Economics', 91. For Horsley's criticism of Theissen's arguments advocating an early Christian itinerant ethos, see his *Sociology*, 116–29. For an extended critique of Theissen's position, see Arnal, *Jesus and the Village Scribes*, 1–95.

village life, as Horsley asserts, but more in the Kingdom of God.[20]

Fourth, W.E. Arnal has recently proposed that Herod Antipas' foundation of new cities in 20's Galilee brought vast social and economic changes that resulted in the loss of scribal independence.[21] As elite patronage increased, so village solidarity eroded. Therefore, the Herodian village scribes—who in Arnal's view were the originators of the Q tradition—espoused a state of idealized reciprocity that belonged to the past but which expressed the newness of Kingdom of God in the present. In sum, Arnal views the Q 'love your enemies' speech (Q 6:27–35) as 'the pinnacle of an ethical revolution'.[22]

Fifth, H.D. Betz claims that Jesus' citation of the Golden Rule in v. 31 serves as an ethical principle which functions in precisely the same way as Greek ethical discussions did (*do ut des* ['I give so that you may give']).[23] Luke proceeds to refute incorrect understandings of the Golden Rule (vv. 32–34) and 'its misapplication to the commandments of Jesus' (v. 27).[24] The correct understanding of the Golden Rule is then enunciated in vv. 35–36. Thus, in Betz's view, v. 35 reflects general Hellenistic debates on beneficence, in which benevolence was not to be confused with business investments.[25] Conversely, in v. 36, the 'mercifulness of the deity was also a generally recognised element of Hellenistic religiosity',[26] as much as it was the case in Jewish covenantal piety.

Sixth, J. Marshall explores vv. 27–36 within the wider pericope of Luke 6:17–38.[27] He argues that the passage should be understood in light of Hellenistic reciprocity and benefaction rituals, operative in the Greek East, as opposed to the conventions of *patrocinium*, the Roman practice of benefaction, found in the Latin West. The rule of the Herod

---

20 Reed, *Archaeology*, 97–98.
21 Arnal, *Jesus and the Village Scribes, passim*. Arnal builds upon the Q stratigraphy of Kloppenborg. However, the claim that one can chart a progression in Q from an early sapiental layer to a later eschatological layer, especially when we do not possess the original Q document (if there ever was one), creates a hypothetical reconstruction of early Christianity which we cannot possibly verify from our later documentary texts (Matthew, Luke) without being highly subjective in our judgements.
22 Arnal, *Jesus and the Village Scribes*, 58.
23 Betz, *Sermon on the Mount*, 599.
24 Betz, *Sermon on the Mount*, 604.
25 Betz, *Sermon on the Mount*, 608.
26 Betz, *Sermon on the Mount*, 613.
27 Marshall, *Jesus, Patrons, and Benefactors*, 191–247.

client-kings provides no real evidence for the evidence of *patrocinium* but rather for the Hellenised rituals of reciprocity, benefaction, and friendship flourished in Palestine.[28] While the Lukan portrait of Jesus demonstrate strong Jewish interpretative models (i.e. prophetic, Jubilee, Passover imagery),[29] Jesus, conversant with the benefaction system, does not reject the reciprocity system per se but only its improper adoption.[30] As Marshall observes, in Jesus' teaching 'new forms of reciprocity, friendship, and benefaction replace normal patterns which existed among the audience'.[31] Indeed, Jesus depicts God the Father as a generous Benefactor (Luke 6:35b) who reciprocates those who are generous to the marginalised (6:38).

But one wonders whether Marshall's tight distinction between 'Hellenised' and 'Romanised' models is overly prescriptive given the fluidity of intercultural contact that characterised the imperial world of the eastern Mediterranean basin. P.-S. Seo, for example, argues that Jesus' emphasis on loving the enemy in Luke 6:27–38 has the spiral of violence in the Roman Empire clearly in view.[32] While one would not want to restrict Luke 6:27–38 to a counter-imperial understanding, Jesus was nevertheless realistic about the threats and impositions wielded by the imperial rulers against their subjects (Luke 22:25a; 23:26), the violence of the Roman magistrates (13:1–3), and their Herodian clients (13:32; Matt 14:6–12; Mark 6:21–29) could bring to the rule of their subjects, even if they publicly projected the highly positive image of 'Benefactor' (22:25b: εὐεργέται καλοῦνται).[33] But imperial violence is only one aperture through which we can view the 'enemy' in our pericope: the enmity arising from the disruption of benefaction rituals, from the violation of φιλία, and from external enemies of the polis, among many other scenarios, are in view.

Despite the differences in emphasis outlined above, many modern scholars believe that reciprocity is at the heart of the social revolution

---

28 Marshall, *Jesus, Patrons, and Benefactors*, 38–41, 44–49, 53–124, 331–33.
29 Marshall, *Jesus, Patrons, and Benefactors*, 239–43, 288–89.
30 Marshall, *Jesus, Patrons, and Benefactors*, 328–33.
31 Marshall, *Jesus, Patrons, and Benefactors*, 330.
32 Seo, *Luke's Jesus*, 147–55.
33 On 'Benefactor' see Marshall, *Jesus, Patrons, and Benefactors*, 286–323; Seo, *Luke's Jesus*, 96–115.

that Jesus is launching.³⁴ What Jesus intends is a revitalization or transformation of traditional reciprocity ethics, either as the dynamic of Judean village life or as the actualization of the Kingdom of God. What is unclear in this consensus, however, is the relation of v. 31 to vv. 27–30 and vv. 32–34. Does the Lucan Jesus endorse reciprocity only to undermine its operations subsequently in a searing exposé of the reciprocity system? Or is reciprocity a daring illustration of love for the enemy?

Scholars have responded in vastly different ways to these issues.³⁵ Several scholars dismiss the authenticity of v. 31 in its present context. R.A. Piper posits that Luke 6:31 could be a 'floating unit of tradition,' even though the consensus is that Matthew's placement of the Golden Rule (Matt 7:12) is redactional.³⁶ J.S. Kloppenborg proposes that because v. 31 interrupts the elaboration of vv. 27–30 by vv. 32–34, Luke 6:31 must be a later insertion, a position earlier articulated by R. Bultmann.³⁷ The Jesus Seminar rates v. 31 as grey ('Well, maybe') as far as authentic Jesus tradition. This is because, the Jesus Seminar asserts, the logion has a 'calculating egoism' and is widely attested in the ancient sources.³⁸

Other scholars argue that v. 31 is correctly placed in its context, with vv. 32–35 clearly in view. A. Dihle considers v. 31 to be an instance of the general human behaviour which, as vv. 32–34 elucidates, must be

---

34 Not all scholars believe that reciprocity is at the core of Luke 6:31–36. Kirk, '"Love Your Enemies"', 667–86, argues that while the 'Love your enemy' command presupposes reciprocity rituals, Luke 6:32–34 challenges the ancient reciprocity system. In the view of Kirk, however, no new understanding of χάρις emerges. Ricoeur, 'The Golden Rule', speaks of the presentation of a spirit of superabundant generosity and unilateral mercy in vv. 32–36 which empties reciprocity of its self-interest. For another 'non–reciprocal' interpretation, see Topel, 'The Tarnished Golden Rule'.
35 Curiously, Piper, '*Love Your Enemies*', 54, does not address the issue. For an incisive coverage of the Golden Rule in Matthew and Luke, see Bock, *Luke*, 595.
36 Piper, *Wisdom in the Q Tradition*, 80.
37 Kloppenborg, *The Formation of Q*, 177; Bultmann, *History of the Synoptic Tradition*, 96. Discussions as to which traditions in Luke 6:27–36 are either pre–Q, the work of the Q editor/community, or later than Q are precarious due to their inherent subjectivity. While the Q hypothesis is our best explanation of the similarities between Mathew and Luke, the absence of documentary evidence for Q renders our speculation about the pericope's tradition–history improbable. Note Ehrman's caustic evaluation (*Jesus*, 132) of the 'cottage industry' in Q studies that has risen out of a 'nonexistent source'. For stimulating discussions of the (proposed) tradition-history, see Tuckett, *Q and the History of Early Christianity*, 300–307; Catchpole, *The Quest for Q*, 101–34. Note, however, the correct observation of Schottroff, 'Non Violence', 22, that the words 'bless those who curse you' (Luke 6:28) are 'substantially pre–Lukan' because they are alluded to in Rom 12:14.
38 Funk, *The Five Gospels*, 296.

surpassed,[39] a point which R. A. Piper—because of his indecisiveness over the issue[40]—is willing to concede.[41] Other scholars, while agreeing that v. 31 admirably fits its context, relate v. 31 to the preceding verses. R.C. Douglas, for example, states that v. 31 provides the rationale for vv. 27–30.[42] In a mediating position, J.B. Green argues that v. 31 is well integrated into the entire context of vv. 27–30 and vv. 32–35 by means of the repetition of the word 'do' throughout (ποιέω: vv. 27, 31 [2x], 33 [3x], 35).[43] C.S. Sunil also argues that the Golden Rule acts as a commentary both on Luke 6:27b–30 and 6:32–34. Its 'totally other-centred approach' in both pericopes is designed to 'reinforce the initial commands set forth in 6:27b–30: v. 32 recalls v. 27b (love your enemies), v. 33 recalls v. 27c (do good) and v. 34 recalls v. 30 (give)'.[44] As such, Jesus' application of the Golden Rule in verse 31 'sharply overturns the principle of equal retribution (*lex talonis*)'.[45]

In contrast to the contextual approaches outlined above, there are scholars who argue that v. 31 is not clearly linked either with what precedes or follows. In this regard, V.P. Furnish writes that the Golden Rule in Luke 6:31 is '*separate* counsel *only generally illustrative* of the love command in vs.27'.[46]

---

39 Dihle, *Die Goldene Regel*, 113–14. Similarly, Evans, *Saint Luke*, 335. Oakman, *Jesus and the Economic Questions*, 78–79, sees Luke 6:31 as a case of 'balanced reciprocity' where exchanges occur on a quid pro quo basis. However, Oakman (pp.162–63) goes on to argue that Jesus undermines the notion of balanced reciprocity with the commands to love the enemy and to lend without expectation of return (Luke 6:32–35). As Oakman (p.163) observes, 'Loaning to enemies or strangers without the expectation of repayment goes against village commonsense'.
40 Rightly, Vaage, *Galilean Upstarts*, 127.
41 Piper, *Wisdom in the Q Tradition*, 80.
42 Douglas, '"Love Your Enemies"', 118. Similarly, Fitzmyer, *Luke I–IX*, 639; Stein, *Luke*, 208. Catchpole, *Quest for Q*, 114, says that the Q editor relates v. 31 more to vv. 27–28 than the 'detour' of vv. 29–30. Vaage, 'Composite Texts', 82, concedes that v. 31 undergirds and elaborates by example the preceding instructions of vv. 27–30.
43 Green, *Luke*, 273.
44 Ranjar, *Be Merciful Like the Father*, 188–89.
45 Ranjar, *Be Merciful Like the Father*, 185 (cf. Exod 21:24; Lev 24:20; Deut 19:21).
46 Furnish, *The Love Command*, 57 (my emphasis). The contention of Vaage, 'Composite Texts', 77, that Luke 6:31 finds a parallel in *Gos.Thom* 6:2 ('do not do what you hate') is overstated. It reflects the more negative formulations of the Golden Rule (e.g. Tobit 4:15; *b. Sabb.* 31a; '*Abot. R. Nat.* B. §26; *t. Ketub.* 7.6; Sir 31.15; *Ep. Arist.* 207; *m. 'Abot* 2.10) rather than the positive rendering of Luke 6:31. Dunn, *Jesus Remembered*, 1.587, points out the same tendency is observed in the echo of the Golden Rule found in *P. Oxy.* 6546.2. Note the comment of Marshall, *Luke*, 262, regarding the negative form of the Golden Rule in contemporary Judaism: 'Jesus thus goes beyond the negative form, citing the rarer and more demanding form'. For a comprehensive coverage of the parallels to the Golden Rule, see Bock, *Luke*, 596–97.

Finally, scholars such as F.C. Downing interpret v. 31 against the backdrop of Cynic teaching on reciprocity.[47] Interestingly, L.E. Vaage entertains the possibility that v. 31—considered to be the *lectio difficilior* due to its inelegant placement—is authentic Jesus tradition. But he concludes that v. 31 is appropriately placed in its redactional context. For Vaage, the logion is a product of the Cynic-like 'Q' people, because it overturns customary ideas about 'how to manage social conflict in antiquity'.[48]

Clearly, the time is opportune for a re-appraisal of the complex issues raised by Luke 6:31–35. After examining select sources illustrating ancient reciprocity, the article addresses several questions. How far has Luke adapted Jesus' teaching in Luke 6.27–36 for his Hellenistic audience? What evidence is there that the historical Jesus critiqued Hellenistic reciprocity? How far does Jesus modify the traditional understanding of reciprocity in regard to divine beneficence and the return of favour? What alternative models of beneficence does Jesus promote?

I will argue that Jesus critiqued the ancient reciprocity system, subjecting its operations to his messianic appraisal. His intention was to establish a community of servant-benefactors—drawn in many cases (though not exclusively) from the marginalised subgroups of society—who would act beneficently as much towards their enemies as to their friends.

2. Luke 6:27–36 in Its Ancient Reciprocity Context

2.1 What Was the Social and Theological Ideology of Reciprocity in Antiquity?

How did reciprocity work between human beings in antiquity and what were its pitfalls?[49] A first-century AD decree from Cardamylae

---

47 Downing, *Christ and the Cynics*, 27; Vaage, *Galilean Upstarts*, 40–54; Vaage, 'Deeper Reflections'. For criticism of the 'Cynic' Jesus thesis, see Betz, 'Jesus and the Cynics'; Eddy, 'Jesus as Diogenes?'.
48 Vaage, *Galilean Upstarts*, 127; cf. also 104.
49 This section draws upon a variety of genres of evidence from my book, *Paul's Language of Grace*. Far too many discussions of ancient reciprocity restrict their investigation of the ancient evidence exclusively to the popular philosophers or to the representatives of the major philosophical schools (e.g. Seneca, Aristotle), with the result that the complex social operations of the ancient 'pay-back' system are only discussed within specific ethical frameworks (e.g. Kirk, '"Love Your Enemies"'). For a sound social–scientific critique of the methodology of Kirk's article, see Crook, 'Reflections on Culture and Social–Scientific Models'.

best represents orthodox first-century belief and practice regarding reciprocity. For five centuries prior to the Christian era, acts of beneficence by heads of state, public officials and private individuals had been celebrated in the stereotyped language of generosity and gratitude on the inscriptions. The key word of the inscriptions summing up the ethos of reciprocity is χάρις. It refers to the generosity of the benefactor—thus its meaning of 'favour, kindness, benefit'. Conversely it could designate the response of the person who had received the benefit, and be translated as 'gratitude, thankfulness', or the return of 'favour' to the benefactor. Note how this important inscription illuminates the ethos of reciprocity at a civic level:

> ... it was resolved by the people and the city and the ephors to praise Poseidippos (the son) of Attalos on account of the aforesaid kindnesses and also to bring never-ending gratitude (ἀτελῆ χάριν) in recompense of ([ἀμοι]βῆς) (his bestowal) of benefits; and also to give to him both the front seats at the theatre and the first place in a procession and (the privilege of) eating in the public festivals which are celebrated amongst us and to offer willingly (χαρ[ιζομέ]ους) all (the) honour (τειμήν) given to a good and fine man in return for (ἀντί) the many [kindnesses] which he provided, while giving a share of the lesser favour (ἐλάττονος χάριτος), (nevertheless) offering thankfulness (εὐχαριστίας) to the benefactors of ourselves as an incentive to the others, so that choosing the same favour (χάριν) some of them may win (the same) honours (τειμῶν). And (it was resolved) to set up this decree on a stone slab in the most conspicuous place in the gymnasium, while the ephors make the solemn procession to the building without hindrance, in order that those who confer benefits may receive favour (χάριν) in return for (ἀντί) love of honour (φιλοτειμίας), and that those who have been benefited, returning honours (ἀποδιδόντες τειμάς), may have a reputation for thankfulness ([εὐ]χαριστίας) before all people, never coming too late for the sake of recompense (ἀμοιβήν) for those who wish to do kindly (acts).[50]

---

50 *SEG* 11(948).

Here we see a careful tabulation of the reciprocal benefits for the benefactor (Poseidippos) and his beneficiaries (the citizens of Cardamylae). Poseidippos receives 'favours' (public honours) in return for his 'love of honour' (his civic benefactions). Cardamylae receives the coveted reputation of gratitude in its return of honour to Poseidippos. The groveling reference to the 'lesser favour' on the part of the city underscores how city-states ensured that no touch of hubris could cause affront and spoil the smooth operation of the reciprocity system.[51] The ethos of reciprocity, as formulated in the Cardamylae decree, is striking for its calculation of the benefits to both parties. Furthermore, the decree is replete with the terminology of exchange. Apart from the obvious words 'recompense' (ἀμοιβῆς) and 'in return for' (ἀντί), χάρις shifts in its meaning as it moves its reference point from the beneficiary to the benefactor.

The ethos of reciprocity also operated in private patron-client relationships. Pseudo-Demetrius acknowledges that he returns the 'lesser' (ἔλαττον) thanks to his benefactor—the same terminology being employed as in the Cardamylae decree. Notwithstanding, the benefactor is encouraged to demand his rightful return (χάρις):

> I hasten to show in my actions how grateful I am to you for the kindness you showed me in your words. For I know that what I am doing for you is less (ἔλαττον) than I should, for even if I gave my life for you, I should not be giving adequate thanks (ἀξίαν ἀποδώσειν χάριν) for the benefits I have received. If you wish anything that is mine, do not write and request it, but demand a return (χάριν). For I am in your debt.[52]

We sense in Pseudo-Libanius the amazement that the ancients felt over the cardinal sin of ingratitude. It violated the principle of reciprocity where the benefactor was publicly recompensed with honours. More fundamentally, this negligence on the part of the beneficiary was an act of enmity since it deprived the benefactor of his prized status as a man of merit (ἀρετή):

---

51 For criticism of Malina's 'agonistic' model of social relations in the ancient honour system, see. Harrison, 'The Fading Crown', 494–95.
52 Pseudo–Demetrius, *Epistolary Types*, 21. II cent. BC –III cent. AD.

> You have received many favours from us, and I am exceedingly amazed that you remember none of them but speak badly of us. That is characteristic of a person with an ungrateful (ἀχαρίστου) disposition. For the ungrateful (ἀχάριστοι) forget noble men, and in addition ill-treat their benefactors as though they were enemies (ὡς ἐχθρούς).[53]

Seneca, too, comments on the problem of ingratitude towards the benefactor. The benefactor must carefully choose the recipients of his benefits.[54] However, the failure of a client to return a favour should not necessarily discourage the benefactor from beneficence. In a saying reminiscent of Matt 5:45, Seneca reminds his readers of the undiscriminating beneficence of the gods towards the ungrateful. Nonetheless, in Seneca's view, those who are intentionally ungrateful should not be accorded generosity:

> If you are imitating the gods, you say 'then bestow benefits also upon the ungrateful; for the sun rises upon the wicked, and the sea lies open to pirates'. This point raises the question whether a good man would bestow a benefit upon one who was ungrateful, knowing that he was ungrateful ... Understand that according to the system of the Stoics, there are two classes of ungrateful persons. One man is ungrateful because he is a fool ... Another man is ungrateful, and this is the common meaning of the term, because he has a natural tendency to this vice. To an ingrate of this first type ... a good man will give his benefit ... To the ingrate of the second type ... he will no more give a benefit than he will lend money to a spendthrift, or entrust a deposit to a man whom many have already found false.[55]

We will not linger on the theme of the reciprocation of parental favour. We simply note that Hierocles in his work, *On Duties*, observes that the measure of childrens' gratitude (εὐχαριστία) towards their parents

---

53   Pseudo-Libanius, *Epistolary Styles*, 64. IV–VI AD.
54   On the importance of the benefactor assessing the character of recipients prior to the conferral of benefits, see Harrison, *Paul's Language of Grace*, 70, 256 n. 170.
55   Seneca, *Ben.* 4.26.

is measured by their 'perpetual and unyielding eagerness to repay their beneficence (τὸ ἀμείβεσθαι τὰς εὐεργεσίας αὐτῶν)'.[56] The incentive given for the perpetuity of this obligation is seemingly the status that parents possessed as images of the gods.

Finally, Dio Chrysostom reveals the hidden pressure that arises when a favour promised by a benefactor is inadvertently forgotten. According to Dio, on such an occasion, the promised favour rapidly escalates into an obligation that demands payment:

> For there is nothing more weighty, no debt bearing higher interest, than a favour (χάριτος) promised. Moreover, this is the shameful and bitter kind of loan, when, as one might say, because of tardy payment the favour (χάριν) turns into an obligation, an obligation the settlement of which those who keep silent demand altogether more sternly than those who cry aloud. For nothing has such power to remind those who owe you such obligations as your having utterly forgotten them.[57]

How did the ethos of reciprocity affect the relationship between the gods and human beings? In a first-century BC decree in honour of Aristagoras we hear of the gods being placed under obligation to the benefactor. On acount of Aristagoras' cultic donations and piety as a priest of Apollo, he obtained 'double gratitude both from the gods and from those he benefited'. This idea of the gods reciprocating gratitude for human benefactions is entirely alien to the New Testament (e.g. Rom 11:35; 1 Cor 4:7), but it was ubiquitous in the ancient world:

> ... he honoured the city and the gods with festal gatherings to which all were invited and by sacred processions and by donations to the tribes, wishing to make this clear, that there is gratitude (χάρις) alike from gods and from men who receive

---

56 Hierocles, *On Duties*, 'How to Conduct Oneself Towards One's Parents', Stob. 3.52. On parental favour in the reciprocity system, see Harrison, *Paul's Language of Grace*, 340–42.

57 Dio Chrysostom, *Or.*, 40.3-4. On the importance of this text for our understanding of the Jerusalem collection, see Harrison, *Paul's Language of Grace*, 312–14. The reverse side of the problem is seen when a beneficiary is overwhelmed by a benefactor's benefits. Ammonius (*P. Oxy. XLII.* 3057. I–II cent AD) pleads with his superior in the Egyptian bureaucracy to stop inundating him with kindnesses, because (in his words) 'I can't repay them (ἀμείψασθαι)'.

benefits for those who conduct themselves in the life of the city with reverence and with noble purpose ...

... again, three years later, when the people ... were seeking a priest of Apollo, the Healer, men's private resources being under severe pressure, he made offer of himself and coming forward before the assembly he assumed the same crown, so obtaining double gratitude (χάριτας) for himself both from the gods and from those he benefited.[58]

The Emperor Hadrian envisages a similar exchange in an inscription from 125 AD. In the inscription Hadrian presents a sacrificial offering—a recently killed she-bear—to the god Eros. By way of reciprocation for his cultic piety, Hadrian makes the request for favour or (possibly) the sexual beauty of Eros:

> Child with the bow of Cyprus and the melodious voice, you who live in Thespiae on Helicon, near the flowery garden of Narcissus, grant me your favours. What Hadrian offers you, receive it as the first fruits of a she-bear which he has killed in striking it from the top of his horse. But you, in return (ἀντί), O Sage, breathe to him the grace (or 'beauty', χάριν) of Aphrodite Ourania.[59]

In another revealing inscription, the Emperor Nero announces his (short-lived) liberation of the province of Greece in AD 67. His act requites the good will and piety of Greece towards himself. More importantly, it reciprocates the care of the Greek deities for the Emperor. As Nero pithily concludes:

> At present it is not out of pity (οὐ δι' ἔλεον) for you but out of good-will (δι' εὔνοιαν) that I bestow this benefaction, and I give it in exchange (ἀμείβομαι) to your gods, whose forethought on land and sea for me I have always experienced, because they granted me the opportunity of conferring such benefits.[60]

---

58 *SIG*³ 708. 100 BC. Provenance: Istropolis.
59 Pouilloux, *Choix D'Inscriptions Grecques*, §48. c. AD 125. Provenance: Thespies.
60 *SIG*³ 814. Provenance: Acraephiae. AD 67.

Significantly for our context, Nero claims that his beneficence was not motivated by 'pity' (or 'mercy,' ἔλεος), but was a reciprocation of the 'good-will' (εὔνοιαν) of the Greeks. As we shall see, in the Jewish worldview of Jesus, the motivation for all beneficence is God's mercy.

By contrast, in a papyrus the socially inferior Hermaios admits that he cannot reciprocate his benefactor's generosity and leaves his requital with the gods. Here we see the vast gulf that exists between Nero, who had the social capital and largesse to reciprocate the gods, and the 'small' Hermaios, who has neither the status nor resources to do so:

> Hermaios greets the most esteemed Aelius Apollonius. Both in this and in all the rest, Lord, you supply to me the good will (εὔνοιαν) fitting for you and friendship (φιλίαν) and while I am small (μικρός) to know gratitude (χάριν) to you, the Gods will requite (ἀμείψονται) you.[61]

Finally, a funerary epigram (North Galatia: mid III cent. AD) speaks of parents faced with the fickleness of the gods who have snatched all their children from them through their premature death. The gods must be reciprocated, as per the reciprocity system. But how does one reciprocate such callous and uncaring gods? The answer is that one bitterly returns to them 'thankless thanks' (ἄχαρις χάρις):

> The fates have seen the place which is always just, and fixed the end of life as our portion. For they have snatched away the finest bloom of beloved youth and we shall no more arrive at the prime (?) of life. This tomb conceals first of all our virgin sister, called Olympias, and then to us, prematurely dead. Theseus was the eldest brother, and my name was Amemptos, a child, younger in age. His cheeks bloomed with a thin down and he was in the flower of youth, like the gods. Theseus died in the winter, then Amemptos in the fourth month, at the beginning of summer. Here may be seen the thankless thank offering (ἄχαρις χάρις) of their wretched parents, a libation on the tomb for their children who died before their wedding day. First virgin Olympias, then Theseus with the unflawed bloom on his cheeks, then a third

---

61 *P. Brem.* 49. II cent. AD. For additional Jewish critiques, see nn.13 and 17 above.

end took away Amemptos. They lie here as a common family and the tomb has joined their remains together.⁶²

2.2 Jewish Critiques of the Ancient Reciprocity System

What evidence is there for a critique of Graeco-Roman reciprocity in our sources? The rarity of such critiques of the Graeco-Roman benefaction system underlines how dominant reciprocity conventions were and their axiomatic status. In this instance, we will confine ourselves to two Jewish critiques of the reciprocity system as the appropriate backdrop to Jesus' own critique.⁶³ First, Philo probes each side of the benefaction ritual, exposing (what he perceives to be) the mercenary nature of the relationship between benefactors and their beneficiaries:

> Look around you and you shall find that those who are said to bestow (χαρίζεσθαι) benefits sell rather than give (δωρουμένους), and those who seem to us to receive them (λαμβάνειν χάριτας) in truth buy. The givers are seeking praise (ἔπαινον) or honour (τιμήν) as their exchange (ἀμοιβήν) and look for the repayment (ἀντίδοσιν) of the benefit (χάριτος), and thus, under the specious name of gift (δωρεᾶς), they in real truth carry out a sale; for the seller's way is to take something for what he offers. The receivers of the gift (τὰς δωρεάς), too, study to make some return (ἀποδοῦναι), and do so (ἀποδιδόντες) as opportunity offers, and thus they act as buyers. For buyers know well that receiving and paying (ἀποδοῦναι) go hand in hand. But God is no salesman, hawking his goods in the market, but a free giver of all things, pouring forth fountains of free bounties (χαρίτων), and seeking no return (ἀμοιβῆς). For He has no needs Himself and no created being is able to repay His gift (ἀντιδοῦναι δωρεάν).⁶⁴

In the view of Philo, benefaction is at heart a financial transaction. Benefactors 'sell' their benefits in exchange for praise and honour; conversely, the beneficiaries 'buy' their benefits, with gratitude and

---

62 Mitchell, *Regional Epigraphic Catalogues of Asia Minor*, §392.
63 For Graeco-Roman critiques of reciprocity in the papyri, see Harrison, *Paul's Language of Grace*, 83–84.
64 Philo, *Cher.*, 122–123.

public honours to the benefactor the currency of trade. The Cardamylae inscription, discussed above, bears a strong resemblance to Philo's portrait of the benefaction system and represents best the view that Philo is caricaturing. Last, while Philo highlights the spontaneous generosity of God, his theology is Stoic rather than Jewish.

Finally, of particular interest is Ben-Sira's insightful exposé of the hostility implicit in benefaction rituals, engendered by the grudging hospitality of the benefactors, and by the ingratitude of their beneficiaries:

> The chief thing for life is water, and bread, and clothing, and a house to cover shame. Better is the life of a poor man in a mean cottage, than delicate fare in another man's house. Be it little or much, hold yourself contented, for it is a miserable life to go from house to house: for where you are a stranger, you dare not open your mouth. You shall entertain, and feast, and have no thanks (ἀχάριστια): moreover you shall hear bitter words: Come, stranger, and furnish a table, and feed me of that you have ready. Give place, stranger, to an honourable man; my brother comes to be lodged, and I have need of my house. These things are grievous to a man of understanding; the upbraiding of houseroom, and the reproaching of the lender.[65]

Ben-Sira's portrayal of the social humiliation implicit in the benefaction system stands in stark contrast to the positive inscriptional catalogues of honours that were rendered to benefactors in recompense of their munificence to their local communities. Clearly Jews other than Jesus were critical of the Graeco-Roman reciprocity system, whether it be the civic munificence of the Hellenistic city-state or the traditional household hospitality of the village.[66]

We turn now to Jesus' critique of the reciprocity system in Luke 6:31–36. Does this tradition originate with the historical Jesus or is it a case of Lucan redaction for his Gentile audience?

---

65 Sir 29.21–28.
66 Note too the logion of Antigonos of Sokho (II. cent BC) who rejects any expectation of reciprocation of one's service: 'Be not like servants who serve the master for condition of receiving a reward, but be like servants who serve the master not on condition of receiving a reward'. As noted, see the rabbinic criticism of Roman benefactors (b Shabbat 33^b; cf. 'Abodah Zarah 2^b) in n. 17 above.

3. The Historical Jesus as Social Critic

3.1 The Relationship of Matthew 5:43–48 to Luke 6:27–36

Matthew 5:43–48	Luke 6:27–36
⁴³ You have heard that it was said, 'You shall love your neighbour and hate your enemy.'	
⁴⁴ <u>But I say unto you, Love your enemies,</u>	²⁷ <u>But I say to you</u> that hear, <u>Love your enemies</u>, do good (καλῶς ποιεῖτε) to those who hate you, ²⁸ bless those who curse you,
and <u>pray for those who</u> persecute <u>you</u>, ⁴⁵ *so that <u>you</u> may be sons of your Father who is in heaven*; for he makes his sun rise on the evil and on the good, and sends rain on the just and unjust.	<u>pray for those who</u> abuse <u>you</u>.
	²⁹ To him who strikes you on the cheek, offer the other also; and from him who takes away your coat do not withhold even your shirt. ³⁰ Give to every one who begs from you; and of him who takes away your goods do not ask them again. ³¹ And as you wish that men would do to you, do so to them.
⁴⁶ For <u>if you love those who love you</u>, what reward (τίνα μισθόν) have you?	³² <u>If you love those who love you</u>, what credit (χάρις) is that to you? For even sinners love those who love them. ³³ And if you do good to those who do good to you, what credit (χάρις) is that to you?

Do not <u>even</u> the tax-collectors <u>do the same</u>?	For <u>even</u> the sinners <u>do the same</u>.
⁴⁷ And if you salute only your brethren what more are you doing than others?	³⁴ And if you lend to those from whom you hope to receive, what credit (χάρις) is that to you?
Do not even the Gentiles do the same?	Even the sinners lend to sinners, to receive as much again. ³⁵ But love your enemies, and do good (ἀγαθοποιεῖτε) and lend, expecting nothing in return; and your reward (μισθός) will be great, and *you will be <u>sons of</u> the Most High*; for he is kind (χρηστός) to the ungrateful (τοὺς ἀχαρίστους) and selfish.
⁴⁸ You, therefore, must <u>be</u> perfect, <u>as your</u> heavenly <u>Father is</u> perfect.	³⁶ <u>Be</u> merciful, even <u>as your Father is</u> merciful.
Gos. Thom. 64	**Luke 14:12–14**
The servant came, he said to his master: 'Those whom you have invited to the dinner have excused themselves'. The master said to his servant: 'Go out to the roads, bring those you shall find, so that they may dine. Tradesmen and merchants [shall] not [enter] the places of my Father".	¹² He said also to the man who had invited him, 'When you give a dinner or a banquet, do not invite your friends or your brothers or your kinsmen or rich neighbours, lest they also invite whom you in return (ἀντικαλέσωσίν σε), and you be repaid (ἀνταπόδομά σοι). ¹³ But when you give a feast, invite the poor, the maimed, the lame, the blind, ¹⁴ and you will be blessed, because they cannot repay you (ἀνταποδοῦναί σοι). You will be repaid (ἀνταποδοθήσεται) at the resurrection of the just'.

The fundamental issue is the degree to which Luke has adapted Jesus' teaching in 6:27–36 and 14:12–14 for his Hellenistic audience. Does the Lucan account—with its sharp rebuttal of reciprocity conventions—retain elements of the authentic teaching of Jesus? If so, how radical is Jesus' critique of reciprocity? Jesus' comments on reciprocity are found in the Q tradition common to Matthew and Luke. As noted, D. Lührmann has argued that the Sermon on the Mount and the Sermon on the Plain have significant parallels throughout and that the order of the subject matter is the same.[67] The parallelism between Matt 5: 44a/b, 46a/b, 48 and Luke 6:27, 28b, 32a, 33b, 36 underscores this feature. Notwithstanding the attempt of many scholars to dismiss the Matthean antitheses (Matt 5:21ff, 27ff, 33ff, 38ff, 43ff) as redactional creations,[68] the partial antithesis in Luke 6:27a confirms that Jesus did speak in a way that accentuated his authority over against the scriptural traditions of the Old Testament and the religious traditions of Second Temple Judaism.[69]

However, care must be taken with our pericope. D.A. Hagner observes that while there are common elements, the material is quite different in its order and wording.[70] First, as regards order, the motif of divine sonship, common to Matthew and Luke, is located differently in each pericope (Matt 5:45a; Luke 6:35b), whereas the Golden Rule occurs in different redactional contexts (Matt 7:21; Luke 6:31).

Second, as regards wording, there are also clear differences. A few examples will suffice. In Matthew 5:46, 47 the Jewish terminology of 'tax-collectors' (οἱ τελῶναι) and 'Gentiles' (οἱ ἐθνικοί) is rendered as 'sinners' (οἱ ἁμαρτωλοί) in Luke 6:32, 33, 34. Accordingly, there might be a temptation to view Matthew's account as closer to the teaching of the historical Jesus precisely because of its Jewishness. However, it is quite

---

67 See Lührmann, 'Liebet eure Feinde'.
68 E.g. Suggs, 'The Antitheses as Redactional Products'.
69 See Jeremias' defence (*New Testament*, 1.250–55) of the authenticity of the Matthean antitheses. See, too, Daube's helpful discussion of the antitheses in their rabbinic context (*New Testament and Rabbinic Judaism*, 55–66). Daube allows for the possibility that Jesus might have prophetically expressed his consciousness of supreme authority in the 'I say unto you' logion (p. 58), but he unnecessarily plays down the force of Matthew's contrast in its rabbinic context (pp. 59ff; contra, Matt 28:20a; Mark 1:22, 27a). Contra, see Ranjar, *Be Merciful Like the Father*, 84.
70 Hagner, *Matthew 1–13*, 133. See also the helpful comments of Horsley, 'Ethics and Exegesis', 80–81.

feasible that Matthew is heightening the Jewishness of Jesus for his own theological ends. Furthermore, although there are Hellenistic phraseology and themes in Luke 6:32–35 (ἀγοθοποιεῖν: vv. 33, 35; χάρις: vv. 32, 33, 34; ἀχαρίστους: v. 35) and the presence of reciprocity terminology in 14:12–14,[71] Luke retains his own Jewish emphases. One such example is Luke's emphasis on the mercy of God (Luke 6.36: οἰκτίρμων), in contrast to Matthew's perfection of God (Matt 5:48: τέλειος).[72] In my opinion, the Lucan paradigm coheres better with the concentration of the historical Jesus upon the mercy-code—over against the boundaries imposed by the Pharisees' extension of the temple holiness code to everyday life—throughout his ministry.[73]

In sum, we are probably dealing with two independent traditions, each deriving from Jesus, but with common elements of teaching underlying each.[74] We must therefore leave open the possibility that Luke did capture the authentic voice of Jesus in Luke 6:27–36. But what about the Lucan material on reciprocity (Luke 6:32–35; cf. 14:12–14) paralleled nowhere else in the Gospel tradition? Is this merely a case of Lucan redaction for his Gentile auditors in a later generation or do we have here an authentic critique of the reciprocity system delivered (substantially) by the historical Jesus?

3.2 Jesus' Critique of the Reciprocity System (Luke 6:32–36/14:12–14)

It is simplistic to dismiss the special Lucan material in 6:32–36 and 14:12–14 as theological invention. Referring to Luke 14:12–14, I.H. Marshall has astutely commented: 'the sentiments are those of 6:32–35, and while the thoughts would be congenial to Luke, there is no

---

71 Jesus' critique of reciprocity ideology in Luke 14:12–14 is underscored by the use of ἀντί compounds in vv. 12 and 14. A spread of reciprocity ideology, including ἀντί is employed in the Cardamylae inscription (*SEG* 11 [948]), discussed above. For discussion of the reciprocity terminology in that decree, see Harrison, *Paul's Language of Grace*, 51–52.
72 In defence of Luke's 'mercy' terminology, Ranjar, *Be Merciful Like the Father*, 96, cites Manson, *Sayings of Jesus*, 55: '... in the Old Testament the epithet "merciful" is given to God, hardly ever to man; and the epithet "perfect" to man, never to God'.
73 E.g. Mark 1:41. See Borg, *Conflict*.
74 By contrast, Ranjar, *Be Merciful Like the Father*, 112–14, argues that the Q-Sermon existed as one unit, with Luke and Matthew making their respective redactional changes to it, even if some of the sayings independently were circulating at a pre-Q stage. But, as noted above (n. 4), if the 'chaotic' theory of Q has credence, we are more likely dealing with independent traditions in this instance.

evidence that they are created by him or the early church'.⁷⁵ There are sound reasons for accepting Luke 6:32–35 and 14:12–14 as authentic Jesus tradition.

First, there were other first-century Jews such as Philo (*Cher.*, 122–123) and Josephus (*AJ* 6. 341–342) who were critical of elements of the Graeco-Roman reciprocity system. As noted, the writings of Ben Sira (Sir 29.21–28: c. 180 BC) exposed the tensions and humiliation accompanying reciprocity conventions in households. It begs the question: could not Jesus have mounted a similar critique as well? Such an astute observer as Jesus of contemporary ruler-benefactors (Luke 13:31–32; 22:25–27; Mark 12:16–17) would hardly have missed the reciprocity rituals supporting the power base of the Herodian Kings, the imperial rulers, and their prefects in Judaea.⁷⁶ Even in the case of the synagogues of Galilee and the treasury of the Jerusalem Temple, there were the benefactors who drew the stinging criticism of Jesus for a variety of reasons (Matt 6:2–4; 23:6; Mark 12:41–44). It should be no surprise that Jesus attacked the *do ut des* mentality ('I give so that that you may give') animating patronage in antiquity.

Second, there are elements of teaching in Luke 6:27–36 and 14:12–14 that are striking in both their Jewish and Graeco-Roman context. We have already observed how Jesus' emphasis on God's *mercy* flew in the face of Nero's stated policy of only reciprocating the good will of his Greek subjects (*SIG*³ 814). Further, this mercy of God is unilateral and unconditioned. The God of Jesus, unlike the Greek deities, cannot be put under counter-obligation (*SIG*³ 708; J. Pouilloux, *Choix D'Inscriptions Grecques*, §48). Moreover, Jesus' command of unconditional beneficence towards the enemy—not simply the ungrateful—would certainly have earned the disapproval of people like Seneca (*Ben.*, 4.26). The postponement of reward till the eschaton and its democratisation would have puzzled the honour-driven city of Cardamylae and undermined the meritocracy associated with the reciprocity system more generally (*SEG* XI[948]). The admission of people with disabilities to the eschatological banquet (Luke 14:12–14)—who were marginalized by the priestly holiness system and

---

75 Marshall, *Luke*, 583.
76 In regard to Mark 12:17, Reed, *Archaeology*, 98, notes Jesus' wry observation that the coin would 'soon enough return to Caesar'.

who were unable to reciprocate favour precisely because of their disability—would have shocked the Qumran community. The Qumran covenanters, as the new Temple community, excluded people with disabilities from their fellowship as they awaited their eschatological vindication over the 'sons of darkness' on the Day of the Lord.[77]

Of particular interest is the way that the Gospel of Thomas 64 excludes tradesmen and merchants from the Parable of the Marriage Feast. This quasi 'Gnostic' Gospel excises the Lucan reference to the inclusion of people with disabilities at the eschatological marriage. The second century AD writer replaces the motif with an ascetic ideal that scorned the accumulation of personal wealth (*Gos. Thom.* 54; 110), symbolised in this context by the merchant.[78] This highlights how offensive Jesus' teaching in Luke 14:12–14 about the inclusive nature of the Kingdom community was to various groups.

Third, several features of Jesus' teaching elsewhere cohere with the sketch outlined above. Jesus reminds his disciples that in their healing ministries they were to demand no reciprocation at all because of God's unilateral beneficence towards themselves: 'You have received without paying, give without pay' (Matt 10.8). Jesus eschews the imposed demands of reciprocity. In Luke 7:1–10 the Jewish elders remind Jesus that a centurion benefactor (in the parlance of the inscriptions) was worthy of counter-favour because he had funded the construction of a synagogue. Significantly, Jesus resists the cultural pressure of reciprocation, healing the sick slave of the centurion only because of his master's remarkable faith. The independent logion of Jesus ('It is more blessed to give than to receive' [Acts 20:35]) is another instance of the up-ending of the reciprocity system.

Further, Jesus inverts the models of benefaction. Now an impoverished widow—not celebrated benefactors like Poseidippos (*SEG* XI[948])—images true generosity (Luke 21:1–4) and the disciples themselves are to be servant-benefactors (Luke 2:24–30). Although

---

77 1QM 7:3–9; 1QSa 2:3–10; 11QT 45:12–14; *CD* 15:15–18; 4QMMT 40–53; cf. 2 Sam 5:6–8 [Josephus, *AJ* 7:61]; *m. Bek.* 7:1; *b. Ber.* 58b; Josephus, *Ap.* 2.1–32. For further discussion, see Shemesh, '"The Holy Angels Are in Their Council"'.
78 Marjanen, 'Is *Thomas* a Gnostic Gospel', 129. Note the comment of Hultgren, *The Parables of Jesus*, 336: 'commerce is incompatible with the contemplative life required of the true Gnostic'.

Jesus affirms a continuing care for parents, its motivation flows from the Torah and not from the Hellenistic benefaction system (Mark 7:9–13; cf. Hierocles, *On Duties*, 'How to Conduct Oneself Towards One's Parents', Stob. 3.52). Indeed, Jesus' hard sayings concerning the burial of fathers (Matt 8:21–22), division within the household (Matt 10:35–39; Luke 12:52–54), and the relativisation of family ties (Luke 11:27–28; Mark 3:21, 31–34) would have seemed to many a savage betrayal of family reciprocity ethics.[79]

Fourth, Jesus' emphasis on the politics of mercy (Luke 6:35) over the politics of holiness (Matt 5:48), while sitting comfortably within mainstream Judaism and the Old Testament covenantal tradition,[80] would not have been endorsed by the Qumran covenanters. The enemy, in their view, was to be accorded no mercy (1QS 2.5–8):

> Be cursed in all the works of our guilty wickedness,
> May God make you an object of terror by the hands of all the
>   avengers of vengeance ...
> Be cursed, *without mercy*, according to the darkness of your works.
> Be damned in the place of everlasting fire.

Similarly, in the context of Graeco-Roman reciprocity conventions, mercy was not the primary motivation for beneficence. As noted, Nero had offered the Greeks 'good will' in liberating Hellas, not 'mercy', in repayment of the Greek gods' care for him on land and sea (*SIG*³ 814). D. Senior draws out the significance of Jesus' teaching here most effectively:

> The teaching is rooted in an experience of God as gracious, merciful and indiscriminately loving. This element, common to Matthew and Luke, was surely part of Jesus' own teaching: his boundary-breaking ministry to outcasts and sinners, his many parables about the mercy of God, and his interpretation

---

79 On the eschatological urgency of mission subordinating household ties, see Barton, *Discipleship and Family*. See also the discussion of Harrison, *Paul's Language of Grace*, 340–42.
80 E.g. TBenj. 4.1–5.4. Cited by Perkins, *Love Commands*, 18. Catchpole, *The Quest for Q*, 116, cites *Tg. Yer. I* Lev 22:28: 'As our Father is merciful in heaven, so be merciful on earth'. See also Stendahl, 'Hate, Non–retaliation, and Love'; Seitz, 'Love Your Enemies'.

of law with love and compassion as first principles all reflect Jesus' own experience of God as lavishly merciful.[81]

Fifth, this cross-cultural critique challenges first-century assumptions about who 'the enemy' actually is,[82] as defined by the operation of the reciprocity system.[83] As noted, Pseudo-Libanius defines the enemy thus: 'the ungrateful (ἀχάριστοι) forget noble men, and in addition ill-treat their benefactors as though they were enemies (ὡς ἐχθρούς). Jesus, as depicted by Luke, multiplies the phrases describing the enemy in Luke 6:27ff (vv. 27b: 'who hate you'; vv. 28a/28b: 'who curse you', 'who abuse you'; vv. 29a/29b, 30b: 'who strikes you', 'who takes away your coat', 'if anyone takes away your goods'),[84] charting thereby a progression of provocation and social domination that ranges from insult to injury and theft.[85] By contrast, the believer's 'love' is progressively amplified in vv. 29b, 30b, 35 (v. 29b: 'do not withhold even your shirt'; v. 30b: 'do not ask for them again'; v. 35: 'love ... do good ... lend'), but without any reference as one might expect to the reciprocity system or its rewards ('expecting nothing in return').

The practical care towards the enemy enjoined by Jesus in this context finds a strong parallel in Proverbs 25:21–22 (cf. Rom 12:20): 'If your enemy is hungry, give him food to eat; if he is thirsty, give him water to drink' (v. 21).[86] Although the human motivation for this act is notoriously unclear in Proverbs 21:22b (is the beneficence extended

---

81 Senior, 'Jesus' Most Scandalous Teaching', 61. My emphasis.
82 For excellent discussions of the 'enemy' in ancient context, see Schottroff, 'Non Violence', and the Love of One's Enemies'; Wink, 'Neither Passivity nor Violence'. Note the perceptive comment of Klassen, 'The Authenticity of the Command', 400: 'between the time Jesus spoke these words, and the Gospel editors transmitted them the definition of enemy changed; few definitions change as quickly'.
83 Meier, *A Marginal Jew*, 4.528–51, has powerfully shown that Jesus 'Love your enemies' command is without real precedent in both the Old Testament, Second Temple Judaism, and the Graeco-Roman world.
84 Note Edwards, *Luke*, 198, regarding Luke 6:29b: 'the instruction to surrender not only your "coat" (Gk. *himation*, outer garment) but also your "shirt" (Gk: *chiton*, undergarment worn next to skin) is not to arm oneself in the face of evil and injustice, but to become naked in the face of it'. Wolter, *Luke*, 1.279, adds the following qualification: 'This could, of course, also be a completely sensible survival strategy, but the rational of the exhortation certainly does not reside in this'.
85 Kirk, '"Love Your Enemies"', 681.
86 Noted by Wolter, *Luke*, 1.278. The heavy ethical emphasis upon practical outcomes is underscored by Jesus' use of sixteen imperatives in Luke 6:27–38: eight imperatives in vv. 27–34, four in vv. 35–36, four in vv. 37–38 (Just, *Luke 1:1–9.50*, 291–92).

to the enemy designed to exacerbate his resentment or elicit his repentance?),[87] the prospect of divine reward is nevertheless held out ('the Lord will reward you': Prov 25:22b). This is the case, too, in Luke 6:35 where Jesus says: 'your reward will be great, and you will be sons of the Most High.' But, in sharp contrast, Jesus expands unequivocally on the divine motivation undergirding beneficence towards the enemy. The believer is to act with the same impartial kindness (χρηστός) as the divine Benefactor does towards those who reject his beneficence (τοὺς ἀχαρίστους) and who respond in ways contrary to his will (τοὺς πονηρούς). According to Jesus, the paradigm for believers is God's covenantal mercy (Luke 6:36b: οἰκτίρμων [Rom 12:1]; cf. οἰκτίρμων: Ex 34:6; Joel 2:13; Jonah 4:2; Pss 86:15[LXX Ps 85:15]; 103:8[LXX 102:8]; 145:8 [LXX 144:8]).[88] It expresses 'the profligate generosity of the Father and his sons toward men who give nothing in return'.[89] Ultimately, it is the Father who undermines the reciprocity system by refusing to restrict in advance his beneficence to the grateful.

In sum, we are witnessing a highly original and wide-ranging theological critique of aspects of Graeco-Roman and Jewish reciprocity. It stands in marked contrast to the Stoic clichés of Philo (*Cher.*, 122–123) and the moralistic stance of Josephus (*AJ* 6. 341–342). We pay Luke too high a complement when we assign the entire tradition to his theological creativity. More likely, Luke has faithfully rendered Jesus' inversion of reciprocity rituals and has added several deft Hellenistic touches of his own.

Curiously, J.P. Meier has suggested that Jesus was disconcertingly silent on the social issues of his day.[90] I remain uneasy about this observation. In the case of Jesus' searing critique of reciprocity,[91] a central pillar of Graeco-Roman social ethics was pulled askew. The edifice would continue to crumble under the weight of history when Paul radically redefined beneficence and located its supreme expression in an

---

87 See Klassen, 'Coals of Fire'.
88 Marshall, *Jesus, Patrons, and Benefactors*, 237.
89 Minear, *Commands of Christ*, 73. Note the telling comment of Constan, *Pity Transformed*, 124: 'Although the pagan Greek and Roman gods might feel pity on occasion, it was not their primary trait, and philosophers never endorsed it as such.'
90 Meier, *A Marginal Jew*, 2.332. Meier omits any discussion of Luke 6:27–36. Similarly, Cadbury, *The Peril of Modernising Jesus*, 95, and Bultmann, *Jesus and the Word*, 103.
91 Wolter, *Luke*, 1.282, speaks of 'the nullification of the principle of ethical reciprocity in vv. 32–34'.

impoverished benefactor (2 Cor 8:9; cf. Mark 12:41–44).[92]

Nor can we assert, as several scholars do, that Jesus intended a revitalization or transformation of *traditional* reciprocity ethics, either within Judean village life or as a social expression of the Kingdom of God. Rather, if Luke 6:31–36 and 14:12–14 are any indication, Jesus was supplanting the traditional reciprocity system with a radically new Kingdom community, stripped of any suggestion of hierarchy and meritocracy (Matt 23:5–10; Luke 22:24–27). It operated with divine mercy towards its enemies and honoured the marginalized by including them at the core of its beneficence. Whatever vestiges of reciprocity remained, they have been profoundly transformed. This is emphasized by the Lucan threefold repetition of χάρις, the leitmotiv of the reciprocity system, in vv. 32a, 33a, and 34a. In each case, the inadequacy of the traditional reciprocity ritual is spotlighted by the reference to the ubiquity of its operation among 'sinners' (vv. 32b, 33b, 34b). Only by loving, doing good, and lending without expectation of return (v. 35) and by one's motivation being informed by divine mercy (v. 36) will a new understanding of χάρις emerge.[93]

---

92 See Harrison, *Paul's Language of Grace*, 250–68.

93 By contrast, Kirk, '"Love Your Enemies"', 682, posits no new understanding of χάρις: 'The salient feature of vv. 32–34, however, is not repudiation of reciprocity behaviour and its animating principle, χάρις, but the turning on its head of the evaluative ancillary evaluative framework'. It is also interesting to speculate whether Jesus might have delivered his teaching occasionally in Greek (including Luke 6:27–36?), as Porter, 'Jesus and the Use of Greek in Palestine' has recently proposed. Did Jesus himself inaugurate the redefinition of χάρις that Paul later brought to fruition in his theology of the 'reign of grace'? While this proposal is initially attractive, its force is lessened when one remembers that the language of grace is especially prominent in the Lucan writings (ἀχάριστος: Luke 6:35; εὐχαριστέω: Luke 17:16; 18:11; 22:17, 19; εὐχαριστία: Acts 24:3; χάρις: Luke 1:30; 2:40, 52; 4:22; 6:32, 33, 34; 17:9; Acts 2:47; 4:33; 6:8; 7:10, 46; 11:23; 13:43; 14:3, 26; 15:11, 40; 18:27; 20:24, 32; 24:27; 25:3, 9; χαρίζομαι: Luke 7:21, 42, 43; Acts 8:14; 25:11, 16; 27:24; χαριτόω: Luke 1:28). Therefore, it is argued, this profuseness of Lukan usage points to the evangelist's adept literary accommodation to the dominant leitmotif of the Graeco–Roman benefaction system. However, the objection is not insurmountable. While it could be legitimately argued that χάρις represents Luke's redaction for the Matthean μισθός ('reward': Matt 5:12//Luke 6:23), Matthew's own use of μισθός could equally be redactional, being a favourite of the evangelist, used some 10 times in his gospel (Rainar, *Be Merciful Like the Father*, 86). More likely Luke's explosion of 'grace' language was occasioned by the impetus of Jesus' radical redefinition of the reciprocity system in terms of gift-giving without any expectation of recompense. Thus Jesus' rejection of reciprocity ethics through the paradigm of the unconditioned mercy of God towards his enemies is expanded upon throughout the Gospel of Luke in the evangelist's presentation of beneficence under the rubric of the operation of divine χάρις. In other words, we must not mistake in this instance the historical phenomenon of social innovation for mere literary dependence upon popular tropes or as an expression of the redactional activities of the evangelist.

But what about the reciprocity envisaged in the Golden Rule (Luke 6:31)?[94] How does this relate to Jesus' critique of the reciprocity system in vv. 32–36? For Jesus and many other Jews, the Golden Rule represented a popular formulation of the Levitical love command (Lev 19: 18b: 'You shall love your neighbour as yourself'),[95] an ethic that marked off Israel as God's holy people (Lev 19:2b: 'You shall be holy, for I the Lord your God am holy'). It is against the backdrop of the Levitical tradition that Jesus' authoritative introduction (Luke 6:27a: 'But I say to you' [ἀλλά ὑμῖν λέγω]) is probably to be understood.[96] Moreover, whereas in Second Temple Judaism the Golden Rule is largely negative in its orientation,[97] Jesus opts for the more positive rendering of the Golden Rule found in some quarters of Judaism (e.g. TNaph. 1; 2 En. 61.1). The reason why Jesus prefers the Golden Rule over the Levitical love command is because of its strong emphasis on 'doing' (Luke 6:31: ποιῶσιν, ποιεῖτε). In a bold move, Jesus expands the boundaries of beneficence from the 'neighbour' to the 'enemy' (Luke 6:27: καλῶς ποιεῖτε).[98] Further, by insisting that his disciples do good to the enemy (Luke 6:35: ἀγαθοποιεῖτε), Jesus destroys the *do ut des* expectation of the Graeco-Roman reciprocity system (6:33–34, 35 ['expecting nothing in return']).

---

94 For discussions of the Golden Rule, see Dihle, *Die Goldene Regel;* Furnish, *The Love Command;* Fuller, *Essays on the Love Commandment;* Piper, *'Love Your Enemies';* Perkins, Love; Klassen, *Love of Enemies;* Klassen, 'The Authenticity of the Command'; Flusser, 'Jesus, His Ancestry, and the Commandment of Love'; Swartley, *The Love of the Enemy;* Theissen, 'Nonviolence and Love of Our Enemies'; Alexander, 'Jesus and the Golden Rule'; Meier, *A Marginal Jew,* 4.551–57. Meier, *A Marginal Jew,* 4.557, argues that the historical Jesus did not teach the Golden Rule, though he concedes that his case is not 'airtight'. But why wouldn't Jesus endorse such a commonplace in Judaism and the Graeco-Roman world more generally? The real question is *how the logion functions* in Luke 6:27–36. For example, Bovon, *Luke,* 1.241, expounding the Golden Rule in Luke 6:31, proposes that 'Christian ethics in Luke aim at a new form of reciprocity, with its roots in God'. This, however, is still too minimalist an interpretation. Rather, as Johnson, *Luke,* 112, argues, 'Luke has Jesus demand of his followers a standard for human relationships that involves a "going beyond" or "more" than the norm of reciprocity, of *do ut des*. The "golden rule" of "do as you want done" is not the ultimate norm here, but rather, "do as God would do"'.
95 Bock, *Luke 1.1–9.50;* Johnson, *Luke,* 109; Just, *Luke 1:1–9:50,* 293.
96 Note the comment of Fitzmyer, *Luke I–IX,* 639–40: 'It is useless to try to establish that the positive form used by Jesus in Matthew and Luke is actually superior to the negative; it all depends on *the context* in which the rule is set' (emphasis added).
97 Sources cited by Marshall, *Luke,* 262. Contra, see Ranjar, *Be Merciful Like the Father,* 187: 'Luke presents the Golden Rule without the support of the Hebrew Scriptures'.
98 Green, *Luke,* 273.

Therefore, v. 31 looks back to vv. 27–30. In including the enemy within the boundaries of beneficence,⁹⁹ Jesus asserts his messianic understanding of the Kingdom community (Luke 6:27a; cf. 4:16–21; 7:18–23 [Isaiah 35:5–6; 52:7; 61:1–2; 11QMelchizedek 2.13–20; 4Q521]) over the restriction of the love command to covenantal members (Lev 19:18a, 18b).¹⁰⁰ Jesus also sets his messianic understanding against the negative expression of the love command in Second Temple Judaism. So far Jesus' critique is confined to the intra-mural debates of Judaism.

But v. 31 also looks forward to vv. 32–36. Here Jesus moves beyond the Torah-based controversies of his contemporaries to a cross-cultural critique of the ancient reciprocity system per se. There is nothing improbable about attributing this strategy to the historical Jesus. The reciprocity system reached from the imperial rulers to the Herods, embracing both the Sadducean and Pharisaic parties,¹⁰¹ as much as the local benefactors in the villages and larger cities of Palestine. These networks of privilege and status defined in advance who the 'neighbour' was and who was worthy of beneficence. Furthermore, as noted, Philo, Ben-Sira, and later rabbinic traditions were critical of the Graeco-Roman benefaction system.¹⁰² By contrast, Jesus' Kingdom community of the marginalized (Luke 14:13–14, 21–24), founded on divine mercy towards the enemy (6:36), experienced and embodied an overflow of divine grace (6:38) that would eventually challenge the social relations of the day (22:24–27). Jesus' critique of the reciprocity system represented an important building block in this new social vision.¹⁰³

---

99 Note the astute observation of Flusser regarding the mentality of the writers of the Dead Sea Scrolls ('A New Sensitivity', 121): 'The biblical command of mutual love is in the Scrolls restricted to the Sons of Light (1QS i.9–11) and is paralleled by the sectarian command of hatred towards the Sons of Darkness'.
100 On Jesus' messianic consciousness, see Evans, 'Jesus and the Messianic Texts from Qumran', esp. 118–24, 128–29.
101 For client–patron relationships in the high priesthood of Caiaphas, see Bond, *Caiaphas*, 43.
102 See above n.17 and §2.2 above.
103 Ranjar, *Be Merciful Like the Father*, 191, writes: '[Luke] also intends to overturn the popular notion of human reciprocity and, at the same time, to emphasize God's grace on those who go beyond the normal human practice of reciprocity'.

4. Conclusion

'Q' studies have flourished in the Third Quest for the historical Jesus. The possibility is sometimes overlooked that 'Q' might render independent historical traditions regarding Jesus' critique of social relations in the Jewish and Graeco-Roman world. We have argued that the 'Q' tradition of Luke 6:27–36 is a case in point.

By the first century AD, the reciprocity system shaped social relations in the eastern Mediterranean basin, flowing from the capital of the imperial rulers to the palaces of the Herods to the villages of Galilee. As important as reciprocity was for social stability, there were dissenting voices, including Philo and Ben Sira in a Jewish context, that were critical of the darker social realities behind the benefaction system. Luke 6:27–36 presents Jesus as one such figure.

Jesus emerges as one who critiques the reciprocity-based social relations of his day. According to the messianic perspective of Jesus, his eschatological community of the marginalised, at least as depicted in Luke 4:18–19 and 14:12–14, 21,[104] would extend beneficence to those in need without any expectation of return. We are witnessing the emergence of a new understanding of divine and human χάρις—pressed down, shaken together, running over (Luke 6:38)—that would up-end the ancient benefaction system and undermine our perception of those we treat as our 'enemy'.

---

[104] Luke, however, reveals elsewhere that there were also socially high-placed believers who belonged to Jesus' eschatological community (e.g. Luke 8:2–3, 27; Acts 6:7; 13:7, 12; 16:14; 17:33; 18:8).

Bibliography

Alexander, P. S.   'The Family of Caesar and the Family of God: The Image of the Emperor in the Heikhalot Literature', in L. Alexander (ed.), *Images of Empire* (Sheffield: Sheffield Academic Press, 1991), 276–97.

Alexander, P.S.   'Jesus and the Golden Rule', in J.H. Charlesworth & L.L. Johns (eds.), *Hillel and Jesus: Comparisons of Two Major Religious Leaders* (Minneapolis: Fortress, 1997), 363–88.

Arnal, W.E.   *Jesus and the Village Scribes: Galilean Conflicts and the Setting of Q* (Minneapolis: Fortress Press, 2003).

Barton, S.C.   *Discipleship and Family Ties in Mark and Matthew* (Cambridge: Cambridge University Press, 1994).

Bertschmann, D.H.   'Hosting Jesus: Revisiting Luke's "Sinful Woman" (Luke 7:36–50) as a Tale of Two Hosts', *JSNT* 40.1 (2017), 30–50.

Betz, H.D.   *The Sermon on the Mount: A Commentary on the Sermon on the Mount, including the Sermon on the Plain (Matthew 5:3–7:27 and Luke 6:20–49)* (Hermeneia; Minneapolis: Fortress, 1995).

Betz, H.D.   'Jesus and the Cynics', *JR* 74.4 (1994), 453–75.

Bock, D.L.   *Luke. Volume: 1:1–9:50* (Grand Rapids: Baker, 1994).

Bond, H.K.   *Caiaphas: Friend of Rome and Judge of Jesus?* (Louisville: Westminster John Knox Press, 2004).

Borg, M.J.   *Conflict, Holiness, and Politics in the Teachings of Jesus* (Lewiston/Queenston: Edwin Mellen Press, 1984).

Bovon, F.   *Luke 1: A Commentary on the Gospel of Luke 1.1–9.50* (Fortress: Minneapolis, 2002).

Briones, D.E.   *Paul's Financial Policy: A Socio–Theological Approach* (London and New York: Bloomsbury T&T Clark, 2013).

Brooten, B.J.   *Women Leaders in the Ancient Synagogue* (Atlanta: Scholars Press, 1982).

Bultmann, R.   *History of the Synoptic Tradition* (Oxford: Basil Blackwell, 1963).

Bultmann, R.   *Jesus and the Word* (New York: Scribner's, 1934 [German: 1926]).

Cadbury, H.J.	*The Peril of Modernising Jesus* (London: Macmillan, 1937).
Capper, Brian	'*Reciprocity* and the Ethic of *Acts*', in I.H. Marshall & D. Peterson (eds.), *Witness to the Gospel: The Theology of Acts* (Grand Rapids: Eerdmans, 1998), 499–518.
Catchpole, D.	*The Quest for Q* (Edinburgh: T&T Clark, 1993).
Collins, J.J.	'The Sibylline Oracles, Book 8', in J.H. Charlesworth (ed.), *The Old Testament Pseudepigrapha: Apocalyptic Literature and Testaments* (Garden City NY: Double Day, 1983), 317–472.
Constan, D.	*Pity Transformed* (London: Duckworth, 2001).
Crook, Z.A.	'Reflections on Culture and Social–Scientific Models', *JBL* 124.3 (2005), 515–32.
Daube, D.	*The New Testament and Rabbinic Judaism* (London: School of Oriental and African Studies, University of London, 1956).
de Lange, N.R.M.	'Jewish Attitudes to Roman Empire', in P.D.A. Garnsey & C.R. Whittaker (eds.), *Imperialism in the Ancient World* (Cambridge: Cambridge University Press, 1978), 255–81.
de Silva, D.A.	'Patronage and Reciprocity: The Context of Grace in the New Testament', *ATJ* 31 (1999), 32–84.
Dihle, A.	*Die Goldene Regel* (Göttingen: Vandenhoeck and Ruprecht, 1962).
Douglas, R.C.	'"Love Your Enemies": Rhetoric, Tradents, and Ethos', in J.S. Kloppenborg (ed.), *Conflict and Invention: Literary, Rhetorical, and Social Studies on the Sayings Gospel Q* (Valley Forge: Trinity Press International, 1995), 116–31.
Downing, F.G.	*Christ and the Cynics* (Sheffield: JSOT Press, 1988).
Dunn, J.D.G.	*Christianity in the Making*. Volume 1: *Jesus Remembered* (Grand Rapids: Eerdmans, 2003).
Eddy, P.R.	'Jesus as Diogenes? Reflections on the Cynic Jesus Thesis', *JBL* 115.3 (1996), 449–69.
Edwards, J.R.	*The Gospel According to Luke* (Nottingham: Apollos, 2015).
Ehrman, B.D.	*Jesus: Apocalyptic Prophet of the New Millennium* (Oxford: Oxford University Press, 1999).

Elliott, N.	'Paul and the Politics of Empire', in R.A. Horsley (ed.), *Paul and Politics: Ekklesia, Israel, Imperium, Interpretation* (Harrisburg: Trinity Press International, 2000), 17–39.
Evans, C.A.	'Jesus and the Messianic Texts from Qumran: A Preliminary Assessment of the Recently Published Materials', *Jesus and His Contemporaries: Comparative Studies* (Leiden-New York-Köln, 1995), 83–154.
Evans, C.F.	*Saint Luke* (London: SCM, 1990).
Fitzmyer, J.A.	*The Gospel According to Luke I–IX* (Garden City NY: Doubleday and Co., 1981).
Flusser, D.	'A New Sensitivity in Judaism and the Christian Message', *HTR* 61 (1968), 107–27.
Flusser, D.	'Jesus, His Ancestry, and the Commandment of Love', in J.H. Charlesworth (ed.), *Jesus' Jewishness: Exploring the Place of Jesus in Early Judaism* (New York: Crossroad, 1991), 153–76.
Freyne, S.	'The Geography, Politics, and Economics of Galilee and the Quest for the Historical Jesus', in B. Chilton & C.A. Evans (ed.), *Studying the Historical Jesus: Evaluations of the State of Research* (Leiden-New York-Köln: Brill, 1994), 75–121.
Fuller, R.H., (ed.)	*Essays on the Love Commandment* (R.H. & I. Fuller, transls.; Philadelphia: Fortress Press, 1978 [German: 1975]).
Funk, R.W. *et al.*, (eds.)	*The Five Gospels: The Search for the Authentic Words of Jesus* (New York: Macmillan, 1993).
Furnish, V.P.	*The Love Command in the New Testament* (London: SCM, 1972).
Gerhardsson, B.	*Memory and Manuscript with Tradition and Transmission in Early Christianity* (Grand Rapids: Eerdmans, 1998).
Gibson, J.C.	*Syrian Semitic Inscriptions.* Volume III: *Phoenician Inscriptions Including Inscriptions in the Mixed Dialect of Arslam Tash* (Oxford; Clarendon Press, 1980).
Gill, C., N. Postlethwaite, & R. Seaford (eds.)	*Reciprocity in Ancient Greece* (Clarendon Press: Oxford, 1998).
Green, J.B.	*The Gospel of Luke* (Grand Rapids: Eerdmans, 1997).
Hagner, D.A.	*Matthew 1–13* (WBC; Dallas: Word Books, 1993).

Harrison, J.R.	'The Historical Jesus as "Social Critic": an Investigation of Luke 6:27–36', *Journal of Gospels and Acts Research* 2 (2018), 53–74.
Harrison, J.R.	'The Fading Crown: Divine Honour and the Early Christians', *JTS* 54.2 (2003), 493–524.
Harrison, J.R.	*Paul's Language of Grace in Its Graeco–Roman Context* (Tübingen: Mohr Siebeck, 2003; reprint: Eugene: Wipf and Stock, 2017).
Horsley, R.A.	'Ethics and Exegesis: "Love Your Enemies" and the Doctrine of Nonviolence', in W.M. Swartley (ed.), *The Love of Enemy and Nonretaliation in the New Testament* (Louisville: Westminster/John Knox Press, 1992), 72–101.
Horsley, R.A.	*Jesus and the Spiral of Violence: Popular Jewish Resistance in Roman Palestine* (San Francisco: Harper and Row, 1987).
Horsley, R.A.	*Sociology and the Jesus Movement* (New York: Continuum, 1989).
Hultgren, A.J.	*The Parables of Jesus: A Commentary* (Grand Rapids: Eerdmans, 2000).
Jeremias, J.	*New Testament: Theology Volume 1* (London: SCM Press, 1971).
Johnson, L.T.	*The Gospel of Luke* (Collegeville: Michael Glazier/Liturgical Press, 1991).
Joubert, S.	*Paul as Benefactor: Reciprocity, Strategy and Theological Reflection in Paul's Collection* (Tübingen: Mohr Siebeck, 2000).
Just, A.A.	*Luke 1:1–9.50* [St. Louis: Concordia Publishing House, 1996).
Keener, C.S.	*A Commentary on the Gospel of Matthew* (Grand Rapids: Eerdmans, 1999).
Kirk, A.	'"Love Your Enemies," the Golden Rule, and Ancient Reciprocity (Luke 6: 27–35)', *JBL* 122.4 (2003), 667–81.
Klassen, W.	'Coals of Fire: Sign of Repentance or Revenge?', *NTS* 9 (1963), 337–50.
Klassen, W.	'The Authenticity of the Command: "Love Your Enemies"', in B. Chilton & C.A. Evans (ed.), *Authenticating the Words of Jesus* (Leiden-Boston-Köln: Brill, 1999), 385–404.

Klassen, W.	*Love of Enemies: The Way to Peace* (Philadelphia: Fortress, 1984).

Kloppenborg, J.S.	*The Formation of Q: Trajectories in Ancient Wisdom Collections* (Harrisburg: Trinity Press International, 2000).

Knowles, M.P.	'Reciprocity and "Favour" in the Parable of the Undeserving Servant', *NTS* 49 (2003), 256–60.

Lifshitz, B.	*Donateurs et Foundateurs dans les Synagogues Juives* (Paris: Gabalda, 1967).

Llewelyn, S.R., (ed.)	*New Documents Illustrating Early Christianity* Vol. 8: *A Review of the Greek Inscriptions and Papyri Published 1984–85* (Macquarie University, NSW & Grand Rapids: AHDRC & Eerdmans, 1998).

Lührmann, D.	'Liebet eure Feinde: Lk 6:27–36; Mt 5:39–48', *ZTK* 69.4 (1972), 412–38.

Maas, M.	*Readings in Late Antiquity* (London & New York: Routledge, 2000).

MacGillivray, E.D.	'Re-Evaluating Patronage in Antiquity and New Testament Studies', *JGRCh* 6 (2009), 37–81.

Malina, B.J., & R.L. Rohrbaugh (eds.)	*Social–Science Commentary on the Synoptic Gospels* (Minneapolis: Fortress Press, 1992).

Manson, T.W.	*The Sayings of Jesus* (London: SCM Press, 1971).

Marjanen, A.	'Is *Thomas* a Gnostic Gospel', in R. Uro (ed.), *Thomas at the Crossroads. Essays on the Gospel of Thomas* (Edinburgh: T&T Clark, 1998), 89–106.

Marshall, I.H.	*Commentary on Luke* (Grand Rapids: Eerdmans, 1978).

Marshall, J.	*Jesus, Patrons, and Benefactors: Roman Palestine and the Gospel of Luke* (Tübingen: Mohr Siebeck, 2009).

Matthews, V. H.	'The Unwanted Gift: Implications of Obligatory Gift Giving in Ancient Israel', *Semeia* 87 (1999), 91–104.

Meier, J.P.	*A Marginal Jew: Rethinking the Historical Jesus.* Volume 4: *Law and Love* (New Haven & London: Yale University Press, 2009).

Meier, J.P.	*A Marginal Jew: Rethinking the Historical Jesus.* Volume 2: *Mentor, message, and miracles* (New York: Doubleday, 1994).

Minear, P.S.   *Commands of Christ* (Nashville-New York: Abingdon Press, 1972).

Mitchell, S.   *Regional Epigraphic Catalogues of Asia Minor: The Ankara District Inscriptions of North Galatia II* (Oxford: BAR, 1982).

Molm, L.M.   'The Structure of Reciprocity', *Social Psychology Quarterly* 73.2 (2010), 119–31.

Montefiore, C.G., & H. Loewe (eds.)   *A Rabbinic Anthology* (New York: Shocken Books, 1977).

Moxnes, H.   'Patron–Client Relations and the New Community in Luke–Acts', in J.H. Neyrey (ed.), *The Social World of Luke–Acts* (Peabody: Hendrickson, 1991), 241–68.

Moxnes, H.   *The Economy of the Kingdom: Social Conflict and Economic Relations in Luke's Gospel* (Philadelphia: Fortress Press, 1988).

Novick, T.   'Charity and Reciprocity: Structures of Benevolence in Rabbinic Literature', *HTR* 105.1 (2012), 33–52.

Oakman, D.E.   *Jesus and the Economic Questions of His Day* (Lewiston: Edwin Mellen Press, 1986).

Perkins, P.   *Love Commands in the New Testament* (New York/Ramsey: Paulist Press, 1982).

Piper, J.   *'Love Your Enemies': Jesus' Love Command in the Synoptic Gospels and the Early Christian Paraenesis* (Cambridge: Cambridge University Press, 1979).

Piper, R. A.   *Wisdom in the Q Tradition: The Aphoristic Teaching of Jesus* (Cambridge: Cambridge University Press, 1989).

Porter, S.E.   'Jesus and the Use of Greek in Palestine', in B. Chilton and C.A. Evans (eds.), *Studying the Historical Jesus. Evaluations of the State of Current Research* (New Testament Tools & Studies, 19; Leiden: Brill, 1993), 123–54.

Pouilloux, J.   *Choix D'Inscriptions Grecques: Textes, Traductions et Notes* (Paris: Belles Lettres, 1960).

Rajak, T.   'Benefactors in the Greco–Jewish Diaspora', in P. Schäfer (ed.), *Geschichte-Tradition-Reflexion: Festschrift für Martin Hengel zum 70. Geburtstag*. Band I: *Judentum* (Tübingen: Mohr Siebeck, 1996), 305–319.

Ranjar, C.S.	*Be Merciful Like the Father: Exegesis and Theology of the Sermon on the Plain (Luke 6:17–49)* (AB 219; Rome: Gregorian & Biblical Press, 2017).
Reed, J.L.	*Archaeology and the Galilean Jesus: A Re-examination of the Evidence* (Harrisburg: Trinity Press International, 2002).
Richardson, P.	*Herod: King of the Jews and Friend of the Romans* (Columbia: University of South Carolina Press, 1996).
Ricoeur, P.	'The Golden Rule: Exegetical and Theological Perplexities', *NTS* 36 (1990), 392–97.
Schottroff, L.	'Non Violence and the Love of One's Enemies', in R.H. Fuller (ed.), *Essays on the Love Commandment* (R.H. & I. Fuller, transls.; Philadelphia: Fortress Press, 1978 [German: 1975]), 9–39.
Schwartz, S.	*Were Jews a Mediterranean Society? Reciprocity and Solidarity in Ancient Judaism* (Princeton & Oxford: Princeton University Press, 2010).
Seaford, R.	'Introduction', in C. Gill, N. Postlethwaite, & R. Seaford (eds.), *Reciprocity in Ancient Greece* (Clarendon Press: Oxford, 1998), 1–12.
Seitz, O.J.F.	'Love Your Enemies: The Historical Setting of Matthew v.43f.; Luke vi.27f.', *NTS* 16 (1969–1970), 39–54.
Senior, D.	'Jesus' Most Scandalous Teaching', in J.T. Pawlikowski & D. Senior (eds.), *Biblical and Theological Reflections on the Challenge of Peace* (Wilmington: Michael Glazier, 1984), 55–69.
Seo, P.S.	*Luke's Jesus in the Roman Empire and the Emperor in the Gospel of Luke* (Eugene: Pickwick Publications, 2017).
Shemesh, A.	'"The Holy Angels Are in Their Council": The Exclusion of Deformed Persons from Holy Places in Qumranic and Rabbinic Literature', *Dead Sea Discoveries* 4 (1997), 179–206.
Stansell, G.	'The Gift in Ancient Israel', *Semeia* 87 (1999), 65–104.
Stein, R.H.	*Luke* (Nashville: Broadman Press, 1992).
Stendahl, K.	'Hate, Non-retaliation, and Love: 1 QS 10.17–20 and Rom 12:19–21', *HTR* 54.4 (1962), 343–55.

Suggs, M.J.   'The Antitheses as Redactional Products', in R.H. Fuller (ed.), *Essays on the Love Command* (R.H. & I. Fuller, transls.; Philadelphia: Fortress Press, 1978), 93–107.

Swartley, W.M., (ed.)   *The Love of Enemy and Nonretaliation in the New Testament* (Louisville: Westminster/John Knox Press, 1992).

Theissen, G.   *Social Reality and the Early Christians: Theology, Ethics, and the World of the New Testament* (Edinburgh: T&T Clark, 1993).

Theissen, G.   'Nonviolence and Love of Our Enemies (Matthew 5:38–48; Luke 6:27–38)', in G. Theissen, *Social Reality and the Early Christians: Theology, Ethics, and the World of the New Testament*, (M. Kohl, transl.; Edinburgh: T&T Clark, 1992), 115–56.

Theissen, G.   *The Gospels in Context: Social and Political History in the Synoptic Tradition* (Minneapolis: Fortress Press, 1991), 26–42.

Theissen, G.   *The First Followers of Jesus: A Sociological Analysis of the Earliest Christianity* (London: SCM Press, 1978).

Topel, J.   'The Tarnished Golden Rule (Luke 6:31): The Inescapable Radicalness of Christian Ethics', *TS* 59 (1998), 475–85.

Tuckett, C.M.   *Q and the History of Early Christianity* (Edinburgh: T&T Clark, 1996), 300–307.

Vaage, L.E.   'Composite Texts and Oral Mythology: The Case of the "Sermon" in Q [6:20–49]', in J.S. Kloppenborg (ed.), *Conflict and Invention: Literary, Rhetorical, and Social Studies on the Sayings Gospel Q* (Valley Forge: Trinity Press International, 1995), 75–97.

Vaage, L.E.   'Deeper Reflections on the Jewish Cynic Jesus', *JBL* 117.1 (1998), 97–106.

Vaage, L.E.   *Galilean Upstarts: Jesus' First Followers According to Q* (Valley Forge: Trinity Press International, 1994).

Van Unnik, W.C.   'Die Motivierung der Feindesliebe in Lukas VI 32–35', *NovT* 8.2 (1966), 284–300.

Wansbrough, H., (ed.)   *Jesus and the Oral Gospel* (Sheffield: Sheffield Academic Press, 1991).

Wilfred, Y.	*Poverty, Charity and the Image of the Poor in Rabbinic Texts from the Land of Israel* (Sheffield: Sheffield Phoenix Press, 2014).
Wink, W.	'Neither Passivity nor Violence: Jesus' Third Way (Matt. 5:38–42 par.)', in W.M. Swartley (ed.), *The Love of Enemy and Nonretaliation in the New Testament* (Louisville: Westminster/John Knox Press, 1992), 102–32.
Wolter, M.	*The Gospel According to Luke*. Volume 1: *Luke 1–9:50* (Waco: Baylor University Press, 2016).

CHAPTER 7

Usury and the Interpretation of the Sacred Text

Robert Tilley

Abstract

Modernity can be understood as a 'secularisation' of time, by which is meant that in place of both universal and localised rhythmic patterns of liturgy and festival there arose a more standardised conceptualisation of time, one that had more to do with matters economic than matters religious or pastoral. Time was abstracted from its religious and agricultural context and made into something better able to be quantified by reference to new 'global' markets and their attendant financial systems. It became an economic system that was increasingly defined by the relaxing of laws against usury, which made possible the rise of financial capitalism proper. The rise of modern Biblical Criticism was concomitant with these changes, and yet it is not common to question how the two were related, and yet how one reads creation will have a profound effect on how one reads the Scriptures. As a prolegomenon to answering this question, this article examines Matthew and Luke in order to ascertain how the issue of time and economics informs the rise of the early Church, with Jesus championing the Law's 'heavenly usury' for the covenant community.

In his work on the Jewish concept of time in early modern Europe, Elisheva Carlebach writes, 'One of the most crucial moments a human society can create is a system accounting for time'.[1] For it is the concept of time that will inform and shape a society in the most basic of ways. Kant was not the first to understand that time and space are fundamental to how it is we conceive of all else, how it is they form something of a given to all understanding. The early modern period being a case in point.

Modernity can be understood as a 'secularisation' of time, by which is meant that in place of both universal and localised rhythmic patterns of liturgy and festival there arose a more standardised conceptualisation of time, one that had more to do with matters economic than matters religious or pastoral.[2] Time, it can be said, was abstracted from its religious and agricultural context and made into something better able to be quantified by reference to new 'global' markets and their attendant financial systems. It became an economic system that was increasingly defined by the relaxing of laws against usury, which change made possible the rise of financial capitalism proper.[3]

Especially significant for our purpose is the fact that concomitant with this change was the rise of modern biblical criticism (hereon, MBC), a discipline that came to define itself by way of a historical method that instantiated the dominant themes of this secularising of

---

1 Carlebach, *Palaces of Time*, 5.
2 For an overview and discussion see: Kaye, *Economy and Nature; A History of Balance*.
3 The simplest definition of usury is when more is required to be paid back on a loan than the principle. However, some have argued that this does not include when one invests in another's business. But technically speaking this is not a loan but an investment. This is not the place to go into the vagaries of the definition of usury for it is a very complex history in that in order to get around the proscription against usury increasingly complex and ingenious arguments have been employed. One could even say that it is these arguments and the necessary sub-laws devised to check them that has given rise to the increasingly complex financial vehicles that inform contemporary global financial markets. For a discussion on this history see Noonan, *The Scholastic Analysis of Usury*. Noonan's work is still the primary one on the topic, albeit not without criticism. See, McCall, *The Church and the Usurers*. On the general cultural and theological effects of usury in respect of biblical religion and developments in the Church, see, Nelson, *The Idea of Usury*. Ohrenstein & Gordon, *Economic Analysis in Talmudic Literature*, detail the ways in which in later Talmudic literature the Torah and Mishnah came to be read such that certain of the laws were made more amenable to current circumstances. This included getting around the prohibitions against usury, as well as being able to avoid having to lend money to a fellow Israelite if the jubilee year was close and the creditor would lose their money (the pruzbul/prozbul). The authors approve of this as being economically enlightened, a view I do not share. It should go without saying that the same kind of rationalisations can also be found in Christian literature.

time (and space, but we will be focusing only on time). These themes being an antipathy to Scholastic metaphysics (and increasingly *all* metaphysics), and an attendant anti-clericalism.[4] The question rarely raised in MBC, let alone in any systematic manner discussed, is how the above changes shaped the thinking and methods of the dominant streams of that discipline.[5] It is not so much the intention of this work to address this aspect of MBC, as to write a kind of prolegomena to just such a work. To do so by way of exploring how the issue of time and economics informs the rise of the early Church and that by way of the Gospels of Saints Matthew and Luke.

Time and space, the economy and the sacred text are all inextricably entwined. Or to put it another way, the reading of creation and the reading of the Scriptures are both read being informed by many of the same fundamental principles; how one reads creation will have a profound effect on how one reads the Scriptures. It is something evident in second temple period (hereon, STP) literature, and that especially so in respect of those texts we refer to under the term 'eschatological'. Here, the fulfilment of the meaning of the Scriptures is correlate with the fulfilment of the meaning of creation and the locus and culmination of this process is the covenantal communion of the elect. A communion defining itself, rigorously so, by way of its liturgy and festivals as well as by its economy. Concerns which found their clearest expression by reference to the jubilee.

---

4   There has been a good deal written on this topic in the last few decades, but by way of example see the essays by Kraynak, 'Hobbes and the Dogmatism of the Enlightenment' and Bagley, 'Spinoza, Biblical Criticism, and the Enlightenment'. Also: Kwakkel, 'The Reformation and Historical-Critical Research'; Morrow, 'The Politics of Biblical Interpretation'; Hahn & Wiker, *Politicizing the Bible*; Harrison, *The Bible, Protestantism, and the Rise of Natural Science*; Reventlow, *The Authority of the Bible*, especially pp. 21–31, 290–4; Sheehan, *The Enlightenment Bible*, especially pp. 14–15, 27–30. Insofar as this article is concerned, although these and other works like them are very good they rarely if ever discuss in any depth what effect developments in the modern economy, vis a vis the rise of financial capitalism, had on the scholarly study of the Bible.

5   Three books in particular I have found both helpful and stimulating in respect of the background to the period that gave rise to Modern Biblical Criticism (albeit these books do not touch specifically on that discipline), are: Jones, *God and the Moneylenders*; Kerridge, *Usury, Interest and the Reformation*; and Hawkes, *The Culture of Usury in Renaissance England*.

The Liturgical and Economic Nature of Time

As is generally accepted, the first chapter of Genesis expresses a priestly cosmology, one that presents time and space as being by their very nature liturgical in character. Creation as a whole being presented both in its 'construction' and form as a temple.[6] Perhaps the most obvious feature in this respect is the use of the number seven and its derivatives. It is a number that not only serves to structure the account of creation but which plays a significant role in the priestly literature, such as Leviticus, doing so by reference to sacrifice, festivals, ordination, and periods of purification.[7] There is, however, another aspect to this number the significance of which is not as commented upon as it might, and this is how it serves to inform the economy of the covenantal communion of Israel and that especially so in respect of credit and debt; by way of usury. Thus, not only was an Israelite not to ask for a return above the value of the principle, after seven years any such debt was to be forgiven. In the great jubilee (the seventh of a sequence of seven years) all debts were to be scrubbed and any land alienated was to be restored to the family.[8] It is the jubilee that comes to define the nature of time as understood within latter STP Judaism and early Christianity and that eschatologically so in that it marks out the period as one in which the eschaton is imminent. John Bergsma in his book *The Jubilee from Leviticus to Qumran* charts in detail how the jubilee developed from earlier periods in both Israel's history and that of the wider ancient near east, through to the period under discussion.[9]

---

6   Much has been written on this theme in the last two or three decades, the following is only a representative sample of these works: Lioy, *Axis of Glory*; Morales (ed.), *Cult and Cosmos*; Morales, *The Tabernacle Pre-figured*; Walton, *The Lost World of Genesis One* and his *Genesis One as Ancient Cosmology*.
7   For example: Lev. 4:6, 17; 8:11, 33, 35; 12:2; 13:4–5, 21, 26, 31; 14:7–8, 16, 38, 51; 15:13; 16:19, 29; 22:27; 23:3, 5–8, 15–16, 24, 27, 34, 39–42; 25:2–4, 8–9; Numbers 8:2; 19:14, 19; 31:19, 24.
8   Deuteronomy 15:1–2, 9: 31:10; Leviticus 25:28, 33.
9   Bergsma, *The Jubilee from Leviticus to Qumran*. For further discussion on the ancient near eastern background to the problem of usury and the attempts by various states to rein it in see the essays in Hudson & Van De Mieroop, *Debt and Economic Renewal*. One of the significant points is that at intervals the State had to force a cancellation of all debts not least due to the fact that usury inevitably ends up concentrating wealth and land ownership in fewer and fewer hands and this to the detriment of all the economy.

Following the lead of Daniel[10] certain groups including those 'communities' associated with the Dead Sea Scrolls divided time up into series of jubilees all of which culminated in the period of the eschaton.[11] This eschaton came to be seen in terms of the time of the coming of the Messiah/s and the purging of the land of Israel, from both the pollution of the nations as well as the apostates. The consequent reestablishment of the proper Zadokite priesthood and the concomitant presence of the angelic host in the camp of the elect. In sum, the vindication of the community of the elect and the presence of the glory of God in the newly cleansed temple. Now were the Law and the Prophets fulfilled and so too creation in that now a purified Jerusalem reigns over the nations, one that accords with a proper economy. As Bergsma notes, integral to the jubilee fulfilment of all things was the cessation of usury, the scrubbing of all debts, and the equitable sharing of wealth (at least among the elect).[12] From what we can discern in the Dead Sea Scrolls (hereon, DSS) those texts that have to do with the rules of the community set out a practice that proleptically realises something of the imminent eschaton, not least by way of having all things in common.[13] As

---

10 Daniel 9:24–27. Although Bergsma writes that Isaiah 61:1–3 may be the first messianic reinterpretation of the jubilee (*The Jubilee from Leviticus to Qumran*, 202).

11 It is a difficult thing to say how widespread the use of texts such as *Jubilees* or the Enochian literature and like texts was, nor should we assume that the Dead Sea Scrolls represent only one community. It is with these qualifications in mind that reference to second Temple literature is made. On this matter see, Collins, 'Beyond the Qumran Community'.

12 As foreign as it may sound to us there was an integral relationship between the sacrificial cult of the temple and the abolishment of debt. Bergsma writes that the jubilee was the socio-economic 'expression of the Day of Atonement' (*The Jubilee from Leviticus to Qumran*, 91–2, 227, see too pp. 30–31, 188 on the Torah's tying together of jubilee with the Day of Atonement). Psalm 15 asks in a series of questions who shall sojourn in the tabernacle and the conclusion forms a climax of sorts which is that the one who will deal therein is one who does not practise usury or take bribes (15:5). The equating of the scrubbing of economic debt with sins to be remitted by sacrifice is not one of mere metaphor, but in fact describes how the heavens and the earth are to be brought into accord (this being the argument of this paper).

13 See Stone, *Scripture, Sects and Visions*, 67. Here too we need to qualify ourselves. As Collins, 'Beyond the Qumran Community', 358, notes: there are some differences between the Community Rule and the Damascus Document, not least that the former demands full community property, while the latter requires the members to submit two days salary a month. But Herda, Reed, & Bowlin, 'Relationship', 123–4, note that, although this was the case, nevertheless the accent in both was on the 'redistribution of resources and support' for those in the community in economic need. Further that intra-sectarian commerce was forbidden, hence there was neither any usury or, for that matter, exchange of wealth (pp.119–20, 125). See too the discussion in Murphy, *Wealth in the Dead Sea Scrolls*.

wealth properly belongs to the community and is distributed according to need, then there is no debt and no usury. Just as their purity both proleptically realises and brings about the eschaton, so too does their economy—indeed, to treat purity and economy as if they were separable is to introduce a division that is not warranted by either the Law or the rules of the community/s.[14]

In the jubilee informed eschatology, time follows a recurrent pattern albeit one with a goal; time is cyclical, characterised by the priestly number seven and its multiples, yet is also teleological in that the cycles repeat themselves culminating in the eschaton. It is this recurrent sequence teleologically oriented that properly describes the character of time qua time. As might be expected it is also the dynamic that informs the way in which Scripture is fulfilled, a dynamic that can be summed up under a term favoured by scholars, namely 'recapitulation'. The Torah itself is informed by this dynamic in that creation is *reversed* in the flood, only to be recapitulated following the flood a process that revolves around Noah who is represented as a second Adam.[15] Creation and the flood are in turn recapitulated at the parting of the sea in Exodus with Moses being the representative figure. Moses, who is saved from the waters while a baby by way of a 'micro-ark' and who in turns saves the covenant communion of Israel bringing them safe through some rather more dramatic waters.[16] Both the event and the person are themselves recapitulated later in the Book of Joshua when Joshua takes over from Moses and leads the people through the separated waters of the Jordan.[17] The prophets too employ the dynamic of recapitulation, not least in the promise that the return from exile will be a new exodus and

---

14 On the treatment of wealth in those texts in the DSS that are non-sectarian in origin (such as Enoch) see, Matthews, *Riches, Poverty, and the Faithful* (especially chapter two).
15 Thus the separation of the waters above and below (and on earth) in Gen. 1:6–10 are again brought together (Gen. 7:11–12, 17–20) only then to be again separated and that by way of a wind that echoes the spirit of God on the deep (compare Gen. 1:2 and 8:1). Noah is depicted as being one who might reverse the fall (5:29) and this is said just prior to the reader being told that Noah's father lived till he was 777 years old which is when Noah comes into his own (5:31), at least in the way the narrative is told. Noah after the flood is given the blessing to be fruitful and multiply (compare Gen. 1:28 with 9:1, and we are reminded of the fact that man is made in the image of God (9:6). Etc.
16 Exodus 2:1–6; 14:21–30.
17 Joshua 3:7, 14–17.

Judah presently a wasteland will soon bloom becoming a foretaste of a new Eden.[18] The Gospel writers employ recapitulation and they do so by way of the covenantal figure Jesus Christ who is depicted as fulfilling the covenant/s with Israel thereby bringing them to their eschatological perfection.[19] And then there is Revelation, a book that more than other biblical book employs a recapitulative dynamic and that within a sevenfold structure.[20]

It is important to underscore the fact that the process of recapitulation takes place *within* the context of the covenant community (in the STP often referring to itself as the elect), and is centred upon chief representative of that community.

In sum, there is a dynamic nature to time in which events repeat themselves but do so in a way that is not simply a repetition of the same. Rather, what went before is brought into the present such that both past and present are brought that bit more to proleptically participate in what is to come. Recapitulation is a dynamic that is liturgical in character.[21] Liturgy is not imposed upon time as if time were a *tabula rasa*,

---

18   See Estelle, *Echoes of Exodus*, 182–207. Space does not permit our going any deeper into the following, recapitulation tends to revolve not just around the covenantal representative (be it Adam, Noah, Abraham, Moses and, of course, later Jesus) and the community he represents, but around sacrifice. This aspect is made evident in the way that the tabernacle/temple especially the Holy of Holies is a recapitulated Eden. On this see, Beale, 'Eden, the Temple, and the Church's Mission in the New Creation'. See too the references given above in footnote 3.

19   For an overview of this theme in the Gospels but specifically in Matthew see, Kennedy, *The Recapitulation of Israel*.

20   One finds it as well in Paul, not least in Romans where Jesus is depicted as recapitulating Adam, albeit by way of bringing life not death (Romans 5:12–21), and Ephesians 1:10 (assuming Pauline authorship) where all things are 'headed up' in Christ, the term being the Greek form of what since St Irenaeus would be translated as 'recapitulation'. So too Hebrews and its understanding of the relationship between the sacrifices of the Law and that of the Cross.

21   As good as Kennedy's book is, in my opinion his definition of recapitulation is a little bit inadequate insofar as it too much leans towards the default position of many scholars, this being to the effect that recapitulation is treated merely as a literary device that instantiates the theological reflections of the NT writers (*The Recapitulation of Israel*, 20–21). However, it should also be noted that Kennedy writes that typology and recapitulation (which are associated in the NT) work within a concept of 'corporate personality', and that Jesus is the climax of the history attendant upon this personality (p.21). Later, that recapitulation involves 'the repetition, reliving, and representative embodiment of Israel's history' (p.230). These and like statements do justice to the topic, only by implicitly accepting that these factors only really apply to the literary text and not to time itself, Kennedy and the authors cited by him too easily assent to a secular understanding of time. And this is the point: this secular understanding informs MBC since its inception, indeed arises out of it and has thus shaped its assumptions and thereby its methods – and that to its detriment.

rather is time liturgical by reason of *its very nature*.²² Usury, however, is inimical to this liturgical nature and thereby obscures the understanding of time's proper dynamic. And it is so, as we will see below, by reason that usury is corrosive of the representational and reflexive logic that is constitutive of the dynamic unity of the covenantal community of the people of God, the elect. A logic that is the social correlate to the liturgical-cosmological character of recapitulation.

As creation and Scripture are coterminous one with the other in that both are fulfilled by means of the same dynamic and to the same end then, just as usury obscures the meaning proper of time and thereby of creation so too does it do the same to Scripture. Usury blinds one as to how both creation and Scripture are to be read. It is in respect of interpretation where the effects of usury are most clearly seen, or would be seen except the effects are so potent that we become blind to our own blindness. It is a problem that Jesus addresses, one that came to be a pressing concern for the first century Church, a concern evident in the Gospels of Matthew and Luke.

The Rich Young Ruler

In each of the Synoptics we meet with the episode of what has popularly come to be known as the 'rich young ruler'. It is too well known to need repeating but the gist of it is that the man in question claims to have kept all the commandments. In reply Jesus tells him that 'one thing he lacks, go and sell all, give it to the poor and follow me'. The rich man cannot do this and leaves. Jesus then remarks how difficult if not impossible it is for a rich man to enter into the kingdom of God. The disciples express astonishment at this and exclaim, 'Who then can be saved!?' To which Jesus responds to the effect that although it is impossible for men, nothing is impossible for God.²³

More often than not, commentators both pious and scholarly take from this passage a teaching on salvation to the effect that keeping the

---

22 Scholer, *Proleptic Priests*, observes that the locus of the proleptic dynamic in Scripture is the priesthood and liturgy.
23 Matt.19:16–26; Mark 10:17–27; Luke 18:18–27.

Law will not bring a person into the kingdom of God.[24] While this reading might have some justification it can also serve to blind us to something else happening within the text and with the reader. Something that implicates not only the rich man and the disciples, but the reader as well. The conclusion drawn by Jesus and the reaction of those present not only makes a soteriological point but serves to reveal a blindness that is at the heart of how it is we read matters sacred, not least in respect of the Law but also in respect of grace and the mission of Jesus. Both Matthew and Luke, as we will see below, elaborate on these matters by way of a language of an economy that contrasts worldly to heavenly usury. The astonishment that the disciples express at Jesus' remarks to the effect that it is humanly impossible for a rich (and in this instance an ostensibly pious) man to be saved betrays a system of values both at odds with the Law and with grace.

It may be obvious but when we speak of the rich there is an implied comparison being made, and the basis of this comparison as well as its promulgation is the economy. More often than not a comparison implies a sliding scale of values, and especially when it concerns human affairs. All of this may be obvious but like many other obvious things it may rarely be addressed, because of its very obviousness. An economy

---

24 As might be expected the writing on this passage is voluminous, but I think that by and large the following are representative. Hagner, *Matthew 14–18*, writes that 'the episode shows that discipleship requires more than mere obedience to the Law. Besides, the rich man almost certainly [had] given some of his wealth to the poor, as the righteous man would have done' (p.558); Witherington, *Matthew*, 384, notes that we learn from this episode that salvation is 'not a human self-help program' (384); Mary Healy, *The Gospel of Mark*, that it shows us the temptations to trust in one's status, and that although the man was a 'faithfully observant Jew' he was nevertheless 'bound by his possessions' (p.203); Culpepper, *Mark*, that the man was 'Torah observant' and sincere (p.336) but that he thought that by his doing he could attain eternal life (p.335); Wilson, *Luke and the Law*, 28–29, that eternal life is not merely of obedience to the Law but needs to be supplemented; Noland, *Luke 9:21–18:34*, 885, that the demands of discipleship reach beyond but do not detract from the Law. For an overview of sorts of the reading of this passage by the Fathers see, Clarke, '"Do not Judge who is Worthy and Unworthy"'. However, see too the comments by Carter, *Matthew and the Margins*, that the inaccuracy of the rich man's claims are 'exposed by his considerable wealth'; That the implication is that his abundant wealth has come from an exploitation of and indifference to the poor (p. 388); That his being called to give all to the poor is 'an act of restitution' (p.389). See too Hays, *Luke's Wealth Ethics*, 169, to the effect that Jesus' teaching 'reasserts an essential element of the Law and Prophets'. St Augustine expressed something a little bit similar when he wrote that the rich man's piety was feigned and that 'I think he spoke with more pride than truth', Letters, 157 *To Hilarius*, cited in Oden & Hall, *Mark*, 142.

operates by way of market values, using 'market' in the broadest possible way to denote not just tangible goods that are bought and sold but also *the means* by which the market in tangible goods functions. The values attendant upon the market attach as well to *the means* of trade, namely the different forms of currency and the different forms of speculation attendant upon that currency. This is often referred to under the term financial capital (including forms of currency speculation), and it is debt that informs capital's most basic as well as its more advanced forms. The comparison that an economy gives rise to and which expresses those values that inform the 'market' is often a comparison predicated upon the distinction between creditor and debtor (albeit this becomes very complex in more advanced forms of financial capital).

It could be said that the intent of most cultures is to keep these market values separate from and distinct to the higher values. 'Higher' because these values constitute what is held to be conducive to virtue and good moral character, and for this reason are seen as being necessary for a culture's unity and flourishing. Again, I use the term 'higher values' in the broadest sense, hence it can include matters religious, ethics and the arts, as well as the sciences. All too often, however, the boundary between the economy and culture becomes porous. The higher values begin to resemble the values attendant upon the economy, and in ways that are often, at first, not obvious. Indeed, matters economic can begin to shape how it is a people view such basic categories as time and space, and, of course, life itself.[25] More to our point, the economy begins to shape how matters religious and divine are read and interpreted.

The values of the market and attendant 'financial vehicles' come to inform the world and shape its values. They inform the conceptual basis by and through which all else is understood and, thereby, they become hidden in plain sight, for they are simply assumed to be a matter of common sense or simply of the very nature of things.[26] In critical parlance, they shape the consciousness of the people. So natural do these values seem that one is astonished when an authority one respects suggests otherwise.

Which brings us back to the rich young man.

---

25 For an extended discussion on this with references see my, 'The Biopolitical Economy of Anti-Essentialism'.
26 On this topic in relation to the reading of Scripture see my, 'The Birth of Ideology'.

Each of the Synoptics presents the episode as taking place while Jesus and his disciples enter Judea and approach Jericho with the intent of heading to Jerusalem.[27] This is the landscape that provides the backdrop to our episode. Now, in order to trace out the blindness present in and around the text we need to bring to mind how it is the Synoptics present life in Palestine, and Judea in particular. There are beggars, destitute cripples, outcast lepers, demoniacs, and ever present poverty. Through it all we are presented with a picture of what is at times a rather striking disparity in wealth, and this continues on (one might even say it becomes more pointed in Jesus' discourse) as Jesus and his disciples draw closer to Jerusalem.[28] The comparison becomes more pronounced and this ought not to surprise us, for the poor will gravitate to urban centres by reason that that is where the wealth is. It's where people might be more inclined to give a coin or two.[29]

The account presents the rich man as needing little introduction, his status as being both righteous and wealthy is accepted by all. Except, that is, for Jesus who calls his status into question. Jesus reveals to those present (and to the subsequent audience who hear or read the account) something of the man's real standing before God. It is the apparent fact of the man's piety and wealth that is the ground for the disciples' astonishment; he of all people should be a shoe-in to be saved! But here's the rub: the rich man claims to keep the Law and a few of its laws are listed. He says he keeps all of these and by implication all of the Law

---

27 Matt. 19:1; 20:29; 21:1; Mark 10:10, 32; Luke 18:31, 35.
28 For example see: Matt. 4:23–25; 8:2, 28; 9:2, 20, 27, 32, 35: 10:1; 11:5; 12:9–10, 15, 22; 14:14, 35; 15:22, 30–31; 17:14–15; 20:29–34; 21:14; 25:36–46. Luke 4:33, 40; 5:12, 15, 18; 6:6, 17–18; 7:22; 8:2, 27, 43; 9:49; 13:11; 14:2, 21; 17:12; 18:35; 21:2. As to how these passages and others like them sit with those concerning the economy as well as how Jesus deploys these matters, see below. The point here is that the major part of the Gospels is taken up with dialogue and less with setting the scene, as it were. However, when the scene is set more often than not we are told of the presence of the disabled, the disturbed, and the indigent. The way in which the material has been edited, it is reasonable to suppose, reflects the concerns of the early Church, not least those of the Apostles and disciples and, thereby, Jesus' own understanding of his mission and the means by which it was to be realised.
29 On the state of Jerusalem at the time of Christ I still think that one of the best books on the subject (with due qualifications made for the use of later rabbinic texts) is Jeremias, *Jerusalem in the Time of Jesus* (see especially pp. 23–33, 56). More recent works that are helpful in this respect are: Fiensy, *Christian Origins* (though I disagree with his thesis that the issue of debt was not a critical one until A.D. 66); Sawicki, *Crossing Galilee*; and Vaage, *Borderline Exegesis* (especially chapter two). See too Hays, *Luke's Wealth Ethics* (especially chapter two).

besides—only he doesn't. The Law commanded the rich in Israel to help their poorer brethren, not least by way of interest free loans that if not able to be repaid in seven years were to be forgiven, the slate scrubbed clean.[30] However, here is this young man overtly rich claiming to keep the Law in circumstances where the poor and destitute are thick upon the ground. Like the rich man in the parable, he seems to be blind to Lazarus at his gate.

When Jesus tells the rich man that there is 'one thing you lack, sell all you have and give to the poor' it is not in the order of a pious recommendation, an evangelical counsel of sorts.[31] Rather is it a command that here serves as a foil to the claim of the rich man to keeping the Law. He is revealed as both lying to himself and to others. It may be objected that Jesus' command is over and above what the Law required. After all, the sharing of wealth did not require the impoverishment of the one with the wealth, merely an equitable redistribution of wealth to answer to the needs of the poor. Perhaps so. Whether or not the Law would require his stripping himself of all his wealth so as to compensate for many years of disobeying the Law is debatable. What is *not* debatable is that this rich man did *not* keep the Law, that he was lying to himself and to others in thinking he did.

More remarkable is the response of the disciples: they are *astonished* that this man and others like him, rich and ostensibly pious, are not saved. If we are to tease out what values inform the thinking of the disciples we need to speculate somewhat as to the cause of their astonishment.

---

30 For some of the relevant passages see: usury is banned among Israelites, though not with other nations, Exodus 22:15; Leviticus 25:36–37; Deuteronomy 23:19–20; a person with wealth was expected to help those without, Deuteronomy 15:7–11; a loan was to be scrubbed after seven years, Deuteronomy 15:1–2, 9; 31:10; the law of the Jubilee entailing not only the forgiving of debt (as it was the seventh of seven period of seven years) but the return of any alienated land to the 'family' Leviticus 25:28, 33. Among other laws involving the running of the economy included the Sabbath rest even for slaves, Exodus 23:12; Deuteronomy 5:14; laws concerning leaving the gleanings that fell to the ground for the poor, Leviticus 19:9–10.

31 On the two-tiered reading of this passage see, Fink, 'Un-Reading Renunciation'.

Interpretation and Ownership

What can loosely be called 'prosperity doctrines' crop up through history and they are certainly not the sole provenance of more modern varieties of Pentecostalism or for that matter New Age. The idea being that divine blessings express divine approval, which blessings translate into present riches.

It is a way of thinking that can find support by way of a fundamental misreading of the Law, especially in respect of its blessings and cursings.[32] If Israel keeps the Law and is thereby faithful to the covenant then she will be blessed with prosperity and progeny; if she doesn't, then curses will ensue. Depending on whether one reads this as applying *immediately* to an individual, or to the individual as *derivative of* the covenant communion one will end up with two very different even opposed interpretations. To read it as first and foremost applying directly to an individual is to undermine the covenantal logic of the Law and, thereby, the integrity of the communion itself. The blessings attendant upon the Law are addressed to the covenant community of Israel, they are of a *communal* nature, and they are mediated through that community to the individual. The blessings to individuals are *derivative* of those given to Israel as a covenantal communion, and when blessings such as wealth are given to an individual it is so that he or she becomes *a means* by which God gives these blessings to Israel. This process of mediation and the means of its application both grounds and defends a social dynamic that is reciprocal and reflexive in nature, a dynamic that not only promulgates the covenantal and communal identity of the people of God but constitutes its very life and integrity. As the covenantal community is the locus of the fulfilment of both creation and Scripture, then this social dynamic of reflexivity and representation instantiates the process of recapitulation just as much as the community's liturgy does. Indeed, they are of a piece.

An 'individualistic' reading, however, does the very reverse; it atomises and is destructive of social reciprocity and reflexivity. Furthermore, it sets in motion a process in which the sacred text is increasingly decontextualized, abstracted from the community to which it belongs,

---

32 For example, Deuteronomy 30:8–10. Culpepper, *Mark*, 338–9, writes that wealth was generally viewed as being a result of God's blessing and that this was rooted in Deuteronomic theology.

insofar as the promises therein now apply directly to the individual and not, first and foremost, to the covenantal communion. The good of the covenantal communion is increasingly subordinated to that of an individual's status.

In the covenantal reading of the Law, individuals are stewards of the wealth entrusted to them and, thereby, they have the honour of being a means of the blessing of all Israel. The wealth is *not* per se theirs, they do not own it but are to manage it and to equitably distribute it, principally to those in need. In what we might call an individualistic reading, the wealth *does* belong to the recipient by reason of their own righteousness and, as a consequence, they are free to do with it what they will. If they feel charitable and give of their wealth then they accrue credit in the form of righteous merit, a merit *they* alone own. Through this reversal of values a duty commanded by the Law has been transformed into a means of boosting individual status. By reason of this, the Law has been subordinated to the logic of a market economy wherein comparison is made in respect of righteous merit; the reflexive and reciprocal relation that is constitutive of the communion is turned into a relation of competition, something that is corrosive of communion and the dynamic of recapitulation. Each individual is free to act as they think fit and if they decide to share their wealth then it is to *their* credit and merit. Whereas the covenantal reading undercuts this for as the 'unworthy servants' of the parable say, 'We have only done what was our duty'.[33]

So it is that the Law is read in a manner that not only justifies great wealth when there is poverty all around, but which also serves to mark out a rich person as being blessed of God, as being among the pious, hence of the elect of Israel. But Jesus reveals that the very opposite applies; the rich and ostensibly pious man *is not saved*. What Jesus reveals in respect of the rich man serves as well to reveal something of the blind spot around which the Law is read and understood, and again this is made evident by the disciples' astonishment. But as blind as the disciples may have been is there not a similar blindness afflicting the reader of this episode when they read it as little more than a lesson on the necessity of grace, to the effect that keeping the Law is not enough. Indeed, that the

---

33 Luke 17:10.

Law may even be irrelevant. Here, grace becomes a means of obfuscation such that the rich young man's self-deception and the disciples' sharing in that deception is simply not seen. Thereby is the command that is meant to ensure a communal equity made a matter of individual counsel and is rendered irrelevant to the individual's salvation.

Opposing Economies

In the Synoptics it is the issue of how Scripture is to be read that more often than not proves to be the locus of contention between Jesus, the religious authorities, and even those sympathetic to his mission.[34] So much so is this the case that one can argue that, among other reasons, these Gospels are written not only to present the mission and work of Jesus but thereby to serve as kind of *primer* on how it is the Church is to read the Scriptures and, thereby, all claims to righteous status. As Jesus read the Law and the Prophets, so too are Christians to read. The Gospels show how it is the grace of the gospel which illuminates and perfects the Law and the Prophets while revealing the blindness of the reader/hearer and that, not least, through the record of the blindness of the Apostles.

If there is one overarching theme in Torah (if not the whole Tanach) it is that of the promise of fruitfulness and multiplication, a promise that came to be associated with faithfulness to the covenant stipulations of the Law.[35] As a consequence, sterility, the lack of agricultural produce, and death became associated in the prophets with unfaithfulness to the Law, especially in respect of injustice and the neglect of the care for the poor, even for their exploitation and oppression. Suffice to say that the fundamental sign of being blessed by God had to do with

---

34 Well to be precise, at the beginning it is with the Devil, but this serves to set the tone. See for example: Matt. 4:1–11; 5:17–48; 7:28–29; 9:2–6, 13; 11:2–6, 13–15; 12:1–14, 38–42; 13:10–17, 34–35; 15:2–11; 16:13–15; 17:10–13; 19:3–9; 21:12–16; 22:23–33, 34–40, 41–46; 23:1–3, 16–22, 27–36.
35 To be more precise the first mention of fruitfulness and multiplication is a command, the first command it could be said in Torah, this is in Genesis 1:22 (to the animals) and 28 (to humans). In the course of Torah the command becomes a promise, so for example: Gen. 9:7 (Noah); Gen.13:16; 15:5; 16:10; 17:5–6; 17:20; 26:4 (Abraham including Ishmael and Isaac); Gen. 28:3, 14 (Isaac of Jacob); Gen. 35:11 (Jacob); Gen. 47:27; 48:4, 19 (Israel in Egypt); Exodus 1:7–12 (Israel in Egypt); Leviticus 26:9; Deuteronomy 7:13; 8:13; 13:17; 28:3–5, 11, 15–18; 30:5.

multiplication and fruitfulness (of progeny and goods). Only, as noted above, the means by which this blessing was bestowed involved the just and faithful stewardship of those elected to be those means, and this includes his Apostles. Jesus' denunciations of the corrupt religious authorities in Jerusalem often elide with and culminate in a warning to the Apostles to be faithful stewards and managers (a warning that, by extension, applies as well to those who have positions of Church governance derived from them).[36] There would seem to be an especial temptation to blindness attendant upon those who hold valid office such that they can feel justified in abusing their office and its authority.

In light of the foregoing it is especially pertinent to note the denouement proper of the rich young man pericope. The denouement is not, in fact, Jesus' words to the effect that nothing is impossible to God, rather it is this point expanded upon by reference to the means of God's working the impossible. In answer to Peter's statement that they have given up all to follow him, Jesus responds that all who do so will receive a hundredfold in return. The promise of abundance attendant upon the Law is fulfilled, but it is so through an act of renunciation here presented as a form of investment that can expect a great rate of return. The contrast being drawn is stark: the rich man goes back to his home sad but presumably comfortable; while the disciples who have left all will receive as a reward a manifold number of homes and families etc. in return.

In Matthew and Luke, Jesus is often presented as identifying matters associated with salvation with those to do with the economy, specifically with what one can expect in return for an initial outlay. The implicit (and sometimes explicit) contrast being drawn is one between a worldly and sinful practise of usury and what can be called a heavenly usury, to which we will return. Often Jesus speaks of salvation by reference to 'reward' (in Greek '*misthos*'), a term that more often than not referred to wages earned hence of what one is owed.[37] But also a term that had other meanings including what is owed by way of 'debt' and/

---

36 Matthew 16:5–12, 23; 18:1–9 (see too 19:13–14), 21–35; 20:1–16, 20–28; 24:36–51; 25:1–46; Mark 10:35–45; 13:32–37; Luke 9:46–48; 12:1–12, 35–48; 17:1–10; 19:11–27; 21:34–26.
37 On the language of economy in soteriology see, Eubank, 'Storing up Treasure with God in the Heavens'; on the term 'Misthos' and its Greek background, see Hansen, '*Misthos* for Magistrates in Fourth-Century Athens'.

or investment.[38] At times the Gospels accent a disproportionate return where 'reward' is concerned, not least in respect of when a debt is written off; in forgiving a minor debt owed to one, one gains access to that which wipes away one's greater debt.[39] In the parable of the talents, Jesus goes so far as to represent his mission (as entrusted to the Apostles) by reference to an expected return over and above the principle.[40]

In Matthew and Luke, salvation is presented in economic terms hence Jesus contrasts serving God to serving Mammon.[41] The distinction can be summed up as either one loves Mammon and thereby loves one's life, practises usury and makes a career of devouring widows' houses,[42] or one loves God, loses one's life, and practises divine usury by lending expecting no return.[43] It needs to be stressed that here the dynamic by which the world works, namely its economy, is the principle means by which Jesus contrasts the way in which God works. It is by reference to the economy that one invests in and thereby participates in, that the possibility or impossibility of being saved turns. A matter that turns upon that economy's attitude to credit and debt, in short to usury.[44]

---

38 The theme is more pronounced in Matthew and Luke than it is in Mark, though this may not be due to any ideological reason but for reasons of space. An argument can also be made that it evidences Matthew's and Luke's priority in that Mark could be seen to be a Gospel more acceptable for general dissemination. See for example Matthew 5:3–12 where the beatitudes show the reversal of worldly power giving eschatological privilege to the poor (a theme that answers to the temptations of the Devil in 4:1–11 where he is depicted as offering up worldly power); in 6:1–34 the reward of God is contrasted to the reward of treasures on earth; see too Matt. 16:26–27; 18:23–34; 19:16–25; 20:1–16; 21:12–17; 23: 16–23.; 25:14–30, 31–46; Luke 1:46–55; 3:18–19; 6:20, 24–26, 34–36; 8:14; 11:39–41; 12:13–21, 22–34; 16:1–13, 19–31; 18:18–30; 19:1–10; 20:47; 21:1–4; Mark 4:18–19; 10:17–31; 12:13–17, 41–44.
39 So Matthew 18:23–34. See too: Matthew 5:12, 46; 6:1–6, 12, 16–18; 7:7–12; 16:26–27; Luke 6: 23, 27–38; 7:36–47; 8:18 and 19:26; 9:25; 11:4, 9–13; 12:15–21, 57–59; 14:12–14; 16:1–14.
40 Matthew 25:14–30 and Luke 19:12–27.
41 Matthew 6:24 and Luke 16:13.
42 Matthew 23:14 (in some recensions); Mark 12:40; Luke 20:47. It is pertinent that in Mark and Luke, and to a slightly lesser degree Matthew, present the sin of devouring widows' houses (the means by which this is done is classically through usury) as the apex of the hypocritical practices of the corrupt religious authorities in Jerusalem.
43 Matthew 5:40–42; Luke 6:34–36. And see too Matt. 25:31–46 where one's outlay on earth is not expected to be repaid. The same can be said of the Good Samaritan in Luke 10:29–37. This parable is especially significant because in Torah one could not practise usury with a 'neighbour', which is to say a fellow Israelite, but one could with the nations (after all, they practised it). But, as is well known, in this parable everything turns on Jesus redefining 'neighbour' such that it now includes non-Israelites (and this contrary to the attempt by Jesus' interlocutor to 'justify himself').
44 On this topic, though from a different angle, see: Anderson, 'From Israel's Burden to Israel's Debt'; Eubank, *Wages of Cross-Bearing and Debt of Sin*.

In the Lord's Prayer, the request is made to have heaven and earth be in accord by reference to God's will, it is thus significant that the only action that the petitioner does to co-operate in bringing about this accord is to forgive the debts owed to him or her, for thereby will their debts be forgiven.[45]

It is here that St Augustine's comments are particularly astute. Usury, he wrote, is a heinous crime, a crime that is of the devil. There is, however, a form of usury that is approved of by God, indeed positively encouraged by God, and that is to lend to God expecting a great return. How does one lend to God? The answer is by giving to the poor, in other words to those who cannot repay you.[46] It should also be added that what it is one lends to God was, in the first place, given to one by God.

It is not that the essence of this teaching is original to Jesus, rather is he bringing out and extending upon what has already been commanded in the Torah. He is fulfilling the Law and the Prophets, not destroying them as some thought he would be doing.[47] It is perhaps significant that this economic language is not anywhere near as evident in the epistles as it is in Matthew and Luke (and to a lesser degree in Mark).[48] But what the significance is must be the topic of another paper.

---

45   Matthew 6:9–13, see too Jesus' 'explanation' of his prayer in vss. 14–15. Also Luke 11:2–4.
46   St Augustine Sermons 36 on Matthew 19:21: 'Give to God, and press God for payment', writes St Augustine. 'Yes rather give to God and thou will be pressed to receive payment'. See too his On the Psalms (Psalm 37) where he notes by way of Matthew 25:31–46 that God shows himself to be 'surety for the poor'. 'Give earth', writes Augustine, 'and receive heaven'.
47   Matthew 5:17–20.
48   Perhaps this should be qualified by reference to St Paul's argument concerning justification by works as contrasted to justification by grace/faith in *Romans* chapters 3 to 5. The argument could be made that the accent in Paul's argument is one that contrasts merit understood in an individualistic reading with one that belongs first and foremost to the covenantal communion. That is, a merit that is earned as if it were a proper income belonging to the individual who did the work, contrasted to a merit that comes in abundance by reason of faith as an investment in the promise fulfilled in Jesus. A merit which belongs to Jesus but is given freely to the covenant communion namely the Church, and through the Church is participated in, derivatively so, by an individual. One does not 'own' one's wealth in such a scheme, just as one does not 'own' one's righteousness, in both cases one participates in the blessing by reason of participating in the covenantal communion. The 'works' view of justification accents the ownership of the individual and is thus self-interested, while the 'faith' view of justification accents the ownership that belongs properly to the covenant communion in which an individual participates. In Romans 13:8–9 Paul applies in a practical manner the arguments of the early part of the letter and writes again using economic language: 'Owe nothing to anyone except to love one another, for the one who loves the other has fulfilled the Law. All the commandments are summed up under this word 'You shall love your neighbour as yourself''. Whether or not it is pertinent we might also note that although a similar argument concerning justification by works or by grace is found in Galatians the language of an economic-soteriology is absent (or at least insofar as I can make out).

Economy and Salvation

In Luke 20:45–47 Jesus denounces in severe terms those religious authorities who make great play on the appearance of pious office but who, behind the scenes, devour widows' houses. As touched upon above, the time honoured way in which the homes of the vulnerable are 'devoured' is lending at interest using the victim's property as collateral. The author has edited his account such that straight after Jesus' denunciation he sees one of these poor widows putting some of her meagre savings into the Temple treasury.[49] A moment's reflection on the way the account is structured will reveal a bitter irony indeed: the very source of the money that is loaned at interest to the likes of this poor widow, which interest helps towards purchasing the glorious robes the corrupt authorities wear in the market place, is the same temple into which she donates her savings. It is this scene that serves to make obvious the dissimulating play of appearance and reality attendant upon the operation of usury. And yet, what is most obvious is not seen. In a similar manner to how the episode of the rich man is presented, here too the Gospel writer has so ordered his material to make a telling point as to the power of a corrupt economy to inculcate blindness. In this episode, however, the disciples are *not* astonished. Indeed, so taken are they by appearances that they can only stand in praise and awe at the temple, *the locus of the very corruption Jesus has just been denouncing.*[50] It is in response to their obtuse praise that Jesus launches into his eschatological discourse, a discourse that begins with him telling them that this wonderfully impressive building will utterly be destroyed.[51]

It seems reasonable to suppose that this is where any reader/hearer of the Gospel would be led to ask: How it is that those who have been with Jesus (in some cases for close on to three years), who have been privy to his teaching and instruction and witnessed his miracles, are nevertheless so taken by appearances that they are still afflicted with a blindness that does not even know it is blind? Reasonable to suppose, yes, but then again how many ask this question?

---

49 Luke 21:1–4.
50 Luke 21:5.
51 Luke 21:6.

The Gospels arose out of the Church some decades after the events they describe, and although this is not the place to rehearse something of the never-ending history of scholarly attempts to reconstruct the way in which the Gospels came to be in the form we have them, nevertheless we *can* say something definite about this process. The Gospels are edited accounts of what Jesus said and did and they have been edited with certain themes in mind—just as any historical account is edited. It is reasonable to suppose that informing this editing and writing were certain issues that, over time, those in the Church felt needed addressing, some of which concerns are seen in those Epistles that precede the Gospels. This involved having the authoritative accounts of the mission of Jesus show how those who founded the Church were, even after some years of direct instruction, blind to the ideological power of a usurious economy to dissimulate itself under the appearance of fulfilling the Law. How was it possible for rich people to be given pride of place in the early Church? How was it possible for them to think that they did not have to share their wealth with those in the Church who were poor and hungry? How was it possible for them to then claim to faith? I refer, of course, to the situation set out in the Letter of James, but much the same questions arise in respect of the episode of the rich young man and the 'widow's mite' and that in respect of the Apostles themselves!

It is pertinent too that the Synoptics also record that Jesus' strongest denunciations and his threats of hell are made rarely if ever to what we might call the ordinary laity, rather are they directed at those with valid religious authority. Further, his denunciations of the corrupt in Jerusalem can often elide into a just as severe (if not severer) warning to the Apostles and, thereby, by extension to those who have positions of Church governance derived from them.[52] There would seem to be an especial propensity to blindness attendant upon those who hold valid office such that they can feel justified in abusing this office and its authority.

Though what follows is speculative, I do not think it is invalid. I think it likely that the popularity of the episode of the rich young man

---

52 Matthew 16:5–12, 23; 18:1–9 (see too 19:13–14), 21–35; 20:1–16, 20–28; 24:36–51; 25:14–30, 31–46; Mark 10:35–45; 13:32–37; Luke 9:46–48; 12:1–12, 35–48; 17:1–10; 19:11–27; 21:34–26.

(evident in its being in all the Synoptics) is because it provided an exemplary lesson in how one can miss what is obvious and, thereby, how powerful the 'blind spot' can be. It would be an easy thing to compose such an account so that the obtuseness of the disciples is spelt out, but in easily seeing their obtuseness the readers would fail to see it in themselves—they would not *experience* it in themselves. However, after having heard this passage read out and then being instructed in what informs it then the audience can have the 'aha!' moment and reflect upon why it was they did not see what is now so obvious. They would, in other words, have the conscious experience of how it is one can hear but *not* hear, see but *not* see—a passage from Isaiah that informs the meaning of the parables as given in that of the sower of the seed, a parable that is in some shape or form in all the Synoptic Gospels; a parable that more than any other encapsulates the power of blindness.[53] A parable that has as its denouement an abundant yield from a very small principle.

It is not enough to tell people that an ideology works such that the plain meaning of a passage can be obscured, rather it must be demonstrated; the student must be made to experience this ideological blindness in the very act of becoming aware of it. That the Gospels may have a performative character to them, if only in respect of the early Church's liturgy, is no new insight, but what I am arguing for here is a 'performance' that is both liturgical and critically reflective; that the two are inextricably entwined, for both are essential to the integrity of the covenantal communion that is the Church.

---

53 Matthew 13:1–23; Mark 4:3–20; Luke 8:1–15 (citing Isaiah 6:9–10). Indeed the parables are a case in point insofar as it is not uncommon even today to hear people say that Jesus was a master communicator in that he told easy to understand stories, namely the parables. Of course, the reason Jesus is recorded as giving for speaking in parables is somewhat different; it is to have people think they understand when they do not, or at least do not fully understand the meaning of the story all the while thinking that they do. Given the theme of Apostolic obtuseness presented in the Synoptics it is interesting to speculate as to what degree these Gospels represent an expansion upon and an extension of the theme of the parables as told by Jesus. That is they use the theme of 'seeing but not seeing' which when attended by the necessary instruction in the Apostolic Church enables the 'reader' to see how it is was he or she was seeing while all the time not seeing.

The Loss of Reciprocity and the Loss of Sight

When Jesus gives what has come to be known as the 'Golden Rule', that one ought to do to others what one would like done to oneself, as has often been pointed out he is saying little that is new, it being a principle that can be found in some shape or form in many disparate cultures and times.[54] What can be referred to as the 'principle of reciprocity' could be said to underlie and inform most law codes, if only in the most basic form of the *Lex Talionis*. It likewise informs the Torah being implicit in one of the 'greatest of the commandments' to love your neighbour as yourself.[55] By derivation this commandment can then be held to inform *all the laws*, hence it is *the* principle by which the covenant communion that is Israel existed and was preserved. But it is a principle that is itself derivative of the first and the greatest commandment, namely to love God with all one's heart and strength. Although there is a formal order between these two commandments they are not able to be abstracted one from the other: the love of neighbour which is the basis of and is the essence of communion is the necessary means by which the love for God is realised and nurtured. Thus, this principle of reciprocity is a transcendentally oriented principle, in that love directs our heart to that which we treasure, and if to God then our heart is oriented to that which is other to all creation.

If there is no love of neighbour as oneself then there can be no love of God.[56] And if there is no love of God then we have lost any real transcendent orientation; we are trapped within an immanent system of thinking and being.[57] The laws of Torah oriented Israel to the love of neighbour not least by prohibiting that which would work against this; that which would 'in-structure' an economy that is destructive of transcendence, namely an economy that practises usury and allows for the accumulation of wealth while impoverishing others. Usury is

---

54 Matthew 7:12 and Luke 6:31. For an overview of its different forms in different cultures see, Wattles, *The Golden Rule*.
55 Leviticus 19:8, 34. Matthew 22:39; Mark 12:30–31; Luke 10:25–28; also Galatians 5:13–15 and Romans 13:9.
56 Thus 1 John 4:20.
57 Usury, the scholastics argued, sins against natural justice and is thus inimical to the very constitution of creation; it has ontological ramifications. See Noonan, *Scholastic Analysis of Usury*, 54–55, 58. See too Franks, *He Became Poor*, 49–50.

destructive of the reciprocity and reflectivity necessary for the integrity of the covenant communion of the people of God, and is thus destructive of transcendence. As it is this transcendent orientation that informs the proper and full meaning of both creation and the Scriptures, as was understood in the STP by reference to time as constituted through the pattern of the jubilee, then a usurious economy will work to create a thoroughly immanentistic culture, a culture that is so powerful that it can blind us *to being blind*. A blindness that Jesus came to cure, which mission was then given to the Church. And this brings us back to the issue at the heart of biblical criticism, of which this work is intended to be a prolegomena of sorts.

Conclusion: The Return to Modern Biblical Criticism (MBC)

Much is made in MBC of its being defined by the practice of historical-criticism. Indeed, the term serves like something of a talisman to wave in the face of anything like a critique of MBC's right to authority over any competing theological claims. What is meant by the term 'historical-criticism', although not as a rule discussed or even defined, is in fact a particular form of criticism with a particular understanding of what constitutes history proper. It is this understanding that in turn informs the identifying of claimed sources and their authenticity or not. In the nineteenth and twentieth centuries, MBC would claim for itself the status of a science, by which was meant an objective and thus neutral discipline the method of which had recognisable procedures that had results that were testable. Few today would be so bold as to claim this for the discipline, indeed it is *de riguer* for any scholar who wants to be taken seriously to voice their critical reservations as to the historical-critical method. Yet rarely are the fundamental assumptions of the historical-critical method properly critiqued. I refer here to the topic that began this paper, namely what exactly is the concept of time that informs the use of the term 'history' in MBC? How does this inform its claimed ability to identify sources and then plot them in a posited history, thereby allowing a scholar to not only date the putative source but to pass judgement on its historical authenticity or not?

Whatever concept of time it is that informs MBC it is *not* a liturgical one, and it certainly is not one that is informed by a metaphysical and cosmological antipathy to usury and its diverse economic forms. Rather MBC operates within a concept of time that is attendant upon the rise of modern financial capitalism, the growth of international markets informed by such, and the rise of the modern nation state.

As was noted earlier this article is more in the way of a prolegomena for a critique rather than the critique itself. But with that proviso, there are two things that can be said to inform MBC—two things mentioned earlier. These are an antipathy to metaphysics and an attendant anti-clericalism, both of which inform the rise to dominance of a secular cosmology devoid of any intrinsic religious or moral value. A cosmos that having been abstracted from any transcendent authority can be subject to an atomising logic that renders all creation plastic. All can be fragmented, manipulated, and then reconstituted closer to the desires of those who hold power. It is a procedure that mirrors both the methods and the results of MBC. As with the jubilee eschatology of the STP, how the cosmos is read is how the Scriptures are read, albeit with a very different outcome for the modern period.

In practical terms what did this modern turn look like? First and foremost, it looked like the abstraction of the Scriptures from the covenantal community of the Church and their coming under the authority of the increasingly secular university.[58]

Certainly, there has been a move within biblical scholarship that argues that the place of the proper study of the Bible is the Church, only too much of this still implicitly accepts that the concept of time that informs the historical method of MBC is, at root, the right one.[59] Albeit there are some voices in the last few decades beginning to suggest otherwise.[60]

---

58 David Legaspi details this process in *The Death of Scripture and the Rise of Biblical Studies*, noting how it is often said that there is a crisis in biblical studies, and so there is but, he argues, this is resolved by accepting that the place of the Bible is in the secular university. Thus he writes, that the 'discipline is best understood as a cultural-political project shaped by the realities of the university' (p.7). Legaspi is in favour of this development.
59 See for example the essays in, Braaten & Jenson, *Reclaiming the Bible for the Church*.
60 For example: Evans, *The Historical Christ and the Jesus of Faith*; Rae, *History and Hermeneutics*.

Perhaps most alarming is the far too prevalent blindness to the necessity of a thorough going critique. Even when it is allowed that the method has failed, by reason, say, that its criteria is too loose such that it produces a myriad of different often contradictory results, this failure is not put down to the fundamental wrongness of those assumptions that inform the method, but to the intractability of the material being studied. The failure of the method is the fault of the text itself! The clearest example of this (in my opinion at least) is the recent avowal of the failure to arrive at the authentic words of Jesus by way of criteria that were always arbitrary at best, but a failure slated to the Gospels themselves as being hostile to historical vindication and not to the method itself.[61]

It has been said that since at least the 1970s there has been a growing crisis in biblical studies, and although there *should* be a crisis, in fact there is no such crisis; it is business as usual. Whatever else this tells us it says that there is so great an ideological investment in certain fundamental assumptions to MBC and the methods they inform that nothing short of a sustained revolution and purge will suffice to effect the radical change that is so urgently needed. Either that or the eschaton.

---

61 See the essays in Keith & Le Donne, *Jesus, Criteria, and the Demise of Authenticity*. I for one find it remarkable that even though M.D. Hooker, 'On Using the Wrong Tool', made some very trenchant criticisms of the 'criteria' almost 40 years ago they seemed to cause little concern. But then again if one looks back through the mainstream biblical studies journals one will find not a few such criticisms of the methods and sometimes assumptions employed, and yet all of this is far too easily assimilated, hence there is no 'crisis'.

Bibliography

Anderson, G. — 'From Israel's Burden to Israel's Debt: Towards a Theology of Sin in Biblical and Early Second Temple Sources', in E. Chazon (ed.), *Reworking the Bible: Apocryphal and Related Texts at Qumran* (Leiden: Brill, 2005), 1–30.

Bagley, P. — 'Spinoza, Biblical Criticism, and the Enlightenment', in J. McCarthy (ed.), *Modern Enlightenment and the Rule of Reason* (Washington D.C.: The Catholic University Pr. of America, 1998), 124–149.

Beale, G. — 'Eden, the Temple, and the Church's Mission in the New Creation' *Journal of the Evangelical Theological Society* 48.1 (2005), 5–31.

Bergsma, J. — *The Jubilee from Leviticus to Qumran: A History of Interpretation* (Leiden: Brill, 2007).

Braaten, C., & R. Jenson (eds.) — *Reclaiming the Bible for the Church* (Grand Rapids: Eerdmans, 1995).

Carlebach, E. — *Palaces of Time: Jewish Calendar and Culture in early Modern Europe* (Cambridge, Mass.: Belknap, 2011).

Carter, W. — *Matthew and the Margins: A Sociopolitical and Religious Reading* (Maryknoll, NY: Orbis Books, 2001).

Clarke, A. — '"Do not Judge who is Worthy and Unworthy": Clement's warning not to Speculate about the Rich Young Man's Response (Mark 10:17–31)' *Journal for the Study of the New Testament* 31.4 (2009), 447–468.

Collins, J. J. — 'Beyond the Qumran Community: Social Organization in the Dead Sea Scrolls', *Dead Sea Discoveries* 16.3 (2009), 351–369.

Culpepper, R. Alan — *Mark* (Macon: Smyth & Helwys, 2007).

Estelle, B. — *Echoes of Exodus: Tracing a Biblical Motif* (Downers Grove: IVP Academic, 2018).

Eubank, N. — *Wages of Cross–Bearing and Debt of Sin: The Economy of Heaven in Matthew's Gospel* (Berlin: de Gruyter, 2013).

Eubank, N. — 'Storing up Treasure with God in the Heavens: Celestial Investments in Matthew 6:1–21', *Catholic Biblical Quarterly* 76 (2014), 77–92.

Evans, C. Stephen — *The Historical Christ and the Jesus of Faith: The Incarnational Narrative as History* (Oxford: Clarendon Pr., 1996).

Fiensy, D. — *Christian Origins and the Ancient Economy* (Eugene: Cascade Books, 2014).

Fink, D. — 'Un-Reading Renunciation', *Modern Theology* 32.4 (2016), 569–593.

Franks, C. — *He Became Poor: The Poverty of Christ and Aquinas's Economic Teaching* (Grand Rapids: Eerdmans, 2009), 49–50.

Hagner, Donald — *Matthew 14–18* (WBC; Dallas: Word Books, 1995).

Hahn, S., & B. Wiker — *Politicizing the Bible: The Roots of Historical Criticism and the Secularization of Scripture 1300–1700* (New York: Crossroad, 2013).

Hansen, M. — '*Misthos* for Magistrates in Fourth-Century Athens', *Greek, Roman, and Byzantine Studies* 54 (2014), 404–419.

Harrison, P. — *The Bible, Protestantism, and the Rise of Natural Science* (Cambridge: Cambridge University Pr., 1998).

Hawkes, D. — *The Culture of Usury in Renaissance England* (New York: Palgrave Macmillan, 2010).

Hays, C. — *Luke's Wealth Ethics: A Study in their Coherence and Character* (Tübingen: Mohr Siebeck, 2010).

Healy, Mary — *The Gospel of Mark* (Grand Rapids: Baker Academic, 2008).

Herda, D., S. Reed, & W. Bowlin — 'The Relationship between Religious Beliefs and the Accounting and Economic Practices of a Society: Evidence from the DSS', *The Accounting Historians Journal* 40.2 (2013), 115–143.

Hooker, M. — 'On Using the Wrong Tool', *Theology* 75:629 (1972), 570–581.

Hudson, M., & M. Van De Mieroop (eds.) — *Debt and Economic Renewal in the Ancient Near East* (Bethesda, Maryland: CDL Pr., 2002).

Jeremias, Joachim — *Jerusalem in the Time of Jesus: An Investigation into Economic and Social Conditions during the NT Period* (London: SCM, 1969).

Jones, N. — *God and the Moneylenders* (Oxford: Basil Blackwell, 1989).

Kaye, J. *Economy and Nature in the Fourteenth Century: Money, Market Exchange, and the Emergence of Scientific Thought* (Cambridge: Cambridge University Press, 1998).

Kaye, J. *A History of Balance: 1250–1375* (Cambridge: Cambridge University Press, 2017).

Keith, C., & A. Le Donne (eds.) *Jesus, Criteria, and the Demise of Authenticity* (New York: T&T Clark, 2012).

Kennedy, J. *The Recapitulation of Israel; The use of Israel's History in Matthew 1:1–4:11* (Tübingen: Mohr Siebeck, 2008).

Kerridge, E. *Usury, Interest and the Reformation* (Aldershot: Ashgate, 2002).

Kraynak, R. 'Hobbes and the Dogmatism of the Enlightenment', in J. McCarthy (ed.), *Modern Enlightenment and the Rule of Reason* (Washington D.C.: The Catholic University Pr. of America, 1998), 77–91.

Kwakkel, G. 'The Reformation and Historical–Critical Research in Biblical Interpretation', in P. Berthoud & P. Lalleman (eds.), *The Reformation: Its Roots and its Legacy* (Eugene: Pickwick, 2017), 74–87.

Legaspi, David *The Death of Scripture and the Rise of Biblical Studies* (Oxford: Oxford University Pr., 2010).

Lioy, D. *Axis of Glory: A Biblical and Theological Analysis of the Temple Motif in Scripture* (New York: Peter Lang, 2010).

Matthews, M. *Riches, Poverty, and the Faithful: Perspectives on Wealth in the Second Temple Period and the Apocalypse of John* (Cambridge: Cambridge University Press, 2013).

McCall, B. *The Church and the Usurers: Unprofitable Lending for the Modern Economy* (Ave Maria University: Sapientia Press, 2013).

Morales, L. Michael *The Tabernacle Pre-figured: Cosmic Mountain Ideology in Genesis and Exodus* (Leuven: Peeters, 2012).

Morales, L. Michael (ed.) *Cult and Cosmos: Tilting Toward a Temple Centred Theology* (Leuven: Peeters, 2014).

Morrow, J. 'The Politics of Biblical Interpretation: A "Criticism of Criticism"', *New Blackfriars* 91.1035 (2010), 528–545.

Murphy, C.   *Wealth in the Dead Sea Scrolls and the Qumran Community* (Leiden: Brill, 2002).

Nelson, B.   *The Idea of Usury: From Tribal Brotherhood to Universal Otherhood* (Chicago: The University of Chicago Press, 1969).

Nolland, J.   *Luke 9:21–18:34* (WBC; Dallas: Word Books, 1993).

Noonan, J. T.   *The Scholastic Analysis of Usury* (Cambridge, Mass.: Harvard University Press, 1957).

Oden, T., & C. Hall (eds.)   *Mark: Ancient Christian Commentaries on Scripture* (Downers Grove: InterVarsity Press, 1998).

Ohrenstein, R., & B. Gordon   *Economic Analysis in Talmudic Literature: Rabbinic Thought in the Light of Modern Economics* (Leiden: Brill, 2009).

Rae, M.   *History and Hermeneutics* (New York: T&T Clark, 2005).

Reventlow, H. Graf   *The Authority of the Bible and the Rise of the Modern World* (London: SCM, 1984).

Sawicki, M.   *Crossing Galilee: Architectures of Contact in the Occupied Land of Jesus* (Harrisburg: Trinity Press International, 2000).

Scholer, John   *Proleptic Priests: Priesthood in the Epistle to the Hebrews* (Sheffield: JSOT, 1991).

Sheehan, J.   *The Enlightenment Bible* (Princeton: Princeton University Press, 2005).

Stone, M.   *Scripture, Sects and Visions* (Oxford: Blackwell, 1982).

Tilley, R.   'The Birth of Ideology: Genesis and the Origins of Self-Deception', *Crucible* 5:1 (2013), 1–22.

Tilley, R.   'The Biopolitical Economy of Anti-Essentialism', *Solidarity: The Journal of Catholic Social Thought and Secular Ethics*. 7.1 (2017), 1–27.

Vaage, l.   *Borderline Exegesis* (University Park, Pennsylvania: The Pennsylvania State University Press, 2014).

Walton, J.   *Genesis One as Ancient Cosmology* (Winona Lake: Eisenbrauns, 2011).

Walton, J.   *The Lost World of Genesis One* (Downers Grove: IVP Academic, 2009).

Wattles, J. *The Golden Rule* (Oxford: Oxford University Press, 1996).

Wilson, S. *Luke and the Law* (Cambridge: Cambridge University Press, 1983).

Witherington, Ben, III *Matthew* (Macon: Smyth & Helwys, 2006).

MATTHEW

CHAPTER 8

The Hermeneutical Significance of the 'Double Love Commandments' in Matthew's Gospel

Wendy Turnour

Abstract

This chapter argues that according to Matthew's Gospel, Jesus understands 'the Law and the Prophets', together with his own ministry (as the fulfillment of 'the Law and the Prophets'), in hermeneutical relation to the 'double love commandments'. They are embedded in the Gospel as its theological hermeneutical centre, their hermeneutical efficacy deriving from their being formative of God-centred community in response to divine grace. Understood in this way, they are the lens through which the Gospel, as a theological document, is best understood. Supported by historical, literary, and other analyses, their hermeneutic engagement resonates richly and harmoniously with key contours and content within the Gospel. The hermeneutic generates a different frame of reference within which to understand the text, different questions to ask of the text, and a different way of reading the text—producing a God-centred, relational and communal reading of Jesus' life, death, and resurrection, with major implications for the contemporary praxis of Christian discipleship.

Whether or not the Matthean 'double love commandments' (Matthew 22:37–39) are employed hermeneutically, and how their hermeneutic function is realised, significantly impacts our understanding of Matthew's Gospel and its expression in Christian discipleship.[1] The issue touches on complex questions lacking a scholarly consensus. In addressing the hermeneutical significance of the 'double love commandments', this essay argues three propositions. First, that the 'double love commandments' are foundationally about the formation of a God-centred community, in response to divine grace. Second, so understood, the Matthean love commandments are embedded as the theological hermeneutical centre within Matthew's Gospel, and therefore the interpretive lens through which the Gospel, as a theological document, is best understood. Third, engaging the 'double love commandments' hermeneutically in this way significantly impacts our understanding of Matthew's Gospel and its expression in Christian discipleship.

1. The 'Double Love Commandments' are Foundationally about the Formation of God-centred Community, in Response to Divine Grace

The 'double love commandments' are fundamentally about the formation of relationships in a God-centred community. Their hermeneutical significance is only fully appreciated when they are seen in the context of community formation as opposed to the perspective of western individualism, and when seen as response to divine grace rather than from a humanistic framework.

a. The First Love Commandment as Formative of Community

In Matthew 22:37 Jesus quotes from Deuteronomy 6:5, which, as part of the Shema, was integral to Jewish worship and culture and was therefore intimately familiar to the Jewish readers of Matthew's Gospel. Deuteronomy 6:4–5 has a complex history of interpretation, but the identity and unity of the people of God have remained central to its

---

1   Unless otherwise specified, biblical quotations are from the New International Version.

exegesis.² The text crystallises the very essence of Israel's identity as a people.

> 'Yahweh our God! Yahweh alone' ... This is what makes an Israelite a true Israelite. Whether they are descended from Abraham or not, the true covenant community consists of all and only those who make this their cry of allegiance, and who demonstrate this commitment with uncompromising covenant love.³

Patrick D. Miller recognises that '[a]s the people are addressed with the words "Hear O Israel, Our God is the Lord", they, too, are being identified'.⁴ However, not only identity, but also unity is effected through the proclamation of God's oneness and in the response. The communal response expresses total allegiance to God, who is separate from and over and above all other dominions, and those bound to God are also bound together into God's kingdom.⁵ Referrring to the use of these verses in Jewish liturgy, Laura Suzanne Lieber writes that 'The moment of recitation of the Shema is one of profound unity: Israel is united as one in the act of unifying God's name as one'.⁶ 'Affirmation of divine unity begets human unity'.⁷

The text is also communal in its context and its address. While love and obedience must spring from each individual heart, the text addresses a community of people about their relationship with God, which is covenanted at a communal level and manifested in its community life. Exegesis of the text in its context makes clear that the love-response to God forms the centre of community life in all its dimensions.⁸

In sum, whatever other exegetical emphases there may be, the first love commandment in its Deuteronomic context is basically concerned with the God-centred formation, identity, unity, and everyday life of the community of Israel. It is formative of community. Since Matthew's

---

2   McBride, 'Yoke of the Kingdom', 274–79, 304–06.
3   Block, 'How Many Is God?', 21.
4   Miller, 'The Most Important Word', 18.
5   McBride, 'The Yoke of the Kingdom', 278.
6   Lieber, 'Yannai on Exodus 3:1 and Deuteronomy 6:4', 211.
7   Lieber, 'Yannai on Exodus 3:1 and Deuteronomy 6:4', 215.
8   Block, 'How Many Is God?', 204.

Gospel has fulfillment of 'the Law and the Prophets' as a major theme, it is entirely reasonable to suggest that the first love commandment would have been understood in this way by both its author and its Jewish readers. This is borne out by the strong emphasis on community formation in early Christian exegesis of Matthew 22:37 which urges God's new chosen people 'to abide as one, bound together in the spiritual love manifested through the Christ'.[9] Individual love for God is integral to the commandment, but a reading solely focused around the individual's relationship with God is a reading conditioned by western individualism.

Both Deuteronomy 6:4–5 and Matthew 22:37, therefore, are directed towards the formation, identity, unity, life, and culture of a God-centred community.

b. The Second Love Commandment as Formative of Community

Turning to the second love commandment (Matthew 22:39), it is clear that if each individual authentically and habitually manifests loving attitudes and actions towards their neighbours, what is created over time is a networked community of people, characterised and held together by genuine mutuality in relationships, through which all members of the community benefit. The command to love one's neighbour is thus not only about being a 'nice' individual, as is sometimes the emphasis in contemporary Christianity, but about building and sustaining community.[10]

In a broader discussion of historical Jewish interpretation of this commandment, Ulrich Luz references the 'the overarching interests of the community', stating '[t]he concern of Leviticus 19:18 is to accommodate one's own claims with those of one's fellow Israelite within the totality of the community of Israel'.[11] Historical Christian interpretation, such as Calvin's exegesis of verse 39, draws attention to this function of the second love commandment: '[K]indness unites all in one body. And by correcting the self-love (φιλαυτίαν) which separates some

---

9   McBride, 'The Yoke of the Kingdom', 279.
10 Carson rightly objects to the tendency in western culture to reduce Christian discipleship to 'niceness'. 'Applied to Christians, the sentimental view breeds expectations of transcendental niceness. Whatever else Christians should be, they should be nice'. Carson, *Love*, 38.
11 Luz, *Matthew 21–28*, 83–84.

persons from others, he brings each of them into a common union, and—as it were—into a mutual embrace'.[12]

The formation of God-centred community is therefore foundational to both the first and second love commandments, in their Deteronomic, Matthean, and historical Christian contexts.

c. Relationship with God in This God-centred Community

Love, including love for God, cannot exist in isolation, but necessarily involves the existence of a relationship. In the Old Testament context, the God who is revealed in Deuteronomy 6:4 is a God who desires relationship.[13] However, Jesus' 'strongly relational teaching' remains challenging for Matthean scholars.[14] It is regrettable that the inherently relational nature of love for God has often been obscured by scholarly approaches which have subsumed the first commandment within the second, having too narrowly circumscribed the nature love for God, or focused on the theological and legal aspects of covenant rather than the relationship brought about through the covenant.

d. Subsuming the First Commandment within the Second

With respect to the first of these issues, Luz points to the error of earlier liberal theologians who, in conjoining the two love commandments, subsumed and lost the first commandment in the second.[15] Love of neighbour, insists Luz, 'is rooted in the relationship to God'.[16] Knox Chamblin's analysis of the Greek text makes clear that the second commandment 'is distinguishable from the first *(prōtē)*; nor does it rank with the first—which alone is the greatest *(megalē)* of all'.[17]

e. Delineating the Nature of Love for God

With respect to the second issue, we are indebted to Luz' expansive knowledge of the history of Christian thought concerning what it means

---

12 Calvin, 'Calvin's Commentaries'.
13 Lowcock Harris, 'Deuteronomy 6:4–9', 330.
14 Green, *The Message*, 236.
15 Luz, *Matthew 21–28*, 80.
16 Luz, *Matthew 21–28*, 87.
17 Chamblin, *Matthew*, 1099.

to love God. Luz loosely approves Fromm, who states that in the western theological and exegetical tradition the love of God is 'essentially a thought experience', and thus draws from Calvin's primary emphasis on love as obedience.[18] Notwithstanding the importance of this emphasis, it is nevertheless clear from Calvin's commentary on Matthew 22:34–40 that love and obedience are not to be entirely equated.[19] Luz's discussion of the issue gives significant weight to earlier Jewish interpretation of what it means to love God, justifying the western accent on love as knowledge and obedience.[20]

But since Jesus 'defines neighbor love much more radically than was customary in Judaism (Luke 10:25–37)', one must allow that his understanding of love for God may also differ from the Jewish interpretation of his contemporaries.[21] Daniel Patte affirms that this is the case:

> The Pharisees (and the Sadducees) totally misconstrue the relationship between God and human beings. For them there are two separate realms and thus one's relationship with God cannot be compared with one's relationship with one's neighbor. By contrast, for Jesus these two relationships are alike, and thus God is present ('close by') with human beings as the neighbor who shares someone's daily life.[22]

In sum, it seems that the relational nature of the first love commandment has been obscured by an interpretation of love for God within the western theological tradition as cognitive knowing and practical obedience. Even the Torah, with its emphasis on absolute holiness, does not exclude the possibility of a close and personal relationship with God, as demonstrated by the nature of the relationship that Moses and David experienced with God, and further illustrated by prophecies such as Jeremiah 31:31–34.[23] The astounding news of Matthew's Gospel is that, with the advent of Christ's birth, 'Immanuel [...] God [is] with us'

---

18 Luz, *Matthew 21–28*, 77.
19 Calvin, 'Calvin's Commentaries'.
20 Luz, *Matthew 21–28*, 85.
21 Blomberg, *Matthew: An Exegetical and Theological Exposition*, 335.
22 Patte, *Matthew*, 315.
23 Exodus 33:11; Acts 13:22; Psalms 18:1–6, 19; 23; 26:8; 27:4; 31:7–8; 34:8–10, 18; 51:10–12.

(1:23). This is the turning point at which relationship with God takes on radical new dimensions. Possibilities only foreshadowed earlier (for example in Exodus 33:11), here find fulfillment and become reality.

In Matthew's Gospel, the type of relationship that Jesus, Son of God, nurtured with his disciples is represented as indicative of the type of relationship that God desires with humanity—face to face, personal, rich in intimacy, holistic, and embracing the fullness of the human capacity of love.[24] It is noteworthy that throughout Matthew's Gospel, the cognitive elements of teaching and knowing are never extricated and sanitised from the messiness of actual human relationships.[25] Matthew's Gospel as a whole, therefore, cannot support 'accenting' knowledge and obedience to the relative detriment of other aspects of relationship; nor can exegesis of Matthew 22:34–40, which in Craig L. Blomberg's analysis involves 'wholehearted devotion to God with every aspect of one's being, from whatever angle one chooses to consider it—emotionally, volitionally, or cognitively'.[26] Neither analysis of the Gospel, nor exegesis of Matthew 22:34–40, support 'accenting' knowledge and obedience to the relative detriment of other aspects of a personal, holistic, loving relationship with God. The 'double love commandments', therefore, are foundationally concerned with the formation of relationships in a God-centred community.

---

24 The personal intimacy with God that characterised Jesus teaching about love for God is evident in many ways. For example, his teachings about prayer to God as Father (6:9) reference familial intimacy, as does his advocacy for prayer to take place in the secret privacy of one's room (6:6). In 12:48–50 Jesus refers to the disciples as brothers and family. Jesus is regarded as a friend' of tax collectors and sinners (11:19), and he even calls Judas 'friend' in 26:50, after he betrays him with a kiss (26:48). The King (God) refers to a wedding guest as 'friend' in 22:12. Jesus has significant conversations 'in private' with his disciples (17:19; 24:3), and their heart-felt horror (16:22) and grief (17:23; 26:75) on learning of the forth-coming crucifixion reflects the reality of a close, personal friendship between Jesus and the disciples. Consistent with intimacy with his disciples, Jesus spends his final hours together and shares the deepest agony of his soul with them at Gethsemane (26:36–42).

25 Jesus' ministry of teaching is inseparably interwoven with face to face touching and healing of people (Matthew 4:23–25; 8:1–3; 9:1–7, 11–13, 18–22, 31–32; 17:14; 19:1–2; 20:29–34; 21:14). Teaching and preaching happens in physical proximity to the people and in the context of the personal informality of everyday life, such as sitting together on a mountain side (5:1; 15:29; 26:30; 28:16), in people's homes (8:14–16; 9:10–11; 9:27–30; 12:46; 17:25; 26:6, 18, 57), in boats (8:23–27; 14:25–32), in cornfields (12:1–8), around children (18:1–6; 19:13–15; 21:15–16), travelling along the road (21:18–22), and over meals (14:18–21; 15:32–39; 26:19–29).

26 Blomberg, *Matthew: An Exegetical and Theological Exposition*, 335.

f. Love for God and Neighbour is in Response to Grace

The 'double love commandments' may not be reduced to humanism, but they are a response to divine grace. In Deuteronomy, Yahweh is identified to the people as 'your God'.[27] God chose and loved Israel, initiated the Abrahamic covenant, called them his people, and blessed them with salvation from Egypt and the promised land. All of these things were acts of grace initiated by God. The love that the people were commanded to give is in response to God's prior and sovereign grace.[28] 'The people are led out with the goal of service in response and gratitude to the one who sets people free'.[29]

Matthew's Gospel retains continuity with this theme. Jesus comes to his people as the promised Messiah (Matthew 1:1,6,17,18; 2:2,4; 11:2; 16:16,20; 22:42; 23:10; 26:68; 27:17,22). God's grace is manifested through his life, death, and resurrection.[30] He is the one who saves people from their sins (1:21; 9:2–6; 26:28), fellowships with diverse groups as his friends (11:19; 26:50), heals sicknesses and diseases, delivers from evil (4:24; 8:16,28–33; 9:32–33; 12:22; 15:22; 17:18), guides through the challenges of life (2:6; 9:36; 26:31), gives meaning in the face of hopelessness, conducts mission to the lost (6:25–33; 10:8,39; 16:25; 28:16–20), and offers eternal life (19:29).

Reading Matthew's Gospel through a relational lens, how could one do otherwise than respond in love to God's grace in Jesus Christ? Love for God, both in its Deuteronomic and Matthean context, is a response to the prior grace of God. Hence a relational understanding of the 'double love commandments', which while necessarily including individual love for God and neighbour, is foundationally concerned with the

---

27 God is identified as 'your God' 240 times in the book of Deuteronomy.
28 Willoughby, 'A Heartfelt Love', 37, 85. Osborne and Arnold, *Matthew*, 823.
29 Miller, 'The Most Important Word', 21.
30 Matthew's seven references to 'righteousness' (significantly more than the other synoptics) in no way undercut the pervasive presence of grace in Matthew's Gospel, as some scholars suggest (nor are they grounds for driving a wedge between Matthew and Paul). As the exegesis of Matthew 22:34–40 below makes clear, Matthew is keen to stress that the absolute, total love which God commands necessarily includes lived-out obedience. As is pointed out below, it is not necessary for the words 'grace' and 'love' to be everywhere used in the text for them to constitute a major thrust of the Gospel. Although the Gospel is a theological document, it is presented in narrative form, and good narratives depict 'grace' and 'love' descriptively, pictorially, and graphically—not linguistically as found for example in the theologically-grounded exhortations of the Pauline letters.

formation of God-centred community in reponse to divine grace. As will be discussed below, this understanding is central to fully appreciating their hermeneutical function in Matthew's Gospel.

2. The Double Love Commandments are the Theological Hermeneutical Centre of Matthew's Gospel

In regards to the the second proposition, in Matthew's Gospel Jesus understands both 'the Law and the Prophets' and their affirmation in and continuity with his own ministry to be in hermeneutical relation to the 'double love commandments'. This will be established by four arguments, outlined below (§§a–d), demonstrating that the 'double love commandments' are the theological hermeneutical centre of Matthew's Gospel. Further, it will be advanced that since the Matthean love commandments are embedded as the theological hermeneutical centre of the Gospel, they are the interpretive lens through which Matthew's Gospel, as a theological document, is best understood.

a. There is a Hermeneutical Relation between the Ministry of Christ and 'the Law and the Prophets'

According to Matthew 5:17, Jesus understood his ministry as the fulfillment of the Law and the Prophets: 'Do not think that I have come to abolish the Law or the Prophets; I have not come to abolish them but to fulfill them'. 'Fulfilment' has been identified by scholars as a major theme, if not, the major theme of the Gospel.[31] Since redactional studies have established that the New Testament authors were theologically intentional in their writing, it can be reasonably concluded that the author of Matthew's Gospel wanted his readers to understand and interpret Jesus' entire ministry as the fulfilment of 'the Law and the Prophets'. 'Fulfillment' here has hermeneutical import. The precise meaning of 'fulfill' in Matthew's Gospel is a matter of considerable scholarly discussion. The fulfilling of prophecy is relatively clear, but

---

31 Luz, *Studies in Matthew*, 76; Blomberg, *Matthew: An Exegetical and Theological Exposition*, 22, 30–32; Foulkes, *A Guide*, 3; Mitch et al., *Matthew*, 17; Talbert, *Matthew*, 8; Turner, *Matthew*, 25; Green, *The Message*, 53.

the fulfilling the commandments is less obvious.[32] Scholarly discussion becomes entangled with the complexities of the relationship between the Old and New Testaments, and the relationship between the Law and the Gospel.[33] Employing the 'double love commandments' hermeneutically, when understood as response to grace and formative of God-centred community, has implications for the meaning of fulfilment, to which we now turn.

b. There is a Hermeneutical Relation between the 'Law and the Prophets' and the 'Double Love Commandments'

In Matthew 22:36–39 Jesus references Deuteronomy 6:5 as the greatest, and Leviticus 19:18 as the second greatest, commandment. In Matthew 22:40 Jesus goes further by indicating the nature of the relationship between the 'Law and the Prophets' and the two love commandments. Most English versions translate κρέμαται (*krematai*) in verse 40 as 'hang on',[34] although almost as many translate it as 'depend on'.[35] Several translate it as 'based on',[36] with four other versions respectively using the phrases 'take their meaning from', 'stem from', 'are but variations on', and are 'about'.[37] D. A. Carson, translates the phrase thus: 'All the Law and the Prophets hang [lit., 'are suspended from'] on these two commandments'.[38]

In saying that 'all the Law and the Prophets hang on these two commandments', Jesus gives this relationship enormous significance. In Matthew's Gospel, 'the Law and the Prophets', and the 'double love commandments' do not exist as isolated entities. Rather they exist in

---

32 Moo, 'Jesus', 24.
33 Regarding Matthew 5:17–20 Carson comments: 'The theological and canonical ramifications of one's exegetical conclusions on this pericope are so numerous that discussion becomes freighted with the intricacies of biblical theology. At stake are the relation between the testaments, the place of law in the context of the gospel, and the relation of this pericope to other N.T. passages that unambiguously affirm that certain parts of the law have been abrogated as obsolete'. Carson, *Matthew (Chapters 1–12)*, 141.
34 ASV, BRG, DARBY, DLNT, GNV, JUB, KJV, KJ21, AKJV, NIV, NIVUK, NKJV, NRSV, NRSVA, NRSVACE, NRSVCE, OJB, WYC, YLT, MSG, MEV.
35 AMP, CEB, CJB, DRA, ESVUK, GW, GNT, HCSB, ISV, PHILLIPS, LEB, MOUNCE, NOG, NASB, NET, RSV, NLV, WEB, EXB.
36 CEV, NIRV, NLT.
37 ERV, TLB, VOICE, WE.
38 Carson, *Matthew (Chapters 13–28)*, 464.

relationship to each other, depending on each other. One ought not therefore seek to understand either 'the Law and the Prophets' or the 'double love commandments' in isolation or abstraction, or through some artificially imposed connection. Instead they are best understood in the context of their mutual relation. The visual picture created by verse 40 portrays a hermeneutical relationship, and they are properly understood in the interpretive light of this mutual relation. In fact, according to the redactional analysis of Eugene Eung-Chun Park, this is the point of this passage.[39] The religious experts here are testing Jesus on textual interpretation (Matthew 22:35-36).

Furthermore, in what sense do 'the Law and the Prophets' hang on the 'double love commandments', and what does this mean for the way in which 'the Law and the Prophets' are interpreted? By definition, these are hermeneutical questions.[40] This is not new. It is widely, though not universally held by Matthean scholars, that the passage intentionally establishes a hermeneutical relation between the 'Law and the Prophets', and the 'double love commandments'.[41] In coming to this conclusion, most scholars reference Birger Gerhardsson, who writes that 'Jesus' answer in verses 37-40 is [...] a very carefully formulated *hermeneutic program*. What we are faced with in these verses is nothing less than the Matthean Church's principles for interprertation and application of the inherited holy scriptures'.[42] The scholarly difficulty lies in delineating and explaining how it is that the 'double love commandments' function hermeneutically. Günther Bornkamm and others have argued for a 'new righteousness, which distinguishes the disciples of Jesus from the Pharisees and scribes'.[43]

From a canonical perspective, Jesus' words in Matthew 5:17-20, make it very difficult to sustain such a disjunction between the person and ministry of Christ and 'the Law and the Prophets'. Bornkamm and Gerhardsson's work has been widely discussed and critiqued. Carson and Moo correctly argue that Jesus did not pit the love commandments

---

39 Park, 'A Soteriological Reading', 64.
40 Thiselton, 'Hermeneutics', 279.
41 Luz, *Studies in Matthew*, 80. Osborne and Arnold, *Matthew*, 824.
42 Gerhardsson, 'The Hermeneutic Program', 134.
43 Bornkamm, Barth, & Held, *Tradition*, 31.

against the 'jot and tittle' of the Law (Matthew 5:18), but instead taught both. Nor does the passage establish 'the priority of love over the law', but rather it establishes 'the priority of love within the law'.[44] Luz's commentary on Matthew's Gospel also rejects such approaches:

> Whether the double commandment of love is a new principle for the interpretation of the law and the prophets is also a new question that presumably could have been posed in this manner only after the Reformation. Its guiding interest probably is to distinguish between Christianity (understood from the perspective of the Reformation) and Judaism. The answer will have to be negative: for Matthew also, as in Judaism, great commandments and the smallest commandments stand side by side (cf. 23:23), and the double love commandment probably does not constitute (as does perhaps Paul's 'law of Christ' (Gal 6:2) a 'canon' on the basis of which certain Torah commandments-for example, the ritual laws-could also be abolished.[45]

No clear consensus has emerged concerning exactly how the hermeneutical relationship between 'the Law and the Prophets' and the 'double love commandments' is to be delineated or explicated. The meaning of 'hang on' in verse 40 is not made explicit in the pericope, and scholars deduce the meaning from intratextual and intertextual references.[46]

But, as noted, the hermeneutical function of the 'double love commandments' is only fully and accurately grasped when these commandments are understood relationally, as formative of God-centred community, in response to grace. The love commandments truly *are* 'the Law and the Prophets' (Matthew 7:12) because they capture the divine purpose (i.e. ultimate aim, destination, goal, or end) of creating and shaping a God-centred community.[47] In Matthew's Gospel, God's on-going purpose expressed through Jesus', incarnation, life, death, and

---

44 Carson, *Matthew (Chapters 13–28)*, 465.
45 Luz, *Studies in Matthew*, 86.
46 Park, 'A Soteriological Reading', 68; Luz, *Matthew 21–28*, 80.
47 In regard to Matthew 22:40, Bertram writes: 'In the NT the law of love is everywhere regarded as preeminent. (cg. Rom. 13:9; Gal 5:14). The fact that love of neighbor is sometines mentioned alone, sometimes made secondary, and sometimes set alongside love of God, is of no essential significance'. Bertram, 'Κρεμάω', 468.

resurrection remains the creation of such a community.

Viewed hermeneutically in this way, 'the Law the Prophets' comprise a complex, dynamically evolving plan,[48] developed over centuries, and comprising various inter-related processes all directed towards these ends. These processes include progressive revelation, narrative, celebration, ritual, object lessons, teachings, instructions, correction, encouragement, hope, exhortation, rebuke, discipline, judgement, and so on. Concepts such sovereignty, holiness, faithfulness, sin, judgement, grace, forgiveness, redemption, and reconciliation, each of which relate to the restoration of a love relationship between God and humanity, were taught and then progressively ingrained in mind and culture, becoming integral to the framework and world-view of everyday life. They were not communicated at an intellectual level as abstract doctrines, but rather were explained by being played out once for all time, in a real-life drama in which people participated. In their historical context, all of the processes referenced in the 'Law and the Prophets', contributed some short or longer-term role in the teaching, building, shaping, preparing, and forming of this God-centred community over time. Everything in 'the Law and the Prophets' addresses some aspect of relationship with God, or relationships between people within this community. Not only the major commandments, but even the 'jot and tittle', the smallest letter or stroke of the law, had some purpose or role, at a particular point in time, in a complex, dynamic, and evolving process. According to the analysis of the 'double love commandments' above, this is the sense in which they function hermeneutically with respect to the 'Law and the Prophets'.

This perspective also brings some clarity to the question of how Jesus fulfills 'the Law and the Prophets'. In Matthew 5:17 Jesus speaks against abolishing the Law, and in 5:18 against even a dot passing from the Law. Given that these are related ideas, it reasonable to suggest that the terms 'fulfillment' and 'accomplishment' in the same two verses are also related. In fact, some translations actually translate γίνομαι (*ginomai*) in verse 18 as 'fulfilled', 'come to pass', 'has happened' or 'takes place'. The Greek word here, meaning 'to be', can also mean coming into existence or being born. The connotation in this context would be that not an

---

48 Deut. 4:32–40; Jer. 29:10–14; Eph. 1:4–12.

iota or dot would pass from the Law until everything comes into existence in the sense of having been given birth. The moment of birthing is the moment of a new beginning, and yet it is continuous with that which has gone before. The image is a powerful one and adds a new a dimension to our understanding. The process of forming a God-centred community bears some relation to the process of forming and birthing a baby. The Law is thus as an integral part of a dynamic process in preparation for everything coming into a new state of being, or being given birth through Jesus Christ. A child in utero in the early stages of pregnancy is substantially different from the child that is birthed at nine months. The existence in utero has completely gone, but at the same time nothing has been lost, not even the smallest jot or tittle of genetic coding.[49] Understanding the meaning of γίνομαι (*ginomai*) in Matthew 5:18 in this way potentially sheds light on some of the interpretive difficulties in relation to 'fulfillment' referenced above, including the Matthean 'antitheses'.

The hermeneutic suggests that in Jesus' interpretation of Law nothing has been abolished or removed, even though his interpretation may appear on the surface to be quite different from the original. Rather, the seed temporarily embedded and developing in and through the Law has been fully formed and birthed. Jesus is the pivotal point in the on-going process, or birthing, by which God is bringing everything to fulfillment. For example, with respect to the laws defining uncleanness, certain animals, menstruation, semen, child-bearing, sexual immorality, discharges and skin diseases, dead bodies and animals, and things touched by something unclean, were declared to be unclean or impure. Almost

---

49 We find a similar idea in the letter to the Hebrews. The reference to abolishing the Law in Hebrews 10:9 must be understood in a manner which is consistent with the reference to the Law in Hebrews 10:1—namely that 'the law has only a shadow of the good things to come and not the true form of these realities'. This perspective resonates with the analogy to childbirth above, the baby in utero being observed only as a shadow of the good thing that is to come. The form of the baby in utero early in his or her development is not in the same form as the final reality. Similarly, death is declared to be abolished in 2 Timothy 1:10 yet we know that people still die. Death is abolished in the sense that our earthly bodies are but a shadow of our heavenly bodies that will be revealed at the resurrection, when the process is completed. It would seem from Romans 8:22–23 ('the whole creation has been groaning as in the pains of childbirth right up to the present time. Not only so, but we ourselves, who have the firstfruits of the Spirit, groan inwardly') that the process of birthing is an on-going one.

every aspect of life appears affected in some way, possibly because of alienation from God and the associated curse in Genesis 3:16–19. Before relationship with a holy God can be restored, this general impurity or uncleanness must be addressed and remedied. This involves a long process—teaching people about existence, nature, and problem of un-cleanness, defining and recognising uncleanness, understanding the magnitude of the issue, learning to abhor uncleanness in everyday life, and finally completly eliminating uncleanness. The Law having prepared the way, the ministry of Christ is decisive in completely eliminating uncleaness (Matthew 8:2–3; 10:8; 11:5; 12:44; 23:25–26; 26:28; 28:3). This end could be not be achieved in any other way, and certainly not by obedience to the Law. Thus, when Jesus declares all foods clean, he is not abolishing anything, bur rather he is fulfilling the Law by completing the process which it began, and the end to which it points.[50]

Matthew's Gospel is broadly regarded as addressing Jews and constituting a 'bridge' between the Old and New Testaments.[51] In the parable of the wine and the wineskins in Matthew 9:14–17, Jesus interprets his ministry as bringing new wine in new wineskins, thus defining a new season: but he locates that new season within a continuing tradition, namely, the long, continuing tradition of wine-making.

To gather up our thoughts, there is a hermeneutical relation between 'the Law and the Prophets' and the 'double love commandments'. In the context of a question about textual interpretation (Matthew 22:34–40), Jesus' statement that '[a]ll the Law and the Prophets hang [lit., 'are suspended from'] these two commandments' intentionally establishes a hermeneutical relation. The meaning of 'hang on' in verse 40 is not made explicit in the pericope, and scholars have been left to deduce the meaning from intratextual, and intertextual reference. The nature of this hermeneutical relation is only fully and accurately grasped when the 'double love commandments' are understood relationally, as formative of God-centred community, in response to grace. Thus understood,

---

50 This declaration is made in Mark's Gospel, however, Donaldson writes that 'while Matthew softens the pericope dealing with ritual purity (15:1–20) by omitting Mark's editorial comment that Jesus "declared all things clean" (Mark 7:19), he nevertheless includes all the statements of Jesus (especially 15:11) implying just such a conclusion'. Donaldson, 'The Law That Hangs'.
51 Green, *The Message*, 37.

'the Law the Prophets' comprise an embryonic and complex, dynamically evolving plan comprising numerous inter-related processes, but all directed in some way towards the end of creating a God-centred community. In Matthew's Gospel, God's on-going purpose expressed through Jesus', incarnation, life, death, and resurrection remains the creation of such a community. Christ fulfills 'the Law and the Prophets' because he furthers this on-going process by bringing it to birth. Understanding the meaning of γίνομαι in Matthew 5:18 in this way sheds further light on some of the interpretive difficulties in relation to 'fulfillment' and the Matthean 'antitheses'.

c. There is a Hermeneutical Relation between the Ministry of Christ and the 'Double Love Commandments'

Consequently, in the Gospel of Matthew, the ministry of Christ is also to be interpreted in the light of the 'double love commandments'.[52] According to Matthew's Gospel, Jesus viewed both the 'Law and the Prophets' and his own ministry of fulfilment in hermeneutical relation to the 'double love commandments'. Just as the 'Law and the Prophets' are an expression of God's on-going grace in forming Israel into a God-centred community, so in Matthew's Gospel God's on-going purpose expressed through Jesus', incarnation, life, death, and resurrection remains the creation of such a community. This is now extended globally in the making of new disciples who are taught what Jesus originally taught the twelve (Matthew 28:18–20).[53] What the 'Prophets and the Law *prophesied* (ἐπροφήτευσαν) until John' (Matthew 11:13) is now fulfilled in the dominical teaching of Jesus on the Law (5:17–48;

---

52 This conclusion is consistent with that of Leonard Doohan who writes: 'Jesus centers his teachings on love [...] The greatest holiness to which the disciples are called is a life of faith in Jesus, manifested by love for others. All laws are secondary to and must be interpreted in the light of this commandment of love' (Doohan, *Matthew*, 134), and also with Stephen Barton's view 'that the double command to love God and neighbour expresses in a nutshell what practical spirituality is about according to Matthew'. Barton, *The Spirituality*, 22.

53 This analysis provides a more satisfactory answer to the question of how Matthew's Gospel helps Jewish readers and followers resolve issues and questions about Jesus and the Law, than Terence Donaldson's view which suggests that Matthew's Gospel merely papers over the cracks of dissonance. Donaldson, 'The Law That Hangs'.

28:20a ['teaching them to obey everything I have commanded you']).[54] Relatedly, in view of the hermeneutical centre of the double love commandments, it is also fulfilled in the continuing ministry of the risen Jesus through the promise of his Spirit to his community of love (Matt 3:11b; 10:20; 28:19).[55]

d. The Nature of this Hermeneutical Relation is that of Hermeneutical Centre

R. T. France describes the use of the word 'hang' in Matthew 22:40 as being 'graphic'.[56] It communicates a clear, visual picture of the situation. The 'double love commandments' belong at the centre of this picture for two reasons. First, everything in the picture hangs or is suspended from them.[57] The word 'hang' was used to describe things connected to an overarching principle;[58] so graphically, the metaphor creates a picture of just two overarching love commandments from which are suspended the massive corpus of 'the Law and the Prophets'. The picture created focuses the reader's attention on the central point from which everything hangs.

Second, the love commandments are the greatest and most important thing in the hermeneutical picture. The central focus of any picture is on the most important thing in the picture, and the love commandments are the most important thing in this picture. The text uses superlative force in testifying that these are the greatest commandments.[59] They demand absolute priority over the entire life and being of all humanity. They are at the centre of life in every possible way. Even hermeneutics itself must come under these commandments.

Therefore, in this graphic picture, Jesus is not depicting a hermeneutical relationship which is minor, peripheral or incidental. The love

---

54 In regard to Luke 16:16 and Matthew 11:13, Banks, *Jesus and the Law*, 217, notes that: 'Whereas Luke 16:16 simply states that the Law and the prophets were until John, Matthew inverts the order of prophets and Law, and inserts a reference to the fact of their "prophesying"'.
55 On the Spirit in Matthew, see Deines, 'The Holy Spirit in Matthew's Gospel'.
56 France, *Matthew*, 847.
57 Contrary to widespread understanding regarding 'hang' in this context, 'the image lying behind the concept is not, as Bauer (BAGD, *S.V.* 2.b) suggests, that of a door "hanging" on its hinges. No door "hangs" on a Greek "turner" (= socket in which the pivot of a door moved)'. Luz, *Matthew 21–28*, 85.
58 Luz, *Matthew 21–28*, 84–85.
59 Weber, *Matthew*, 358.

commandments are not one interpretive lens amongst numerous other interpretive lenses. Textual interpretation was a much debated issue at the time of Christ and Jesus, as a great and authoritative teacher, is here graphically depicting the interpretive centre of both 'the Law and the Prophets' and his own ministry which is in continuity with them. In Matthew's Gospel, they form the theological 'hermeneutical centre' through which Jesus' ministry is understood.

Understanding Matthew's Gospel 'in its own terms', requires endeavouring to understand the Gospel through its own hermeneutical centre—namely, the 'double love commandments'. Understanding the Gospel is this sense echoes Gadamer's project of seeking 'understanding' of a historical text, which is quite a different interpretive task from that of elucidating the historical context of a text, assessing the historical accuracy of the text, modernising a historical text for contemporary audiences, or finding meaning for 'me' the reader with varying regard for the text's literary or historical meaning.[60] While all of these scholarly approaches fall under the umbrella of 'biblical interpretation', they are quite different, though related, undertakings. Hermeneutics as 'the science of the methods of exegesis'[61] brings clarity to the differing objects that the differing methods of exegesis are designed to achieve, together with the contributions and weaknesses of each approach.[62] My primary concern here is with furthering the understanding of the final canonical form of Matthew's Gospel 'in its own terms'. Understanding Matthew's Gospel in this sense requires endeavouring to understand it through its own hermeneutical centre— namely, the 'double love commandments'.

e. As the Theological Hermeneutical Centre of Matthew's Gospel, the 'Double Love Commandments' are the Lens through which the Gospel is Best Understood

Biblical scholarship has established that Matthew's Gospel is theological in its content, purpose, and emphases. Anna Case-Winters writes

---

60 Gadamer, *Truth and Method*.
61 CODCC, 'Hermeneutics'.
62 Boxall, *Discovering Matthew*, 13, supports the necessity of a 'multi-pronged approach' for a 'well-rounded understanding of the Gospel'.

that 'Matthew is a blatantly theological book'.⁶³ The Gospel was written primarily with religious intention, about religious subjects, for religious purposes, and with particular religious emphases. Consequently, Matthew's Gospel must be viewed and understood primarily as a theological document, notwithstanding its historical and literary characteristics.⁶⁴ Just as it is appropriate and necessary to study historical and literary documents using historical and literary hermeneutics, it is appropriate and necessary to study a theological document using a theological hermeneutic.

Historical and literary methodologies provide valuable data concerning the historical and literary aspects of the Gospel, particularly concerning details which can only been seen under a historical or literary microscope. Such methods however were never designed and are limited in their capacity to understand the theological composition and meaning of Matthew's Gospel. As will be explained below, in comparison with other approaches, engaging the 'double love commandments' hermeneutically generates a theological frame of reference within which to understand the text, a different way of reading the text, and different questions to posit in relation to the text. All of this significantly impacts one's understanding of Matthew's Gospel.

3. Engaging the 'Double Love Commandments' Hermeneutically Impacts Understanding of Matthew's Gospel and the Praxis of Christian Discipleship

Reading Matthew's Gospel through the lens of the 'double love commandments' provides a different frame of reference within which to understand the text, different questions to ask of the text, and a different way of reading the text. This impacts the reader's understanding of Matthew's Gospel, and in turn, the praxis of discipleship by contemporary Christian communities.

---

63   Case-Winters, *Matthew*, 'Introduction'.
64   I do not mean here that Matthew's Gospel, as an historical theological document, should be treated in the same manner as contemporary theological documents.

a. A Different Frame of Reference Within Which to Understand the Text

First, the 'double love commandments' used hermeneutically create a God-centred, rather than an anthropocentric view of life and being. Absolute and central to every dimension of life and being, including biblical interpretation, is love for God, understood relationally, and having both individual and communal dimensions. The hermeneutic points the reader to this broad theological frame of reference from which the Gospel was written, and within which it is best understood.

Second, within this broad frame of reference, the hermeneutic brings the love and grace of God in the person of Jesus into the foreground of Matthean interpretation, because the 'double love commandments' are understood as response to grace. God first manifests and imparts grace and love, and (ideally) this is met with a personal and reciprocal response of love. This hermeneutic resonates richly and harmoniously with the text. Matthew narrates God's love and grace expressed through Jesus' life, death, resurrection and his on-going presence with his disciples. Grace is specifically identifed in Matthew 10:8 in a way that covers Jesus' entire ministry: 'Freely you have received; freely give'. Moreover, the word 'love' is referenced in a number of important contexts (Matthew 3:17; 5:43–46; 6:24; 10:37; 12:18; 17:5; 19:19; 22:37–39; 24:12). Reading from within this hermeneutic, the cross as the climax of the Gospel is the decisive act of love and grace. Matthew's descriptions of Jesus as one who will 'save his people from their sins'(1:1) and as a servant who came 'to give his life as a ransom for many' (20:28) point to this supreme manifestation of love and grace. Jesus' words in Matthew 26:27–28, referring to his blood being poured out for the forgiveness of others, are similarly to be interpreted as an act of love and grace.

Third, within the broad God-centred frame of reference created by the hermeneutical use of the 'double love commandments', the love and grace of God, which is foregrounded in the person of Jesus, has a particular purpose. The 'double love commandments' are understood as forming God-centred community. Hence in Matthew's Gospel, the purpose of the love and grace of God, manifested through Jesus is the bringing to birth of God-centred community. Again, the hermeneutic resonates richly and harmoniously with the text, with the overall purpose of God-centred community being reflected in numerous ways.

In the Gospel of Matthew, God-centred community is portrayed as 'God with us' (1:23). Matthew uses 'God with us' as an *inclusio* framing the entire Gospel, and the idea is everywhere present. The Gospel begins with the geneological characterisation of the community in Chapter 1, identifying Jesus as Immmanuel, God with us, in 1:18, and 1:23. The Gospel ends similarly. R.T. France writes that 'the last words of Jesus [...] echo the title with which he was first introduced in 1:23, 'Immanuel—God with us'.[65] According to Talbert, Matthew uses 'Emmanuel [...] when speaking of the divine presence in Jesus' and 'the ripple effect [...] is seen throughout the Gospel'.[66] Matthew's use of 'God with us' as an *inclusio* is in perfect alignment with the identification of the double love commandments, understood as formative of God-centred community as the Gospel's embedded hermeneutical centre.

The hermeneutic gives coherence to the five Matthean discourses, which together address the on-going formation of the kingdom community. The Sermon on the Mount outlines the foundational way of life in the kingdom community, centring on relationships between God and neighbours. The mission discourse in chapter 10 commissions and equips the disciples to go out and gather the lost sheep, incorporating them into the kingdom community. In the chapter 13 discourse Jesus encourages the fledgling kingdom community in a time of considerable difficulty: their future will bring growth and fruitfulness, even though for now they live as a minority amongst a wider community whose hearts are calloused, whose lives are like tares, and whose wickedness will eventually be punished. The chapter 18 discourse addresses the on-going maintenance of relationships within the kingdom community. The discourse in chapters 24 and 25 looks to the future, and encourages the community to persevere in faithfulness through persecution and hardship to final glory.

The hermeneutic draws attention to the communal dimensions of the cross as the pivotal point within a much larger narrative focusing

---

65 See France, *Matthew*, 'VI Galilee:The Messianic Mission is Launched 28:16–20'.
66 Talbert, *Matthew*, 16.

on the restoration of God-centred community.[67] Under the covenant, with which Jewish readers would have been very familiar, restoration of relationship with God through atonement was made not just for individuals, but for the whole Israelite community (Leviticus 16:29–34). The covenantal and communal dimension of the cross is referenced by Jesus at the Last Supper —'This is my blood of the covenant, which is poured out for many [...]' (Matthew 26:28).

Reading from within this hermeneutic, the much discussed 'Great Commission'of 28:17–20, is not an end in itself, nor does it supercede the primacy of the 'double love commandments'. The 'Great Commission' is also enclosed and framed by 'God with us'. Verses 17–18 reference Jesus, who now has all authority, being worshipped by the disciples, and verse 20b concludes with 'I am with you aways'.[68] In addition, the command is to make disciples of nations or people groups, who are to be baptised corporately into the triune name of God (verse 19), thus forming a God-centred community. They must then be taught 'all that I have commanded you' (verse 20a), presumably beginning with the greatest and most important commandments, which command love for God and neighbour, not evangelism as taught by some contemporary communities.[69] In commissioning the on-going formation of God-centred commmunity, the 'Great Commission' necessarily includes but transcends the evangelisation of individuals.

Fourth, within this broad God-centred frame of reference, the love and grace of God which is manifested in Jesus, whose purpose is the formation of God-centred community, is advanced by focusing primarily on relationships. Again the hermeneutic resonates richly and

---

67 In defining 'the gospel', Carson, 'Eight Summarizing Words', notes the following: 'For some Christians, "the gospel" is a narrow set of teachings about Jesus and his death and resurrection which, rightly believed, tip people into the kingdom. After that, real discipleship and personal transformation begin, but none of that is integrally related to "the gospel". This is a far cry from the dominant New Testament emphasis that understands "the gospel" to be the embracing category that holds much of the Bible together, and takes Christians from lostness and alienation from God all the way through conversion and discipleship to the consummation, to resurrection bodies, and to the new heaven and the new earth'.
68 Leim, 'Worshiping the Father', 83, writes 'Matthew navigates this unity-in-distinction [the relation between the Father and the Son] through his paternal-filial idiom; Israel's "Lord" has a "Son," who is likewise "Lord," the "I am he" who rescues and redeems (see the discussion above of 14:22–23). He too, therefore, receives the worship reserved for the one true God'.
69 See Hagner, 'Holiness', 179.

harmoniously with the text. The Sermon on the Mount outlines the foundational way of life in the kingdom community, expounding the qualities characterising relationships with God and with each other. In addition, the way Jesus goes about building the kingdom with his disciples is inherently relational.[70] His numerous everyday interactions with people are personal in nature, not distant and removed. His teaching discourses are not formal institutional lectures, but are relational in nature, invovling a relaxed low-key environment, with people gathering around Jesus, who is usually seated.[71] Finally, relationships of love for God, and love for neighbours are identifed as the greatest and second greatest commandments for Christian disciples.[72] The formation of a God-centred community is advanced by focusing on relationships.

Understood through this hermeneutic, the interpretive emphasis of the 'blood of the covenant, which is poured out for many for the forgiveness of sins' (Matthew 26:28), falls on the restoration of relationship with God, not on escape from divine judgement as has been emphasised by some Christian communities, historically. Matthew's Gospel gives considerable weight to divine judgement (for example 21:18-22,28-46; 22:1-14; 23:1-25:46), but the hermeneutic use of the 'double love commandments' focuses the reader on the restoration of relationships,

In conclusion, the hermeneutical use of the 'double love commandments' points the reader to the broad God-centred frame of reference from which Matthew's Gospel was written, and within which it is best understood. This perspective resonates richly and harmoniously with the contours and content of the text. It significantly impacts the reader's understanding of Matthew's Gospel, bringing into the foreground the love and grace of God manifested in the person of Jesus, drawing attention to Jesus' purpose of birthing a God-centred community, and the priority of relationships within the kingdom community.

---

70 Robert Coleman's small but iconic work excellently describes the authentic and personal relationships that Jesus had with his disciples. Coleman and Graham, *The Master Plan*.
71 Matthew 5:1; 13:1; 18:2; 24:3.
72 Matthew 22:34-40.

b. Different Questions Are Asked of the Text

Just as a literary hermeneutic asks literary questions of the text, and a historical hermeneutic asks historial questions of the text, so a relational and communal hermeneutic asks relational questions of the text. Since the 'double love commandments' are understood relationally, readers of the Gospel will ask of the text: Who exactly is this God who is to be loved? What is God's nature and his identity, character, actions, and purposes? What does the text portray as the nature and means of relationship with God? What is biblical love? Who are biblical neighbours? Such questions focus not only on individuals, but on their location-within-community, and the dynamic location of individuals and communities in relation to God's on-going and ultimate purposes.

c. A Different Way of Reading the Text

The 'double love commandments' (including the synoptic parallels in Mark 12:30 and Luke 10:27) are insistent that engagement with religion is comprehensive, and, necessarily, includes the cognitive capacities, as well as the 'heart', the 'soul', and the 'strength' as expressed through the resources and capacities of everyday life. As a religious text, the Gospel is intended to be understood and therefore it is only *fully* understood when it is read in a way that engages not only the mind, but also the heart, the soul, and the reader's everyday life. The hermeneutic requires that cognitive analysis and response together with 'heart and soul' responses, and lived out obedience are necessary and unified aspects of biblical interpretation and scholarly understanding.

Using the 'double love commandments' hermeneutically therefore invites readers to engage the text holistically, not only cognitively, but also with their hearts and souls, as well as through praxis. The text was not designed to be understood in abstraction and at a distance.[73] Like its hermeneutic, the text is personal. Questions asked by the reader may include: Who am *I* in relation to the text, the God in the text, and the communities of the text? Who are *my* neighbours? Do *I* love

---

73 Cf. Barton, *Spirituality*, 3: '[T]he Gospels are "faith documents" from start to finish — written expressions of profound encounters with the divine, intended to mediate those experiences to others as the basis for faith, repentance and new life'.

God and neighbour? What does this mean for me in relation to my will, my passions and desires, my innermost being, my feelings, my thinking about life and being, and my practical everday existence? Consistently approaching the text through a personal and relational hermeneutic over time opens up the possibility of encountering God in Christ, and of such encounters being life-transforming, as they were for the original disciples.[74] Consistently approaching the text through a personal and relational hermeneutic challenges readers concerning their relationships with their neighbours. Self awareness locates the reader as being somewhere on a continuum, between completely closed or completely open, either being completely positive or completely negative to the possibilities presented by the text. Readers will validly form different understandings and make diverse responses, some helpful and others deletarious relationally.

Employing the 'double love commandments' hermeneutically thus creates a different way of reading the text, one which, in Gadamer's words embraces 'the whole of our hermeneutic experience'.[75]

---

[74] In Matthew's Gospel through a relationship with Jesus, the disciples were transformed from fishermen (4:21–22) and tax collector (9:9), to religious leaders commissioned to go and make disciples of all nations (28:19). In discussing the way in which the indicative of divine enablement underlies the imperative in an ongoing way in Matthew's Gospel, Talbert, *Matthew*, 16, writes 'one would have to conclude that when Matthew uses the formula "with you" or "in your midst", he is speaking of God's prior enabling activity (the indicative), activity that empowers individuals to do the tasks set before them [...] In Matthew scholars have frequently noted the use of the phrase "with you" or "in your midst" in three texts: 1:23; 18:20; and 28:20'.

Talbert also notes (p.23) the transformative effects of being 'with' Jesus. 'In the Sermon on the Mount [...] Jesus says to his disciples that they are salt and light (5:13–14) and are sound trees that bear good fruit (7:17–18). That is, Jesus assumes that transformation of the disciples' characters has begun to take place. From the Gospel's plot, the only thing so far that could explain their transformation is the fact that, having been called, they followed Jesus (4:20,22). That is, they were with him, and this association had a transforming quality [...] The disciples' being "with him" has not only the philosophic frame of reference but also the overtones of being changed by beholding deity. In Matthew, then, for the disciples to be "with Jesus" is for them to be transformed by their vision of God-with-us'.

Further (p.18): 'For the period between Jesus' resurrection and parousia, there are the oft-noticed duo 18:20 ("Where two or three are gathered in my name, I am there among them"; (NRSV) and 28:20 ("I am with you always, to the end of the age" (NRSV) [...] In Matthew's schema, when Jesus is with the disciples, God is present with them. Moreover, in most cases the presence is obviously an enabling one'. Talbert, *Matthew*, 17. Similarly '[t]o be baptized into the triune name, therefore, is to enter into a bonded relationship that will provide one with the divine resources to enable following the guidance of what comes next (all that I have commanded you)'. He points also to the enabling power of revelation—from Jesus and the Father (pp.18–20).

[75] Gadamer, *Truth and Method*, xxii

d. The Implications for Christian Discipleship

Because of their hermeneutic centrality, their theological weightiness and force, and the importance that the text attaches to their priority, the 'double love commandments' should form the foundation for contemporary theologies of discipleship. First, the 'double love commandments' are embedded in Matthew's Gospel as its hermeneutical centre. They are the interpretive lens through which the huge volume of material on discipleship in Matthew's Gospel is to be understood. Used hermeneutically, they provide a God-centred, relational and communal framework within which to understand the text, bringing into the foreground the grace and love of God manifested in the person of Jesus Christ.

Second, the 'double love commandments' have the theological weight-bearing capacity to encompass all the life and being of the Old Testament and New Testament communities, and, crucially, contemporary Christian disciples. When Jesus declared in Matthew 7:12 that the command to 'do to others what you would have them do to you' *'sums ups'* or *'is'* 'the Law and the Prophets', he is saying that the great volume of material in 'the Law and the Prophets' can be reduced to a summary statement, without 'reductionism' in the sense of losing its integrity or meaning.[76] Detailed exegesis of the 'double love commandments' in their New Testament context reveal them to be broad umbrella

---

76 Bertram writes: 'In the NT the law of love is everywhere regarded as preeminent. (e.g. Rom. 13:9; Gal. 5:14). The fact that love of neighbor is sometimes mentioned alone, sometimes made secondary, and sometimes set alongside love of God, is of no essential significance'. Bertram, 'Κρεμάω', 468.

commandments, able to encompass all of life and being.⁷⁷

Third, the text, as noted, forcefully underscores that these are the greatest commandments. They demand absolute priority over the entire life and being of humanity.

The 'double love commandments' properly form the foundation for contemporary theologies of discipleship. It comprises thee key elements.

(a) Since the 'double love commandments' are understood as response to the grace of God manifested in the person of Jesus, Christian discipleship will be concerned initially with discerning the presence of Jesus and the manifestation of God's prior and continuing love and grace in any given context. Jesus'

---

77 Numerous scholars make this point. Osborne states that the double love commandments provide 'the vertical (God-oriented) and horizontal (others-oriented) poles of the Christian life'. Osborne and Arnold, *Matthew*, 824.

'Jesus answered in words that came from the Law (from Deuteronomy 6.5 and Leviticus 19.18) and that covered everything in relation to God and in relation to people. ... No one has ever given a better summing up of what God from human lives. It stands for us today, whatever our culture or circumstances, giving us what is most basic for those who would live as God's people in the world'. Foulkes, *A Guide*, 197.

'Combining Jesus' teaching here with his approach to the law, as, e.g., in the Sermon on the Mount, demonstrates that while the principle of love remains constant, applications vary for different circumstances'. Blomberg, *Matthew: An Exegetical and Theological Exposition*, 22, 335.

Chamblin, *Matthew*, 1106–07: '[t]he other OT commands do not therefore cease to matter; rather, they all depend upon — "hang on"... these two. God knows that his people need clear direction for obeying the two foundational commands; by means of all those other teachings in the "the law and the prophets" he expounds a host of ways in which love for him and for neighbour can find concrete expression. Jesus does the same, beginning with his discourse in Matthew 5:3–7:27... The primary ways to obey the commands of Deuteronomy 6:5 and Leviticus 19:18 are set forth in the Decalogue ... which both verses presuppose. The perspective of Jesus in Matthew 22:37–40 is one with that of the duplicate tables of the covenant, which comprehend the whole duty of man within the unity of his consecration to his covenant Lord'.

Davies and Allison, *Matthew*, 382: 'Love the Lord your God and love your neighbour: all the rest is commentary'.

France, *Matthew*, 843, 847: 'It is these two foci [ie the double love commandments] which provide the framework of the Decalogue, with its two "tables" covering these two aspects in turn. If the Decalogue is itself a sort of epitome of the law, these two quotations in turn sum up the Decalogue'; and (on 22:34–40) in relation to the 'graphic use of "hang" as a term for dependence ... the two texts chosen by Jesus are together sufficiently strong to bear the weight of the whole OT. This does not mean as some modern ethicists have argued, that "all you need is love," so that one can dispense with the ethical rules set out in the Torah. It is rather to say that those rules find their true role in working out the practical implications of the love for God and neighbour on which they are based. Far from making the law irrelevant, therefore, love thus becomes the primary hermeneutical principle for interpreting and applying the law'.

words 'surely I am with you always, to the very end of the age' (Matthew 28:20) create the faith-expectation that Jesus' presence and grace will continue into the future. Beginning with the awareness of, and responsiveness to the love and grace of God, corrects the anthropocentric and/or humanistic orientation of Christian discipleship often evident in contemporary western culture, as well as the barrenness of discipleship devoid of a deep experience and understanding of grace.

(b) Since the 'double love commandments' are inherently relational, it follows that Christian discipleship will prioritise the practice of love for God and neighbours. As reflected in the Matthean narrative, love is not abstract but necessitates authentic and personal relationships. Love for God is paramount and involves the whole of one's being—the mind, the heart and soul (including the will, passion, desire, and feeling), as well as social, economic, and political expressions.[78] Following the example of Jesus, love for neighbours is multi-dimensional and impacts the physical,[79] social,[80] emotional,[81] relational,[82] psychological,[83] mental,[84] and/or spiritual[85] well-being of neighbours.[86]

---

78 In relation to Deuteronomy 6:5, Block, 'How Many Is God?', 204: 'The common rendering of the last expression, *me'ōd* as "strength" follows the Septuagint, which reads [...] "power" [...] but again it flattens the nuanced reading of the Hebrew [...]. It should be understood in the sense of economic or social strength'. McBride, 'The Yoke of the Kingdom', 299: 'Moran brilliantly illumines the legal and political implications of the biblical concept which all too often has been characterized in largely moral, antinomic, and psychological terms'.
79 Matthew 4:23–24; 8:5–13, 14–15, 23–27; 9:1–7, 23–25, 27–31, 32–33, 35; 14:13–20, 34; 20:29–34.
80 Matthew 8:1–3; 9:1–7; 8:10–12; 9:20–22, 27–31; 11:19; 12:18; 19:13–14; 18:1–4; 26:8–10.
81 Matthew 5:3, 4; 11:28–30; 12:20; 14:27; 17:6.
82 Matthew 5:3, 7, 8, 21–48; 7:1–6; 12:7, 23, 48; 15:1–7; 17:27; 18:21–35; 19:1–11; 20:20–28.
83 Matthew 5:3, 10; 6:25–34; 11:28–30; 12:20.
84 Matthew 8:28–33; 11:1; 13:1–3.
85 Matthew 4:16–17, 23; 5:3; 6:1–24; 7:1–29; 8:16–17, 28–33; 9:1, 35; 11:4–5, 28–30; 12:13, 15, 22; 13:1–3; 15:8–20, 28–38; 18:15–17; 21:12–14, 28–45; 22:1–14; 25.
86 Not all of these dimensions are present in all relationships or all interactions. At the same time, the authentic, real-life interations and relationships in which Jesus participated were wholistic in their mulit-facetedness, and resist being separated out into physical, social, relational, psychological, mental, and spiritual dimensions as attempted here, in order to point to their full and multi-facted nature.

This approach impacts the contemporary praxis of discipleship, challenging many commonly found deficits within Christian communities—for example, institutional religion lacking an authentic, intimate, and life-transforming relationship with God; a limited understanding of what love for God entails and how it is expressed in everyday life; a limited understanding of who neighbours are, what love for neighbours entails, and how this is expressed in everyday life; engagement in social reform in the absence of authentic personal relationships with 'neighbours'; the practice of humanitarian work without due regard for the importance of evangelism in restoring each individual's relationship with God; the growing of authentic and loving churches, reflecting both God-ward and neigbour-focused love; and the focusing of churches on themselves rather than on their neighbours, who according to Jesus' explanation of the commandment in Luke 10:25–37 are the 'outsiders', not the 'insiders'.

(c) It follows that Christian discipleship is strategically directed towards the ultimate purpose of forming God-centred communities. Love for God and neighbours are not simply isolated interactions between individuals, but are the process by which community is formed. This community is brought about by reaching out to neighbours, embracing them, and forming networks of authentic relationships. The formation of God-centred community does not require that God is at the centre for all members of that community in the initial instance, or indeed, at any point in time. The testimony of the Gospels as well as contemporary experience suggests that the process often works in reverse; people become part of communities before coming to God (Matthew 4:24–25; 9:10–13; 13:33; 16:13–16). It is expected that 'the wheat' and 'the tares' will grow alongside each other, and will not always be distinguishable (Matthew 13:24–29).[87] The formation of God-centred

---

87 'Modern scholarship has made it plain that in the gospels the Kingdom cannot be identified with the Church'. Browning, 'Kingdom of God'.

community is complex and multi-dimensional, glimpsed partially now, but only ultimately brought forth at the eschaton (Matthew 23:37–39; 24:30–31). It differs from utopian visions of community rooted in human philosophy or ideology, and achieved by human effort.[88]

This further impacts the contemporary praxis of discipleship, challenging the individualism of western Christians. Examples are easily cited: the compartmentalisation of the spiritual life into the realm of 'private' rather than 'public', and 'individual' rather than 'communal'; the tendency within western culture towards an individualised spirituality without due regard for its communal dimensions; the perception of every-day (including vocational) tasks in isolation or abstraction rather than as a contribution to the God-ordained building of community; the passive acceptance of every-day institutions and organisations lacking the types of neighbourly relationships that would transform them into communities; every-day participation in systems or the achievement of outcomes without regard for the effect on 'neighbours' locally and globally; the priority of power, status, money, and things over people and relationships in everyday life, including individual, family, government, corporate, and cultural life; the reluctance to view people holding power and authority equally, as neighbours and servant-leaders within a given community, thus aiming ideally to estalish a community characterised by universal other-centeredness and mutual submission.[89]

In growing God-centred community, Christians imbued with the individualism of western culture may require insight and correction from other cultures in going forward with some of these aspects of Christian discipleship and vice versa. In pursuit of spiritual growth, those with power may require

---

[88] '[T]he kingdom of God is not to be equated with a human Utopia'. Browning, 'Kingdom of God'.

[89] '[T]here *are* important ethical and social consequences of embracing or entering the Kingdom, the coming of which is to be sought (Matt. 6:10). Social hierarchies and class discriminations are irrelevant (Matt. 22:9–10)'. Browning, 'Kingdom of God'.

insight and correction from those without power, and those with wealth insight and correction from those in poverty, and vice versa.

In sum, the 'double love commandments' form the foundation for contemporary theologies of discipleship. The hermeneutical employment of those commandments has significant implications for Christian discipleship. Discipleship begins with discerning the presence of Jesus and the manifestation of God's prior and continuing love and grace. In response, it prioritises authentic and wholistic relationships of love for God and neighbours, which embrace the totality of everyday life. Such relationships are to be more than isolated interactions between individuals; they are to be recognised as having communal dimensions, and directed towards the on-going formation of God-centred family, church, local, national, and global communities. A theololgy of discipleship founded on the 'double love commandments' comprehends the totality of everyday life in God-centred, relational, and communal terms.

Conclusion

This chapter has argued for three propositions. The 'double love commandments' are foundationally about the formation of God-centred community, in response to divine grace. They are the theological hermeneutical centre of Matthew's Gospel and the lens through which the Gospel is best understood. Last, engaging the 'double love commandments' hermeneutically impacts the understanding of Matthew's Gospel and the praxis of Christian discipleship.

Bibliography

Banks, Robert	*Jesus and the Law in the Synoptic Tradition* (Cambridge: Cambridge University Press, 1975).
Barton, S.C.	*The Spirituality of the Gospels* (London: Wipf & Stock, 2006).
Bertram, G.	'Κρεμάω (*Kremaō*) "to Hang" ', in G. Kittel, G. Friedrich, & G.W. Bromiley (eds.), *Theological Dictionary of the New Testament: Abridged in One Volume* (Grand Rapids: Eerdmans, 1985), 468.
Block, Daniel I.	'How Many Is God?: An Investigation into the Meaning of Deuteronomy 6:4–5', *Journal of the Evangelical Theological Society* 47.2 (2004), 193–212.
Blomberg, Craig L.	'Matthew', *Journal of the Evangelical Theological Society* 48.2 (June 2005), 383–85.
———.	*Matthew: An Exegetical and Theological Exposition of Holy Scripture* (The New American Commentary, 22; David S. Dockery, ed.; Nashville: Broadman 1992).
Bornkamm, G., G. Barth, & H.J. Held	*Tradition and Interpretation in Matthew* (London: SCM, 1963).
Boxall, I.	*Discovering Matthew: Content, Interpretation, Reception* (London: SPCK 2014).
Browning, W.R.F.	'Kingdom of God', *A Dictionary of the Bible. Online* (Oxford: Oxford University Press, 2019 2nd ed.).
Calvin, J.	'Calvin's Commentaries' (Westminster Press), ccel.org.
Carson, D.A.	'Eight Summarizing Words on the Gospel', Salem Web Network, www.christianity.com/newsletters/features/eight-summarizing-words-on-the-gospel-11597936.html?p=0.
Carson, D.A.	*Love in Hard Places* (Wheaton: Crossway, 2002).
Carson, D.A.	Matthew Vol. 1 (Chapters 1–12). *The Expositor's Bible Commentary* (Frank E. Gaebelein, ed.; 2 vols.; Grand Rapids: Zondervan, 1995).
Carson, D.A.	Matthew Vol. 2 (Chapters 13–28). *The Expositor's Bible Commentary* (Frank E. Gaebelein, ed.; 2 vols.; Grand Rapids: Zondervan, 1995).

Case-Winters, A. *Matthew: A Theological Commentary on the Bible* (Louisville: Westminster John Knox, 2015).

Chamblin, K. *Matthew (Chapters 14–28)* (A Mentor Commentary; 2 vols.; Dublin: Mentor - CFP, 2010).

CODCC 'Hermeneutics', *Concise Oxford Dictionary of the Christian Church. Online edition* (E.A. Livingstone, ed.; Oxford: Oxford University Press, 2014 3rd Ed.).

Coleman, R., & B. Graham *The Master Plan of Evangelism, Second Edition, Abridged* (Grand Rapids: Baker, 2010).

Davies, W.D., & D.C. Allison *Matthew: A Shorter Commentary* (London: Bloomsbury, 2005).

Deines, Roland 'The Holy Spirit in Matthew's Gospel', in Aaron White, David Wenham, & Craig A. Evans (eds.), *The Earliest Perceptions of Jesus in Context: Essays in Honour of John Nolland* (LNTS 566; London: Bloomsbury T&T Clark, 2018), 213–35.

Donaldson, Terence L. 'The Law That Hangs (Matthew 22:40), Rabbinic Formulation and Matthean Social World', *Catholic Biblical Quarterly* 57.4 (1995), 689–709.

Doohan, L. *Matthew: A Gospel for a Divided Community* (London: Wipf & Stock, 2016).

Foulkes, F. *A Guide to St Matthew's Gospel* (SPCK International Study Guides; London: SPCK, 2001).

France, R.T. *The Gospel of Matthew* (Grand Rapids: Eerdmans, 2007).

Gadamer, Hans-Georg *Truth and Method* (Joel Weinsheimer & Donald G. Marshall, transls.; London: Bloomsbury Academic, 1989, 2013).

Gerhardsson, Birger 'The Hermeneutic Program in Matthew 22:47–40', in R.G. Hamerton-Kelly & R.J. Scroggs (eds.), *Jews, Greeks and Christians: Religious Cultures in Late Antiquity: Essays in Honor of William David Davies* (Leiden: Brill, 1976), 129–151.

Green, Michael *The Message of Matthew: The Kingdom of Heaven* (Leicester: InterVarsity Press, 2000).

Hagner, Donald A. 'Holiness and Ecclesiology: The Church in Matthew', in D.M. Gurtner & J. Nolland (eds.), *Built Upon the Rock: Studies in the Gospel of Matthew* (Grand Rapids: Eerdmans, 2008), 170–187.

Leim, Joshua E. 'Worshiping the Father, Worshiping the Son: Cultic Language and the Identity of God in the Gospel of Matthew', *Journal of Theological Interpretation* 9.1 (2015), 65–84.

Lieber, Laura Suzanne 'Themes and Variations: Yannai on Exodus 3:1 and Deuteronomy 6:4', *Prooftexts* 30.2 (2010), 180–216.

Lowcock Harris, Sue 'Between Text and Sermon: Deuteronomy 6:4–9', *Interpretation* 70.3 (2016), 329–31.

Luz, Ulrich *Matthew 21–28: A Commentary* (J.E. Crouch, transl.; Hermeneia; 3 vols.; Minneapolis: Fortress, 2005).

Luz, Ulrich *Studies in Matthew* (Rosemary Selle, transl.; Grand Rapids: Eerdmans, 2005).

McBride, S. Dean 'The Yoke of the Kingdom an Exposition of Deuteronomy 6:4–5', *Interpretation* 27.3 (1973), 273–306.

Miller, Patrick D. 'The Most Important Word: The Yoke of the Kingdom', *Iliff Review* 41.3 (1984), 17–29.

Mitch, C., E. Sri, P. Williamson, M. Healy, & K. Perrotta *The Gospel of Matthew* (Catholic Commentary on Sacred Scripture; Peter S. Williamson & Mary Healy, ed.; Grand Rapids: Baker, 2010).

Moo, Douglas J. 'Jesus and the Authority of the Mosaic Law', *Journal for the Study of the New Testament* 20 (1984), 3–49.

Osborne, G.R., & C.E. Arnold *Matthew* (Grand Rapids: Zondervan, 2010).

Park, Eung Chun 'A Soteriological Reading of the Great Commandment Pericope in Matthew 22:34–40', *Biblical Research* 54 (2009), 61–78.

Patte, D. *The Gospel According to Matthew: A Structural Commentary on Matthew's Faith* (Minneapolis: Fortress, 1987).

Talbert, C.H. *Matthew* (Paideia Commentaries on the New Testament; Mikeal Parsons, C. & Charles H. Talbert, eds.; Grand Rapids: Baker, 2010).

Thiselton, A.   'Hermeneutics', in B.M. Metzger & M.D. Coogan (eds.), *The Oxford Companion to the Bible* (Oxford: Oxford University Press, 1993).

Turner, D.L.   *Matthew* (Grand Rapids: Baker, 2008).

Weber, Stuart K.   *Matthew* (Holman New Testament Commentary; Max Anders, ed.; Nashville: B&H, 2000).

Willoughby, Bruce E.   'A Heartfelt Love: An Exegesis of Deuteronomy 6:4–19', *Restoration Quarterly* 20.2 (1977), 73–87.

CHAPTER 9

The Now and Not Yet of Seeing Jesus of Nazareth Reading Matthew's Gospel as Narrative

Chris Booth

Abstract

This paper adopts a reader response approach to investigate the role that the sense of vision plays as an embedded textual device in the Matthew's Gospel. We will briefly consider a narrative critical method prior to conducting two close readings on two paragraphs from Matthew's Gospel (Matt 17:1–8 and Matt 28:1–15). This study is a contribution towards the understanding of the kind of discipleship promoted by Matthew's Gospel.

And Lord, haste the day when the faith shall be sight,
The clouds be rolled back as a scroll;
The trump shall resound, and the Lord shall descend,
Even so, it is well with my soul.

Horatio G. Spafford, 1873

βλέπομεν γὰρ ἄρτι δι' ἐσόπτρου ἐν αἰνίγματι,
τότε δὲ πρόσωπον πρὸς πρόσωπον·
ἄρτι γινώσκω ἐκ μέρους,
τότε δὲ ἐπιγνώσομαι καθὼς καὶ ἐπεγνώσθην.

For we see at present by the use of a mirror, indirectly,
But then it will be face to face.
At present I know in part
    But then I will know completely just as I have been known.

1 Corinthians 13.12

Narrative Critical Method

This essay uses standard narrative criticism techniques, with a particular focus on the sense of vision, to evaluate the impact of Matthew's Gospel on compliant readers. Matthew is a biblical narrative that works to substantiate the claims made about Jesus Christ within an eschatological framework.[1]

However, we should build on the definition of narrative a little more to understand what is meant by 'impact'. Donaldson states that 'narrative consists of a story, told in a particular way (to) produce a desired effect in the reader'.[2] This essay argues that the senses are textually embedded devices used by Matthew to engage the reader and produce a desired effect.[3] With the disciples acting as sympathetic characters, the reader is invited into the 'authoritative collegium' of being something of the 13th disciple in the narrative.[4] The minimal impact of the senses would be for the 'flesh and blood' reader to understand why Matthew employed them, only to disregard Matthew's desired outcome for that reader to live as a disciple. The maximal impact is the realization of Matthew's desired effect of flesh and blood readers becoming disciples of Christ.

Before evaluating how this impact occurs, we will briefly examine the framework used in this investigation.

---

1 Webb, 'Biblical Authority and Diverse Literary Genres', 598.
2 Donaldson, 'Guiding Readers — Making Disciples', 31.
3 Bolt, *Matthew: A Great Light Dawns*, 16–17; Cf. Bolt, *Jesus' Defeat of Death*.
4 Bauckham, *Jesus and the Eyewitnesses*, 94, quoting Gerhardsson, *Reliability of the Gospel Tradition*, 74.

Framework

As primary influences, this article draws upon Bolt, *Jesus Defeat of Death*, and Cooper, *Incorporated Servanthood*.[5] Cooper's influence is of particular interest, since it looks at the Gospel as a communicative event with the author sending the message or text to an expected reader profile with the aim of persuasion. The message itself is made up of a) the explicit content, or the text; b) the implicated premises or assumptions the author makes use of; and c) the conclusions that the author intends the receiver to make. This model can be used to examine how Matthew, the sender, uses vision as an implicated premise to assist the receivers to respond successfully with the conclusion of becoming an obedient disciple of Christ. During our close readings we will be working with the various narrative critical tools such as plot, setting and implied reader compliancy, but before we reach the close readings we must consider the key assumption being examined—the sense of vision.

The Sense of Vision and his use of the Old Testament

Matthew's use of the Old Testament is a strong implicated premise, as it is crucial to his desired impact. Matthew's objective in presenting Jesus is underscored by his demonstration of the fulfilment of Scripture. Something of Matthew's beliefs and values are portrayed through his use of Israel's Scriptures, which are present much more explicitly than in his synoptic companions.[6] On the assumption that the author knew the Old Testament particularly well, it is therefore prudent of readers of Matthew to appreciate the quotations, allusions, and echoes that occur throughout the narrative.[7]

Regarding the sense of vision, in *The Senses of Scripture: Sensory Perception in the Hebrew Bible*, Yael Avrahami argues that the sense of sight is the prominent sense within the Hebrew Bible through which the supernatural is perceived: 'The correlation between sight and

---

5   Cooper, *Incorporated Servanthood*, 14–47. Cf. Bolt, *Jesus' Defeat of Death*, for similarities.
6   Matthew contains fifty-nine citations of the Old Testament, compared with thirty-one in Mark, twenty-six for Luke, and sixteen for John. Matthew is the Gospel that most explicitly links with the Old Testament. Webb, 'Biblical Authority and Diverse Literary Genres', 599.
7   Hays, *Echoes of Scripture in the Gospels*, 10.

hearing in the Hebrew Bible is self-evident. There are frequent parallels between sight-hearing and eye-ear in the context of knowledge, learning and understanding'.[8] Avrahami's insight can be a point of departure for analysing how Matthew's OT-saturated mind may have used the senses throughout his narrative, as he pursues the goal of making disciples.

The apostle Paul looked towards the day when Christ's people will directly and perfectly see him face to face (1 Cor 13:12). In no way denying this beatific vision of Christ that is very much part of the Christian hope, Matthew's Gospel has a temporal use constrained to this age. The maximal impact of the narrative is to move the reader towards seeing Christ clearly *now* through *faith*.

With this 'broad brush' understanding in place, let us now consider our two close readings.

Matthew 17:1–8

Matthew's narrative is replete with vision language. It is in Matthew 5:8 (ὁράω), where it is inferred that the beatific vision impacts the present reality. Matthew 14:22–33 illustrates the link between faith and vision as Peter decides to see (βλέπω) the elements in preference to the God who is walking over them. In referring to Mark's successive boat scenes, Tannehill comments:

> Perhaps the reader would like to stand with Jesus, rather than to admit a similarity with the blind and fearful disciples, but this will become increasingly difficult in light of Jesus' demands. The implied criticism of the disciples threatens to become criticism of the reader.[9]

It is in reference to 'blindness' that opponents of Jesus who refuse the discipleship mandate are described as 'blind guides' (Matt 15:14–19). Our focus narrows shortly after Matthew 16:13–20, the turning point in Matthew's Gospel.

From Peter's revelation that Jesus is 'the Christ, the Son of the living

---

8   Avrahami, *Senses of Scripture*, 69–74.
9   Tannehill, 'Mark as Narrative Christology', 70.

God' (Matt 16:16), Jesus begins to show or demonstrate (δείκνυμι) to his disciples what needs to happen (Matt 16:21). Curiously, Matthew does not employ vocabulary of teaching or explaining, but uses a word that primarily means 'to exhibit something that can be apprehended by one or more of the senses'.[10] After Peter's ill-thought expressed in his rebuke of Jesus, Jesus explains the cost of discipleship, concluding that some 'will not taste death until they see (εἶδον) the Son of Man coming in his kingdom' (Matt 16:28). Matthew's regular employment of the sense of vision as an embedded textual device continues as he turns to the transfiguration account (17:1–8).

Matthew 17:1 acts as the stage directions or the setting for this scene. If the reader desires to be compliant, they move with the movement of the disciples up the high mountain. If this is the case, they are being brought up to this privileged location with Jesus. The last time Jesus acted in a similar way was in Matthew 14:22, which raises expectations for the reader even more sharply of something supernatural occurring.[11] Furthermore, Exodus 24 is echoed loudly with the parallel of three people coming up the mountain with Jesus (cf. Aaron, Nadab and Abihu and Peter, James and John).[12] Importantly, with Moses, when the three chosen ones and the other seventy elders went up they saw (ראה/ ὁράω [LXX]) the God of Israel (Exod 24:10). Such a 'shocking anthropomorphism' against the fear-riddled background of humans seeing God (Exod 33:20) and ceasing to live, is now made manifest in Jesus.[13] This suggests that the implied reader is expected to be reading with an anticipation that a similar engagement through the sense of vision is about to occur.

However, Exodus 24:9–10 describes something other than a direct vision of God. It is more of a vision of the heavenly temple.[14] Durham describes the event of Exodus 24:9–11 as less a vision of God and more

---

10 BDAG, 214–15. An illustration of how Matthew employs vision is actually found in BDAG's secondary definition 'to come to the understanding of something, notice, perceive, observe, find' which, contrary to first impressions, does not go against my argument. The NT examples BDAG employs for this secondary definition could fit within the primary use of the word (cf. θεωρέω 2.a.b.c).
11 Carson, 'Matthew', 384.
12 Davies & Allison, *Matthew*, 2.694.
13 Alter, *The Five Books of Moses*, 457.
14 Dozeman, *Exodus*, 567.

a theophany of the Presence of God from the prostrated position.¹⁵ With Jesus being alluded to as greater than Moses the setting begins to shape the reader's expected response.

Nolland describes this scene with people being taken aside as rare in Matthew's Gospel, emphasising the privilege that the disciples are afforded in witnessing such a scene.¹⁶ The rarity of Jesus 'taking' people aside is curious. He has elsewhere called them or approached them, but here, the distance seems to be controlled by the main character and not the narrator. Compliant readers read along with the disciples, particularly with those such as Peter, towards whom they are especially sympathetic (an ongoing effect of Matthew 14), and are therefore best situated to be swept up with the suite of experiences the disciples now encounter.

To summarise the amount of OT allusions to Moses in Matthew 17:1–8 is almost impossible. A survey of OT allusions within this scene, however, reveals a startling, but small, amount of visual language. The scene is described with echoes of Daniel 7:9, Exodus 24, Psalm 2 and Isaiah 42, but this is a scene that forces the disciples' faces to the ground in awe. The sense of hearing is engaged more. It was the hearing of God which terrified them (Matt 17:6), and his command to rise which got them up again (Matt 17:7). This is surprising because, of all Matthew's scenes, something as spectacular as the Transfiguration could be expected to impact the reader through vision as a textually embedded device. In fact, the disciples miss most of the visually stimulating sights. If we notice the saturation of visual language:

> καὶ μετεμορφώθη ἔμπροσθεν αὐτῶν, καὶ ἔλαμψεν τὸ πρόσωπον αὐτοῦ ὡς ὁ ἥλιος, τὰ δὲ ἱμάτια αὐτοῦ ἐγένετο λευκὰ ὡς τὸ φῶς.

> Moreover, he (Jesus) became transfigured before them, and his face shone like the sun, and his clothes became white as light.¹⁷

---

15   Durham, *Exodus*, 344.
16   Nolland, *Matthew*, 699.
17   This is perhaps more illuminating when compared with Mark and Luke. Note the difference. Not only was Jesus' face altered, but it also shone. This engagement creates a recognisable image for the reader, particularly when modified by the sun. Matthew also comments not just on his clothes becoming white but also the brightness. Light carries with it all the motifs associated with what is holy and right and what the disciples themselves should be striving to reflect (Matt 5:14).

it becomes apparent that, for the disciples, the visual action is more restricted (verse 8):

ἐπάραντες δὲ τοὺς ὀφθαλμοὺς αὐτῶν οὐδένα εἶδον εἰ μὴ αὐτὸν Ἰησοῦν μόνον.

And, when they lifted their eyes they saw no one, but only Jesus.

When they lift their gaze, they see Jesus alone. In a very busy scene, the engagement with visual images is rich, and yet perhaps it is the final moment when the disciples raise their eyes (v.8) that has the most impact upon the reader. The disciples raise their fearful eyes in response to Jesus' call and the reader, likewise, is reminded of the simplicity of the discipleship mandate. To raise one's eyes requires the conquering of fear through trusting in the voice of Jesus (Matt 17:6–8).

This is surprising. We read of the transfiguration, an extremely visual scene, and we expect a detailed description of what it looked like. Instead, Matthew alludes to the OT and tells us very little of what it looked like. The compliant reader is impacted with the sense of vision because the reader expects there to be visual cues. Instead, the reader is simply commanded to 'raise their eyes' to Jesus. The simplicity correlates to the profundity. To fulfil the discipleship mandate, the reader is to simply affix their eyes on Jesus—but this need not be in any physical way. Matthew does not directly immerse us in visual language here, but gives the compliant reader an understanding from the OT of who Jesus is. The disciples at Matthew 17:8 raised their eyes because they were obedient to Jesus's command and trusted in who he was. They responded with faith. Approaching the scene through the eyes of the disciples, this is also the appropriate response for those reading, as Matthew makes further disciples.

Matthew 28:1–15

The content of our second close reading, Matthew 28:1–15, forms an interesting contrast to the Transfiguration scene.

Once again, the plot up until this point has many examples of Matthew using vision in an interesting way. The healing of the blind in

Matthew 20:31 is of particular significance, in that it mirrors the call of the disciples but in reverse. Just before Jesus' long-awaited entry into Jerusalem, he heals two more blind men, who call him by his title 'Son of David' (20:31). Jesus responds by asking what they want him to do and, we read (v.33):

λέγουσιν αὐτῷ Κύριε, ἵνα ἀνοιγῶσιν οἱ ὀφθαλμοὶ ἡμῶν.

They said to him, Lord, Let our eyes be opened.

The next thing to flow from the narrative after their request is Jesus restoring their vision καὶ ἠκολούθησαν αὐτῷ, 'and they followed him'. This is almost a reversal of the initial commissioning of the disciples in Matthew 4:18–22. There Jesus called out his disciples and they followed him—well before fully 'seeing'. Here it appears that the physically blind recognise who Jesus is, his significance, and therefore, logically, it is their faith that leads to their healing (cf. Matt 13:15).

Matthew continues to use vision as the narrative pace increases from chapter 26 with some notable moments.[18] The conflict escalates with Israel in Matthew 26 as the plot to betray and arrest Jesus is carried out. Bolt highlights the curious and eschatologically loaded 26:58 as a plot point where Matthew uses vision as a textually embedded device.[19] Following Jesus' arrest 'Peter was following him at a distance, as far as the courtyard of the high priest, and going inside he sat with the guards to see the end'. What Peter has come to witness, 'the end', Bolt argues, is an allusion to Daniel 12:4, 9, 13, stating: 'whatever Peter was expecting as he walked into that courtyard that night, for the reader the language of "the end" is already loaded with overtones of "the end of the world", drawn from both Daniel and Matthew's previous narrative'.[20] The expectation that one should read the narrative via an apocalyptic lens and that 'seeing' is more than physical again impacts the reader by means of Matthew's OT allusions.

The final contextual key in approaching chapter 28 is the death of Jesus in 27:51–53. An interesting exchange occurs as the narrator tells us:

---

18   Cooper, *Incorporated Servanthood*, 208.
19   Bolt, 'Feeling Matthew Changing Us', 151.
20   Bolt, 'Feeling Matthew Changing Us', 151.

Ὁ δὲ ἑκατόνταρχος καὶ οἱ μετ' αὐτοῦ τηροῦντες τὸν Ἰησοῦν ἰδόντες τὸν σεισμὸν καὶ τὰ γενόμενα ἐφοβήθησαν σφόδρα, λέγοντες,

Now the centurion, and those with him who were guarding Jesus, saw the earthquake and what took place, they were filled with extreme fear, saying

Ἀληθῶς θεοῦ υἱὸς ἦν οὗτος.

Truly this was the Son of God.

The obvious question is how could a centurion who was at the foot of Jesus' cross see the temple curtain tear in two? It seems clear that the centurion did not experience some supernatural vision of all these things occurring, but what can be ascertained by his confession is that this group of men 'experienced the power of God' and recognised it as divine witness.[21] Matthew's use of vision here indicates that the centurion and his company understood their part in the greatest crime in the history of the world.

However, perhaps the supreme use of vision in Matthew's narrative is when *nothing* is seen, as chapter 28:1–15 reveals.

We have identified that the disciples are the characters with whom the reader is most sympathetic and yet they are absent from this scene. However, Matthew employs women in this scene, as he did in Matthew 27, as characters with whom the reader naturally empathises. The implied reader is not only sympathetic to the women, but the women are also allied to the disciples, and they respond as the disciples (whether intra- or extra- narrative) should, namely, with obedience.

In contrast to Mark and Luke,[22] Matthew does not load this scene with an abundance of information. Mark recalls that they went to the tomb to 'anoint' Jesus, where Matthew's account simply states they visited 'to see' (θεωρῆσαι) the tomb. It is not until verse 5 that the angel reminds the women of the purpose of their visit (ὅτι Ἰησοῦν τὸν ἐσταυρωμένον ζητεῖτε) and even then, the purpose is vague. The angel states that the reason why

---

21 Osborne, *Matthew*, 1047.
22 Bolt, 'Feeling Matthew Changing Us', 151, observes that Luke uses the sense of smell in his account.

they came to look at the tomb was part of their task in seeking the Jesus who was crucified, not the risen one. And when the angel does speak to them, such as in verse 7, Matthew adds an additional visual imperative (ἰδού, 'behold') that Mark and Luke do not use.²³

Another peculiarity only mentioned in Matthew is how the stone is rolled away. Both Mark (Mark 16:4) and Luke (Luke 24:2) simply have the stone rolled away. Matthew, however, paints a very 'visual picture' of the angel sitting atop of the stone after rolling it away.²⁴

Davies and Allison observe that, in contrast to the other Synoptics:

> The section is held together by several formal features. (καὶ) ἰδού stands near the beginning of each part (vv. 2, 9, 11); ἀπαγγέλλω appears in each (vv. 8, 10, 11); and words having to do with sight are abundant: vv. 1 ('to see the tomb'), 2 ('behold'), 6 ('see the place'), 7 ('you will see', 'behold'), 9 ('behold'), 10 ('will see'), 11 ('behold').²⁵

How this could impact the reader is fascinating.

Mary and the other Mary travel to see (θεωρῆσαι) the tomb.²⁶ The aorist infinitive of this verb has only been used by Matthew one other time, also associated with the women (27:55) observing the death of Jesus from a distance. Bolt notes that such a word is used, not for a passing glance, but a 'long, slow examination; a studied gaze'.²⁷ Now it is reused, perhaps to raise the expectation that their Lord is dead (cf. above, and the purpose of their visit). Again (28:2), much like the last time they looked upon Jesus (27:51,55), there is another earthquake. This time, ἰδού, divine action is far more explicit with the appearance of an angel of the Lord descending from heaven, appearing much like Jesus at his transfiguration (cf. Matt 17:2, 28:3). They see something 'completely unexpected'.²⁸ Verse 3 is rich with the language of vision, at the same time that yet another allusion to Daniel 7:9 is provided in

---

23 Nolland, *Matthew*, 1250.
24 Bolt, 'Feeling Matthew Changing Us', 152.
25 Davies & Allison, *Matthew*, 2.659.
26 Bolt, 'Feeling Matthew Changing Us', 151–53.
27 Bolt, *Matthew*, 254. cf. BDAG, 454. 'to observe with sustained attention'.
28 Bolt, *Matthew*, 254–56.

the mention of the angel's clothes. The women are told not to worry (by this stage the reader expects fear and supernatural events to be coupled together), because, as the angel says, 'he is not here, for he has risen'. After such a visually stimulating scene, the vocabulary of seeing is repeated 3 times (Matt 17:6, 10, which looks to v.17). Bolt comments:

> The angel then commands them to use their sense of vision, dramatically (v.6): 'come, see' (δεῦτε ἴδετε). Though they cannot see Jesus here, they will see him elsewhere (v.7): 'there you will see him' (ὄψεσθε). Just in case the angelic report was not enough, the fleeing women then meet the risen Jesus himself and he repeats the promise about the disciples' future sight (v.10): 'there they will see me' (ὄψονται)…

All this visual language provides a sustained 'inside view', which engages the readers as they see along with the characters and perceive what they perceived.[29]

The immediate response from those who would not fear, but believe in this good news, is to 'come and see'. This contrasts with what Cooper refers to as 'kingdom-blindness'.[30] Indeed, 'kingdom-blindness' is exactly what is on display in Matthew 28:11–15.

Ethically, the reader is left with a decision to make. To be a compliant reader, they must accept what was seen, believe and respond accordingly. The alternative is to still reach communicative alignment, and in one sense, see what happened (like the guards) but not respond in the manner appropriate to truly seeing. What is curious is that in a scene where it is revealed that the tomb is empty, Matthew uses a heavy concentration of graphic language. The absence of Jesus' body is flooded with an engagement of the sense of vision in a manner that is unique to Matthew. When contrasted to the transfiguration scene it is noticeable that this could be a trait of how Matthew tells his story. When there is something significant to see, visual language is reduced. When there is nothing to see, visual language abounds. Seeing, then, is to impact the implied reader to point them towards what is unseen, not what is seen.

---

29 Bolt, 'Feeling Matthew Changing Us', 152.
30 Cooper, *Incorporated Servanthood*, 135, 219.

Vision and the NT

The faith/knowledge and sight relationship extends through to places in the New Testament such as 1 Corinthians 13 when the eschatological vindication of seeing Christ will be realised by believers. Here also we see how Matthew's use of vision in places like Matthew 5:8 is complemented by the ability to actually 'see' something now through eyes of faith. Matthew 17 shows the importance of seeing Jesus is as much centred upon faithful obedience than it is visual impact. And with the absence of a visual cue, Matthew 28 pushes the reader to faithfully accept or reject the evidence. Seeing Jesus of Nazareth today is as simple as knowing Christ and believing. In doing so, the reader jumps the supposed 'historical gap' to live by faith and not by sight (2 Cor 5:7) and stand with the disciples on the mountain receiving the great commission to 'go and make disciples'. What better way to further the impact of Jesus of Nazareth for others today, than by allowing narratives such as Matthew's to do the work and persuade them, via the Holy Spirit, to repent, believe and become disciples.

Bibliography

Alter, Robert (ed.)	*The Five Books of Moses: A Translation with Commentary* (New York: W.W. Norton & Co, 2004).
Avrahami, Yael	*The Senses of Scripture: Sensory Perception in the Hebrew Bible* (The Library of Hebrew Bible Old Testament Studies; New York: T&T Clark, 2012).
Bauckham, Richard	*Jesus and the Eyewitnesses: The Gospels as Eyewitness Testimony* (Grand Rapids, Mich.: Eerdmans, 2006).
Bolt, Peter G.	'Feeling Matthew Changing Us: Sensible Story-Telling', in Peter G. Bolt (ed.), *Listen to Him: Reading and Preaching Emmanuel in Matthew* (London: Latimer Trust, 2015), 137–60.
———	*Matthew: A Great Light Dawns* (Sydney South: Aquila Press, 2014).

	Jesus' Defeat of Death: Persuading Mark's Early Readers (SNTSMS; Cambridge: Cambridge University Press, 2008).
Carson, D. A.	'Matthew', in *The Expositor's Bible Commentary with the New International Version of the Holy Bible* (Frank E. Gaebelein, ed.; Grand Rapids: Zondervan, 1984), 3–602.
Cooper, Ben	*Incorporated Servanthood: Commitment and Discipleship in the Gospel of Matthew* (London: T&T Clark, 2013).
Davies, W. D., & Dale C. Allison	*A Critical and Exegetical Commentary on the Gospel according to Saint Matthew. Vol 2: Commentary on Matthew VIII – XVIII* (ICC; London; T&T Clark, 2004).
Donaldson, Terrance. L.	'Guiding Readers—Making Disciples: Discipleship in Matthew's Narrative Strategy', in Richard N. Longenecker (ed.), *Patterns of Discipleship in the New Testament* (McMaster New Testament Studies; Grand Rapids: Eerdmans, 1996).
Dozeman, Thomas B.	*Commentary on Exodus* (ECC; Grand Rapids: Eerdmans, 2009).
Durham, John I.	*Exodus* (WBC; Waco, Texas: Word Books, 1987).
Gerhardsson, B.	*The Reliability of the Gospel Tradition (*Peabody: Hendrickson, 2001).
Hays, R.B.	*Echoes of Scripture in the Gospels* (Waco: Baylor University Press, 2016).
Nolland, John	*The Gospel of Matthew: A Commentary on the Greek Text* (NIGTC; Grand Rapids: Eerdmans, 2005).
Osborne, Grant R.	*Matthew* (Clinton E. Arnold, ed.; ZECNT; Grand Rapids: Zondervan, 2010).
Tannehill, Robert C.	'The Gospel of Mark as Narrative Christology', *Semeia* 16. *Perspectives on Mark's Gospel* (1980), 57–96.
Webb, Barry G.	'Biblical Authority and Diverse Literary Genres', in D. A. Carson (ed.), *The Enduring Authority of the Christian Scriptures* (Grand Rapids: Eerdmans, 2016), 517–614.

MARK

CHAPTER 10

Sometimes one word makes a world of difference: a return to the origins of Mark's Gospel (Mark 1:38)

Alan H. Cadwallader

Abstract

This essay isolates one Markan *hapax legomenon*, κωμόπολις, and explores its potential contribution to larger questions. When the scribal textual tradition is examined the traditions associated with the west appear ignorant of the word. Its use in Josephus and earlier ancient literature not only clarifies its meaning, but also reinforces its use in the east. The Byzantine use of the term is an appropriation from earlier days. The meaning of the word arising from the survey not only illuminates Mark 1:38, but, being eastern, it provides evidence relevant to the question of the Gospel's provenance.

Introducing the question[1]

In the urbane musings about various orators that Seneca the elder dispensed for sons and students in his *Controversiae*, comes this

---

1   I am indebted to the comments and insights on an earlier draft of the paper from Cilliers Breytenbach, and the participants in the seminar of the Centre for Biblical and Early Christian Studies at the Australian Catholic University, Melbourne, Australia.

double-edged swipe at a contemporary:

> Haterius bowed to the schoolmen so far as to avoid cliché and banality. But he would employ old words that Cicero had used but that had later fallen into general disuse, and these caught the attention even in that break-neck rush of language. How true it is that the unusual stands out even in a crowd!²

So also, the unusual stands out in the Gospel of Mark. The older commentators, trained in philology, noted the seventy-nine *hapax legomena* in Mark's Gospel, taking the New Testament as the parameters for the assignment;³ the number is slashed to thirty-eight if the Septuagint is added to the parenthesis of reference.⁴ Matthew and/or Luke determined that thirty-two words required replacement, by reason of narrative or stylistic considerations, just as Seneca implied about the necessary editing of Haterius' speech. More recent commentators have narrowed their attention to the *hapax legomena* that are found among the Latinisms (κεντυρίων, Mark 15:39, 44, 45; σπεκουλάτωρ, Mark 6:27; more doubtful *hapax* Latinisms are ξέστης, Mark 7:4 and Συροφοινίκισσα, Mark 7:26). These are turned to a study of provenance rather than comparative lexicography, with debates continuing over a Rome or Syria location for the origin of the Gospel.⁵ Either way, the study of Mark's *hapax legomena* is in substantial need of renewed attention. This essay isolates one *hapax legomenon* and explores its potential to contribute to larger questions.

The singular occurrence of κωμόπολις (Mark 1:38) meets all the requirements for the study of a *hapax legomenon*.⁶ *Hapax legomena* not only command attention because they are unusual, as Seneca suggested.⁷ They can also point to compositional interests, sources and contexts

---

2   Seneca *Contr* 4.Pref.9. (Loeb ed. Winterbottom).
3   Swete, *Mark*, xliv; Taylor, *Mark*, 44–45.
4   One *hapax legomenon*, κεφαλιόω (Mark 12:4 ἐκεφαλίωσαν), is probably a ghost, being an early transpositional blunder for κολαφίζω (ἐκολάφισαν) arising in the transmission of the text. Matthew's λιθοβολέω (Mt 21:35) became a ready-made, epexegetical assimilation for the difficult, transmitted Markan reading: λιθοβολήσαντες ἐκεφαλίωσαν. See Taylor, *Mark*, 474.
5   The dominant view has been that Mark writes in Rome; see Incigneri, *The Gospel to the Romans*. No consensus has resulted however, with recent scholarship swinging towards Syria. See Collins, *Mark*, 7–10; Mack, 'The Spyglass and the Kaleidoscope', 181–205.
6   Greenspahn, *Hapax Legomena*; Mardaga, '*Hapax Legomena*'.
7   Of course, other grammatical and syntactical features can arrest attention.

that contribute a wider segment of information than mere semantic content.⁸ This is not to require of such words an expanse of meaning such that if we don't understand them at all we lose the gist of a phrase or sentence. The 'rule of maximal redundancy' can guide us here, that is, 'to make it contribute least to the total message derivable from the passage where it is at home'.⁹ In this case, it is deceptively simple because the word is manifestly a compound word, a combination of κώμη and πόλις. We are invited by the word and the syntactical unit within which it occurs in Mark's Gospel, to recognise places of habitation that lie relatively near to Capernaum where the narrative has, to this point, been based (Mark 1:21–34). The call to depart (ἄγωμεν v.38b) combined with the directional markers ἀλλαχοῦ and εἰς and a relatively rare form of an indication of proximity—τὰς ἐχομένας¹⁰—are sufficient to give a rough idea of what is meant by κωμοπόλεις. These settlements are to be the recipients of Jesus' preaching (ἐκεῖ κηρύξω).

Certainly, the lexical resources and remarks of commentators have unwittingly been scrupulous adherents of this 'rule of maximal redundancy' even if in a misguided fashion. The 1838 lexicon of James Donnegan distilled the obvious 'a town of a size between that of a village and a city',¹¹ although some earlier lexica defined the κωμόπολις as an *oppidulum* (a little town), a colorful diminution of *oppidum*.¹² Most assessments claim that the absence of a wall was a critical characteristic

---

8   See, for example, Trites, 'The Importance of Legal Scenes ', 282.
9   Joos, 'Towards a First Theorem in Semantics', quoted in M. Silva, *Biblical Words*, 154.
10 Some older commentaries imply the expression is found in the LXX (Swete, *Mark*, 27, followed by Taylor, *Mark*, 184). However, the full expression τὰς ἐχομένας πόλεις does not occur in the LXX, though ἐχόμενος in the sense of borderlands (*of* Edom, Gilgal, Kedesh, Gibeah, spring of Enrogel) occurs in Num 34:3; Deut 11:30; Jdg 4:11; 19:14; 3 Rgns 1:9 *et al;* but cf 2 Rgns 13.23 (of Ephraim, closer in form but still with the sense of borderlands); cf also *Prop. Vit.* 1.1, 6. The closest is the synonymous τὰς πλησίον πόλεις which only occurs in 3 Macc 1:6. This last expression does occur occasionally in Josephus (*Ant* 6.1.1, 11.8.6 cf *BJ* 2.18.1).
11 Donnegan, *A New Greek and English Lexicon*, 789. Focant, *Mark*, 75 n17, is almost identical. Marcus, *Mark 1–8*, 202, is similar though tries to summons Mark's use of doublets (as in the temporal marker of 1:35) to elucidate what is here a single word, claiming 'the second term [ie πόλις] makes the first one more precise'. This seems to be stretching the doublet phenomenon into dubious service and does not credit that the word is used by other writers, with no sense of a 'doublet' in mind. Compare the descriptive translations of Mann, *Mark*, 217; Taylor, *Mark*, 184; Donahue & Harrington, *Mark*, 88; Gelardini, *Christus Militans*, 82; cf *LSJ* sv; *TDNT* IV.53.
12 Dawson, *Lexicon Novi Testamenti*; similarly, Schrevel, *Lexicon Manuale*, sv; Pasore, *Lexicon Greco-Latinum*, 425. The lexical suggestion seems to have been made by Erasmus. Cicero's use of *oppidulum* in *Quint. frat.* 2.11.3 shows the use of a diminutive as a ridiculing device; cf *Att.* 10.7.1. For *oppidum*, see Schleusner, *Novum Lexicon*, 968.

of *komopoleis* even allowing that they were more 'city-like' (*stadtähnlicher*)¹³ than villages. But Swete, following later Byzantine usage, allowed that the presence of a wall or even fortifications was not conclusive.[14] From the outset of modern criticism, the expanse of the settlement and the size of the population have been factored as determinative.[15]

The relation and distinction between a *komopolis* and a *polis* has been blurred firstly by a claim that Mark and Luke (in the parallel, Luke 4:43) were simply translating the same Aramaic source (מְחוֹזָא), in two different ways;[16] and secondly by an apparent lack of precision in the application of the terminology. As to the first, Joseph Fitzmyer, rightly, is extremely doubtful both about the handling of the Aramaic evidence and the implicit removal of the dependence of Luke upon Mark: 'It seems more likely that Luke has simply substituted a more usual Greek word for a rare Marcan one'.[17] As to the second, W. M. Ramsay, for example, takes a *komopolis* as distinguished by an ability to mint its own coins, amongst other marks that might generally be thought to apply to a city[18]—and he does not simply garner evidence from a later, Byzantine period. In one instance at least, a *komopolis* seems to be an association of villages.[19] Luke's redactional penchant for the display of *poleis* for the sake of his urbanized and Romanized 'most excellent Theophilos', thus converts even Nazareth into a city (Luke 4:29)—not bad for a settlement of perhaps 150 to 300 people.[20] Little wonder that Luke also

---

13 Strack & Billerbeck, *Kommentar zum neuen Testament*, 2.
14 Swete, *Mark*, 27; Schoff, *Parthian Stations*, 5, tries to bring out the distinction between κώμη and κωμόπολις in the 'Parthian Stations' of Isidore of Charax by translating the former a 'village' and the latter as 'walled village' though sometimes opting for 'town'. John Malalas writes of κωμοπόλεις in the time of Seleukos Nicator receiving walls, with no sense that this was a status advance (τὸ πόλις) but rather a strategic defence measure (*Chron.* 13.39.20–23).
15 Wilke, Clavis Novi Testamenti Philologia, 631, followed by Thayer, *A Greek-English Lexicon*, 367, both citing as a comparison the German *Marktflecken* which is probably the prompt to some modern assessments. Compare Dagron's coinage of 'bourgade': 'Entre village et cité', 29–52, supported by Varinlioğlu, 'Living in a Marginal Environment', 298.
16 Schwarz, '"Auch den anderen Städten"? (Lukas iv.43a)', 344.
17 Fitzmyer, *Luke I–IX*, 557. The word seems to connote significant centers for trade, even becoming the name of a large Jewish trade settlement on the Tigris (Jastrow, *Dictionary*, 757).
18 Ramsay, 'Some Recent Works on Asia Minor', 140.
19 Ramsay, 'Phrygian inscriptions of the Roman period', 387.
20 McIver, 'First-century Nazareth'.

converted Mark's *komopoleis* into *poleis*.²¹ Rhetorical flair has often been forgotten when Luke's adjustment of Mark has been assessed. It is likely that Luke was falling in with standard Greek and Roman literary practice of elevating settlement status as a means of accentuating the importance of events and persons associated with place.²²

So, what is this odd word doing in Mark? The Gospel contains quite common words that postulate a range of places and habitations even allowing that Mark discloses a preference for some over others.²³ These garner multiple appearances in the Gospel, as elsewhere in the New Testament: πόλις (8/164), κώμη (7/27), ἀγρός (8/37), χώρα (4/28), ἔρημος (7/48)²⁴ to which we should probably add γῆ (19/250), περίχωρος (1/9), πατρίς (2/8), ὅριον (4/12), τόπος (9/94)²⁵ θάλασσα (19/91), ὄρος (11/63), ὁδός (16/101),²⁶ even οἶκος / οἰκία (12/114; 17/94),²⁷ ἀγορά (3/11) and βασιλεία (18/162).²⁸ *Komopolis* needs somehow to be factored in relationship to this array of places of human interaction without being subsumed to any one of them,²⁹ especially κώμη, πόλις and ἀγρός given that each of these is sometimes proferred as the meaning

---

21 Compare the designation of Bethlehem in John 7:42 (κώμη) with Luke 2:4 where it gains all the dignity and status of a πόλις.
22 See Safrai, 'The Description of the Land of Israel in Josephus' Lands', 320.
23 Compare the discussion in Incigneri, *Gospel to the Romans*, 70–78.
24 The figures are adopted from Rehkopf, *Septuaginta-Vokabular*, who derives them from the usual lists, checked against Moulton, Geden, and Moulton's concordance. Minute variations may occur but the overall tendency remains secure. Vocabulary from the shorter and longer endings of Mark is excluded.
25 Five uses of τόπος are in combination with ἔρημος (Mark 1:35, 45; 6:31, 32, 35).
26 ἄμφοδον occurs once in Mark (11:4), strictly a 'dislegomenon' in the New Testament (with Acts 19:28).
27 See, especially, the observations of Leveau, 'Territorium urbis', 470.
28 Note τρίβος only occurs in the quotation from Is 40:3 (Matt 3:3, Mark 1:3, Luke 3:4). Τὰ σπόριμα (Mark 2:23) may convey a place designation (cf Xenophon *Hell* 3.2.10; Theophrastus *Hist. Plant.* 6.5.4); similarly, τὰ πετρώδη (Mark 4:16 cf Aristotle *HistP.* 549b14) and τὰ μνημεῖα (Mark 5:2, 5), πύργος (Mark 12:1 cf Josephus, *Jewish War* 3.2.3) and φυλακή (3/47). Κατάλυμα and ἀνάγαιον (Mark 14:14, 15) at least require consideration. Of course, full clarity about how a word is used in the wider discourse unit demands specific, individual analysis, including the use of a word in quotation from the LXX (eg σπήλαιον Mark 11:17) and a recognition that options in a semantic range may be housed by a single word.
29 Rogerson & Vincent, *The City in Biblical Perspective*, 56–57; Louw & Nida, *Greek-English Lexicon*, 1, 17–19.

of the term.³⁰ It is unsatisfactory to reduce the word to a 'Grauzone' between city and village.³¹

Accordingly, the primary aim of this paper is to address *where* the word κωμόπολις was applied and where it was elided. A secondary purpose of the paper, consequent upon the first investigation, is to distill any indications of what is meant by the term. Some observations on how Mark or Mark's source uses the word may then be possible. The analysis of the provenance and usage of the term may foster questions about the provenance of the Gospel itself, even allowing that the provenance of a single word cannot anchor a global assessment of the total work in which it occurs. The argument here cannot address the issue of sources.³² However, whatever conclusions about source(s) behind Mark 1:35–38(or 39) may be made,³³ it is too sweeping to isolate issues of sources from issues of provenance.³⁴ One must allow Mark a similar redactional capacity as that which Luke and the text's transmission history show, to be sure.³⁵ But Luke and later scribes executed their revisions in their own interests (however discerned) and those of their target audience.³⁶ That κωμόπολις remains (without explanation) in the text must be taken seriously—for author and audience alike. It is far too simplistic to wave the surrendering flag of verisimilitude at the use of an unusual word, especially if driven by a polemical intent to defend a certain provenance. At the very least, the consequence of the detailed analysis of this paper is that the common attribution of Mark's provenance to Rome cannot easily accommodate this small piece of evidence. This

---

30 So, for example, David Fiensy, 'The Galilean Village', 178–9 n4, suggests that the word may be equivalent to the phrase πόλεις καὶ κῶμαι in Matt 9:35; *Thesaurus Linguae Latinae* gives the meaning *conciliabulum* for the transliterated Greek *comopolis*.
31 So, Schuler, *Ländliche Siedlungen*, 27. Schuler is content however, and the word receives almost no analysis beyond noting its appearance in Strabo and Mark (only).
32 The quality of the Greek τὰς ἐχομένας κωμοπόλεις was early noted as standing somewhat apart from Mark's predilection for the verb ἔχω: Elliott, *The Language and Style of the Gospel of Mark*, 99–102. By contrast, later commentators could take the unusual phrasing as an indicator of Mark's redactional hand: Kee, *Community of the New Age*, 59. This problem of the isolation of sources and composition preoccupied a number of contributors to the Neirynck Festschrift, van Segbroeck, *The Four Gospels 1992*.
33 The passage is usually assigned to the evangelist's editorial activity (but see the previous note) rather than to a source: Collins, *Mark*, 177.
34 *Contra* Incigneri, *Gospel to the Romans*, 14, *et al.*
35 Compare Henaut, *Oral Tradition*, 120.
36 Best, 'Mark's Readers', 2.841.

hapax legomenon has not usually been factored into such assessments, except in the most general sense by those interested in promoting an agricultural setting.[37] This paper makes no decision about provenance (or the provenance of sources). It simply aims to highlight a neglected piece of evidence for the discussion.

The categories of evidence that gain attention are the variants that occur in the manuscripts of the transmission of Mark's Gospel, the usage of the term in a small coterie of writers during the Roman principate, the expanded frequency of occurrence in the Byzantine period, and the limited occurrence of the term in inscriptions. The cumulative weight points to this term coming from and witnessing to patterns of settlement, or more particularly, as one of the terms to describe certain patterns of settlement in the *eastern* part of the Roman empire, namely, Asia Minor, Syria and Parthia. This *hapax legomenon* re-opens an *a priori* case for a reconsideration of the provenance of Mark's Gospel.

The text itself in transmission

We have already seen that Luke's reworking of Mark 1:35–39[38] shifted the direction of Jesus' mission from *komopoleis* to *poleis* and suggested that Luke's rhetorical interests may have been responsible (rather than any failure to understand Mark's rare usage). This is one of the few passages of Mark that is not paralleled in Matthew. Even though the phenomenon of assimilation is quite widespread between Gospel manuscripts, there is debate about which Gospel receives the most harmonizations. Willem Wisselink argued that the most frequent occurrence of assimilations was applied to, rather than from, the text of Matthew.[39] Tjitze Baarda argued that Mark was most often the receptacle of harmonizations from other Gospels.[40] In any case, one would be unsurprised to find Mark being assimilated here to Luke (as in Mark 2:5

---

37 So, Theissen, *The Gospels in Context*, 238–9.
38 Marshall, *Luke*, 197: 'considerably edited'.
39 Wisselink, *Assimilation*, 86–8.
40 Baarda, 'ΔΙΑΦΩΝΙΑ–ΣΥΜΦΟΝΙΑ', 139. This judgment has a lengthy heritage: see Harris, *The Codex Sangallensis (Δ)*, 47.

from Luke 5:20, Mark 3:14 from Luke 6:13 amongst many examples).⁴¹ However this is not the case. Only one manuscript appears to assimilate to Luke here. Minuscule 69, a fifteenth century manuscript, reads εἰς τὰς ἐρχομένας πόλεις. In strict form, it is closer to Josephus (*Ant* 11.8.6) than Luke's ταῖς ἑτέραις πόλεσιν, if one corrects what appears to be a slip of the scribe's pen in the addition of a *rho* to the participle.⁴² But it is merely the shift of a single word that is apparent when it would have been as simple to adopt Luke's dative construction in its entirety. Earlier interpretation compensated for this in any case, with Luke, under John Chrysostom's control, providing the accepted channel for understanding the passage in Mark.⁴³

However, another variation that sequesters *poleis* occurs in Codex Sangallensis (Δ, 037) a ninth century bilingual (interlinear) manuscript. Its Greek text reads εἰς τὰς ἐχομένας κωμο καὶ πόλεις. The smaller Latin text added above the Greek reverts, as occasionally elsewhere, to the Old Latin, reading *in proximos vicos et civitates*.⁴⁴ It is likely that the Latin, even though in smaller script, has influenced the Greek here, given that the controlling concern is to make the Greek intelligible to Latin readers,⁴⁵ if not provide Greek training for Latin scribes.⁴⁶ The formal appearance of this manuscript is unusual because almost every word is followed by a punct (or point). This Latin practice, common in Latin inscriptions and frequent in Latin manuscripts, means that the *scriptio continua* so familiar in other Greek uncials,⁴⁷ has given way to segmented words. Sometimes the words have been segmented wrongly,⁴⁸ in part compounded by working from a *vorlage* that was constructed by sense lines.⁴⁹ Certainly the prime editor of the manuscript, Heinrich

---

41 So Metzger, *A Textual Commentary*, 77, 80. See also pp. 84, 87–8, 110, 113–4, 114–5, 116, 118, 119.
42 This singular reading, included (correctly) in Legg, *Novum Testamentum Graece*, had already been noted by Alford, *The Greek Testament Vol I*, 299.
43 Cramer, *Catenae Graecorum Patrum*, 1.279–81; see also Hörner, *Catena aurea deutsch*, 2.38–41.
44 The Latin in the codex has been shown to be a blend of Vulgate and several Old Latin forms. See Harris, *Codex Sangallensis*, 3–5.
45 Houghton, *The Latin New Testament*, 78.
46 Trobisch, 'Structural Markers', 178.
47 Compare, amongst uncial manuscripts of similar date, the eighth century Codex Basilensis (07), ninth century Codex Seidelianus (011), and the tenth century Codex Boreelianus (09).
48 So, Nestle, *Introduction to the Textual Criticism of the New Testament*, 72.
49 Rettig, *Antiquissimus quattuor evangeliorum canonicorum Codex Sangallensis*, XIII.

Rettig, noted frequent scribal confusions over letters.[50] Caspar Gregory discerned a 'scribe ... more used to writing Latin than Greek' and suggested that the manuscript may even have been produced at the monastery of St Gallen by an Irish monk.[51] No dot follows κωμο but this is a common (but by no means ubiquitous) practice for end of lines—the manuscript regularly allows part of a word to finish a line and continue the balance on the next. This separation of κωμο and πόλεις occurs in other manuscripts though these omit the separating καί. Rather a ὑφέν (loop) below the line links κωμο to πόλεις to overcome an apprehended separation.[52] The twelfth century minuscule 1282 and an eleventh century minuscule in the National Library of Greece (§118)[53] both carry this rare scribal feature.[54] It suggests that the scribes concerned, whether working orally or visually, were either unfamiliar with this unusual word or were expecting a somewhat more familiar κῶμαι καὶ πόλεις (see Mark 6:56; cf Jud 15:7)—though the usual sequence is the reverse (Matt 9:35; Luke 8:1; 13:22). They certainly were concerned that there be no misapprehension about the word used.

Another variation comes in Codex Bezae. It reads εἰς τὰς ἐγγὺς κώμας καὶ εἰς τὰς πόλεις. The appearance of ἐγγύς, unique in the Greek manuscript tradition for this verse, combined with the separation of the compound word, κωμόπολις, into its constituent parts has also been taken as the influence of the Latin on the Greek text.[55] The Latin reads *in proximos vicos et civitates*. The *proximos* ~ ἐγγύς equation is telling, especially as both recur in Mark 6:36[D], the Greek ἔγγιστα replacing κύκλῳ.[56] This suggests considerable activity expended on the text and thus dismisses, in my view, any speculation that the critical text of Mark

---

50 Rettig, *Antiquissimus quattuor evangeliorum canonicorum Codex Sangallensis*, XXIV–XXV.
51 Gregory, *Canon and Text of the New Testament*, 358. Rettig had indicated multiple monks had worked on the manuscript (XV). Houghton speculates that it may have been produced at the monastery at Bobbio in Ireland and brought across (*Latin New Testament*, 78).
52 For an explanation of this siglum, not noted by the grammarians, see Tsantsanoglou, 'Punctuation', 1331.
53 Not yet catalogued in the Nestle-Gregory enumeration.
54 The *Center for the Study of New Testament Manuscripts* has made possible a vast resource for scholars and I am indebted here to its work that has enabled recognition of this feature.
55 Harris, *Codex Bezae*, long ago recognised that this was a particular characteristic of Codex Bezae. See also, *Codex Sangallensis*, 1.
56 Harris, *Codex Bezae*, 89.

(εἰς τὰς ἐχομένας κωμοπόλεις) might be an adjusted homoioarchton of a Bezan-style reading in a *Vorlage* (εἰς ... εἰς).

The Old Latin, Vulgate, Syriac and Coptic also separate the compound word, though the Old Latin sometimes reads *castella* rather than *vicos*.[57] *Castellum* has the sense of a fortified settlement, such as a tower or a protected shelter and is often taken as the translation of φρούριον.[58] Here we are back to the question of walled townships. But what is clear is that the western tradition does not seem to know the settlement called a κωμόπολις even though the use of *castella* might hint at it. The one Greek manuscript that reads πόλεις (69) seems also to have been produced in the west. If Jean-Claude Haelewyck is correct in his suggestion that the Old Latin of Mark originated in North Africa,[59] the weight on the translation from the Greek is towards the substitution of a familiar word/phrase for an unfamiliar word, albeit a substitution made the easier because of the formal simplicity of the compound word. At the same time, the distinctive Latin then bent its influence back upon the Greek as we have seen in Codex Sangallensis and Codex Bezae. Put bluntly, the evidence of the manuscript traditions generally associated with the west reveals considerable disruption in the transmission of the reading κωμοπόλεις; this is likely to be because of ignorance of the word, or suspicion of a mistake in the form, or concern for the target audience. There was apparently insufficient 'oriental' flavor in κωμόπολις to save it.

Other ancient usage

As we dust ourselves off from this initial foray into manuscript transmission, it is time to turn to the somewhat limited occurrence of the word in other ancient writers. As it turns out, all are eastern in origin. Josephus can be expunged from the frame, even though there have been

---

57 *proxima castella* in ms a; *castella confinia* in ms b, according to Julicher, *Itala II: Marcus-evangelium*, 8.
58 Marquardt, *Römische Staatsverwaltung* I, 15, with supporting evidence.
59 Haelewyck, *Evangelium secundum Marcum*.

some venerable claims that he did use κωμόπολις.⁶⁰ Most scholars recognize that Josephus is inconsistent in the terms he uses for particular settlements, sometimes within his own works (in the exchange of πόλις and κώμη), sometimes in relationship to other writings.⁶¹ Explanations have ranged from the difficulty in expressing Hebrew designations for settlements, to the influence of Greco-Roman historiographical practices. It should also be factored that Josephus is writing in the west, substantially for (Roman) westerners,⁶² though Strabo and Isidore, our main dialogue partners, were hardly exempt from this, even if their purposes were different. Arguments from silence are notoriously fragile, but the absence of κωμόπολις in Josephus's writings is striking.

As we turn to literature earlier than Josephus, we find the hint contained in the transmission and versional history of the New Testament is clearly borne out. Abbott and Johnson's detailed analysis of Roman administration carefully distinguished the manner and terminology of governance in Italy and the west from that deployed in 'the Orient', as they called it. They relied, in their analysis of κωμόπολις, on the occurrences in Strabo, but credited the organization, along with other named groupings, to pre-Hellenistic Persian communities.⁶³ For them, κωμόπολις had no place in the west.

Strabo has an array of words for centres of human population. In addition to the ubiquitous πόλις and κώμη, he also uses πόλισμα and πολίχνιον, the former (πόλισμα) perhaps little more than a stylistic variant on πόλις,⁶⁴ the latter clearly a diminutive form. So, for example, when he turns to describe the district of Cataonia,⁶⁵ he comments on the fertility of the plain and notes that the people of this country

---

60 Swete, *Mark*, 27, claims κωμόπολις is found in *Antiquities* xi.86; Taylor, *Mark*, 184, slots the reference to *Antiquities* xi.8.6. They seem to have been confused by the use of *Ant* 11.8.6 as a demonstration of the passive participle of ἔχω in the phrase τὰς ἐχομένας κωμοπόλεις in the sense of 'surrounding', 'neighboring'. Josephus, as previously noted, writes of neighboring *cities* (πόλεις). I have not sourced their mistake. Wettstein, *Η ΚΑΙΝΗ ΔΙΑΘΗΚΗ*, 557, used *Ant* 6.1.1 to illustrate this use of ἐχομένας.
61 Safrai, 'Description', 320; Cohen, *Josephus*, 45 n79, 70 n5. Bosenius, *Der literarische Raum*, 177.
62 See McLaren, 'Constructing Judean History', 90–108.
63 Abbott & Johnson, *Municipal Administration*, 22.
64 Compare however, Ricl, 'Alexandreia Troas', 89–91, 95–106, who sees Strabo's use of πόλισμα as indicating smaller cities and also those placed in a subservient (and consorting) relationship to another dominant settlement:
65 *Geogr* 12.2.

(Melitene) has no city, a fair indication of Cappadocia as a whole.⁶⁶ Strabo mentions a noteworthy (possibly because singular) city (πόλις ἀξιόλογος) on the edge of the Taurus mountains that houses an important temple of Enyo.⁶⁷ And he uses the term we have previously come across in connection with the Old Latin reading *castella*, namely, φρούρια, for some 'strongholds' (Azamora and Dastarcum) in those mountains. Another Cappadocian district, Sargarausene, is noted for a river and a small town (Herpa), designated a πολίχνιον. Another district gains his attention for their ἐρύματα (Argos and Nora),⁶⁸ here meaning 'strongholds' rather than simply a walled protection, given that he mentions both their elevation and ability to withstand sieges.

When Strabo's documentary travelogue broaches the reign of Archelaus Sisines (36 BCE – 14 CE), he mentions his first royal city, Cadena, pleonastically if not curiously described as πόλεως κατασκευὴν ἔχον, 'having the construction of a city'. Immediately, Strabo moves on to mention Garsaüra, significant probably because this settlement became substantially rejuvenated in Archelaus' Augustan-backed reign and was renamed Archelaïs.⁶⁹ However, when Strabo mentions the place in its initial context, he describes it as a κωμόπολις, albeit a settlement that had previously known glory days: λέγεται ὑπάρξαι ποτὲ καὶ αὕτη μητρόπολις τῆς χώρας, 'This is said even to have existed as metropolis over the region'. Strabo seems particularly alert to the fluctuating fortunes of a settlement. Elsewhere he describes Thebes as a place which 'today does not preserve the character even of a respectable village'.⁷⁰ One can almost hear a prosaic echo of that acerbic wit, Stratonicus of Athens, 'This is no city; it is a pity'.⁷¹

The implications that flow from the beginning of this overview are:

---

66 *Geogr.* 12.2.6 (C 537).
67 *Geogr.* 12.2.3 (C 535).
68 *Geogr* 12.2.6. Elsewhere a φρούριον is indicated by inscription as not being independent of a city proper: *SEG* 4.671. One can readily imagine that stability would demand some formal relationship between φρούριον and πόλις.
69 Levick, 'Greece (including Crete and Cyrprus) and Asia Minor from 43 B.C. to A.D. 69', 672.
70 *Geogr* 9.2.5.
71 Αὕτη οὐ πόλις, ἀλλὰ μόλις *apud* Athenaeus *Deipn.* 8.352a (Loeb ed. Gulick).

i. the all-too-often-forgotten witness that places of settlement rise and decline in influence, size and population. Douglas Edwards reminds us, when commenting on Galilean villages, that they were not static, long-lived entities, not only rising and falling but sometimes disappearing entirely.[72] The same apparently can apply to cities, even metropoleis.

ii. The benchmark for Strabo at least in determining the terminology to apply to a settlement is the πόλις.

iii. A settlement that has gone into decline gains a revision of the terminology by which it is known, in this case from μετρόπολις to κωμόπολις and in the process loses the ability to have control over a wider region,[73] here χώρα, but presumably meaning the other settlements ranked below the metropolis in a designated region.

When we turn to a more famous settlement, Ilium (Augustus' re-naming after re-founding ancient Troy), the element of decline again appears with Strabo's deployment of κωμόπολις. The term is applied to the settlement when it first came under Roman control. It appears to have lain moribund for some time, even though one previous source for Strabo, Demetrius of Scepsis, graced the place with the name of πόλις though not even roof tiles on the buildings had been maintained.[74] Another source, Hegesianax, expected a settlement at Ilium that could sustain the role of an ἔρυμα, a stronghold, but left disappointed because its famous walls had all but evaporated. Strabo then relates further fluctuations in its fortunes until arrested by Rome's intervention (no doubt assisted by the propaganda benefits derived from tracking Aeneas' journey).[75] Strabo's account of Ilium's fortunes have caused some headaches for critics,[76] which need not detain us here. Some further implications can be drawn:

---

72 Edwards, 'Identity and Social Location', 359–62.
73 Note the warning in Robert, *Études Anatoliennes*, 46, about assuming that the loss of reference to a place as 'city' (πόλις) means the demise of settlement.
74 *Geogr.* 13.27 (C 594).
75 See *Geogr.* 13.27 (C 595).
76 Leaf, *Strabo on the Troad,* 141–4. For further consideration of Strabo's misdirection, see Ricl, 'Alexandreia Troas', 105–6.

iv. there is a certain level of flexibility in human settlement that can shift its function and therefore its designation.

v. walls become a key factor in the adjustment of that function. In the light of Ilium's decline, marked by the decay of walls (and roof-tiles!), a settlement can move from a designation of πόλις to κωμόπολις—and back again! It seems that this provided the reductionist basis for the twelfth-century, Byzantine biblical commentator, Euthymios Zigabenos, to hold that, as a city had walls and a village did not, then a *komopolis* partly had walls and partly did not!⁷⁷

Strabo has a third reference to κωμόπολις. It comes in his ventures beyond the region of Galatia, to Lake Tatta on its border with Greater Phrygia. He recalls by way of comparison about the depths of the wells on the plateaus of the Lycaonians, a settlement called Soatra, termed a κωμόπολις. Noteworthy in this regard is not decline but that this κωμόπολις is somehow tied to Garsaüra, a location that, a few lines later, is given the status of πολίχνιον, a 'little city'. This is the same designation given to a nearby (ἐνταῦθα) town more well-known (to us): Iconium. The phrasing is important κωμόπολις Γαρσαούρων πλησίον.⁷⁸ The situation of Soatra as 'nearby' / 'in the neighborhood' is indicated by πλησίον. Whilst this word is not in Mark 1:38, it is one of the three main alternatives used by Josephus to describe villages (in the main) that lie in the region surrounding a city.⁷⁹

Strabo proceeds to talk of the industry associated with this κωμόπολις, namely coarse wool-production, an industry that was highly lucrative and gave to a number of people great wealth (μεγίστους πλούτους). He mentions a contemporary, one Amyntas, ruler of Galatia, as owning more than 300 flocks in the region's territories. From this, we can derive further implications:

---

77 πόλις μέν ἐστιν, ἡ τετειχισμένη· κώμη δὲ, ἡ ἀτείχιστος· κωμόπολις [sic] δὲ, ἡ ἐν μέρει μὲν ἀτείχιστος· ἐν μέρει δὲ τετειχισμένη: *PG* 129.781–4.
78 *Geogr.* 12.6.1 (C 568).
79 So, πλησίον (*BJ* 1.17.3; 2.21.3; *Ant* 20.5.4); cf τὰς πέριξ κώμας (*BJ* 2.19.4, 3.7.1; 4.7.6 *et al.*); ἐχομένας (*Ant* 6.1.1; 11.8.6; cf *BJ* 2.18.1).

vi. a κωμόπολις was often if not usually tied to a larger entity, a πολίχνιον or, as a generalisation, a πόλις.

vii. a κωμόπολις was characterised by a level of industrial output that gave its inhabitants (and the settlement in consequence) a measure of renown and influence.

viii. a κωμόπολις can have a significant tie with a patron or leading man (perhaps even a tie assigned by a ruler as a 'boon').[80]

These eight implications about the meaning of κωμόπολις exhaust the usage in Strabo.

Another geographer adds to our evidence: Isidore of Charax. Again we are placed in the East, plying the trade route from the Levant to India by land. Although referenced by John Wettstein,[81] Isidore's material has been overlooked subsequently, possibly because of the fragmentary remains of his work. Seventeen brief fragments occur in Pliny the Elder's *Natural History*.[82] Though these do not refer to settlements, their presence assists with dating—probably to the period, even to the express commissioning, of Augustus in the first century BCE.[83] It seems that Isidore's writing, now dubbed the *Parthian Stations*,[84] was originally a full-scale, wide-ranging *Geographia*, similar to that of Strabo. What we do possess, outside Pliny's lemmata, is remarkably valuable for the light it throws on the boundaries of the Roman empire in the East and on trade routes connecting the empire through Parthia to the Indian sub-continent. As Fergus Millar writes,

> Isidorus' *Parthian Stations*, written while the area [Mesopotamia] was still part of the Parthian Empire, gives a strong impression of identifiably 'Greek' cities interspersed among other places

---

80 Athenaeus *Deipn.* 29f cf Mark 6:23.
81 Curiously, Schnelle, *Neuer Wettstein,* 82–3, has no reference to Isidore.
82 Pliny's use of 'Dionysius' is taken as meaning 'Isidorus' (*NH* 6.141). Pliny does not make use of any of the material of interest to this inquiry.
83 Schoff, *Parthian Stations,* 17. For further discussion of the question of dating see, Chaumont, 'Étude d'Histoire Parthe V', 63–66.
84 See Jacoby *Die Fragmente der Griechischen Historiker vol IIIC,* 777–85, (inexplicably Jacoby omits the introductory list); Müller, *Geographi Graeci Minores vol 1,* LXXX–XCV and 244–56. The main section of Isidore's writing that has survived, seems to have gained the title of *Parthian Stations* by the time of Pseudo-Lucian: Chaumont, 'Étude d'Histoire Parthe V', 64.

with non-Greek names; very significantly in view of what we have seen of settlement patterns elsewhere in the Near East, he gives several of these other places the label 'kōmopolis' 'village-city'.⁸⁵

The *Parthian Stations* tracks one route between Zeugma (Seleucus on the Tigris River) and the eastern Parthian outpost, Merv. It follows a particular method, providing the names of districts, cities and smaller settlements, sometimes with comments on noteworthy natural and constructed features and the founders. Sometimes also attention is drawn to where there is a place to stay—a station or caravanserai (σταθμός) —and above all, to the methodical provision of distances, measured in schoeni (σχοῖνοι). William Tarn considers that Isidore is following some official survey document serving Mithridates II (ruled 121–91 BCE), albeit adding his own comments. Indeed, Tarn dates this source to about 110–100 BCE.⁸⁶ This route-finder, known from two Paris manuscripts,⁸⁷ mentions four *komopoleis*.

These four settlements are named: Merrha, Nabagath, Allan and, probably, a place that received the name Basileia.⁸⁸ Three of the four places bear (transliterated) Aramaic toponyms. When these are locked into his sequence of cities and smaller settlements stretching along the Euphrates River, the pattern suggests that the Greek cities, identifiable not only through their names but through the occasional express notation in the text about their Macedonian / Greek foundation, had come to assert a measure of control over the population centres around them. The fourth *komopolis*, bearing the name Basileia, is distinguished by a temple of Artemis that was established not by Alexander but by Darius (Artemis Azzanathkona?).⁸⁹ It obviously held a certain pre-eminence and its Greek name may reflect this. Moreover, located in the vicinity

---

85   Millar, *The Roman Near East*, 442.
86   Tarn & Lee, *The Greeks in Bactria and India*, 54–55.
87   *Codd. Par.* 443 and 571. In these manuscripts, Isidore's material is included along with many other ancient writings (such as the Satires of Juvenal, in the former). Two other manuscripts owe their origin to these manuscripts, being copied from them in the sixteenth century; see Chaumont, 'Étude d'Histoire Parthe V', 67–8.
88   Schoff, *Parthian Stations*, 5, took the word descriptively: 'a royal place'; Chaumont, 'Étude d'Histoire Parthe V', 71, 81 [map], 83, 88, recognized, correctly in my view, a place-name.
89   Chaumont, 'Étude d'Histoire Parthe V', 84, 92.

was the engineered 'canal of Semiramis' that seems to have had a particular function of controlling the flow of the Euphrates for agricultural and mercantile interests. Christopher Tuplin suggests that this place-name corresponds to that of Aphphadana (for Apadana) listed in Ptolemy's *Geography* (5.17.5),[90] confirming the sense not only that *komopoleis* were tied in some ways to cities and perhaps *metropoleis* but that such a tie was frequently imposed by incoming foreign powers. Cities became the ongoing instrument of control by these powers as well as indicating the supremacy of the newcomers over antecedent peoples, whether by their location in the cities (if pre-existing) or in settlements in the surrounding countryside. Apadana is mentioned in the margins of a diplomatic instruction for reception of a Parthian ambassador (c. 208–9 CE), which implies that the settlement was a Roman military post.[91] Another of these *komopoleis*, Merrha, is described as an ὀχύρωμα, a stronghold or fortress, but it is not mentioned as such in Roman military correspondence of Dura-Europos, suggesting that Roman appraisal of strategic benefit had privileged Basileia over Merrha. Interestingly, Nabagath, is mentioned as the transit point for infantry (τὰ στρατόπεδα)[92] crossing into or out of Parthian territory. It is likely that the standard mirroring of hierarchical relationships was in place, given the mention that the village of Phaliga was nearby to the *komopolis* of Nabagath (παράκειται δὲ τῆι Φάλιγα κωμόπολις Ναβαγάθ). This implies a tie beyond merely geographical proximity.[93] Two hundred years later, Nabagath will be described as a κώμη, meaning either imprecision in these classifications or a diminution of size and status. The fact that this later reference comes in a contract struck at Dura-Europos for the purchase of a vineyard lying in pastureland at Nabagath, clearly points to a requisite tie of a village to a city, even though the contract was between two brothers, one of whom lived in the village.[94] The land is

---

90 Tuplin, 'On the track of the ten thousand', 355 n42. Chaumont, 'Étude d'Histoire Parthe V', 83.
91 *P. Dura* 60B; see Chaumont, 'Étude d'Histoire Parthe V', 87–8.
92 This probably means Parthian troops (compre Herodotus 1.76; 9.51, 53), though στρατόπεδα was also used of the Roman legion: Polybius 1.16.2.
93 Note however that Michal Gawlikowski, 'Thapsacus and Zeugma', 131, plots the two settlements on either side of the river Khabur and suggests that they were administered under different hyparchies.
94 *P. Dura* 25.21–24 cf l.5.

described as 'epiphyteutic' which the editors take as royal land that had been conferred into local ownership by production (planting and cultivation).⁹⁵ Again the subjection of the settlement to the prerogative and largesse of a higher authority is in view. This confirms a previous observation.⁹⁶

The distances in the *Parthian Stations* between large and small settlements can also be helpful. Occasionally Isidore mentions villages (plural) in a region, noting 'a Greek city' (such as Artemita and Chala), but also observing that there are 'stations' to be found between them in these villages. This seems to imply that such villages, because of distance between settlements, not only needed to provide stop-overs for travellers, but also that they were, consequently, less under that city's control. A district such as Apolloniatis in which is recorded a city and a number of villages is measured as 33 schoeni long, that is approximately 248 miles / 366 kilometers. The Digest of Justinian seems to equate a day's required walk (say, to attend a court hearing) at a maximum of 20 Roman miles (ie 18.3 miles / 29.6 kilometers),⁹⁷ or, by conversion, just under three schoeni. One can therefore envisage such villages beyond a three-schoeni radius operating fairly independently of cities and of one another. Some other districts in Isidore's parade (Carina, Comisena) are without mention of cities, whereas another (Parthyena) is noteworthy for having only one village and another (Margiana) having none, everything being concentrated in a city (Antiocheia). A similar concentration of cities lies in the district of Anauon. Nowhere does Isidore use the language of 'neighboring' or 'surrounding' though occasionally the syntactical linking of city and villages is suggestive and, in one instance, παράκειται may carry this meaning.⁹⁸

The implications that flow from Isidore's treatment are:

    ix. a *komopolis* is to be distinguished from a village and may have some authority or control over such a village.

---

95 Welles, Fink & Gilliam, *The Parchments and the Papyri*, 127.
96 It should be noted that such authority was the point of appeal when disputes between smaller settlements had become intractable: *I.Magnesia* 93a.15–16, 26–27.
97 *Dig. Just* 2.11.1 (Gaius).
98 Compare the only such occurrence in Josephus: μηδεμιᾶς δὲ πόλεως Ἰουδαίων παρακειμένης,(*Vita* 349).

x. sometimes a *komopolis* seems to have developed because of some importance other than or in addition to agriculture, such as being a religious centre, a military post (and hence similar to the κάστρα) or an integral part of far-ranging infrastructure.

xi. a *komopolis* may acquire a reduced status or function because a new power has emerged that has privileged or founded another centre[99] or has exercised a greater control over the settlement's functions. Such relational fluctuations cohere with the observations of archaeologists elsewhere.[100]

Again, the evidence is eastern. Indeed in Isidore, further eastern, albeit aggregated in the western half of the eastern route into Parthia.

Two instances of the use of the term remain. Ptolemy's *Geography* actually has a settlement in Assyria bearing Κωμόπολις as a proper name (6.1.5). Little is known of it but, like Basileia above, the name may indicate something of its origins, in this case, perhaps as a Greek military colony. These instances are drawn from a number of examples of eastern settlements that have their proper name formed from some descriptive allusion.[101]

The remaining forensic sliver might, at first sight, seem to be counter-evidence to the eastern drift of the provenance of *komopoleis*. A fragment from the third century Roman historian and senator, Cassius Dio, is found in the twelfth-century Byzantine writer, Zonaras of Constantinople. Cassius hailed from Nicaea in Bithynia and constantly celebrated its halcyon embrace both in writing and in bodily residence. In his recounting of the period of the Second Punic War (218–201 BCE), he notes the Roman consuls, Claudius Marcellus and Gnaeus Scipio and their efforts, *inter alia*, to shore up Rome's northern frontiers. The strategic center was Mediolanum (Milan), which was finally wrested from the Gallish tribe, the Insubres. Unique to Cassius' account is the mention that, after taking Mediolanum, the victors subdued another town (κωμόπολιν ἑτέραν).[102] No other writer covering

99 Compare Alcock, *Graecia Capta,* 152–54.
100 See, on Beoetia, Bintliff, 'Territorial Behaviour', 226.
101 Tarn, *The Greeks in Bactria and India,* 13; Cohen, *The Hellenistic Settlements in Syria,* 55.
102 Cassius Dio, 12, *apud* Zonaras 8.20.

Republican history mentions the action or the term.¹⁰³ This is the only instance of the use of κωμόπολις for a settlement in the west—in this case seemingly connected with a πόλις, a pattern that we have noted already in the evidence. But we need to recall that Cassius is writing out of his familiarity with eastern arrangements and also applying the terminology of a period almost five hundred years after the occasion being narrated. Consequently, his use of κωμόπολις seems rather to cohere with the witness compiled thus far.

The Byzantine profusion

From the early Byzantine period, κωμόπολις came to be understood as a technical or semi-technical term in the administrative inventory of settlements in the eastern empire, even if subject to the same fluctuations that only military and bureaucratic impulsiveness is capable of delivering.¹⁰⁴ Κωμοπόλεις for example receive letters and heralds that announce various matters;¹⁰⁵ later, they become named in official imperial lists.¹⁰⁶ The term became formally recognized by a calque in translation into Armenian.¹⁰⁷ What does seem to occur in the Byzantine period is a rise in status and, by implication, in the size and capacity of the κώμη. The understanding of a small settlement, perhaps of a few related families, that was often in earlier times described as a κώμη, seems now to be designated by χωρίον, a shift in its sense of a country district. The κῶμαι came to be understood as satellite towns, sometimes aggregated around a κωμόπολις or μητροκομία.¹⁰⁸ Nevertheless, the distinction often seems to rest in bureaucratic or juridical paperwork rather than necessarily lying on the ground.¹⁰⁹ Eusebius' *Onomasticon* does not use κωμόπολις but does distinguish κώμη from κώμη μεγάλη,

---

103 For example, Polybius 2.34.12, Eutropius *Breviarum* 3.6.
104 See Haldon, 'The Idea of the Town'.
105 John Damascene, *Balaam and Joseph* 26.28 (ed. Volk); Theodore Studite PG 99.1476.
106 Constantinus Porphyrogenitus *De thematibus* 1.11; 4.20 (of the place named Meros); 4.22 (of the place named Domateros); 6.9 (of the place named Modrene); cf John Scylitzes, *Chronographia* (continua) 138.9 (of Herakleon).
107 Garsoïan, 'The Early-Medieval Armenian City', 71.
108 Drakoulis, 'Regional Transformation', 85; Sartre, 'Les metrokomiai'.
109 Dagron, 'Entre village et cité'.

πολίχνη and πόλις in ascending order. Possibly κώμη μεγάλη is the same as κωμόπολις,[110] or a μητροκομία.[111] Gilbert Dagron suggests that demographic and economic impact within a region distinguished such a settlement.[112] Nevertheless, it seems clear that by Byzantine times at least, formal recognition of a πόλις required official authorization,[113] though this gained only limited replication in general literature.[114]

I do not wish to attract the axe of anachronism here by applying the same searching microscope used thus far, on the assumption that it might contribute to our understanding, firstly, of the singular instance in Mark's Gospel and, secondly, as another piece of corroboration for the suggestion that the word belongs to an eastern not a western provenance. However, I would suggest that the Byzantine utilisation of the term was not an invention of a later period but an appropriation of a term and understanding from an earlier time, indeed a recognition of the continuation of the term bearing a roughly recognisable association. That κωμόπολις had arrived at some formal meaning and application is shown in an inscription adorning a simple stone from Seleukeia in Cilicia.[115] It is dated to the sixth century, the same period as when John Malalas includes the word in his writings of *komopoleis* in Syria, of settlements becoming reinforced with walls.[116] The inscription is complete but does not provide the name for the settlement. It reads simply Ορος κω|μοπό|λεως and, in its original position, would have marked the boundary of a settlement that was formally identified as a *komopolis*.[117]

Conclusion: implications for Mark's Gospel

Singularly lacking in this study has been any extended examination of the material remains with its complement of demographics, dimensions and infra- and inter-regional connections. The modern application of

110 Hirschfeld, 'Farms and Villages', 38.
111 Sartre, 'Les metrokomiai', 207–8, is inclined to distinguish μητροκωμία and κωμόπολις.
112 Dagron, 'Entre village et cité', 34–35, 43.
113 *ILS* 6090 (of Orcistus); see Jones, *The Later Roman Empire*, 358.
114 Haldon, 'The Idea of the Town', 11.
115 *SEG* 48.1793.
116 See n.10 *supra*..
117 See Dagron & Callot, 'Les bâtisseurs isauriens chez eux', 61–2.

the term κωμόπολις to certain excavated settlements can be evocative but presumes a certain classification of what is perceived, in the absence of a textual or epigraphic reference.[118] Josephus's hyperbole of villages with a population of 15,000 inhabitants has no scholarly backers.[119] But his claim of 204 cities and villages in Galilee[120] is increasingly finding archaeological demonstration. Schurer's schema of a tripartite classification of settlements in Galilee may be too forced,[121] but it does recognize that there were settlements of different size and they do seem to be related to one another in some measure either as hierarchical satellites or, occasionally, in mutual supportive alliances. The difficulty not only is what words to use to describe different settlements but whether such terminology was so deployed at a juridical, descriptive or self-referential level. As Laura Boffo has argued in her negotiation of Strabo's terminology, there is a variability and ambiguity in the word usage.[122] But what is apparent is that there are distinct regional variations. So one might not be absolutely clear on the distinction or application of κωμόπολις but its use is clearly present—as a distinct eastern phenomenon.

Further, the survey indicates that *komopoleis* frequently have noteworthy features—a temple, walls, key nodes of infrastructure, fortifications, significant patronal ties, agro-economic influence. In Mark's text, the implication is that these *komopoleis* have synagogues (Mark 1:39), however we are meant to understand these entities.[123] Of course, these are features that cannot be turned into defining marks, given that at various times alternate labels, from κώμη to πόλις, apply to settlements touting the same features. However, as also common to most settlements, interconnecting ties are crucial, sometimes cultivated, sometimes imposed. Villages, especially in remote areas of mountain or wilderness, are the only settlements that sometimes escape the necessity

---

118 So Finkielsztejn, 'Les mosaïques de la komopolis de porphyreon du sud'; Bintliff, *The Complete Archaeology of Greece*, 270. For the problems involved, see Leveau, '*Territorium urbis*,' 467.
119 *BJ* 3.1.3.
120 *Vita* 235.
121 Schurer, *The History of the Jewish People in the Age of Jesus Christ*, 188–89.
122 Boffo, 'Il Lessico', 135.
123 See Mack, 'The Spyglass and the Kaleidoscope', 188–9.

of ties with other, often aggrandizing, settlements.[124] *Komopoleis* are settlements that operate within significant relational ties with other settlements, most especially cities. Here Mark's expression needs to be noted, τὰς ἐχομένας κωμοπόλεις, 'the surrounding / neighboring *komopoleis*'. This qualification—with alternatives in πλησίον, περί, πέριξ—is frequent in Josephus where it always functions as relational language, though with variations on what is the tie or anchor in such relationships. Of course, the primary tie for a *komopolis*, even as indicated in its compound form, is to a *polis* (above) and a village (below). Mark's reference to *komopoleis*, however, comes in the speech of Jesus who is placed in the wilderness (v.35, ἔρημος). The key term hammered into the structure of the prologue finds an answering echo here. Whether deliberate or not, the expected connection (to Capernaum or even Tiberias—the latter absent in Mark altogether) does not emerge in the text. In Roman imperial terms this would be simply unimaginable, let alone unworkable.[125] The wilderness, not the city, defines the relationships of human settlements in Mark, and in so doing, reconfigures what is meant to constitute aggregations of human habitation. Jesus' 'coming out' (ἐξῆλθεν, v.35) is read by Joel Marcus as applying to Jesus the language 'used of divine envoys' (whether emperor, imperial representative, deity or a deity's representative), indeed (also) of military ones. It points to a battle over disputed territory, he claims.[126] I suggest it is rather an overturning of the configuration of territory, the relationships and their hierarchy. We are now venturing into the symbolic spatialisation of territory that is so much part of Eric Stewart's thesis.[127]

The point will be driven home at the feeding of the 5000. The disciples focus on surrounding villages and pasturelands (εἰς τοὺς κύκλῳ ἀγροὺς καὶ κώμας Mark 6:36) as the source of food (*that can be purchased*—v.37) whereas Jesus provides food in (and indeed from) the wilderness.[128] There, as it turns out, is found green grass, verdant pastures (Mark 6:39 cf Ps 23:2).

124 Occasionally, villages will enter into cooperative relationships with each other (compare Mark 11:1).
125 Gelardini, *Christus Militans*, 82.
126 Marcus, *Mark 1–8*, 204.
127 Stewart, *Gathered around Jesus*.
128 Compare the use of κύκλῳ in this sense in Josephus *BJ* 2.545.

However, whether the term κωμόπολις was familiar in the language of description of or self-identification *within* Galilee itself is moot. Josephus's silence is sonorously ambiguous. It remains to be conclusively decided whether Mark's use of the phraseology is his own, though perhaps one should allow, for argument's sake, that the evangelist was dependent on a source.[129] What is clear is that the use of the term as a designation for a settlement in some sort of relationship with and distinction from a πόλις, a κώμη, the χώρα, ἀγρός and ἔρημος (to confine ourselves to Mark's lexicon) is an eastern phenomenon, and may date back to Seleucid times. The west, especially as manifest in the textual transmission of Mark's Gospel, does not seem to know or recognize the entity. The term is not found, to my knowledge, in the thousands of papyri from Egypt.

Given that the word is marked by a certain provenance, albeit ranging from Ilium / Alexandreian Troas on the eastern shore of the Mediterranean to Merv in Parthia, and that western texts of the Gospel appear disinclined to preserve it (removing any suggestion of versimilitude), this invites an assessment of the provenance of the Gospel of Mark itself. It has been, in recent days, a common-place in scholarship to support an origin of the Gospel in Rome. The attraction of confessional benefits aside (namely Mark as Peter's amanuensis),[130] strong, though often flawed, reliance has been placed on the Latinisms in the Gospel. This eastern Greek term, left unexplained by Mark (unlike the Aramaisms, also in the Gospel), has not entered debates about Mark's provenance.

This detailed study has rested upon one *hapax legomenon* in Mark's Gospel. Much has been extracted as to the parameters of meaning of the term and how and in what circumstances it might be used. Implications for the interpretation of Mark have been suggested, especially in terms of the inversion of the hierarchical ties that structured a *komopolis* into relationships with other settlements. But also I have argued that a single *hapax legomenon* has more to yield than merely a curiosity about a rare word. It needs to be factored into questions of the provenance of Mark's Gospel and, perhaps, of the sources of that Gospel.

129 It is striking that there are two *hapax legamonena* in Mark 1:38, κωμόπολις and ἀλλαχοῦ. The latter word is quite rare: *NDIEC* 4, 28.
130 See Moon, *Mark as Contributive Amanuensis of 1 Peter?*.

Bibliography

Abbott, F. F., & A. C. Johnson — *Municipal Administration in the Roman Empire* (Princeton: Princeton University Press, 1926).

Alcock, S. — *Graecia Capta: The Landscapes of Roman Greece* (Cambridge: Cambridge University Press, 1993).

Alford, H. — *The Greek Testament* Vol. 1 (London: Rivingtons, 1859⁴).

Baarda, Tjitze — 'ΔΙΑΦΩΝΙΑ-ΣΥΜΦΟΝΙΑ: Factors in the Harmonization of the Gospels, Especially in the Diatessaron of Tatian', in W. L. Petersen (ed.), *Gospel Traditions in the Second Century: Origins, Recensions, Text, and Transmission* (London: University of Notre Dame Press, 1989), 133–154.

Best, E. — 'Mark's Readers: A Profile', in F. van Segbroeck et al. (eds.), *The Four Gospels 1992: Festschrift Frans Neirynck* (Leuven: Peeters, 1992), vol. 2, 839–58.

Bintliff, J. — 'Territorial Behaviour and the Natural History of the Greek Polis', in E. Olshausen & H. Sinnabend (eds.), *Stuttgarter Kolloquium zur Historischen Geographie des Altertums Vol 4* (Amsterdam: Hakkert, 1994), 207–249.

Bintliff, J. — *The Complete Archaeology of Greece: From Hunter-gatherers to the 20th Century A.D.* (Oxford: Wiley-Blackwell, 2012).

Boffo, L. — 'Il Lessico dell'insediamento neo libri Straboniani sull' Asia Minore', in A. M. Biraschi & G. Salmeri (eds.), *Studi di storia e di storiografia* (Naples: Edizioni scientifiche italiane, 2000), 114–142.

Bosenius, B. — *Der literarische Raum des Markusevangeliums* (Göttingen: Neukirchen-Vluyn, 2014).

Center for the Study of New Testament Manuscripts www.csntm.org/.

Chaumont, M-L. — 'Étude d'Histoire Parthe V. La Route royale des Parthes de Zeugma à Séleucie du Tigre d'après l'itinéraire d'Isidore de Charax', *Syrie* 61.1–2 (1984), 63–107.

Cohen, G. M. — *The Hellenistic Settlements in Syria, the Red Sea Basin and North Africa* (Berkeley: University of California Press, 2006).

Cohen, S. J. D. — *Josephus in Galilee and Rome: His Vita and Development as a Historian* (Leiden: Brill, 1979).

Collins, A. Y.　　　*Mark* (Hermeneia; Minneapolis, MN: Fortress, 2007).

Cramer, J.　　　*Catenae Graecorum Patrum in Novum Testamentum* (Oxford: 1846), Vol. 1.

Dagron G., & O. Callot　　　'Les bâtisseurs isauriens chez eux: Notes sur trois sites des environs de Silifke', in I. Ševčenko & I. Hutter (eds.), ΑΕΤΟΣ: *Studies in Honour of Cyril Mango* (Stuttgart: De Gruyter, 1998), 55–70.

Dagron, G.　　　'Entre village et cité: La bourgade rurale des IVᵉ – VIIᵉ siècles en Orient', *Koinonia* 3 (1979), 29–52.

Dawson, J.　　　*Lexicon Novi Testamenti* (London: Rivington, 1822).

Donahue, J. R., & D. J. Harrington　　　*The Gospel of Mark* (CP 2; Collegeville, Minn: Michael Glazier, 2002).

Donnegan, J.　　　*A New Greek and English Lexicon* (Boston: Hilliard, Gray & Co, 1838).

Drakoulis, D. P.　　　'Regional Transformation and the Settlement Network of the Coastal Pontic Provinces', in G. R. Tsetskhladze (ed.), *The Black Sea, Paphlagonia, Pontus and Phrygia in Antiquity: Aspects of archaeology and ancient history* (BAR 2432; Oxford: Archeopress, 2012), 79–95.

Edwards, D. R.　　　'Identity and Social Location in Roman Galilean Villages', in J. Zangenberg, H. W. Attridge & D. B. Martin (eds.), *Religion, Ethnicity and Identity in Ancient Galilee* (Tübingen: Mohr Siebeck, 2007), 357–74.

Elliott, J. K.　　　*The Language and Style of the Gospel of Mark: An Edition of C. H. Turner's 'Notes on Marcan Usage' Together with Other Comparable Studies* (Leiden: Brill, 1993).

Fiensy, D. A.　　　'The Galilean Village in the Late Second Temple and Mishnaic Periods', in D. A. Fiensy & J. R. Strange (eds.), *Galilee in the Late Second Temple and Mishnaic Periods* (2 vols; Minneapolis: Fortress, 2014), 177–207.

Finkielsztejn, G.　　　'Les mosaïques de la komopolis de porphyreon du sud (Kfar Samir; Haïfa, Israël), Un évêché (?) entre village et cité', *La mosaïque gréco-romaine* 9 (2005), 435–52.

Fitzmyer, J. A.　　　*The Gospel According to Luke I–IX* (AB 28; New York: Doubleday, 1981).

Focant, Camille — *The Gospel according to Mark: A Commentary* (L. R. Keylock, trans.; Eugene: Pickwick, 2012).

Garsoïan, N. G. — 'The Early-Medieval Armenian City: An Alien Element', *JANES* 16–17 (1986), 67–83.

Gawlikowski, Michal — 'Thapsacus and Zeugma the crossing of the Euphrates in Antiquity', *Iraq* 58 (1996), 123–33.

Gelardini, G. — *Christus Militans: Studien zur politisch-militärischen Semantik im Marcusevangelium vor dem Hintergrund der ersten jüdisch-römischen Krieges* (Leiden: Brill, 2016).

Greenspahn, F. E. — *Hapax Legomena in Biblical Hebrew: A Study of Its Treatment Since Antiquity with Special Reference to Verbal Forms* (Chico, CA: Scholars Press, 1992).

Gregory, C. — *Canon and Text of the New Testament* (Edinburgh: T & T Clark, 1907).

Haelewyck, J-C. (ed.) — *Evangelium secundum Marcum* (Vetus Latina; Die Reste der Altlateinischen Bibel, 17; Fascicle 2 Introduction (fin) Mc 1,1–43; Freiburg, Herder, 2013 [1949]).

Haldon, J. — 'The Idea of the Town in the Byzantine Empire', in G. P. Broglio & B. Ward-Perkins (eds.), *The Idea and Ideal of the Town between Late Antiquity and the early Middle Ages* (Leiden: Brill, 1999), 1–24.

Harris, J. Rendel — *The Codex Sangallensis (Δ). A Study in the Text of the Old Latin Gospels (London: Clay, 1891)*.

Harris, J. Rendel — *Codex Bezae: A Study of the so-called Western Text of the New Testament* (Cambridge: Cambridge University Press, 1891).

Henaut, B. W. — *Oral Tradition and the Gospels: The Problem of Mark 4* (Sheffield: Sheffield Academic Press, 1993).

Hirschfeld, Y. — 'Farms and Villages in Byzantine Palestine', *DOP* 51 (1997), 33–71.

Hörner, P. (ed.) — *Catena aurea deutsch: Band 2: Markusevangelium: Text* (Berlin: de Gruyter, 2012).

Houghton, H. A. G. — *The Latin New Testament: A Guide to its Early History, Texts, and Manuscripts* (Oxford: Oxford University Press, 2016).

Incigneri, B.	*The Gospel to the Romans: The Setting and Rhetoric of Mark's Gospel* (Leiden: Brill, 2003).
Jacoby, F.	*Die Fragmente der Griechischen Historiker vol IIIC* (Leiden: Brill, 1958).
Jastrow, M.	*A Dictionary of the Targumim, the Talmud Babli and Yerushalmi, and the Midrashic Literature* (London: Luzac, 1903). www.tyndalearchive.com/TABS/Jastrow/
Jones, A. H. M.	*The Later Roman Empire, 284–602: A Social, Economic and Administrative Survey* (Baltimore: Johns Hopkins University Press, 1986).
Joos, Martin	'Towards a First Theorem in Semantics', in Semantic Axiom Number One, Lg. 48 (1972), 257–265.
Julicher, A.	*Itala II: Marcus-evangelium* (Berlin: de Gruyter, 1970).
Kee, H.	*Community of the New Age* (Macon, GA: Mercer University Press, 1983).
Leaf, Walter	*Strabo on the Troad: Book XIII, Cap. 1* (Cambridge: Cambridge University Press, 1923).
Legg, S. C. E.	*Novum Testamentum Graece* (Oxford: Clarendon, 1935).
Leveau, Philippe	'*Territorium urbis*. Le territoire de la cité romaine et ses divisions: du vocabulaire aux réalités administratives', *REA* 95 (1993), 459–71.
Levick, B. M.	'Greece (including Crete and Cyrprus) and Asia Minor from 43 B.C. to A.D. 69', in A. K. Bowman, E. Champlin & A Lintott (eds.), *The Augustan Empire 43 B.C. – A.D. 69* (CAH 10; Cambridge: Cambridge University Press, 1996²), 641–745.
Louw, J. P., & E. A. Nida	*Greek-English Lexicon of the New Testament based on Semantic Domains* (New York: UBS, 1988).
Mack, B. L.	'The Spyglass and the Kaleidoscope: From a Levantine Coign of Advantage', in B. S. Crawford & M. P. Miller (eds.), *Redescribing the Gospel of Mark* (Atlanta, GA: SBL, 2017), 181–205.
Mann, C. S.	*Mark* (AB 27; New York: Doubleday 1986)
Marcus, Joel	*Mark 1–8* (AB27; New York: Doubleday, 2000).

Mardaga, H.	'Hapax Legomena: A Neglected Field in Biblical Studies', CBR 10.2 (2012), 264–74.
Marquardt, J.	Römische Staatsverwaltung I (Leipzig: Herzel, 1881²).
Marshall, I. Howard	The Gospel of Luke: A Commentary on the Greek Text (NIGTC; Exeter: Paternoster 1978).
McIver, R. K.	'First-century Nazareth', in B. Oestreich (ed.), Glaube und Zukunft gestaltung (Frankfurt am Main: Lang, 1999), 139–59.
McLaren, J.	'Constructing Judean History in the Diaspora: Josephus's Accounts of Judas', in J. M. G. Barclay (ed.), Negotiating Diaspora: Jewish Strategies in the Roman Empire (LSTS 45; London: T & T Clark, 2004), 90–108.
Metzger, B. M.	A Textual Commentary on the Greek New Testament (United Bible Societies, 1st Edition, 1971).
Millar, F.	The Roman Near East 31 BC – AD 337 (Cambridge, Mass: Harvard University Press, 1993).
Moon, J.	Mark as Contributive Amanuensis of 1 Peter? (Berlin: LIT, 2009).
Moulton, W. F., Geden A. S., and H. K. Moulton	Concordance to the Greek Testament (Edinburgh: T & T Clark, 5th ed., 1978).
Müller, C.	Geographi Graeci Minores vol 1 (Paris, 1855; repr. Hildesheim, 1965).
Nestle, E.	Introduction to the Textual Criticism of the New Testament (William Edie, trans.; London: Williams and Norgate, 1901).
Pasore, G.	Lexicon Greco-Latinum in Novum ... Testamentum (London: Griffin, 1650).
Ramsay, W. M.	'Phrygian inscriptions of the Roman period', Zeitschrift für vergleichende Sprachforschung auf dem Gebiete der Indogermanischen Sprachen 28 (1887), 381–400.
Ramsay, W. M.	'Some Recent Works on Asia Minor', The Classical Review 13 (1899), 136–144.
Rehkopf, F.	Septuaginta-Vokabular (Göttingen: Vandenhoeck & Ruprecht, 1989).

Rettig, H. C. M. *Antiquissimus quattuor evangeliorum canonicorum Codex Sangallensis Graeco-Latinus intertlinearis* (Zurich: Schultess, 1836).

Ricl, Marijana 'Alexandreia Troas in the Hellenistic Period', in *Mélanges d'histoire et d'épigraphie offerts à Fanoula Papazoglou* (Belgrade: Université de Belgrade, 1997), 89–116.

Robert, Louis *Études Anatoliennes: Recherches sur des inscriptions de l'Asie Mineure* (Paris: de Boccard, 1937).

Rogerson, J. W., & J. Vincent *The City in Biblical Perspective* (London: Equinox, 2009), 56–57.

Safrai, Z. 'The Description of the Land of Israel in Josephus' Lands', in L. H. Feldman & G. Hata (eds), *Josephus, the Bible and History* (Leiden: Brill, 1989), 295–324.

Sartre, M. 'Les metrokomiai de Syrie du Sud', *Syria* 76 (1999), 197–222.

Schleusner, J. F. *Novum Lexicon Graeco-Latinum in Novum Testamentum* (Glasgow: Duncan, 1817).

Schnelle, Udo *Neuer Wettstein: Texte zum NT aus Griechentum und Hellenismus: Band I Texte zum Markusevangelium 1.1* (Berlin: De Gruyter, 2008).

Schoff, Wilfred *Parthian Stations by Isidorse of Charax* (Philadelphia: Commercial Museum, 1914).

Schrevel, C. *Lexicon Manuale* (London: Rivington, 1831).

Schuler, C. *Ländliche Siedlungen und Gemeinden im hellenistischen und römischen Kleinasien* (München: Beck, 1998).

Schurer, E. *The History of the Jewish People in the Age of Jesus Christ* (rev. ed. by G. Vermes, F. Millar and M. Black; Edinburgh: T & T Clark, Vol II, 1979).

Schwarz, G. '"Auch den anderen Städten"? (Lukas iv.43a)', *NTS* 23 (1976–7), 344.

Silva, M. *Biblical Words and Their Meaning: An Introduction to Lexical Semantics* (Grand Rapids, Mich: Zondervan, 1994^2).

Stewart, E. C. *Gathered around Jesus: An Alternative Spatial Practice in the Gospel of Mark* (Eugene: Cascade, 2009).

Strack, H. L., & P. Billerbeck — *Kommentar zum neuen Testament aus Talmud und Midrasch* (Munich: Beck, 1978).

Swete, H. — *The Gospel according to St Mark* (London: Macmillan, 1902).

Tarn, W. W. — *The Greeks in Bactria and India* (Cambridge: Cambridge University Press, 1951).

Tarn, W. W., F. Lee — *The Greeks in Bactria and India* (Cambridge: Cambridge University Press, 1951²).

Taylor, V. — *The Gospel According to St Mark* (London: Macmillan, 1966).

Thayer, J. H. — *A Greek-English Lexicon of the New Testament* (Edinburgh: T & T Clark, 1898⁴).

Theissen, G. — *The Gospels in Context: Social and Political History in the Synoptic Tradition* (L. M. Maloney, trans.; Minneapolis: Fortress, 1991).

Trites, A. A. — 'The Importance of Legal Scenes and Language in the Book of Acts', *Nov T* 16 (1974), 278–84.

Trobisch, D. — 'Structural Markers in New Testament Manuscripts, with Special Attention to Observations in Codex Boernerianus (G 012) and Papyrus 46 of the Letters of Paul', in M. C. A. Korpel & J. M. Oesch (eds.), *Layout Markers in Biblical Manuscripts and Ugaritic Tablets* (Assen: van Gorcum, 2005), 177–90.

Tsantsanoglou, K. — 'Punctuation', in A.-F. Christidis (ed.), *A History of Ancient Greek: From the Beginnings to Late Antiquity* (Cambridge: Cambridge University Press, 2007 [2001]), 1326–33.

Tuplin, C. — 'On the track of the ten thousand', *Revue des Études Anciennes* 101.3–4 (1999), 331–66.

F. van Segbroeck et al. (eds), *The Four Gospels 1992: Festschrift Frans Neirynck* (Leuven: Peeters, 1992), vol. 2

Varinlioğlu, G. — 'Living in a Marginal Environment: Rural Habitat and Landscape in Southeastern Isauria', *DOP* 61 (2007), 298–317.

Welles, C. B., R. O. Fink & J. F. Gilliam — *The Parchments and the Papyri (The Excavations at Dura-Europos ... Final Report V, Part I)* (New Haven: Yale University Press, 1959).

Wettstein, John	Η ΚΑΙΝΗ ΔΙΑΘΗΚΗ, Novum Testamentum Graece (Amsterdam: 1751).
Wilke, C. G.	*Clavis Novi Testamenti Philologia* (Leipzig: Arnold, 1850).
Wisselink, W. F. D.	*Assimilation: as a criterion for the establishment of the text* (Kampen: Kok, 1989).

JOHN

CHAPTER 11

The Fourth Gospel and the Beginnings of Jesus' Ministry

Francis J. Moloney

Abstract

Most who have been involved in the three quests for the historical Jesus have dismissed the Fourth Gospel as a possible source for the authentic words and works of Jesus of Nazareth. Taking as a point of departure C.H. Dodd's argument that the Gospel of John draws on independent traditions often closely related to those of the Synoptics, this article explores whether the Gospel of John might provide a better framework for some episodes in Jesus' story. Since this is acknowledged for the end of this ministry, the question is explored for its beginning. Through an examination of the Johannine material on John the Baptist, the vocation of the earliest disciples, and Jesus' action in the temple, potentially genuine historical reminiscences are uncovered and a framework for the beginning of Jesus' ministry is suggested.

The work of the source critics and the first search for the historical Jesus, closed by Schweizer, led to the rejection of the Gospel of John as a reliable source for words and works of the pre-Easter Jesus.[1] The emergence

---

1   For a lucid presentation of the earlier association between John, the son of Zebedee, as the author, and the 'authenticity and genuineness' of the Johannine account, see Lightfoot, *John*, 41–78.

of Form Criticism, the post-World War II redaction critics, and the new quest for the historical Jesus, strengthened the grounds for this rejection. Loss of interest in the historicity of the Fourth Gospel has been accompanied by a vigorous insistence upon the Gospel as testimony for a robust early Christian Theology, witnessed by the great commentaries of Albert Loisy, Marie-Joseph Lagrange, Rudolf Bultmann, Edwyn C. Hoskyns, C. Kingsley Barrett, Rudolf Schnackenburg, and Raymond E. Brown.[2] More recent literary studies, from moderate aesthetic readings, through Reader-Response theory, into more radical contextually determined post-modern readings, do not pose historical questions. As scholarship focusses more fully upon readership, interest in the world behind the text, although sometimes passingly acknowledged, has become less central to the scholarly agenda.

The so-called 'third quest' for the historical Jesus, generated by the Jesus Seminar, largely bypasses the narrative of the Fourth Gospel. The work of John P. Meier is something of an exception to this tendency. In his general introduction to the use of the canonical books of the New Testament as sources for genuine historical data,[3] and throughout his historical reconstructions of Jesus' words and actions, he gives careful consideration to relevant material from the Fourth Gospel. He often decides in its favor. The same could be said for Derek Tovey and Paul Anderson.[4] The former locates the Fourth Gospel within the theoretical model of narrative mediacy where the Beloved Disciple's role as a 'reflector-character', a reliable historical character who tells a 'history interpreted under the impress of a particular understanding of the historical Jesus'.[5] Anderson focuses intensely upon John 6, a narrative which contains episodes which have parallels in the Synoptic Tradition. His investigation of John 6:1–24 and 6:67–71 leads him to conclude that the Johannine version of the bread miracle and the appearance on the sea is a correction of the various Synoptic traditions, and that the report of Peter's confession is a further correction of the Petrine tradition. This corrective re-reading of early tradition is an indication of the

---

2   See the brief remarks in Moloney, *John*, 20–23.
3   Meier, *A Marginal Jew*, 1:41–55.
4   Tovey, *Narrative Art*; Anderson, *Christology*.
5   Tovey, *Narrative Art*, 255.

Evangelist's *'reflective dialogue with his tradition*, in which he continues to find meanings in the significance of Jesus' words and works'.[6] These more creative contributions arrive at conclusions similar to British scholars of some decades ago: behind the post-Easter portrait of Jesus lies some authentic Jesus-material.[7]

The case for some form of dependence of the Fourth Gospel upon one or more of the Synoptic Gospels is still strongly argued by commentators,[8] and by various representatives of the so-called 'Leuven School', inspired by Frans Neirynck.[9] This essay takes as its starting point Charles H. Dodd's work on the historical traditions behind the Fourth Gospel.[10] Starting from the suggestion of P. Gardner-Smith that it is easier to explain the similarities between the Fourth Gospel and the Synoptic tradition *without* a theory of dependence, rather than to explain the differences between the two traditions *with* one, Dodd's carefully argued case has never been systematically dismantled.[11] The sheer number and complexity of the post-Dodd hypotheses, with no sign of a consensus, weighs against the possibility of one of them being the final solution to the question. Gardner-Smith's criterion still holds. Behind the Fourth Gospel lay independent traditions, often bearing a close relationship with those of the Synoptic Gospels. Following the Dodd hypothesis, if the Fourth Evangelist is not directly dependent upon one or several of the Synoptic Gospels in a way that matches, for example, Matthew's dependence upon Mark, some Johannine material may point back to historical traditions associated with the life of Jesus.[12]

---

6   Anderson, *Christology*, 261. Stress in original. For summaries of his conclusions, see 256–57 (on John 6:1–24) and 259–60 (on John 6:66–71).
7   See, for example, Hoskyns, *The Fourth Gospel*, 107–28; Dodd, 'The Portrait of Jesus'; Robinson, 'The Use of the Fourth Gospel'.
8   For a sampling, see Barrett, *John*, 42–54; Brodie, *Quest*; Schnelle, *Das Evangelium nach Johannes*, 13–17; Lincoln, *John*, 26–39. Interestingly, this is an increasing interest for German scholars. For Thyen, *Das Johannesevangelium*, the Fourth Evangelist rewrites the Synoptic tradition creatively; Beutler, *John*, leans favourably towards the dependence of the Johannine tradition on all three Synoptic Gospels, as advocated by Frans Neirynck and the Leuven school (see 13–16). But see the contrary position in Theobald, *Das Evangelium nach Johannes*, 76–81.
9   For a survey of this question, see Smith, *John*. On the Leuven School, see pp.139–76.
10 Dodd, *Historical Tradition*.
11 See Brown, *An Introduction*, 94–104. Dodd, *Historical Tradition*, 8 n. 2, points to the work of Gardner-Smith, *John Among the Gospels*, as 'the turn of the tide' in these discussions.
12 For a concise summary of Dodd's hopes in this regard, see *Historical Tradition*, 423–32.

After years of involvement with the Fourth Gospel, I have no doubt that the Johannine story is *unconditionally* determined by the Johannine theological agenda. But I wonder if it is possible that there are elements in the Fourth Gospel which might provide a better 'framework' for periods of the Jesus' story.[13] This is nowadays widely accepted for the Johannine sequence of the *end of the Jesus' story* in the passion narrative.[14] I would like to test whether John might carry a more reliable 'framework' for the *beginning of the Jesus' story*.[15] I am aware of the maverick nature of this suggestion. I wish to test it by devoting some detailed analysis to the Baptist material (John 1:19–28, 29–34; 3:22–30),[16] the vocation of the first disciples (1:35–51), and the so-called purification of the Temple (2:13–22).

The Johannine Baptist

There is universal agreement that John the Baptist exercised a preaching and baptizing activity in the period immediately before the ministry of Jesus of Nazareth, and that he baptized Jesus.[17] The exact nature of his preaching, the significance of his baptism and the places where he baptized are, as is to be expected, the subject of considerable scholarly

---

13 I make this remark to express my lack of confidence in the 'John, Jesus, and History Project', in the Society of Biblical Literature, founded by Tom Thatcher and Paul N. Anderson. It is good that the question is being asked, but it indicates a 'missionary' agenda, driven by the passion of Paul N. Anderson who sees establishing a close link between the Fourth Gospel and history (whatever that means) as a 'game changer' in New Testament studies. I do not share that passion. On the thorny question of 'history', generally not posed by the above project, see the valuable collection of essays in Luther, Röder, & Schmidt, *Wie Geschichten Geschichte schreiben*.
14 See, among many, Smith, *John among the Gospels*, 111–37, and the many indications of Brown, *The Death of the Messiah*, subsequent to his more general remarks in 1:81–85.
15 The expression 'framework' is, of course, taken from the title of the work of one of the founders of form criticism, Schmidt, *Der Rahmen der Geschichte Jesu*. Schmidt's work put to rest the earlier hypothesis (established in 1863 by H. J. Holzmann) that the Gospel of Mark provided a historically reliable 'framework' (Rahmen) for the ministry of Jesus.
16 I am discounting the Baptist material in the Prologue (1:4–6, 15) and Jesus' words on the Baptist in 5:33–36. As Meier, *Marginal Jew*, 1:53 n. 22, points out, there is more likelihood of unearthing genuine historical reminiscence 'from the narrative part of the Fourth Gospel rather than from the sayings tradition'.
17 Marcus, 'Jesus' Baptismal Vision', 512, remarks: 'The *fact* of the baptism itself ... is a bedrock of historical datum'.

reflection.[18] Dodd identifies three elements which run across all the Johannine Baptist material: he was *not* the Messiah, he bore unique and privileged witness, and he brought others to Jesus. There is also an interesting link between his geographical situation in 1:28, 10:40 and possibly 3:23, depending upon one's location of the unknown Aenon near Salim. Dodd claims that these elements reach back to an original pre-Johannine tradition. Such a tradition, of course, does not necessarily mean that its reported events can be taken as 'historical'. The Baptist's witness to Jesus and the conscious presentation of Jesus to his disciples as the Lamb of God are surely the results of early Christian theologizing.[19]

Meier has shown, in a detailed analysis of the use of ἔρημος, that the Baptist's activities are to be located within the region of the Judean desert, and should not be located in one fixed place. It is reasonable to accept that he was active on both the eastern and western sides of the Jordan, and in the northern region of the desert (Aenon near Salim).[20] It is possible that this impressive prophet-like figure may have been subjected to some form of interrogation by representatives of Jerusalem authorities (1:19b–23), however stylized this interrogation has become in its Johannine dress. Indeed, his activity may have been regularly punctuated by questions from those who came to him, asking about his relationship to the expectations of Israel. The eschatological nature of his baptism and his associated message has been submerged by the Johannine focus upon messianic and subsequent discipleship question (1:19–51).[21] But the Fourth Evangelist alone has a tradition that authorities from Jerusalem questioned him about his messianic status. If the Johannine portrait of the Baptist is simply as the witness *par excellence*, then why did 'the Jews' send 'priests and levites from Jerusalem' to interrogate him? Why bother with this figure if all he did was witness to a coming one who would do even more for the establishment

---

18 For an encyclopedic survey of the discussions and critical conclusions with which I am largely in agreement, see Meier, *Marginal Jew* 2:19–233.
19 Although Dodd, *Historical Tradition*, 269–71, suggests that the title 'the Lamb of God', only found here in the Gospels, could have been used by the historical Baptist, 'or in a traditional account of his preaching'. Of the two, I suggest the latter as more likely.
20 Meier, *Marginal Jew*, 2:43–46. Ernst, 'Johannes der Täufer', also suggests a moving activity. Murphy-O'Connor, 'John the Baptist', 363–65, insists that there was only one place.
21 On the Johannine agenda for 1:19–51, see Moloney, 'The First Days of Jesus'.

of God's design in Israel than he himself was doing? It is possible that this report comes from pre-Johannine tradition. It need not necessarily reflect *wie es eigentlich gewesen war*, but the Johannine account of the interrogation of John the Baptist by representatives of Jewish leadership may rest upon an authentic memory. Although now on the wane, for the purposes of this exercise, using the traditional criteria widely used from testing historical possibility the report of John 1:19–28 adds multiple attestation to the disturbing nature of the Baptist's restless eschatological call to conversion and new life, more thoroughly represented in the Synoptic tradition (see Matt 3:7–12//Luke 3:7–9, 15–18; Matt 11:2–9//Luke 7:18–35).[22]

The question posed to the Baptist in John 1:25: τί οὖν βαπτίζεις εἰ σὺ οὐκ εἶ ὁ Χριστὸς οὐδὲ Ἠλίας οὐδὲ ὁ προφήτης, a link which has no sound first-century background is made between the practice of baptism and figures of the messianic era. This link may simply serve the theological purpose of author, who insists upon 'the Christ', 'Elijah', and 'the prophet' (see also John 1:20–21; Mark 6:15; 8:28–29). This serves the purpose of keeping the messianic question before the reader,[23] despite the Baptist's exaggerated rejection of any association between the Messiah and his own person and mission (ὡμολόγησεν καὶ οὐκ ἠρνήσατο καὶ ὡμολόγησεν).[24] But there are two statements from the Baptist which initially tell of his listeners' ignorance (v. 26: μέσος ὑμῶν ἕστηκεν ὃν ὑμεῖς οὐκ οἴδατε) and then, surprisingly, of his own ignorance (v. 31: καγὼ οὐκ ᾔδειν αὐτόν). This piece of tradition may add to the historical portrait of John the Baptist. He was a charismatic figure, practising a baptism of conversion,

---

22 A good summary of the 'criteria', and how they should be applied to Gospel narratives, is available in Meier, *Marginal Jew*, 1:167–95. For the contemporary widespread rejection of the traditional criteria for historicity, see the important works of Allison, *Constructing Jesus*, and Keith and Le Donne, *Jesus, Criteria*. Significant theological questions surrounding the quest for the historical Jesus can be found in Kelly, 'The Historical Jesus'.
23 See Moloney, *John*, 48–63.
24 Dodd, *Historical Tradition*, 298–300, rightly points to this exaggerated turn of phrase as an indication of the *Sitz im Leben* that gave birth to the Johannine Baptist material. Unlike the Synoptics (see especially Matt 11:12–13; Luke 16:16), the Baptist is the first to confess Jesus. Historically, he belongs to a period before any recognition of Jesus. See Meier, *Marginal Jew*, 2:156–63. Dodd helpfully suggests that the *Sitz im Leben* was 'one in which it was desired that persons who had followed the Baptist should be regarded as adoptive members of the Church'. He suggests that it may come from 55–57 CE. The question of the motivation for the Johannisation of Baptist material will be discussed later in this paper, but Dodd's suggestion should be noted at this stage.

and preaching an eschatological message, but had no precise knowledge of the person or role of the coming figure. In the Synoptic tradition, the Baptist can only speak of ὁ ἰσχυρότερος (see Mark 1:7; Matt 3:11; Luke 3:16).[25] The many possible identifications of 'the stronger one' (Elijah, the Son of Man, the angel Michael, God) may only indicate that 'perhaps ... John never moved much beyond the general idea that he himself was not powerful enough to complete the eschatological task God had begun with him'.[26] There is a certain tension here. We may again be dealing with pre-Johannine tradition, and not history, but the *Johannine* Baptist points to Jesus as the Lamb of God, the Son of God (John 1:29, 33–34, 35), while a *historical reminiscence* is perhaps found in his ignorance concerning the one who was to come after him.[27]

The relationship between the tradition of a future pouring out of the life-giving spirit which would eclipse John's baptism, found in John 1:33 as well as Mark 1:8, Matt 3:11//Luke 3:16 (Q), confirms the results of careful study of the Synoptic Tradition. John the Baptist was a disturbing figure whose presence generated much interest.[28] He, however, could only point beyond himself to an unknown coming figure who would administer the gift of the Holy Spirit, which would bring

---

25 A number of scholars (see Theissen & Merz, *The Historical Jesus*, 199–204) suggest that the historical Baptist also spoke of 'the coming one' (ὁ ἐρχόμενος). For the purposes of this paper, I am limiting myself to ὁ ἰσχυρότερος in the light of Meier's comments (*A Marginal Jew*, 2:79 n. 76).
26 Meier, *Marginal Jew*, 2:35.
27 Dodd, *Historical Tradition*, 267–68, takes this as a reference to 'the hidden Messiah', suggesting that this notion was widespread in first century Judaism, and thus probably an aspect of the preaching of the historical John the Baptist. Despite Mowinckel, *He That Cometh*, 304–308, the notion of 'the hidden Messiah' is difficult to establish with certainty. For the (second century [but see John 7:27]) evidence, see Brown, *John*, 1:53. The suggestion that the expression *originally* reflected his ignorance, whatever literary and theological function John 1:26, 31 may have in the canonical Gospel, appears the more likely solution to this odd claim to 'not know' (John 1:31).
28 Neither Dodd nor the many later considerations of the possible eschatological nature of the historical Baptist's message ever look at John 3:36: ἡ ὀργὴ τοῦ θεοῦ μένει ἐπ'αὐτόν. I have argued elsewhere that John 3:31–36 is an earlier form of the highly Johannanised passage of 3:11–21 (see Moloney, *Belief in the Word*, 127–29). One of the several signs of the primitive nature of vv. 31–36 is the expression ἡ ὀργὴ τοῦ θεοῦ. This is the only appearance of ἡ ὀργή in the Fourth Gospel, but it is part of the Q material on the Baptist's message (see Matt 3:7//Luke 3:7). On this, see Meier, *Marginal Jew*, 2:29–32. It is the regular LXX translation of a number of Hebrew words used to describe God's anger. This not to suggest that John the Baptist ever said anything like John 3:31–36. On the Johannine nature of 3:30–36 as a whole, see Loader, *Jesus in John's Gospel*, 46–67.

'eternal life instead of destruction on the last day'.[29] Dodd's assessment of the historical worth of Johannine Baptist tradition is close. He suggests that it 'may have represented the Baptist, the last of the prophetic succession, as claiming an experience analagous to the prophets of the Old Testament'.[30]

One detail from 1:19–34 remains uninvestigated: the indications in v. 27: ὁ ὀπίσω μου ἐρχόμενος and in v. 30: ὁ ὀπίσω μου ἔρχεται ἀνήρ, that the one to whom he was bearing witness was 'coming after him'. Given the presence of ὁ ὀπίσω μου in Mark 1:7 and Matt 3:11, it has often been suggested that, historically, Jesus was a follower of John the Baptist (see Mark 1:16–20), and that the Baptist pointed to this follower as 'the more powerful one'. Meier argues against this being the case in the Markan tradition, taken over by Matthew and altered in Luke 3:16. He thus also excludes it as a possible meaning for John 1:27. For Meier, Jesus may have indeed been some sort of 'follower', but not in the sense that we might understand a 'disciple' as someone who belonged to the Baptist's retinue.[31] Despite his careful philological and redactional analysis, I suspect that Meier is influenced by his more important conclusion—argued across his study of the Baptist traditions—that the Baptist had no knowledge of the stronger one who would bring about a new era for Israel.

The two are not mutually exclusive. It is possible that Jesus' following of the Baptist, and even the event of his baptism by John the Baptist did not signal him out as someone special. The events which accompany the Synoptic reports of Jesus' baptism (Mark 1:9–11; Matt 3:13–17; Luke 3:21–22), and the Johannine Baptist's recollection of the descent of the Holy Spirit (1:32–34), are surely the result of the later Church's conviction that, on the basis of the *historical fact* that the

---

29 Meier, *Marginal Jew*, 2:39. There are many who would claim that the baptism with the holy spirit is secondary, showing the superiority of Christian Baptism. The Q version (Matt 3:10, 12) 'with fire' would be original. For this case, see Theissen & Merz, *The Historical Jesus*, 203–04. For the position taken above, arguing for a baptism in the holy spirit (see Ezek 36:26–27; Joel 3:1–5; Jubilees 1:23; 1QS IV:20–22), see Meier, *Marginal Jew*, 2:35–40, 81–84.
30 Dodd, *Historical Tradition* 261. The idea of the Baptist's being 'the last of the prophetic succession' has its resonances in Matt 11:12–13; Luke 16:16. Along these lines, see Meier, *Marginal Jew*, 2:156–163.
31 Meier, *Marginal Jew*, 2:83 n. 97; 92 n. 149; 116–119.

paths of these two foundational figures eventually separated, something unique took place at this privileged moment. It can scarcely be questioned that Jesus received the baptism of John, but we cannot rediscover *what actually happened* at that moment, nor do we need to accept as historical that the superiority of Jesus over the Baptist was indicated at that event. What Jesus and John the Baptist made of that brief encounter in the waters of the Jordan lies outside the limits of our scientific control.[32] Indeed, the question the Baptist asks of Jesus, whose response receives no further reaction from the Baptist, most likely indicates that the Baptist went to his death not certain that his former follower, now exercising a ministry of his own, was ὁ ἰσχυρότερος (Matt 11:2–11, 16–19; Luke 7:18–23).[33] At this stage of our argument, I would like to ask that we remain open on the possibility that the Baptist looked to someone from those he had initiated with his baptism, and whom he could rightly but vaguely describe as ὁ ὀπίσω μου ἐρχόμενος (see 1:27), to make that 'more powerful' step which was beyond his understanding of God's design.

The First Disciples

It is universally accepted that the Markan (Mark 1:16–20//Matt 4:18–22) version of the vocation of the first disciples is a highly idealized account, largely based upon the prophetic vocation, especially that of Elishah by Elijah (see 1 Kings 19–21),[34] and that the Lukan version of the same event (Luke 5:1–11) is a more developed presentation of the growing 'psychological' maturation of Simon Peter, resulting the same promise and response. They will henceforth become 'fishers of men' (Mark and Matthew) or 'catching men' (Luke) as they leave everything

---

32 See the reflections of Theissen and Merz, *The Historical Jesus*, 211–213. Recently, however, Marcus, 'Jesus' Baptismal Vision', 512–21, gave five reasons why Luke 10:18 ('I saw Satan falling like lightning from heaven') might be the substance of Jesus' report of that event. An authentic saying of Jesus (for a reconstruction, see pp. 518–19) it was shifted from its original location because the early Church came to regard the death and resurrection as the moment of Satan's overthrow. Ernst, 'Johannes der Täufer', 162–67, insists on the baptismal moment as a turning point in Jesus' messianic self-understanding.
33 See Meier, *Marginal Jew*, 2:130–156 for a detailed analysis of Matt 11:2–11, 16–19 and Luke 7:18–23, arriving at the conclusion sketched above.
34 See Pesch, *Das Markusevangelium*, 1:109–10.

and follow him (Mark 1:17, 20; Luke 5:10–11). The radical demands of early Christian discipleship have played a large part in the formation of these narratives.[35] Despite widespread scholarly opinion that the Johannine account of the call of the first disciples (John 1:35–51) is used by the Evangelist to show an immediate acceptance of Jesus' messianic status, an alternative interpretation is possible. It appears to me that this alternative suggestion may be closer to 'what actually happened' than the theologically impregnated narratives found in the Synoptic Tradition.

The sequence of events in the Fourth Gospel, the encounter between the Baptist and Jesus followed by disciples of the Baptist becoming followers of Jesus does not strain the imagination. It was suggested above that Jesus was a follower of the Baptist in the serious sense implied by the use of ὁ ὀπίσω μου across two traditions (Mark 1:7//Matt 3:11; John 1:27, 30). There may have been a gradual separation of their ways, and this lies behind the episode reported in John 3:22–24.[36] There is nothing particularly 'Johannine' about a report that Jesus and his disciples went εἰς τὴν Ἰουδαίαν γῆν while the Baptist continued his wandering baptismal ministry in the northern reaches of the Judean desert 'at Aenon near Salim'. What lies outside the data provided by our sources is whether or not John's baptism of Jesus (not directly reported in the Fourth Gospel) generated this duplication of ministries, or whether Jesus simply decided to practice his own ministry, much in the tradition of his mentor, John the Baptist, in Judea. I would hypothesize that something along the lines of the latter was the case.[37] The very Johannine response of the Baptist to the question about the respective baptisms in vv. 27–30 should not cloud the possibility that the concerns voiced v. 26 did emerge: ῥαββί, ὃς ἦν μετὰ σοῦ πέραν τοῦ Ἰορδάνου ... ἴδε οὗτος βαπτίζει καὶ πάντες ἔρχονται πρὸς αὐτόν.[38] It is not true to claim: 'He (Jesus) does

---

35 Among many, see Moloney, *Mark*, 159–67. On Luke 5:1–11, its relationship with Mark 1:16–20, and its originality within the Lukan narrative, see Bovon, *Luke*, 1:166–72.
36 For a similar reading of the Johannine material, see Meier, *Marginal Jew*, 2:119–123.
37 Obviously, I am able to provide any solid reason why the separation took place. I would not sensationalize it, but suggest that, in due time, Jesus of Nazareth decided to continue the practice of his mentor, joining other contemporary 'baptists' inspired by his baptizer; see Thomas, *Le mouvement baptiste*.
38 Obviously omitting the words ᾧ σὺ μεμαρτύρεκας which look back to both 1:6–8, 15, and the narrative of vv. 19–34.

not baptize' (4:2, correcting 3:22).³⁹ The comment from the Johannine narrator, inserted into v. 2, shows that the opposite was the case.⁴⁰ There was a time when both the Baptist and Jesus exercised a baptismal ministry.⁴¹

The Baptist, along with his entourage, continued his ministry in the northern regions of the Judean desert, unsure of who the ἰσχθρότερος might be, and whether or not he had come. Indications are that this uncertainty remained with him till the end of his life (see Matt 11:2–3//Luke 7:18–19: 'Are you the one who is to come, or are we to wait for another').⁴² In the meantime, Jesus had begun a parallel ministry, along with an initial group of disciples (John 3:22: ὁ Ἰησοῦς καὶ οἱ μαθηταὶ αὐτοῦ), in Judea. In this reconstruction of a sequence of events, it is possible that Jesus' disciples had also earlier formed part of the entourage of the Baptist. This is the evidence of 1:35–51. In a fully Johannine sense, the Baptist indicates Jesus, as the Lamb of God, to two of his disciples (vv. 35–36). Andrew and the unnamed other disciple set out to follow Jesus (v. 37; see v. 40 for Andrew's name), and from that original core pair come further 'first disciples': Simon Peter (vv. 41–42), Philip (vv. 43–44), and Nathanael (vv. 45–49).

It is impossible to claim historicity for the names of these men, ex-disciples of the Baptist and their friends, the first to follow Jesus.⁴³ Names may have been placed on this first page of the Gospel because of the later roles of these foundational personalities. There is not a great deal of evidence, one way or the other, and thus we cannot be certain. Although Simon Peter, Andrew and Philip (see 6:5–8, 67–70; 12:21–22; 14:8–9; 13:6–11; 18:10–11, 15–18, 25–27; 20:2–10; 21:1–2, 7, 11, 15–19), play cameo roles later in the Gospel, Nathanael disappears from the scene entirely, with the exception of his appearance among the fishing party in 21:2. This may indicate that he was one of those ex-disciples of the Baptist who accompanied Jesus when he began his

---

39 Theissen & Merz, *The Historical Jesus*, 209. Parenthesis mine.
40 See Meier, *A Marginal Jew*, 2:121–23.
41 For a somewhat imaginative reconstruction of that period, see Murphy-O'Connor, 'John the Baptist', 362–66. The possibility of both Jesus and John the Baptism exercising a baptismal activity is rejected by Ernst, 'Johannes der Täufer', 172–76.
42 It is this Q tradition that weighs against the event of Jesus' baptism by John as having been marked by remarkable events.
43 But see Murphy-O'Connor, 'John the Baptist', 362.

separate baptismal ministry in Galilee (3:22). One can only speculate, but perhaps the presence of Nathanael in 21:2 is a hint of his leadership role in the Johannine Church.[44]

One further comment on 1:35–51 is called for. It is a misreading of the Johannine point of view in this passage to see the disciples as rapidly moving to expressions of a correct messianic understanding of Jesus.[45] For the Fourth Evangelist, as the Prologue (1:1–18) has already instructed the reader, the determining principle is that Jesus is the 'Lamb *of God*' (vv. 29, 34) and the 'Son *of God*' (v. 34). *Never* do these first disciples approach such belief. As well as 'Rabbi,' and other messianic terms (including Nathanael's 'son of God', set between 'Rabbi' and 'King of Israel' in v. 49),[46] they speak of Jesus as 'Jesus *of Nazareth*', 'the son *of Joseph*' (v. 45) and 'the King *of Israel*' (v. 49). These first encounters between Jesus and the ex-disciples of the Baptist conclude with a correction of Nathanael's limited faith (v. 50), and a promise of the sight of 'greater things' (v. 51).[47] Behind this Johannine series of 'days', leading to the revelation of the δόξα 'on the third day' (2:1, 11), may also lie the authentic (and perhaps 'embarrassing') memory of the initial difficulties the first disciples had in coming to grips with their new leader. No doubt Jesus himself was working toward a clearer understanding and articulation of his response to God. The limited, culturally, historically and religiously conditioned response of the Johannine first disciples in 1:35–51 may be an elaborated, but basically historical reflection of one side of the confusion. For the Fourth Evangelist, there are no limitations to Jesus' self-understanding (see vv. 42, 48, 50–51), but the disciples struggle to understand him correctly. Unlike the instantaneous *sequela* and the massive conversions that open the Synoptic Tradition, the Fourth Gospel presents a better indication of what might have actually happened when former disciples of the Baptist, who had gone to Aenon near Salim, followed Jesus into Judea (3:22–23).

---

44 On John 21, and its relationship to John 1:1–20:31, see Moloney, 'John 21'.
45 Such an interpretation is widespread. See, for example, Hahn, 'Die Jüngerberufung Joh 1,35–51', and the majority of commentators.
46 For a detailed presentation of this case, see Moloney, 'The First Days of Jesus'.
47 For a more detailed presentation of this case, see Moloney, *John*, 50–63.

The Episode in the Temple

As I have had occasion elsewhere to discuss the possible interference of the Johannine story with the Markan account of the episode in the temple (Mark 11:15–18),[48] I will raise an initial question, touched upon but not developed in that essay, and then offer a summary of my earlier conclusions. An as yet uninvestigated question arises from the two baptismal ministries, as John and Jesus baptize in different parts of the land, reported in John 3:22–23. It closes with a throw-away remark which has no theological significance, and which is left hanging without narrative resolution in the Fourth Gospel. The narrator remarks: οὔπω γὰρ ἦν βεβλημένος εἰς τὴν φυλακὴν ὁ Ἰωάννης (3:24). There is no report of the Baptist's imprisonment or death in the Fourth Gospel. What is the point of 3:24?

This could provide a key to a further piece of information which can be gleaned from the Fourth Gospel concerning the story of Jesus of Nazareth. Earlier we stated that it is impossible to decide what separated the two 'baptists', Jesus and John. I suggested that Jesus initially practiced a ministry parallel to that of his mentor. But at some stage, one cannot question, Jesus' understanding of himself and his ministry changed direction. There is no longer a focus upon the call to repentance, to avoid the terrors of the end time, but Jesus preaches the imminent coming, indeed the incipient presence of the Kingdom of God.[49] It is possible that the Johannine note in 3:24 is an indication of when and why this transformation began.[50] For the Synoptic Tradition, Jesus' baptism by John encapsulates the moment of messianic commissioning. The Fourth Evangelist, in his analepsis recalling of the moment of baptism in 1:33, has no need for any such commissioning. The descent of the Spirit seen by the Baptist (v. 34) merely confirms what was already in place ἐν ἀρχῇ (1:1).

Yet the Fourth Evangelist reports that Jesus and the Baptist carried

---

48 For a fuller development of what follows, see Moloney, 'Revisiting the Temple'.
49 For a detailed discussion of contemporary debates, see Meier, *A Marginal Jew*, 2: 131–64, 399–404. These pages are dedicated to the establishment of what the historical Jesus said about the historical John. The continuity and the difference emerge strongly.
50 This suggestion is rejected by Ernst, 'Johannes der Taufer', 176–77, on the grounds that it is part of the Johannine anti-Baptist polemic.

on baptismal ministries in two different locations before John was put in prison (3:22–24). Is it possible that the Baptist's imprisonment and death, understood by Jesus and many of his fellow-Jews as a martyred prophet,[51] was a turning point in Jesus' own career, and for this reason the totally irrelevant detail of John 3:24 has been preserved? How was Jesus to relate to God, *after* his mentor had been put in prison and slain (see 3:24)? Is it to 'psychologize' too heavily to suggest that the violent death of John the Baptist led to Jesus' self-reflection and eventual further development of the prophetic categories learnt from his master and mentor?[52] Is this the catalyst which began a process which led to his consciousness of a relationship with the traditional God of Israel, expressed his use of the expression *abba* (see Mark 14:36, and especially Gal 4:6 and Rom 8:15),[53] and, at some stage of his brief public career, his teaching his disciples to join him in addressing God in this way (Matt 6:9–13//Luke 11:2–4)?[54] I am not claiming that between the Baptist's death and Jesus' coming to Jerusalem for his first Passover he had taught his disciples to pray to God as *abba*. Such a sequence is impossible to establish, but unlike the Matthean setting for the 'Our Father' (Matt 6:9–15), strongly determined by the literary architecture and theological message of the Sermon on the Mount (Matt 5:1–7:28),[55] the Lukan setting for this Q material (Luke 11:1) is provided by a request from Jesus' disciples to be taught how to pray 'as John taught his disciples'. Is it possible that this Lukan setting is based on a request made of Jesus while the memory of the Baptist and his disciples was still fresh? The introduction of the Baptist in Luke 11:1 comes as a surprise.

---

51 See Meier, *A Marginal Jew*, 2:171–77; Ernst, 'Johannes der Täufer', 176–82.
52 Although clearly Markan in its present composition and temporal location, does Mark 1:14–15 reflect a memory of this turning point? On Mark 1:15, see Meier, *A Marginal Jew*, 2:430–34.
53 Despite the many modifications that have been brought to his argument (see the resumé in Theissen & Merz, *The Historical Jesus*, 526–27), one should still consult Jeremias, *The Prayers of Jesus*, 11–65. See also Meier, *A Marginal Jew*, 2:358–59 n. 20.
54 For a reconstruction of the original prayer to the 'Father' (*abba*), taught by the historical Jesus to his disciples, see Meier, *A Marginal Jew*, 2:291–302. Full documentation of both classical and contemporary discussion of this issue can be found in the notes on pp.353–66. See his remark on p.359: 'If it cannot be established that the more probable hypothesis that Jesus did use father-language for God, I suggest that the criteria for historicity be abandoned along with the quest as a whole'.
55 On the literary use of the Matthean version of the 'Our Father' in the Matthean 'Sermon on the Mount', see Luz, *Matthew*, 1: 172–74, especially the diagram on 173.

There is no call for any 'divine' or uniquely metaphysical 'filial' sense in this consciousness. Whatever early Christian tradition, and especially the Fourth Gospel, made of Jesus' relationship to God, Jesus' transcending prophetic categories would start with a Jewish tradition, inspired by such biblical passages as Ps 2:7 and 2 Sam 7:14, now witnessed to in the Qumran Documents (see 4QFlorilegium I.10–13; 4QAramaic Apocalypse II.1).[56] The basis of the relationship would have been Jesus' decision both to continue and develop the activity of John the Baptist, a prolongation of unconditional adhesion to his understanding of the design of the God of Israel, whom he began to address as *abba*, and to associate his disciples with him in such an approach to God.

There is a necessary level of speculation in these claims.[57] What remains unexplained, because it is undocumented, is *why* the death of the Baptist led to Jesus' shift in focus. I can only hypothesize that the violent elimination of his mentor may have led Jesus to turn more single-mindedly to God. This hypothesis is *at least* the equal of suggestions made by others. For Hollenbach, Jesus' transformation was generated by the sudden discovery of a power, given by God, to overthrow demons (see Matt 12:28//Luke 11:20).[58] Sanders suggests that Jesus, equally convinced that the end was near at hand, transformed the Baptist's traditional call to repentance. He accepted sinners into fellowship without demanding the traditional signs of repentance: 'If the sinners had repented, they would not have been sinners'.[59] Freyne, followed by Murphy-O'Connor, proposes that he was moved by the abysmal social conditions in Galilee that he began to privilege a message about a gracious God over the observance of the Law.[60] The criteria of dissimilarity, coherence and multiple attestation all support the historical possibility that Jesus developed an understanding of his relationship with God,

---

56 See Fitzmyer, '4Q246', for a full presentation, photograph, reconstruction, commentary, and analysis of the importance of the Aramaic Apocalypse text.
57 A feature of the work of Dodd and Robinson (see above, note 7) has been an insistence that the Johannine presentation of Jesus' relationship with God as 'Father' is primitive. It can be found in the Q-logion Matt 11:25–27//Luke 10:21–22, and in a parable about the Father instructing the Son, which probably has its origins in the historical Jesus, now found in John 5:19–20.
58 Hollenbach, 'The Conversion of Jesus', 209–211.
59 Sanders, *Jesus and Judaism*, 200–11. See especially pp.206–07. Citation from 206.
60 This is Murphy-O'Connor's reading of Freyne's suggestion. Freyne, *Galilee*, 155–207 (social conditions in the Galilee) and 220–228 (Jesus). See Murphy-O'Connor, 'John the Baptist', 372–74.

and that he shared this with his disciples. The above speculation suggests why this development took place.

If Jesus' awareness of his relationship with God was heightened by the death of John the Baptist, then the Johannine Jesus' description of the Temple in John as τὸν οἶκον τοῦ πατρός μου (John 2:16) reflects an earlier moment in the traditions found in Mark 11:17 and in Q (Matt 21:13//Luke 19:46), where Jesus cites Isaiah 56:7 to refer to the Temple as ὁ οἶκος μου. Responding to the God he now calls 'Father', on one of his many visits to Jerusalem after the death of the Baptist, possibly on the occasion of the Pilgrim Feast of Passover, he was disturbed by certain practices taking place in the house of *his Father* (John). It was only later in the development of the Jesus-tradition that those who developed this traditional passage were able to make Jesus Lord of the Temple, and thus able to speak of *'my house'* (Mark and Q).[61]

As I have indicated elsewhere, I am not insisting that the Fourth Evangelist correctly locates the historical moment of this event: at the beginning of Jesus' public career. The Johannine location serves the author's literary and theological sensitivities very well. It raises the issue of the death and resurrection of Jesus at the beginning of his narrative. But the Markan (and subsequent Matthean and Lukan) location of the Temple episode is determined by the Markan time-line. Jesus was in Jerusalem only once. For John, he was there regularly.

There is no call for the scene known as 'the purification of the Temple' to have taken place as one of the very first episodes in Jesus ministry, as it appears in John. But the timing of John's report better captures what happened regularly during Jesus' visits to Jerusalem than the widely accepted historical conclusion that it only happened only at the end of Jesus' ministry, and led to his death. Subsequent to the death of John the Baptist (see John 3:24), Jesus' ministry began to focus more intensely upon the reigning presence of God, marked by a strong sense of a relationship between Jesus and the God of Israel as his Father. It was this relationship that generated passion whenever he visited the Jerusalem Temple, and observed what was happening in 'his Father's house'.

---

61 This is not, of course, to detract from the crucial importance that 2:13–22 has in the final redaction of the Johannine narrative. On this, see Moloney, 'Reading John 2:13–22'.

Conclusion

If the reconstruction of a 'framework' for the early part of Jesus' ministry outlined above is correct, these various pieces fit together:

1. John the Baptist's preaching and baptismal ministry disturbed the Jerusalem leadership (John and the Synoptics).
2. Jesus was baptised by John (John [implicitly] and the Synoptics).
3. He became a follower of John (John and the Synoptics).
4. At a certain stage he began a separate baptismal activity (in Judea), while John continued his ministry elsewhere (in the northern regions of the Judean desert?) (only John). There is evidence for subsequent baptized John the Baptist disciples in Acts 18:24–19:7.
5. Departing from their original master, some disciples (John 1:35: μαθηταί) of the Baptist followed Jesus (v. 37: ἠκολούθησαν τῷ Ἰησοῦ) as he began his separate ministry.
6. Within this new group there were tensions between the expectations of the followers of Jesus and his own sense of his mission (only John).[62]
7. The popularity of Jesus' activity created a problem for the Baptist and his disciples (only John 3:25–30), which the Baptist never resolved (only in Q 7:20).
8. The two parallel ministries continued until the Baptist was imprisoned and killed (only John 3:24).
9. This event, the violent death of a prophet-martyr, led to Jesus' development of his own ministry, a continuation of that of his mentor, but enlivened by the centrality of his concern with the

---

62 When I say 'only John' here, I am aware that this tension, to my mind an understandable historical occurrence, becomes a major theme, exploited in different ways, and outstandingly by Mark, of the misunderstanding and failure of the disciples across the whole of the story of Jesus. But it is 'only John' who locates it in his account of the vocation (?) of the first disciples. It is strikingly absent from the Synoptic accounts of the same occasion.

Kingdom of God.[63]

10. His preaching on the Kingdom *of God* impressed because he spoke authoritatively, indicating an immediacy with God, whom he was known (at least by his disciples whom he taught to address God in this way) to call *abba* (the Synoptics and John, implied by Pauline Christology).

11. Early in his career, and then throughout his ministry, Jesus was angered by certain practices in the Temple which he regarded as the House *of God* (and thus, 'my Father'). He objected to such practices (possible early chronology from John; episode in both John and the Synoptics).

This suggestion of a sequence of events used to narrate the essentially theological opening of the Fourth Gospel can never be more than that: a suggestion.

Nevertheless, if we were to look for support from the much used and abused 'criteria' that have been established to determine the possibility of historicity, this sequence could claim the support of multiple attestation and coherence. The figure behind the sequence of events outlined also has a claim to dissimilarity. While he was similar to many who looked for eschatological resolution, and turned to the Baptist in his search, much to the embarrassment of the early Church, he is dissimilar to the Jesus who emerges in the Pauline Letters and the Synoptic and Johannine Gospels. I sense that John's sequence offers support for the historicity of the Baptist's question found in Q: 'Are you the one who is to come, or are we to wait for another?' This investigation into the earliest period in the public life of Jesus at least indicates that the Fourth Gospel should not be dismissed as a possible source, as it has been by most who have been involved in the three quests for the historical Jesus.

---

[63] For an exhaustive—and right-headed—treatment of Jesus' use of 'the Kingdom of God', see Meier, *A Marginal Jew*, 2:237–506. His use of parables indicates both the centrality of his Kingdom teaching, and his unique immediacy with the God of Israel. Among many, see the recent survey of Zimmermann, *Puzzling the Parables of Jesus*, 57–103.

Bibliography

Allison, Jr., Dale C. *Constructing Jesus. Memory, Imagination, and History* (Grand Rapids: Baker Academic, 2010).

Anderson, Paul N. *The Christology of the Fourth Gospel: Its unity and Disunity in the Light of John 6* (Valley Forge: Trinity Press International, 1996).

Barrett, C. Kingsley *The Gospel According to St John* (2nd ed.; London: SPCK, 1978).

Beutler, Johannes *A Commentary on the Gospel of John* (trans. Michael Tait; Grand Rapids: Eerdmans, 2017).

Bovon, François *Luke* (3 vols.; Christine M. Thomas & James Crouch, transls.; Hermeneia; Minneapolis: Fortress, 2002–2012).

Brodie, T. L. *The Quest for the Origin of John's Gospel: A Source-Oriented Approach* (New York: Oxford University Press, 1993).

Brown, Raymond E. *The Gospel according to John* (AB 29-29A; New York: Doubleday, 1966–1970).

⸻. *The Death of the Messiah. From Gethsemane to the Grave. A Commentary on the Passion Narratives of the Four Gospels* (ABRL; 2 vols.; New York: Doubleday, 1994).

⸻. *An Introduction to the Gospel of John* (Francis J. Moloney, ed.; ABRL; New York: Doubleday, 2003).

Dodd, Charles H. *Historical Tradition in the Fourth Gospel* (Cambridge: Cambridge University Press, 1965).

⸻. 'The Portrait of Jesus in John and in the Synoptics', in William R. Farmer, Charles F. D. Moule & R. R. Niebuhr (eds.), *Christian History and Interpretation: Studies Presented to John Knox* (Cambridge: University Press, 1967), 183–98.

Ernst, J. 'Johannes der Täufer und Jesus von Nazareth in historischer Sicht', *New Testament Studies* 43 (1997), 167–72.

Fitzmyer, Joseph A. '4Q246: The "Son of God" Document in Qumran', *Biblica* 74 (1993), 153–74.

Freyne, Sean *Galilee from Alexander the Great to Hadrian 323 B.C.E. to 135 C.E. A Study of Second Temple Judaism* (Wilmington/Indiana: Michael Glazier/Notre Dame Press, 1980).

Gardner-Smith, P.   *St John and the Synoptic Gospels* (Cambridge: Cambridge University Press, 1938).

Hahn, F.   'Die Jüngerberufung Joh 1,35–51', in P.-G. Müller & W. Stenger (eds.), *Kontinuität und Einheit: Für Franz Mussner* (Freiburg: Herder, 1981), 172–90.

Hollenbach, P. W.   'The Conversion of Jesus: From Jesus the Baptizer to Jesus the Healer', *ANRW* 2.25.1 (1982), 196–219.

Hoskyns, Edwyn. C.   *The Fourth Gospel* (Francis N. Davey, ed.; London: Faber & Faber, 1947).

Jeremias, J.   *The Prayers of Jesus* (SBT 6; London: SCM Press, 1967).

Keith, Chris, & Anthony Le Donne (eds.)   *Jesus, Criteria, and the Demise of Authenticity* (London: T&T Clark, 2012).

Kelly, Anthony J.   'The Historical Jesus and Human Subjectivity: A Response to John Meier', *Pacifica* 4 (1991), 202–28.

Lightfoot, J. B.   *The Gospel of John. A Newly Discovered Commentary* (Ben Witherington III & Todd D. Still, eds.; The Lightfoot Legacy Set 2; Downers Grove: IVP Academic, 2015).

Lincoln, Andrew T.   *The Gospel According to John* (BNTC London: Continuum, 2005).

Loader, William   *Jesus in John's Gospel: Structure and Issues in John's Gospel* (Grand Rapids, Eerdmans, 2017).

Luther, Susan, Jörg Röder, & Eckart D. Schmidt   *Wie Geschichten Geschichte schreiben: Frühchristlicher Literatur zwischen Faktualität und Fiktionalität* (WUNT 2.395; Tübingen: Mohr Siebeck, 2015).

Luz, Ulrich   *Matthew* (3 vols.; James E. Crouch, trans.; Hermeneia; Minneapolis: Fortress, 2001–2007).

Marcus, Joel   'Jesus' Baptismal Vision', *New Testament Studies* 41 (1995), 512–21.

Meier, John P. *A Marginal Jew. Rethinking the Historical Jesus* (5 vols.; ABRL/AYBRL; New York/New Haven: Doubleday/Yale University Press, 1991–2016).

Moloney, F. J. *Belief in the Word. Reading John 1–4* (Minneapolis: Fortress Press, 1993).

———. *The Gospel of John* (SP 4; Collegeville: The Liturgical Press, 1998).

———. *Mark. Storyteller, Interpreter, Evangelist* (Peabody: Hendrickson, 2004).

———. 'John 21 and the Johannine Story', in *Johannine Studies 1975–2017* (WUNT 372; Tübingen: Mohr Siebeck, 2017), 521–37.

———. 'The First Days of Jesus and the Role of the Disciples: A Study of John 1:19–51', in *Johannine Studies 1975–2017* (WUNT 372; Tübingen: Mohr Siebeck, 2017), 307–30. A brief form is published in *ABR* 65 (2017), 1–17.

———. 'Reading John 2:13–22: The Purification of the Temple', in *Johannine Studies 1975–2017* (WUNT 372; Tübingen: Mohr Siebeck, 2017), 355–73.

———. 'Revisiting the Temple: Mark 11:15–17 and 13:2'. Forthcoming publication by the Catholic University of America Press, Washington, DC (2020).

Mowinckel, Sigmund *He That Cometh* (Oxford: Blackwell, 1959).

Murphy-O'Connor, J. 'John the Baptist and Jesus: History and Hypotheses', *New Testament Studies* 36.3 (1990), 359–374.

Pesch, Rudolf *Das Markusevangelium* (2 vols.; HTKNT II/1–2; Freiburg: Herder, 1977).

Robinson, John A. T. 'The Use of the Fourth Gospel for Christology Today', in Barnabas Lindars & Stephen Smalley (eds.), *Christ and Spirit in the New Testament. In Honour of Charles Francis Digby Moule* (Cambridge: Cambridge University Press, 1967), 183–98.

Sanders, E. P. *Jesus and Judaism* (Minneapolis: Fortress Press, 1985).

Schmidt, K.-L. *Der Rahmen der Geschichte Jesu. Literarkritische Untersuchungen zur ältesten Jesusuberlieferung* (Darmstadt: Wissenschaftliche Buchgesellschaft, 1964 [original 1919]).

Schnelle, U.   *Das Evangelium nach Johannes* (THZNT 4; Leipzig: Evangelische Verlagsanstalt, 1998).

Smith, D. Moody   *John Among the Gospels* (Columbia: University of South Carolina Press, 2001 2nd ed.).

Theissen, Gerd, & Annette Merz   *The Historical Jesus: A Comprehensive Guide* (Minneapolis: Fortress Press, 1998).

Theobald, Michael   *Das Evangelium nach Johannes: Kapitel 1–12* (RNT; Regensburg: Pustet, 2009).

Thomas, J.   *Le mouvement baptiste en Palestine et Syrie* (Universitas Catholica Lovaniensis; 2nd Series 28; Gembloux: Duculot, 1935).

Thyen, Hartwig   *Das Johannesevngelium* (HNT 6; Tübingen: Mohr Siebeck, 2005).

Tovey, Derek M. H.   *Narrative Art and Act in the Fourth Gospel* (SNTSMS 51; Sheffield: Sheffield Academic Press, 1997).

Zimmermann, Ruben   *Puzzling the Parables of Jesus. Methods and Interpretation* (Minneapolis: Fortress, 2015).

CHAPTER 12

The Woman at the Well, Jesus, and Prejudice In Samaria (John 4:3–43)

Lyn Kidson

Abstract

Many assume that John's Gospel is portraying the Samaritan woman at the well as a sinner. Or at the very least a woman compromised by a relationship with a man Jesus describes as 'not your husband' (John 4:18). This assumption has its roots in ancient prejudices. Both Romans and Jews characterised women who did not fit neatly into the traditional family scheme as sexually promiscuous. This essay will investigate the possibilities in regard to the multiple marriages of the woman in the context of Roman Palestine. It will also consider the various impediments to marriage for this woman. It will be argued that two impediments are the most likely options in the case of a Samaritan woman. As this investigation progresses, it will become apparent that this is a story about poverty and prejudice in regards to gender, race, and social dislocation.

L. L. Welborn in his 'The Polis and the Poor: Reconstructing Social Relations from Different Genres of Evidence' notes the difficulty that the historian has in pinning down any portrait of the urban poor from the historical sources:

> [Ancient] historians and orators write of the urban mob. Doubtless many of those who composed this multitude suffered scarcity, hunger, and destitution, but the poor are not identified in this literature as a distinct group within the populace. Moreover, the sources reflect an elite bias.[1]

I would like to argue that the encounter of Jesus of Nazareth with the Samaritan woman at the well in the Gospel of John offers a unique window into the life of the rural poor of Palestine in the first century.[2] Although Welborn found it difficult to catch glimpses of the urban poor in Rome, there have been some important studies on the economy and the poor in Roman Palestine.[3] In addition, a number of studies provide detailed information about marriage, divorce, death, and widows.[4] This paper will make use of these studies in order to investigate the multiple marriages of the Samaritan woman, as well as the arrangement she now has with the one Jesus says 'is not your husband' (John 4:18).[5]

The story in John 4 begins by locating the reader geographically in Samaria (John 4:3–43).[6] Jesus and his disciples are travelling through Samaria and they come to a 'city' (εἰς πόλιν) 'called Sychar' (John 4:5). The identification of Sychar has caused problems for scholars.[7] It most likely lay in the vicinity of Shechem, known as Neapolis in Roman times.[8] If Jacob's well has been identified correctly by William Thomson then it was two miles, or three to four kilometres, from Neapolis.[9] Neapolis as a polis would have had its own water supply so it is unlikely

---

1 Welborn, 'The Polis and the Poor', 189–190.
2 Keener, *John*, 140–142; Carson, *John*, 82–87.
3 Safrai, *The Economy of Roman Palestine*; Dar, *Landscape and Pattern*; Hamel, *Poverty and Charity*.
4 Satlow, *Jewish Marriage in Antiquity*; Huebner, *The Family in Roman Egypt*.
5 All Scripture is taken from NASB. This study agrees with Margaret Beirne that the character of the woman is drawn in such a way that she is far from 'type cast' and her presentation as a 'feisty and colourful woman' cuts through any stereotyping, while taking on a representative role within the Gospel, *Women and Men*, 101–102.
6 Zangenberg, "Open Your Eyes and Look at the Fields", §3.84–94: the geographical references in the Gospel are significant locators of Johannine tradition beyond any theological concepts.
7 Barrett, *John*, 231.
8 Keener, *John*, 590.
9 Thomson, *The Land and the Book*, 2:206; Strack & Billerbeck, *Das Evangelium*, 2:431; Michaels, *John*, 235 n.16.

that that city was her point of origin.¹⁰ More likely a small village existed near the well, as one did when Thomson wrote his guide in 1860.¹¹ Neapolis was a large centre and sat on a major crossroads between Jerusalem and Scythopolis (north and south), and the western coastal plain and the Jordan Valley (east and west).¹² More recent research has found a pattern of settlement in Roman Palestine that fits with the picture that is given in John 4: 'The *polis* was at the center of the territory. Around the *polis* were the suburbs of villas...in which the rich citizens of the city lived; and the farm region which included, at times, both large and small towns. The territory was divided into village units, each with a mother settlement and a number of satellite or offshoot settlements'.¹³ It is also possible that there were small villages that had no connection with the mother settlement.¹⁴ Sychar was most likely a small village, which left only a small imprint in the literary sources.¹⁵ Therefore, the term *polis* used here in John is being used in a general way to mean any type of settlement rather than in a technical sense to mean a Greek city.

Rabbinic literature understood extended families to be living in villages.¹⁶ The Talmud portrayed villagers to be poor and leading miserable lives because of the lack of services.¹⁷ Archaeological remains reveal two forms: on one hand, that villages could be very poorly constructed, but on the other hand, they could consist of a large dwelling for a rich family surrounded by other dwellings, buildings, and fortifications.¹⁸ Therefore, depending on the social grouping, the village could offer a life that was almost the equivalent to life in a bigger centre or it could

---

10   Michaels, *John*, 235 n.16; Safrai, *The Economy of Roman Palestine*, 30–32.
11   Aschâr: Thomson, *The Land and the Book* 2: 206; Keener, *John*, 590: although Aschâr is approximately 1.5 kilometres from the well known as 'Jacob's well'; Michaels, *John*, 235 n.16: Aschâr had its own spring so is the women 'unwelcome at her own town's spring?'
12   Isaac, *The Limits of Empire*, 430.
13   Safrai, *The Economy of Roman Palestine*, 100: this pattern of settlement reached its height in the 3rd century CE.
14   Safrai, *The Economy of Roman Palestine*, 70.
15   Zangenberg, 'Open Your Eyes and Look at the Fields', §3.84–94; Safrai, *The Economy of Roman Palestine*, 100–103; 146–147, 371–373: the exact number of small villages around Neapolis is unclear. If Aschâr is Sychar then it is mentioned in Ecclesiastes Rabbah 2:11 and Midrash Ha-Gadol on Deuteronomy 8:9, p.179.
16   Safrai, *The Economy of Roman Palestine*, 81.
17   Hamel, *Poverty and Charity*, 30.
18   Safrai, *The Economy of Roman Palestine*, 81–82.

offer a life of impoverishment as the Talmud suggests. If we posit that Sychar was a small satellite village of a few houses then this may suggest a level of impoverishment for the villagers. John describes the disciples as having 'gone away into the city to buy food' (John 4:8). It is unlikely the village that we have conjectured had a baker.[19] It is possible that some villagers offered food for sale to passing travellers.[20]

Therefore, we could postulate that the woman who came to draw water (John 4:7) lived in a small village in relatively modest conditions if not in poverty. Much has been made of the woman coming to the well at the sixth hour or at midday rather than in the cool of the dawn or evening.[21] Her appearance at the sixth hour could be in reference to Rachel's at the well at the same hour (Gen 29:7).[22] However, we have evidence, albeit from the twentieth century, of how wells were used by villagers in Palestine.[23] If we consider the use of a well from this evidence, then women started drawing water at dawn and would continue to come to the well during the day.[24] Often women would meet at the well, converse, and sing usually in the early morning or later in the afternoon.[25] One woman recalled that the task was to fill the large water jar kept at the entrance to the home.[26] Some women would use donkeys to transport the water back to their homes. If we assume that our woman from Sychar had no donkey then this would involve a number of trips depending on how empty the jar was. Further, she appears to be attending to this task alone so her visit to the well may have been delayed because of other necessary tasks. The elderly villagers recall that it was the girls' task to collect the dry animal droppings to fuel the bread ovens.[27] If our woman had to compete for fuel in the morning

---

19 Safrai, *The Economy of Roman Palestine*, 82.
20 Safrai, *The Economy of Roman Palestine*, 79–80: there may have been merchants that travelled between small villages selling their wares, who would have needed food and lodging; Schottroff, *Lydia's Impatient Sisters*, 96–97.
21 Carmichael, 'Marriage and the Samaritan Woman', 336–337.
22 Carmichael, 'Marriage and the Samaritan Woman', 336.
23 Peled, 'The Social Texture of the Baqa Well', 810–825.
24 Peled, 'The Social Texture of the Baqa Well', 815.
25 Peled, 'The Social Texture of the Baqa Well', 815–817.
26 Peled, 'The Social Texture of the Baqa Well', 816.
27 Peled, 'The Social Texture of the Baqa Well', 817; Hamel, *Poverty and Charity*, 112: it was part of a wife's duty to collect the water, as well as wood for the fire.

then drawing water would wait for later in the day. This reflects the gruelling physical labour that village woman experienced.[28] In the more modern Palestinian example men were forbidden from being at the well during the hours that the women would frequent the well.[29] However, we cannot tell if there was such a custom in place in Samaria in the first century. It also appears that Jesus and his disciples are at the well at a strange hour since the first meal of the day was normally at ten in the morning.[30] So perhaps the image is that both the woman and Jesus are out of their expected social domains at midday. In summary, there are certain ambiguities about the woman's appearance at the well at midday, which we will return to in due course.

Jesus asks the woman for a drink (John 4:7). Thus follows an explanation by the woman and the narrator about the social relations between Samaritans and Jews (John 4:9). The conversation which follows between Jesus and the Samaritan woman is unexpected and by rights should never have happened. In the midst of their conversation about water Jesus said to the Samaritan woman,

> 'Go, call your husband and come here'. The woman answered and said, 'I have no husband'. Jesus said to her, 'You have correctly said, "I have no husband"; for you have had five husbands, and the one whom you now have is not your husband; this you have said truly' (John 4:16–18).

The revelation about this woman's life has left many scholars perplexed.[31] First, I would like to consider the five marriages that this woman is said to have had. Then after this I will consider her last relationship.

C.K. Barrett, in his commentary on John, notes that the Rabbis did not approve of more than three marriages although 'any number were legally admissible' citing the Talmud, *b. Niddah* 64a.[32] But this reference takes place in a discussion about patterns in menstruation

---

28   Peled, 'The Social Texture of the Baqa Well', 816; Hamel, *Poverty and Charity*, 112.
29   Peled, 'The Social Texture of the Baqa Well', 818.
30   Hamel, *Poverty and Charity*, 31; Safrai, *The Economy of Roman Palestine*, 105.
31   Keener, *John*, 605–608; Morris, *John*, 234–235.
32   Strack & Billerbeck, *Das Evangelium*, 2. 437; Barrett, *John*, 235: 'the Rabbis did not approve of more than three marriages', but this is not quite the case.

and appears as an insertion. Elsewhere in the Babylonian Talmud there is a more enlightening discussion. In the earlier *b. Yevamot* 64a–65b the problem being dealt with is infertility. A man may divorce his wife after ten years if no children are born. She is entitled to have her *ketubba* handed to her and to remarry (64a). In Rabbinic law the *ketubba* is an endowment pledge by the husband to his wife if he divorces her or she is widowed.[33] It is said that a woman should not remarry more than twice if her husbands have died (*b. Yev.* 64b). In *b. Yevamot* 65a a woman that has been divorced twice because of infertility 'may marry a third man only if [the husband] has children'.[34] The question being discussed here is in relation to her *ketubba*. The next question is if she marries a fourth time and has children. She cannot reclaim her *ketubba* because her third husband may insist that her marriage to her fourth husband be annulled making her children illegitimate. It is 'assumed that she has now been restored to health'.[35] In *b. Yevamot* 64b it is said that a woman may not remarry after the death of the second husband because either there is a disease in her womb that causes a man to die or her ill luck has resulted in her husband's accidental death. However, 'Rabbi. R. Simeon b. Gamaliel said: She may be married to a third, but she may not be married to a fourth' so there was disagreement about the number of times a woman may remarry if her husbands had perished either through accident or disease (*b. Yev.* 64b).[36]

As we can see in this discussion, there is a certain prejudice surrounding an ill-fated woman. Even if her betrothed husband has died in an agricultural accident, this still counts against a woman's reputation. However, Michael Satlow describes the Rabbis' discussion on marriage as an attempt to negotiate between an ideal and an 'engagement in an impossibly conflicted reality'.[37] Further, the discussion taking place among Jewish scholars in Babylon may not reflect the social realities of Palestine in the first century.[38] Death in early adulthood was common enough and many people were remarried.[39] In relation to the rural context we could propose

---

33 Satlow, *Jewish Marriage in Antiquity*, 202.
34 'Come and Hear™'.
35 'Come and Hear™'.
36 'Come and Hear™'.
37 Satlow, *Jewish Marriage in Antiquity*, 262–264 esp. 263.
38 Satlow, *Jewish Marriage in Antiquity*, 264–265.
39 Satlow, *Jewish Marriage in Antiquity*, 183.

a number of possible scenarios for the woman at the well.

Firstly, as a young bride she may have been married to a man living with his family. Compounds with extended families working their land were common.[40] It was expected that if a woman's husband died she would leave her children with her husband's family and return to her family of origin.[41] However, it was possible for a woman to marry within her husband's family to keep her and her children together.[42] This is not a levirate marriage where the brother of the deceased took his brother's wife if they were childless, although, this could also be a possibility.[43]

It could also be that she was divorced because of infertility. It is unlikely that she has had five husbands each divorcing her for infertility after ten years as the Rabbis prescribe.[44] She could have possibly been divorced for adultery, leaving one husband for another. It is hard to imagine this as a possibility for all five husbands.

There is a possibility that she has been widowed five times. If her husbands were agricultural workers then they would have been dependent on productive seasons for work. Even a landowning family might struggle to provide all the nutrition that the household members needed to survive in lean times.[45] Further, as the Talmud depicts agricultural accidents could happen, such as falling out of a date palm (*b. Yev.* 64b). Agricultural work was and is dangerous. Death could come through being gored by an ox, through eating poisonous foodstuffs from foraging, accidents such as falling down a well, a range of infectious diseases and parasites, or septicaemia from an infected wound.[46]

It is impossible to postulate which scenario is in mind here in John.

---

40 Dar, *Landscape and Pattern*, 80–81; 85–87.
41 This might be the case if her husband was living with his family, Huebner, *The Family in Roman Egypt*, 34–35, 43–45, 51, 99–103.
42 Huebner, *The Family in Roman Egypt*, 42–43, 53, 103: census returns in Egypt show unwed brothers and cousins living with married relatives.
43 Satlow, *Jewish Marriage in Antiquity*, 186–189.
44 Satlow, *Jewish Marriage in Antiquity*, 19.
45 Hamel, *Poverty and Charity*, 34, 44–52.
46 Gored by an ox (Exod. 21:28–32); foraging, Hamel, *Poverty and Charity*, 18, 52–54; Poisonous wild fruit (2 Kgs 4:38–41); falling down a well, Peled, 'The Social Texture of the Baqa Well', 815, cf. Jer. 38:6; also accidental death by being struck with a loose axe head (Deut. 19:5); infections (Deut. 28:27); infectious diseases (Lev. 26:16; Deut. 28:22; 2 Sam. 24:15); dysentery? (2 Chr. 21:18; Amos 4:10); parasites (Acts 12:23); wounds (2 Kgs 8:29; Ps. 38:5; Isa. 1:6; Jer. 6:7; Luke 10:34), potential for septicaemia, Botero & Pérez, 'The History of Sepsis'.

The Rabbis' discussions speak of either the widow or the divorcee, but not a combination of life's misfortunes. While it may seem extreme it was not impossible for Rabbi Gamaliel to imagine a woman widowed three times wanting to marry a fourth time. The picture that emerges in John 4 is one of poverty and tragic circumstances. While the Roman ideal was that a woman would be married once, realistically women remarried to survive.[47] It appears that in Jewish society there was no equivalent ideal and women were expected to remarry if their husbands died or divorced them.[48] Even so there was a limit to how many husbands a woman might respectably have. However, this would not be an impediment to the Samaritan woman marrying a sixth time. We come now to consider the arrangement depicted in the Gospel: 'the man you are with is not your husband'.

Greeks and Jews had similar marriage customs. It had been the custom in Egypt that when a girl was married for the first time her father would formally hand her to her husband.[49] This was called *ekdosis* in Greek.[50] There would normally be a wedding lasting a number of days.[51] A girl usually came into a marriage with property, goods, and cash given to her by her father.[52] In Greek this was called a dowry. Jews of Egypt and Palestine in the late Hellenistic period had adopted this custom.[53] Michael Satlow argues that in some Jewish marriage contracts the dowry is called a *ketubba*.[54] He has argued that the dowry 'served as compensation to the husband for the upkeep of a wife'.[55] It was also expected that it would keep a widow until she returned to her family of origin or remarried.[56] A marriage contract could be drawn up, but this normally

---

47 Venour, 'The Roman Widow: A Social Study', 62.
48 Satlow, *Jewish Marriage in Antiquity*, 182.
49 Wolff, *Written and Unwritten Marriage*, 27–29. *ekdosis* as a custom appeared to have waned over time; Satlow, *Jewish Marriage in Antiquity*, 69.
50 Wolff, *Written and Unwritten Marriage*, 15.
51 Satlow, *Jewish Marriage in Antiquity*, 168–180.
52 Satlow, *Jewish Marriage in Antiquity*, 199.
53 Satlow, *Jewish Marriage in Antiquity*, 201.
54 Satlow, *Jewish Marriage in Antiquity*, 200–202: in Jewish marriage arrangements another payment could be made from the husband to the woman's father or brother and this was called a *mohar*. In the documents from the Elephantine this payment was 'usually a small sum of money'.
55 Satlow, *Jewish Marriage in Antiquity*, 209–213 esp. 213.
56 Satlow, *Jewish Marriage in Antiquity*, 213.

came before the wedding.⁵⁷ Sometimes it would be drawn up after the couple had been cohabitating for a number of years.⁵⁸ When a marriage contract was drawn up this was then called a written marriage.⁵⁹ It seems this was normally the case if the bride was bringing property with her. Some marriages had no written contract and these were called unwritten marriages.⁶⁰ There were conventional expectations about the roles that each partner would perform. These were often described in written contracts, but of course in unwritten marriages they were just expected. Wives would be expected to cook, do laundry, grind grain and bake bread.⁶¹ Husbands were expected to feed and clothe their wives.⁶²

While the first marriage of a girl would be accompanied by a formal handing over, a wedding, and a dowry, the second marriage of a woman received little fanfare.⁶³ The couple started cohabitating. The *Tosephta* advised a man to marry a second time on the Thursday so he may have the Sabbath to enjoy his bride before returning to work.⁶⁴ Otherwise he would be married one day and at work the next. The woman could possibly have the consent of her legal guardian, but this was not always the case.⁶⁵ Since men usually married later than women, fathers usually died before mothers, if they made it through their child bearing years.⁶⁶ Depending on the number of years a woman was married before she was

---

57 Pummer, 'Samaritan Marriage Contracts and Deeds of Divorce', 532: the earliest known Samaritan marriage contract dates from 1510/11 CE. Pummer also notes that Samaritans knew of written marriage contracts in the eleventh century CE and argues that it is reasonable to assume that 'like the Jews, Samaritans too possessed written marriage contracts centuries before that date'.
58 Wolff, *Written and Unwritten Marriage*, 44–45; cf. Pummer, 'Samaritan Marriage Contracts and Deeds of Divorce', 532: the contract was read at the wedding ceremony, although these are much later examples of Samaritan marriage contracts.
59 Wolff, *Written and Unwritten Marriage*, 2.
60 Wolff, *Written and Unwritten Marriage*, 2; Satlow, *Jewish Marriage in Antiquity*, 74–75, 84: 'the marriage existed with or without the document'.
61 Hamel, *Poverty and Charity*, 112; Satlow, *Jewish Marriage in Antiquity*, 220: a wife is responsible for seven tasks: grinding, baking, laundry, cooking, breast feeding children, making the bed, and working in wool.
62 Satlow, *Jewish Marriage in Antiquity*, 219–224; Pummer, 'Samaritan Marriage Contracts and Deeds of Divorce', 538: the formulae in the Samaritan marriage contracts appears to reference Exod. 21:10 and states the husband 'shall not diminish her food, her clothing, or her marital rights'.
63 Satlow, *Jewish Marriage in Antiquity*, 183.
64 Satlow, *Jewish Marriage in Antiquity*, 183–184.
65 Llewelyn, 'Paul's Advice on Marriage', 2.
66 Satlow, *Jewish Marriage in Antiquity*, 185.

widowed, a woman could find herself without a father when she remarried. This might even be the case at her first marriage. There are a number of marriage contracts where either the mother of the bride or the bride herself is doing the contracting.[67] In the case of a second marriage a woman would bring her dowry with her.[68] If it was not substantial she would not need a contract to protect her rights to her property. In this case an unwritten marriage would then ensue. This has been called an informal marriage and was in essence a de-facto marriage based on the verbal agreement of the spouses.[69]

We are now in a position to ask why the Samaritan woman and Jesus consider her not to be married to the man she is currently with. There could be a number of impediments to marriage, even an unwritten one. We will consider these now.

First, a freed woman cohabitating with a man was not considered his wife but his concubine.[70] Neither were cohabitating slaves considered married.[71] But this does not apply to the Samaritan woman as she has been married demonstrating that she is a free born woman.

Secondly, under Roman law a Roman citizen had to be married to another Roman citizen to have children eligible to be citizens.[72] A Roman man could cohabit with a non-Roman, who was considered his concubine, but their children would not be Roman citizens.[73] Many couples fell into this category and despite their legal standing they considered themselves married.[74] But this relationship is not what is in view here in John.

Thirdly, Roman soldiers could not marry until they had completed their active service after twenty five years. Many soldiers ignored this and cohabitated with their concubines.[75] Their children were considered to

---

67 Wolff, *Written and Unwritten Marriage*, 60; Llewelyn, 'Paul's Advice on Marriage', 1–18.
68 Satlow, *Jewish Marriage in Antiquity*, 201–202; Mueller, 'Strategies for Survival', 198–199, 202–205: Roman law formally recognised the concubine and this arrangement was distinct from marriage.
69 Wolff, *Written and Unwritten Marriage*, 28, 81–83.
70 Saller, 'Family and Household', 862.
71 Mouritsen, 'The Families of Roman Slaves and Freedmen', 129–144.
72 Rawson, 'Introduction', 1–5; Mueller, 'Strategies for Survival', 206–209.
73 Satlow, *Jewish Marriage in Antiquity*, 193–194.
74 Mueller, 'Strategies for Survival', 207–215.
75 Allison, 'Soldiers' Families in the Early Roman Empire', 161–182.

be illegitimate.[76] Again this type of union was so frequent it was not considered socially inappropriate.[77] It is extremely unlikely that this is the case for the Samaritan woman as the Roman army was primarily stationed in Syria.[78]

Fourthly, she may be cohabitating with a freedman.[79] This is a good point at which to consider the economic possibilities lying behind the depiction of the Samaritan woman. I am assuming that her dowry or her *ketubba* has been depleted through her multiple marriages.[80] A strategy for survival was for the widow to cohabitate with a privileged slave or freedman.[81] However, this is unlikely in a rural setting. She could of course be living with a farmer's freedman.[82] In this case he is hiring himself out as a day labourer. He would therefore be poor. Judging by the disciples' reaction upon seeing her, we can surmise that she looked poor. Their reaction demonstrates the common prejudice against the poor as we saw in Welborn's discussion.[83] Since she is not in a contracted marriage, either written or unwritten, then the man she is with is not obliged to provide for her. She is therefore dressed in either coarse, dark coloured clothes worn by the poor or perhaps she is still in her worn clothes from her last marriage.[84] Most likely she would be barefooted.[85]

76 Youtie, *Scriptiunculae Posteriores*, 1.17–34.
77 Youtie, *Scriptiunculae Posteriores*, 1.17–34.
78 Safrai, *The Economy of Roman Palestine*, 339: 'Until 66 CE the Roman army in Judaea was rather small: 3–6 auxiliary units, some of which were composed of local militia from Sebaste and Caesara'; Isaac, *The Limits of Empire*, 77–83; 139; 336–342; stationed in Syria, 269–270; garrison at Jerusalem pre-70 CE, 279–282.
79 Satlow, *Jewish Marriage in Antiquity*, 193; Safrai, *The Economy of Roman Palestine*, 334–336: slaves and free working on estates.
80 Schottroff, *Lydia's Impatient Sisters*, 92–95: see the discussion on the precariousness economic position of women widowed more than once.
81 Mueller, 'Strategies for Survival', 300–301.
82 Mueller, 'Strategies for Survival', 282–299: those in the 'lower classes' mixed socially and children from their relationships, though illegitimate were not stigmatized; Mouritsen, 'The Families of Roman Slaves and Freedmen', 137: freedmen frequently stayed with their household of origin.
83 Hamel, *Poverty and Charity*, 199: perhaps we should see the disciples' reaction based on twin prejudices; a prejudice against Samaritan women and the notion among Jews that impurity was linked to poverty.
84 Hamel, *Poverty and Charity*, 60, 72–73: provision of clothes was a part of a marriage contract; quality and colour of clothes, 76–78; 81–82, 86–88; Pummer, 'Samaritan Marriage Contracts and Deeds of Divorce', 538: note that in Samaritan marriage contracts it was the husband's duty to provide clothes for his wife.
85 Hamel, *Poverty and Charity*, 63–64, 65–66, 75–76: it was expected that a husband would provide shoes for a wife but these were not as durable as sandals.

There is one last possibility: the man she is with is a Jew. And this explanation fits the context of this narrative. As the narrator himself says, Jews do not associate with Samaritans. Jews were not to intermarry with Samaritans, therefore, a Jew cohabitating with a Samaritan would not consider her his wife.[86] This would mean that there was no verbal contract between them and therefore their relationship was not a marriage. Even so, by his association with her, he would be unclean.[87] The Mishnah considered Samaritan women to be perpetually unclean, as if they were continually menstruating (*m. Nid.* 4:1).[88] This prejudice would have worked the other way.[89] This may explain in part the reluctance of the woman to associate with the other women when drawing water from the well.[90] It also explains her knowledge and interest in the differences between Jews and Samaritans (John 4: 19–20).

This is not a picture of forbidden love. It is a picture of people at the economic extremity trying to survive. I would like to speculate that there were relationships like this throughout Palestine.[91] I suggest, that like the freedman described above, our conjectured Jew was a day labourer forced by economic circumstances to work in Samaria.[92] Economically it was beneficial for the two individuals we have pictured

---

86 Satlow, *Jewish Marriage in Antiquity*, 149–150, 152–153; Jeremias, *Jerusalem in the Time of Jesus*, 356; Kasher, 'Josephus on Jewish-Samaritan Relations', 217–236: Josephus tells us that Herod had married a Samaritan woman Malthace. The evidence suggests that she was not converted to Judaism, therefore he had transgressed the Jewish prohibition against marrying Samaritan women.
87 Jeremias, *Jerusalem in the Time of Jesus*, 357.
88 Crown, 'Qumran, Samaritan Halakha and Theology, and Pre-Tannaitic Judaism', §2.23–24: it is somewhat ironic that Samaritan *halakha* was stricter in regard to women's purity than Rabbinic Judaism; cf. Ruairidh and Bóid, *Principles of Samaritan Halachah*, 317–320.
89 Racial prejudice in the Greco-Roman world, Benjamin, 'Ethnic Prejudice and Racism', 329–339; Crown, 'Qumran, Samaritan Halakha and Theology, and Pre-Tannaitic Judaism', §2.13–31: there was a marked difference between Samaritan and Jewish interpretation of the Pentateuch.
90 Jeremias, *Jerusalem in the Time of Jesus*, 353–354.
91 Jeremias, *Jerusalem in the Time of Jesus*, 352–358: Jeremias paints a checked picture of Jewish and Samaritan relations. Herod the Great had married a Samaritan woman, perhaps to ease the tensions between them.
92 Other options: tenant farmer or sharecropper, or he came to work in the flax industry that operated around Neapolis, Safrai, *The Economy of Roman Palestine*, 335–337, 451–452; There is evidence that Jews did have business dealings with Samaritans, Pummer, 'Religions in Contact and Conflict', §3.48.

to live together.⁹³ Hired labourers were often paid in kind.⁹⁴ His work would feed them both. Either she or he may have had a cloak to keep warm at night.⁹⁵ Important for our scenario here is our conjectured village. If the village was indeed without a baker, then a woman who possessed a millstone would be exceedingly advantageous.⁹⁶ The ability to grind one's own grain was an important factor in providing enough nutrition for a family.⁹⁷ The picture I am suggesting is one of two people thrown together by necessity; neither believes they are cohabiting with an ideal partner but together they are surviving. Their life together is made possible by living in a small village with others, who may be also social misfits.⁹⁸ The woman's story is known to her neighbours, who are impressed that Jesus somehow knew of the intricate story of widowhood, divorce, and compromise this Samaritan woman has had to live through (John 4:28–29, 42).

If this was indeed the assumed background to the Samaritan woman, then why would the narrator not make this explicit? I suggest that the image of a Samaritan cohabiting with a Jew was believed by the writer to have the potential to overwhelm the point of the story: Jesus came to bring living water to all of Israel, even the Samaritans (John 4:13–14, 39–42). For those in the audience who were familiar with Sychar and Samaria the clues were obvious enough, but for those without this knowledge a number of options could fit the picture that is presented in John 4. For some readers the picture of the Samaritan woman fitted in with their assumptions of Samaritans and women. For both Romans and Jews, women who did not fit neatly into the traditional family

---

93 Safrai, *The Economy of Roman Palestine*, 358–365; 371–373: it is possible the women owned a house with a small plot of land or the couple rented a room in a house; Huebner, *The Family in Roman Egypt*, 39, 97–99. A widow could also have life tenure of her husband's property if she did not remarry. However, tenure would only be possible if her husband had inherited his property.
94 Hamel, *Poverty and Charity*, 37–38.
95 Hamel, *Poverty and Charity*, 71.
96 Hamel, *Poverty and Charity*, 32, 34: purchasing bread from a baker was not ideal. It exposed a person to fluctuating supply so that one lacked food security and also it was not as nutritious and filling as home baked bread.
97 Hamel, *Poverty and Charity*, 39, 52–53, 112: 'malnutrition meant that poor people were also more prone to diseases'. However, grinding grain consumed a significant proportion of the day.
98 Safrai, *The Economy of Roman Palestine*, 71.

scheme were characterised as sexually promiscuous.[99] This is an assumption that has stayed with us to the present day.[100]

In conclusion, the encounter of Jesus with the Samaritan woman pictured in John 4 is ambiguous.[101] The woman coming to the well at such a late time in the morning suggests some kind of shunning by the other women of the town. On the surface this appears to be related to her five husbands and the admission that the man she is now with is not her husband. It is possible, judging by the discussion of the Rabbis, that her five husbands were a matter of some shame to her. However, this might not have been out of the ordinary for women in rural Palestine. It is, after all, firmly established in the narrative that these men were her husbands. It is unlikely that divorce was a social impediment. However, as we have seen in the discussion of the Rabbis, women with multiple marriage partners were viewed with suspicion. And it would appear that we are to understand from John that this widow or divorcee was not able to remarry, but had to cohabitate with a man, who could not legitimately marry her. We investigated the options for this circumstance and brought it down to two possibilities. Either she was cohabitating with a freedman or with a Jewish man. The weight of evidence from within the narrative implies that the man was Jewish. However, only an informed reader would see this possibility, so that the narrative otherwise glides over this awkward idea. The story of the woman at the well is not so much about the relations between genders, but a story about poverty and prejudice in regards to gender, race, and social dislocation. Prejudices overcome by Jesus' response to her as his disciple.[102]

---

99 Strong, 'Labeled Women: Roman Prostitutes and Persistent Stereotypes', 1—9; Sly, *Philo's Perception of Women*, 173; Jeremias, *Jerusalem in the Time of Jesus*, 359–360.
100 Beirne, *Women and Men*, 82 n. 64; For example, Keener, *John*, 605–608; Morris, *John*, 234: 'It is best taken as his way of bringing the woman's sin into the open...Jesus' reply is devastating. It shows that he knows all about her marital misadventures'; cf. Carmichael, 'Marriage and the Samaritan Woman', 332–346; Eslinger, 'The Wooing of the Woman at the Well', 167–183.
101 Beirne, *Women and Men*, 95: assuming a gendered pairs scheme between Nicodemus and the Samaritan woman.
102 Beirne, *Women and Men*, 99–100.

Bibliography

Allison, P.   'Soldiers' Families in the Early Roman Empire', in B. Rawson (ed.), *Companion to Families in the Greek and Roman World* (S.l.: John Wiley & Sons, 2011), 161–82.

Barrett, C. K.   *The Gospel According to St. John: An Introduction with Commentary and Notes on the Greek Text* (Philadelphia: The Westminster Press, 1978 2nd ed.).

Beirne, M. M.   *Women and Men in the Fourth Gospel: A Genuine Discipleship of Equals* (London: Sheffield Academic Press, 2003).

Benjamin, I.   'Ethnic Prejudice and Racism', in B. Graziosi et al (eds.), *The Oxford Handbook of Hellenic Studies* (Oxford: Oxford University Press, 2009), 329–39. DOI:10.1093/oxfordhb/9780199286140.001.0001; www.oxfordhandbooks.com/view/10.1093/oxfordhb/9780199286140.001.0001/oxfordhb-9780199286140 [accessed August, 2017]

Botero, J.S.H, & M. C. F. Pérez   'The History of Sepsis from Ancient Egypt to the XIX Century, Sepsis—An Ongoing and Significant Challenge' (ed. Luciano Azevedo; 2012). DOI: 10.5772/51484; www.intechopen.com/books/sepsis-an-ongoing-and-significant-challenge/the-history-of-sepsis-from-ancient-egypt-to-the-xix-century [accessed August 2017]

Carmichael, C. M.   'Marriage and the Samaritan Woman', *NTS* 26 (2009), 332–46.

Carson, D. A.   *The Gospel According to John* (PNTC; Grand Rapids & Cambridge: Eerdmans, 1991).

Crown, A. D.   'Qumran, Samaritan Halakha and Theology, and Pre-Tannaitic Judaism', in V. Morabito et al (eds.), *Samaritan Researches* 5 (Studies in Judaica; Sydney, Australia: Mandelbaum Publishing, 2000), §2.13–31.

Dar, S.   *Landscape and Pattern: An Archaeological Survey of Samaria 800 B.C.E.–636 C.E.* (S. Applebaum, ed.; Oxford, UK: B.A.R, 1986).

Eslinger, L.   'The Wooing of the Woman at the Well: Jesus, the Reader and Reader-Response Criticism', *Literature and Theology* 1 (1987), 167–83.

Hamel, G. H.	*Poverty and Charity in Roman Palestine, First Three Centuries C.E.* (Berkeley and Los Angeles, CA: University of California Press, 1990).
Huebner, S. R.	*The Family in Roman Egypt: A Comparative Approach to Intergenerational Solidarity and Conflict* (Cambridge: Cambridge University Press, 2013).
Isaac, B. H.	*The Limits of Empire: The Roman Army in the East* (New York; Oxford: Oxford University Press; Clarendon Press, 2000 rev. ed.).
Jeremias, J.	*Jerusalem in the Time of Jesus: An Investigation into Economic and Social Conditions During the New Testament Period* (F. H. & C. H. Cave, transls.; London: SCM, 1969).
Kasher, A.	'Josephus on Jewish-Samaritan Relations under Roman Rule (BCE 63–CE 70)', in A. D. Crown et al (eds.), *Essays in Honour of G.D. Sixdenier: New Samaritan Studies* 3&4 (Studies in Judaica; Sydney: Mandelbaum Publishing: n.d.), 217–36.
Keener, C. S.	*The Gospel of John: A Commentary* (2 vols.; Peabody: Hendrickson Publishers, 2003).
Llewelyn, S.R.	'Paul's Advice on Marriage and the Changing Understanding of Marriage in Antiquity', in S.R. Llewelyn (ed.), *New Documents Illustrating Early Christianity* 6 (North Ryde, NSW: Macquarie University, 1992), 1–18.
Michaels, R.	*The Gospel of John* (NICNT; Grand Rapids: Eerdmans, 2010).
Morris, L.L.	*The Gospel According to John* (NICNT; Grand Rapids: Eerdmans, 1995 rev. ed.).
Mouritsen, H.	'The Families of Roman Slaves and Freedmen', in B. Rawson (ed.), *A Companion to Families in the Greek and Roman Worlds* (Wiley-Blackwell, 2010), 129–44.
Mueller, I.	'Strategies for Survival: Widows in the Context of Their Social Relationships' (unpublished Ph.D. diss., University of Chicago, 2004).
Peled, K.	'The Social Texture of the Baqa Well: Drawing History from an Old Well in a Palestinian Arab Town in Israel', *Middle Eastern Studies* 50 (2014), 810–25.

Pummer, R. 'Samaritan Marriage Contracts and Deeds of Divorce', in A.D Crown et al (eds.), *Essays in Honour of G.D. Sixdenier: New Samaritan Studies* 3&4 (Studies in Judaica; Sydney: Mandelbaum Publishing, n.d.), 4.529–50.

Pummer, R. 'Religions in Contact and Conflict: Samaritans of Caesarea among the "Pagans", Jews and Christians', in V. Morabito et al (eds.), *Samaritan Researchers* 5 (Studies in Judaica; Sydney: Mandelbaum Publishing, 2000), §3.29–53.

Rawson, B. 'Introduction', in B. Rawson (ed.), *Marriage, Divorce, and Children in Ancient Rome* (Canberra; Oxford, UK; New York: Humanities Research Center; Clarendon Press; Oxford University Press, 1991), 1–5.

Ruairidh I, & M. Bóid, *Principles of Samaritan Halachah* (Studies in Judaism in Late Antiquity; Leiden; New York; København; Köln: Brill, 1989).

Safrai, Z. *The Economy of Roman Palestine* (London; New York: Routledge, 1994).

Saller, R. 'Family and Household', in A. Bowman et al (eds.), *The High Empire, A.D. 70–192* (Cambridge: Cambridge University Press, 2000), 855–74.

Satlow, M. L. *Jewish Marriage in Antiquity* (Princeton: Princeton University Press, 2001).

Schottroff, L. *Lydia's Impatient Sisters: a Feminist Social History of Early Christianity* (B. & M. Rumscheidt, transls.; Louisville: Westminster John Knox Press, 1995).

Sly, D. *Philo's Perception of Women* (Brown Judaic Studies; Atlanta: Scholars Press, 1990).

Strack, H. L., & P. Billerbeck *Das Evangelium Nach Markus, Lukas Und Johannes Und Die Apostelgeschichte* (Kommentar Zum Neuen Testament Aus Talmud Und Midrasch 2; München: Beck, 1969).

Strong, A. 'Labeled Women: Roman Prostitutes and Persistent Stereotypes' (unpublished Ph.D. diss., Columbia University, 2005).

Thomson, W. M. *The Land and the Book* 2 (New York: Harper & Brothers 1860).

Venour, K. C.   'The Roman Widow: A Social Study' (unpublished Ph.D. diss., University of Victoria, 1992).

Welborn, L.L.   'The Polis and the Poor: Reconstructing Social Relations from Different Genres of Evidence', in J.R. Harrison & L.L. Welborn (eds.), *The First Urban Christians 1: Methodological Foundations* (Atlanta: SBL Press, 2015), 189–243.

Wolff, H. J.   *Written and Unwritten Marriage in Hellenistic and Postclassical Roman Law* (Philological Association 9; Lancaster, PA; Oxford, UK: Lancaster Press; Blackwell, 1939).

Youtie, H. C.   *Scriptiunculae Posteriores* 1 (Bonn: R. Habelt Verlag, 1981).

Zangenberg, J.   '"Open Your Eyes and Look at the Fields" Contacts between Christians and Samaria According to the Gospel of John', in V. Morabito et al (eds.), *Samaritan Researches* 5 (Studies in Judaica; Sydney: Mandelbaum Publishing, 2000), §3.84–94.

Web Resources

'Come and Hear™: An Educational Forum for the Examination of Religious Truth and Religious Tolerance', www.come-and-hear.com/yebamoth/yebamoth_65.html [accessed July 2018].

CHAPTER 13

Johannine Altruism: A Biblical Tonic for the Randian Plague

Dr Debra Snoddy

Abstract

Ayn Rand and Jesus of Nazareth are opposites on the altruism-individualism continuum! Recent seismic shifts in the socio-political landscape globally are ample confirmation of this. Behind these shifts is a brand of individualism that, I believe, finds its natural home with the mid-twentieth century author/philosopher Ayn Rand. An individualism that values the other only in so far as they are a reflection of oneself, based on transactional or trader model of virtue. This is essentially the 'virtue in selfishness' understood as 'a concern for one's own interests' above all others, protecting one from the social collectivist mindset. In this model of understanding, altruism is 'self-inflicted loss, self-inflicted pain and the gray, debilitating pall of an incomprehensible duty'.[1] 'Altruism cannot permit a recognition of virtue; it cannot permit self-esteem or moral innocence. Guilt is altruism's stock in trade, and the inducing of guilt is its only means of self-perpetuation. If the giver is not kept under a torrent of degrading, demeaning accusations, he might take a look around and put an end to the self-sacrificing. Altruists are concerned only with those who suffer—not with those who provide relief from suffering, not even enough to care whether they are able to

---

[1] Rand, *The Virtue of Selfishness*, viii.

survive. When no actual suffering can be found, the altruists are compelled to invent or manufacture it'.[2]

> It is your mind that they want you to surrender—all those who preach the creed of sacrifice, whatever their tags or their motives, whether they demand it for the sake of your soul or of your body, whether they promise you another life in heaven or a full stomach on this earth. Those who start by saying: "It is selfish to pursue your own wishes, you must sacrifice them to the wishes of others"—end up by saying: "It is selfish to uphold your convictions, you must sacrifice them to the convictions of others".[3]

The contradiction of the 'virtue of selfishness' implies that its corollary is the 'vice of selflessness' best understood as a mindless act of self-immolation, self-abnegation, self-denial, and self-destruction. Is this true? Or has the Johannine Jesus of Nazareth something more substantial to offer our world as it struggles with the consequences of Randian individualism? How can the message of the Gospel of John heal the Randian plague? This article sets out to show that the true opposite for Randian individualism is altruism and a Johannine altruism at that.

1. Introduction

Ayn Rand and Jesus of Nazareth are opposites on the altruism-egoism/individualism continuum![4] This may be seen as stating the blindingly obvious but there is a reason I want to start here. This past year (2016–17) has seen seismic shifts in the socio-political landscape globally. Britain is brexiting the EU, the US Presidential elections of 2016

---

2   Rand, 'Moral Inflation', The Ayn Rand Letter, III, 13, 2.
3   Rand, *For the New Intellectual*, (Galt's Speech), 142.
4   If one searches the antonyms for individualism in any dictionary, the opposite of individualism appears to be collectivism, understood as a form of either communism or of National Socialism (fascism). However, this simply does not work with the conceptual world of Ayn Rand. As this article sets out to show. The true opposite for Randian individualism is altruism and a Johannine altruism at that.

revealed deep-seated divisions and resulted in the election to the office of President of the United States of America of cult personality figure and billionaire, Donald Trump and the One Nation Party now boasts a Federal Member in the Senate in Australia. What do these events have in common? A determination to 'save our way of life from the onslaught of foreigners, migrants, and other nefarious ne'er-do-wells' and the promise to make Britain/ America/ Australia 'great again'. But more importantly, there is within each 'cause' a brand of individualism that, I believe, finds its natural home with the mid-twentieth century author/ philosopher Ayn Rand. However, I hear you say, how can individualism be at the root of such a diverse global paradigm shift? Allow me to explain.

2. What is Randian Individualism?

Ayn Rand was born in Russia in 1905 to a Jewish family, and in the course of 1917 experienced both the Kernesky Revolution, which she supported, and the Bolshevik Revolution, which she denounced from the outset. She completed studies in Philosophy and History at the University of Petrograd in 1924. On the pretext of visiting relative in the US, in 1925, she obtained permission to leave Soviet Russia and never returned. She spent the next nine years in Hollywood working in different jobs including as a screenwriter, married actor Frank O'Connor in 1929, and began working on her novel, *The Fountainhead*, in 1935. It was finally published in 1943 and began a best seller through word-of-mouth, but initially had a mixed reception from literary critics. This is our first encounter with her version of man as 'he could be and ought to be', the ideal man, the kind of hero whose depiction was the chief goal of her writing.[5]

In *The Fountainhead*, we meet Howard Roark, an individualistic young architect who refuses to compromise his artistic and personal vision for worldly recognition and success. The novel, champions

---

5   It also contains a sex scene that has been described as advocating rape by some scholars. See Brownmiller, Against Our Will, 348–350; Brown, 'Ayn Rand: The Woman Who Would Not Be President', 63–65; Grizzuti Harrison, 'Psyching Out Ayn Rand', 74–75 to mention but a few.

his battle against the conformity ideals of the establishment in order to bring to birth his vision of modern architecture. The plot revolves around Roark's quest for success on his own terms, which eventually lands him in court for dynamiting a building rather than seen his design comprised. His courtroom speech has gone done in history as the championing of individualism over collectivism and gained for Rand the lasting recognition as the champion of individualism.

Throughout the 1940s Rand was involved in both free-market and anti-Communist activism and she and her husband were active in the Republican campaign for the Presidential elections of 1940 and 1947. She also testified to the House Un-American Activities Committee in 1947 about her experiences in the Soviet Union. The couple moved to New York in 1951 where Rand established a group called 'the collective,'[6] to discuss philosophy and this group were privy to earlier drafts of her work.

Her last work of fiction, and her *opus maior*, *Atlas Shrugged*, was published in 1957. Having experienced great difficulty in getting *The Fountainhead* published, Rand now found herself courted by many publishers for her second and last work of fiction. Twelve years in the writing, the plot takes the form of a mystery story, centred on the question 'Who is John Galt?' and is a dramatization of her vision of existence and of man's highest potential. In order to create heroic fictional characters Rand had to identify the philosophic principles which make such individuals possible. In *Atlas Shrugged*, her unique philosophy integrates ethics, metaphysics, epistemology, politics, economics and sex. The themes dealt with are many and varied from, 'the role of the mind in man's existence,'[7] to good versus evil, to the nobility of business such that those who pursue business rationally receive profound moral recognition and those who enter the realm to expropriate values receive condemnation, which includes the absolutism of reason and its natural

---

6   A young Alan Greenspan, future Chairman of the Federal Reserve, was a notable member of her clique.

7   Ayn Rand, *Capitalism: The Unknown Ideal*, 1 and *id.*, 'Basic Principles of Literature' in *The Romantic Manifesto: A Philosophy of Literature*, 81. The fuller statement reads as follows, 'the role of the mind in man's existence and, as a corollary, the presentation of a new code of ethics – the morality of rational self-interest' as espoused in *id.*, 'Is Atlas Shrugging?' in *Capitalism*, 15 and *id.*, *For the New Intellectual*, 88.

corollary freedom from all constraints, as well as her unique take on love and sex. What emerges is a code of rational self-interest as a 'Morality of Life' and the conventional code of selflessness and self-sacrifice as a 'Morality of Death'.

When her *magnum opus* eventually came out in 1957, it was carped by critics on both the left and right, but it became an international bestseller. Indeed, in 1991, the US Library of Congress and the Book of the Month Club ranked it the second most influential book among American readers.[8] The Bible was ranked first! After this, Rand dedicated her life to her brand of philosophy which she termed as Objectivism, 'a philosophy for living on earth'.[9] She wrote seven books of philosophy, but other volumes appeared after her death (March 6, 1986).

Rand was never taken seriously in *academia* while she lived, but her way of thinking has been a key influence on American conservatives and libertarians. Whole Foods CEO John P. Mackey is one of many of the corporate elite who cites Rand as key to his success. Leonard Peikoff, her heir and former member of 'the collective' established the Ayn Rand Institute in 1985 and makes sure her fiction continues to influence new generations, giving copies of her novels to high schools.[10] There is much that one could write in rebuttal of Rand's stance on most things, I have chosen just one—her objectivist ethics and mostly particularly her definition and understanding of altruism and its relationship to humanity.

3. Humanity and its Relation to Altruism According to Rand

I find an inherent dichotomy in her understanding of humanity that directly contradicts her declaration that 'Man [is] the highest living species on this earth—the being whose consciousness has a limitless capacity for gaining knowledge'.[11] Yet she favours the view that all human

---

8   www.nytimes.com/1991/11/20/books/book-notes-059091.html (Accessed 20/09/17).
9   Ayn Rand, 'Philosophy: Who Needs It'.
10 www.haaretz.com/jewish/this-day-in-jewish-history/.premium-1.674065 (Accessed 6/2/17).
11 Rand, *The Virtue of Selfishness*, 21.

interactions ought to be based on the trader principle, '[t]he principle of trade is the only rational ethical principle for all human relationships, personal and social, private and public, spiritual and material. It is *the* principle of justice'.[12] 'A trader is a man who earns what he gets and does not give or take the undeserved. He does not treat men as masters or slaves, but as independent equals. He deals with men by means of a free, voluntary, unforced, un-coerced exchange—an exchange which benefits both parties by their own independent judgment. A trader does not expect to be paid for his defaults, only for his achievements. He does not switch to others the burden of his failures, and he does not mortgage his life into bondage to the failures of others'.[13]

This all sounds so familiar! Anyone hearing an echo of Karl Marx? He, too, advocated for naked self-interest in its time and place and for similar reasons to Rand, in that, it defeated religion and give reign to cognate accomplishments. Marx and Rand differ on its ultimate goal: he proffers freedom from necessity and self-alienation as his meaning and message while she delivers a message of forthright philosophic materialism, and her ardent atheism is a secondary consequence. Consistent materialism begins by rejecting God and religion and so Randian Man, in much the same manner as Marxian Man, is the ultimate value. Further, freed from the burden of religion, man's happiness is firmly in his own hands. 'The moral purpose of a man's life is the achievement of his own happiness'.[14] However, what, exactly, constitutes happiness?

Happiness is according to Rand, '...the successful state of life, suffering is the warning signal of failure, of death'.[15] 'Happiness is that state of consciousness which proceeds from the achievement of one's values'.[16] 'Happiness is a state of non-contradictory joy—a joy without penalty or guilt, a joy that does not clash with any of your values and does not work for your own destruction... . Happiness is possible only to a rational man, the man who desires nothing but rational goals, seeks nothing but rational values and finds his joy in nothing but rational

---

12 Rand, *The Virtue of Selfishness*, 34, emphasis added.
13 Rand, *The Virtue of Selfishness*, 34-35.
14 Rand, *The Virtue of Selfishness*, 49.
15 Rand, *The Virtue of Selfishness*, 30.
16 Rand, *The Virtue of Selfishness*, 31.

actions'.[17] '"Happiness" can properly be the purpose of ethics, but not the standard'.[18] Unfortunately, the pursuit of happiness, often mutates into the pursuit of pleasure with the attendant softening of the will, intelligence and spirit. This is likely why Rand insists that man must be 'a heroic being with his own happiness as the moral purpose of his life, with productive achievement as his noblest activity, and reason as his only absolute'.[19] Without this nobility, man becomes no more than the most consuming of all, constantly seeking satiation.

Altruism then, is seen as antithetical to her philosophy. To quote Rand:

> Altruism declares that any action taken for the benefit of others is good, and any action taken for one's own benefit is evil. Thus, the beneficiary of an action is the only criterion of moral value-and so long as that beneficiary is anybody other than oneself, anything goes.[20] [Altruism] is ... the ethical theory which regards man as a sacrificial animal, which holds that man has no right to exist for his own sake, that service to others is the only justification of his existence, and that self-sacrifice is his highest moral duty, virtue and value... Altruism holds death as its ultimate goal and standard of value—and it is logical that renunciation, resignation, self-denial, and every other form of suffering, including self-destruction, are the virtues it advocates.[21]

It becomes increasingly clear that Rand has little time for her understanding of altruism since it permits no view of men except as 'sacrificial animals and profiteers-on-sacrifice, as victims and parasites...'[22] But what is altruism? Has Rand rather gilded the lily?

---

17 Rand, *The Virtue of Selfishness*, 32.
18 Rand, *The Virtue of Selfishness*, 33.
19 Rand, *Atlas Shrugged*, 'About the Author,' Appendix.
20 Rand, *The Virtue of Selfishness*, 6.
21 Rand, *The Virtue of Selfishness*, 37–38.
22 Rand, *The Virtue of Selfishness*, 7.

4. What is altruism?[23]

In popular culture, altruism is identified in opposition to egoism as, '[d]isinterested and selfless concern for the well-being of [the] other'.[24] Philosophy understands it as 'motivated by a desire to benefit someone other than oneself for that person's sake... [also] the word is used more broadly to refer to behaviour that benefits others, regardless of its motive.'[25] In psychology it is '[p]utting others' interests before one's own sometimes to the point of sacrificing one's own interests or life in the process.'[26] '[T]he prototypical altruistic situation involves someone who gives (a benefactor), and someone who receives (a recipient). In some cases, characteristics of the benefactor affect altruism, and in other cases it is characteristics of the recipient'.[27]

What is common to all these definitions is the concept of disinterestedness for another's well-being wherein one gives and the other receives. Here it is important to make a philological distinction. 'Disinterested' does not mean 'uninterested', which is a fundamental mistake in Rand's thinking. However, even the Oxford Dictionary notes that there is controversy over the usage of the two terms:

> Nowhere are the battle lines more deeply drawn in usage questions than over the difference between disinterested and uninterested. According to traditional guidelines, disinterested should never be used to mean 'not interested' (i.e. it is not a synonym for uninterested) but only to mean 'impartial', as in the judgements of disinterested outsiders are likely to be more useful. Ironically, the earliest recorded sense of disinterested is for the disputed sense. Today, the 'incorrect' use of disinterested is widespread: around a quarter of citations in the Oxford English Corpus for disinterested are for this sense.[28]

---

23 From the Latin *alteri huic* 'to this one' or 'to this other'. Author's translation.
24 https://en.oxforddictionaries.com/definition/altruism (Accessed 30/1/17).
25 https://plato.stanford.edu/entries/altruism/ (Accessed on Monday, 30 /1/17).
26 Matsumoto, *Cambridge Dictionary of Psychology*, 31. See also Krebs, 'Altruism', which appears to be the standard from which research in the field is conducted.
27 Krebs, 'Altruism', 262.
28 https://en.oxforddictionaries.com/definition/disinterested (Accessed 22/9/17).

Correctly understood the adjective 'disinterested' means that one is 'not influenced by considerations of personal advantage'.[29] The adjective 'uninterested' is, in fact, its antithesis, meaning, as it does, that one is 'not interested in or concerned about something or someone.' A common enough error.

A further aspect that Rand does not take sufficiently into account is that altruism is typified by empathy.

> Empathy is the experience of understanding another person's condition from their perspective. You place yourself in their shoes and feel what they are feeling. Empathy is known to increase prosocial (helping) behaviors. While American culture might be socializing people into becoming more individualistic rather than empathic, research has uncovered the existence of 'mirror neurons,' which react to emotions expressed by others and then reproduce them.[30]

It appears then, that the human person is essentially hard-wired for empathetic response! This response has been shown to have both emotional and cognitive elements. One such emotional element of relevance for this study is empathetic concern and its role in triggering pro-social and helping behaviors. Research consistently finds a positive correlation between how much empathic concern individuals report feeling for another person (or group of people) and their willingness to help those people, even when helping requires some sacrifice (e.g., time, effort, or money). '[31] However, there continues to be debate within psychology as to how empathy and altruism are linked. Some scholars hotly defend a link, others do not. 'Attempts to decide whether the helping behavior is selfless or selfish are complicated by the fact that self-interest and

---

29 https://en.oxforddictionaries.com/definition/disinterested (Accessed 22/9/17).
30 www.psychologytoday.com/basics/empathy (Accessed 25/9/17).
31 https://psychology.iresearchnet.com/social-psychology/emotions/empathy/ (Accessed 25/9/17). This article also names the other two elements of emotional empathy, emotional contagion understood as feeling what the other feels and personal distress understood as 'one's own feelings of distress in response to perceiving another's plight'. Batson, Ahmad, & Stocks, 'Benefits and Liabilities', 359–385; Davis, *Empathy*; Hodges & Biswas-Diener, 'Balancing the empathy expense account', 389–407; Ickes, *Everyday Mind Reading*.

benefits to the other person may overlap'.³²

'Cognitive empathy refers to the extent to which we perceive or have evidence that we have successfully guessed someone else's thoughts and feelings...cognitive empathy (often called empathic accuracy) entails having more complete and accurate knowledge about the contents of another person's mind, including how that person feels'.³³ How a person achieves cognitive empathy is a matter of debate still. What is clear is that empathy is the social glue that holds human society together. Frans de Waal argues that modern psychology and neuroscience research supports the concept that 'empathy is an automated response over which we have limited control'.³⁴ De Waal challenges the view that humans are slaves to a 'selfish gene' making it clear that while humanity has competing genes some of which are aggressive and 'selfish' and others that are empathetic and 'selfless', these competing genes are continually vying for dominance. People are not instinctively cruel or selfish, but complex and complicated, and just as capable of caring and empathy. The argument as to whether altruism is caught or taught, by nature or nurture I leave to the psychologists and cultural anthropologists.³⁵

An altruistic person gives and shares what belongs to them with others without reservation (usually at the expense of their convenience, or at times survival). The altruist identifies the one who needs their help, responds and does their best to assist without expecting any reward in return for such assistance. Further, many altruists clearly understand that some people see them as foolish and/or people pleasing but they choose to express and confirm this altruistic character nonetheless. Lastly, a truly altruistic person is driven by the ideology, or more appropriately, the charism summed up best of all by John 15:12. Altruism then can be seen as typified by ἀγάπη *agápē*.

---

32 https://psychology.iresearchnet.com/social-psychology/emotions/empathy/ (Accessed 25/9/17).
33 https://psychology.iresearchnet.com/social-psychology/emotions/empathy/ (Accessed 25/9/17).
34 De Waal, *The Age of Empathy*.
35 Krebs, 'Altruism...', *ad loc.*; Biddle, *Role Theory, ad loc.* Christopher Boehm a cultural anthropologist, director of the Jane Goodall Research Center and professor of Anthropology and Biological Sciences at the University of Southern California, has conducted fieldwork with both human and non-human primates and has published more than 60 scholarly articles and books on the problem of altruism. In his 2012 book, *Moral Origins: The Evolution of Virtue, Altruism, and Shame*, Boehm synthesizes this research to address the question of why, out of all the social primates, are humans so altruistic?

5. The Johannine Jesus: a Counter-cultural Referent in a Hostile World

This empathy that is rooted in ἀγάπη *agápē* needs to be correctly understood. While Christians did not create the word ἀγάπη *agápē*, they did make it a defining word for Christian life and teaching.[36] I expend much time and effort in class is helping students understand the differences, quantitatively, between the four loves, but that is currently beyond the scope of this paper.[37] Briefly, ἀγάπη (the noun, and so by extension its cognate verb ἀγαπάω *agapaō* from which it cannot be separated)[38] in its theological and exegetical understanding is love centred in moral preference based on a divine imperative. There is an active agency inherent in it that leads to a dynamic engagement with the world, *not* disenfranchisement from it. Thomas Jay Oord defines it as 'acting intentionally, in sympathetic response to others (including God) to promote overall well-being when responding to acts, persons or structures of existence that promote ill-being'.[39] Therefore, one may say that ἀγάπη *agápē* is exactly 'disinterested love'.[40]

This understanding is what lies behind John 15:12 (and 13:34).[41] This verse is theologically and structurally at the heart of the farewell discourse of John 13–17. In this long discourse, a transition takes place in the relationship between Jesus and his disciples. Earlier during the foot-washing scene the master-servant relationship was highlighted and subverted as Jesus portrayed the humility necessary to fulfill his mission (13:12ff). Within this very pericope a decisive change takes place—Jesus moves them from disciples to friends and this has consequences not only for them for all who believe.

The ἀγάπη *agápē* Jesus typifies is that which ultimately takes its form

---

36 Willis, 'agápē', 27.
37 Lewis, *The Four Loves,* is still the most useful guide in this regard.
38 Culpepper, *Johannine Literature: With an Introduction*, 177.
39 Oord, *Defining Love*, 43.
40 Ἀγάπη *agápē* – properly, *love* which centers in moral *preference*. So too in secular ancient Greek, *agápē* focuses on *preference*; likewise the verb form ἀγαπάω *agapaō* in antiquity meant, 'To *prefer*' (*TDNT*, 7). In the NT, *agápē* typically refers to *divine love* i.e. what *God prefers*. ἀγαπάω in its usage in the NT properly means, to *prefer*, to *love*; for the believer, *preferring to 'live through Christ'* (1 Jn 4:9, 10), i.e. embracing God's will (choosing His choices) and obeying them through His power. It preeminently refers to what *God prefers*, as He 'is love' (1 Jn 4:8, 16).
41 Indeed, John uses ἀγάπη *agápē* more than any other NT source and about one third of all uses.

as the self-giving act of Jesus on the cross (15:13; 10:11, 15) and it is this sacrifice that is to be the model and paradigm that the disciples are to manifest to each other.[42] It is through the sharing of ἀγάπη *agápē* that the disciples become friends. 'Precisely the consciousness of the humanity of Jesus, and his death as loss, give the love command it moral force and exemplary power'.[43] Indeed, in the Johannine understanding of ἀγάπη agape forms the basis for three relationships

a. Between members of the community

b. The community's relationship with God/ Jesus and Spirit

c. The commissioning of the disciples as Jesus' representatives in a hostile world.[44]

Since we have no other form of ethical preaching in John the love command 'bears all the weight of Christian ethical obligation'.[45]

There can be little doubt about the connection between the love command of 15:12 and the vine and branches metaphor immediately preceding it. Its hortatory purpose is clear; loving as Jesus loved is a consequence for true discipleship, referring back as it does to the parable of the Good Shepherd (10:12–18).[46] The love of which Jesus speaks has its source in God. Such is the ultimate ἀγάπη *agápē* for which disciples must prepare. However, unlike 14:15, which uses a plural form of the verb ἀγαπάω *agapaō*,[47] here in 15:12 and 14 it is in the singular stressing the singular focus to this new friendship between Jesus and the disciples. The mutuality of Jesus and the disciple is based on the mutuality that already exists between God and Jesus,[48] where mutuality is understood as the indissoluble bond of love between Father and Son (15:9).[49] Out of loving friendship, they will be obedient to Jesus who now shares the things of God with them. No slave could expect to share

---

42 Smith, 'John', 1069.
43 Smith, 'John', 1069.
44 Perkins, *Love Commands in the New Testament*, 107.
45 Perkins, *Love Commands in the New Testament*, 107.
46 Scott, 'John', 1198.
47 14:15 has ἀγαπᾶτέ wherein the verb is in subjunctive present active 2nd person plural from of ἀγαπάω.
48 Scott, 'John', 1198.
49 Willis, '*agápē*', 27.

such intimacy with their master.⁵⁰ Jesus' mission is to become theirs as the language of commissioning in 15:16 makes clear and through Jesus they are under the authority of the same God (15:17).

Jesus takes the initiative choosing them to bear fruit that will last (15:16) because of the unity they now share with the Father through him. The fruit that will last is the fulfillment of the ἀγάπη *agápē* command of 15:12 by bearing witness to Jesus in a hostile world (15:27). The believer's obedience to Jesus is equivalent to Jesus' perfect obedience to the Father making true friendship possible between those equal in virtue exemplified by obedience.⁵¹ Therefore, just as Moses was the friend of God in the past with the ability to speak boldly to God in prayer, so now with the disciples (15:16) who becomes friends of God, not through any merit of their own but because they have been chosen by Jesus.

6. The Benefits of Johannine ἀγάπη agápē

Discipleship is fundamentally about correct relationship with God and the world around us. To know God is to acknowledge one's neighbour and '*love of God* is *love of neighbor*'.⁵² Moreover, even if the practice of ἀγάπη *agápē* does not make perfect, it will make the trait of ἀγάπη *agápē* permanent. Humans will not always get it right, but the continual practice of ἀγάπη *agápē* will make it an ingrained pattern of behaviour, a way of life. 'Johannine ἀγάπη *agápē* is above all a nature, considered sometimes as transcendent, sometimes immanent, precisely because it is both divine and incarnate'.⁵³

Further, the Christian practicing ἀγάπη *agápē* is in a stable condition, which testifies to their spiritual authenticity. The love received surpasses them and is greater than their own hearts, binding them with God in mutual attachment and reciprocal indwelling (1 John 4:16).⁵⁴ In short, it allows humanity to participate in God, by allowing God to participate

---

50   Scott, 'John', 1199.
51   Perkins, *Love Commands in the New Testament*, 110.
52   Bruggemann, *Journey to the Common Good*, 111.
53   Spicq, *Agape in the New Testament*, 3.171–172.
54   Spicq, *Agape in the New Testament*, 3.172.

through us to the point of realizing a presence. It is this presence that allows one to become more than merely human, it fosters growth to become a child of God with its innate tendency to unity—Father, Son and through the total ἀγάπη *agápē* of the Son God's children.⁵⁵ One no longer belongs to oneself, but to God and in this is found true freedom to be, not a self-deified individual as Rand would have it, but utterly human endowed with divine ἀγάπη *agápē* that was first made manifest in Jesus' incarnation. This incarnation may be understood as the gift of self and the desire for the happiness of one's friends to the point of sacrificing one's life for them (15:13). 'To love as Christ loves is to love both religiously and humanly, to share in God's love and to extend it to others'.⁵⁶

The psychology of the Christian and the community of believers, changes as ἀγάπη *agápē* is practiced. There is no fear in love (1 John 3:14) and the notion of fearing God is nullified as mutuality between the believer and God grows through the continuing encounter in Christ. John lists no works of charity like James and his virtues are considerably poorer in number than the Synoptics, Peter and especially Paul. That is not to say that John is not interested in morality; his genius lies in his organization of the Christian ethic as a function of ἀγάπη *agápē* conceived as total gift of self.⁵⁷ This kind of heroism requires a sanctity that can come only from God—all the rest flows from this. As one is given over to the love of God, one's heart is filled with the confidence and assurance, of one who triumphs (1 John 5:4) as God inspires the beloved in whom God himself dwells. The most important benefit of ἀγάπη *agápē* is that it allows one to be fully human in an increasingly inhuman world. ἀγάπη *agápē* does not consider the worth of the person, but their need and in seeking to meet that need ἀγάπη *agápē* allows them the possibility for full human flourishing, or to use a Johannine phrase, abundant life (John 10:10).

---

55 Spicq, *Agape in the New Testament*, 3.173.
56 Spicq, *Agape in the New Testament*, 3.180.
57 Spicq, *Agape in the New Testament*, 3.192.

7. Conclusion

Rand's idea of human worth, based on her philosophy of individualism, is devoid of any humanity and if one can deal with humans thusly, what hope is there for God's good creation? A purely materialistic view of humanity necessitates a purely materialistic view of reality, which 'has not only resulted in disregard for the environment, but also undermined the worth of a human life, especially those forms viewed as having little or no utility—human embryos, the poor, or people with disabilities'.[58] If a person worth is to be measured only by 'productive achievement as his noblest activity' than those incapable or disenfranchised from productive achievement like human embryos, the poor and marginalised, people with disabilities are cast on the scrap heap. In her philosophy, the principle of trade becomes deified and priority is given to speculation and the pursuit of happiness through financial gain and this becomes the only rule. Therefore, the fragile of this world are defenseless against the interests of the deified market.[59] The freedom proffered by Rand is illusory, turning its eyes from the ills of others so as to dispense oneself from relieving them.

> Yet all is not lost. Human beings, while capable of the worst, are also capable of rising above themselves, choosing again what is good, and making a new start, despite their mental and social conditioning. We are able to take an honest look at ourselves, to acknowledge our deep dissatisfaction, and to embark on new paths to authentic freedom. No system can completely suppress our openness to what is good, true and beautiful, or our God-given ability to respond to his grace at work deep in our hearts. I appeal to everyone throughout the world not to forget this dignity which is ours. No one has the right to take it from us.[60]

---

58 https://thejesuitpost.org/2015/06/an-overview-of-laudato-si/ (Accessed 27/9/17).
59 Here I would like to acknowledge my debt to the thinking behind *Laudato Si* §56.
60 *Laudato Si* §205.

Bibliography

Batson, C. D., N. Ahmad, & E. L. Stocks, 'Benefits and Liabilities of Empathy-induced Altruism', in A G Miller (ed.), *The Social Psychology of Good And Evil* (New York: Guilford Press 2004), 359–385.

Biddle, Bruce J. *Role Theory: Expectations, Identities, and Behaviors* (New York: Academic Press, 1979).

Boehm, Christopher *Moral Origins: Social Selection and the Evolution of Virtue, Altruism, and Shame* (New York: Basic Books, 2012).

Brownmiller, Susan *Against Our Will: Men, Women, and Rape* (New York: Simon and Schuster, 1975).

Bruggemann, Walter *Journey to the Common Good* (Louisville: Westminster John Knox, 2010).

Culpepper, R. Alan, J.M. Court, R. Edwards, B. Lindars *Johannine Literature: With an Introduction* (Sheffield Academic Press, 2000).

Davis, M. H. *Empathy: A Social-Psychological Approach* (Madison: Brown & Benchmark. 1994).

De Waal, Frans *The Age of Empathy: Nature's Lessons For A Kinder Society* (New York: Three Rivers Press Random House, 2009).

Dunn, James D. G., & John W. Rogerson (eds.) *The Eerdmans Commentary on the Bible* (Grand Rapids: Eerdmans, 2003).

Farrow, T. F. D., & P. W. R. Woodruff (eds.), *Empathy In Mental Illness and Health* (Cambridge: Cambridge University Press, 2007).

Gladstein, Mimi Reisel, & Chris Matthew Sciabarra (eds.) *Feminist Interpretations of Ayn Rand. Re-reading the Canon* (University Park, Pennsylvania: Pennsylvania State University Press, 1999).

Grizzuti Harrison, Barbara 'Psyching Out Ayn Rand', in Mimi Reisel Gladstein & Chris Matthew Sciabarra (eds.), *Feminist Interpretations of Ayn Rand. Re-reading the Canon* (University Park, Pennsylvania: Pennsylvania State University Press, 1999), 67–78.

Hodges, S. D., & R. Biswas-Diener   'Balancing the empathy expense account: Strategies for regulating empathic response', in T. F. D. Farrow & P. W. R. Woodruff (eds.), *Empathy In Mental Illness and Health* (Cambridge: Cambridge University Press, 2007), 389–407.

Ickes, W.   *Everyday Mind Reading: Understanding What Other People Think and Feel* (Amherst: Prometheus Books, 2003).

Krebs, Dennis L.   'Altruism: An Examination of the Concept and a Review of the Literature', *Psychological Bulletin* 73.4 (1970), 258–302.

Lewis, Clive Staples   *The Four Loves* (London: HarperCollins, 2012 rep., 1960 orig.).

Love Brown, Susan   'Ayn Rand: The Woman Who Would Not Be President', in Mimi Reisel Gladstein and Chris Matthew Sciabarra (eds.), *Feminist Interpretations of Ayn Rand. Re-reading the Canon* (University Park, Pennsylvania: Pennsylvania State University Press, 1999), 275–298.

Matsumoto, David (gen. ed.)   *The Cambridge Dictionary of Psychology* (Cambridge: Cambridge University Press 2009).

Mays James L. (gen. ed.)   *Harper's Bible Commentary* (San Francisco: Harper and Row, 1988).

Miller, A. G. (ed.)   *The Social Psychology of Good And Evil* (New York: Guilford Press 2004).

Oord, Thomas Jay   *Defining Love, A Philosophical, Scientific and Theological Engagement* (Grand Rapids: Brazos Press, 2010).

Perkins, Pheme   *Love Commands in the New Testament* (New York: Paulist, 1982).

Rand, Ayn   *Capitalism: The Unknown Ideal* (New York: Signet, 1967).

Rand, Ayn   'Basic Principles of Literature', in *The Romantic Manifesto: A Philosophy of Literature* (New York, 1975), 71–90.

Rand, Ayn   *For the New Intellectual* (New York: Signet, 1963).

Rand, Ayn   'Philosophy: Who Needs It', *The Ayn Rand Letter* 3 (7, 1974, 12). Reprinted in Ayn Rand, *Philosophy: Who Needs It* (New York: New American Library, 1982).

Rand, Ayn   *Atlas Shrugged* (New York: Plume, 1999 [original: 1957]).

Rand, Ayn	*The Virtue of Selfishness* (London & New York: Penguin Books, 1964).
Scott, J. Martin C.	'John', in James D. G. Dunn & John W. Rogerson (eds.), *The Eerdmans Commentary on the Bible*, (Grand Rapids, Mich.: Eerdmans, 2003).
Smith, D. Moody	'John', in James L Mays (gen. ed.), *Harper's Bible Commentary* (San Francisco: Harper and Row, 1988), 1044–1076.
Spicq, Ceslaus	*Agape in the New Testament*. Vol. 3: *Agape in the Gospels, Epistles, and Apocalypse of St John* (London: Herder, 1965).
Willis, Wendell	'Agape', in David Noel Freedman (ed.), *Eerdmans Dictionary of the Bible*, (Grand Rapids: Eerdmans, 2003), 27–28.

Websites

www.haaretz.com/jewish/this-day-in-jewish-history/.premium-1.674065 (Accessed 6/2/17).

https://en.oxforddictionaries.com/definition/altruism (Accessed 30/1/17).

https://en.oxforddictionaries.com/definition/disinterested (Accessed 22/9/17).

https://plato.stanford.edu/entries/altruism/ (Accessed 30/1/17).

https://psychology.iresearchnet.com/social-psychology/emotions/empathy/ (Accessed 25/9/17).

https://thejesuitpost.org/2015/06/an-overview-of-laudato-si/ (Accessed 27/9/17).

www.nytimes.com/1991/11/20/books/book-notes-059091.html (Accessed 20/9/17).

www.psychologytoday.com/basics/empathy (Accessed 25/9/17).

CHAPTER 14

The Johannine Messiah and the Isaianic Servant: Identity And Response

Chris Seglenieks

Abstract

The Gospel of John uses the Old Testament in the portrayal of Jesus' identity. The role of different elements is debated, with Isaiah as well as Passover often identified as significant. The acclamation of Jesus as 'Lamb of God' (1:29) has been a focal point for the debate and will provide an initial focus for this investigation. It will be argued that the Passover connections in the Gospel have been overemphasised. Instead, the role of Isaiah is critical for the Johannine presentation of Jesus' identity. The Johannine use of Isaiah contributes to presenting Jesus not only as God's servant, but as divine himself. The role of Isaiah goes further, for Isaianic language provides some of the key Johannine language for conveying the necessary response to Jesus which the Gospel seeks to evoke (20:31). As the God of Isaiah calls for belief and witness, so too does the Johannine Jesus.

The Gospel of John has a significant focus on the identity of Jesus, as well as on how people ought to respond to Jesus, both of which feature in the statement of purpose in 20:31. Both the identity of Jesus and the response to him are connected to Old Testament language and categories, although this has primarily been considered in terms of identity but not response. Two key influences on the identity of the Johannine Jesus are those of the Passover lamb, and the Isaianic servant. A focal point for discussing these connections has been the identification of Jesus as 'the Lamb of God, who takes away the sin of the world' (John 1:29).[1] The argument that this refers to Passover is symptomatic of an overemphasis on Passover imagery, and overlooks the central role of Isaiah across the Gospel both for Jesus' identity but also for the intended response to Jesus. The argument that follows will first establish that while Passover imagery has a role in John, its significance for Jesus' identity has been overplayed. Then John 1:29 will be used as a starting point to show the influence of Isaiah in shaping the Johannine presentation of Jesus' identity.[2] The connections to Isaiah regarding Jesus' identity will lead to a consideration of the role of Isaiah in shaping the Johannine language of responding to Jesus, and in particular the characteristic Johannine emphasis on belief.

1. The Passover Motif in John

The initial point at which Passover may be linked to the identity of Jesus is in John the Baptist's identification of Jesus as the Lamb of God (1:29). The source of the image is most commonly identified as Passover or Isaiah.[3] While many identify a Passover reference, that identification is not without problems.[4] While Jesus is identified with the Passover lamb elsewhere in the New Testament (1 Cor. 5:7), there are no explicit links in John 1:29 or its context. Even the use of ὁ ἀμνός is a weak connection, as the LXX usually refers to the Passover victim with πρόβατον, and

---

1   All English quotations of Scripture come from the NIV.
2   John appears to have primarily used a form of the LXX when using the Old Testament, therefore connections will be drawn primarily with the LXX. See Menken, 'Observations', 93.
3   For other possible interpretations see Morris, *John*, 144–147; Brown, *The Gospel According to John*, 1.58–63.
4   For the view that Passover imagery is primary see Lee, 'Paschal Imagery'; Hoskins, 'Deliverance from Death'; Porter, 'Traditional Exegesis', 396–429. For the view that it is Passover along with one or more other elements see Schneiders, 'Lamb of God'; Nielsen, 'Lamb of God'; Skinner, 'Another Look'; Grigsby, 'The Cross'.

ὁ ἀμνός only appears in Exodus 12:5 in some manuscripts.[5] In addition, there is a lack of evidence to assert that the Passover sacrifice was understood as expiatory in first-century Judaism.[6] Thus, while a Passover allusion is possible, it is unlikely to be the primary referent.

Aside from John 1:29, the other passage that may link Passover with Jesus' identity is John 19.[7] By placing Jesus' death at the time of the Passover sacrifice, in the afternoon of the day of preparation (19:14), it may be that Jesus is to be identified with the Passover lamb.[8] The differences between the Synoptic and Johannine accounts could be evidence that John has altered the story to facilitate the identification of Jesus with the Passover sacrifice.[9] Yet a Johannine theological reworking is not certain, as other resolutions of the relative chronologies are possible, and therefore a symbolic significance to the time of Jesus death cannot be assumed.[10] The case for the timing being theologically significant is undermined by the failure to draw the reader's attention to the connection. The Passover sacrifice is not mentioned, while the three references to Passover in connection with Jesus death have no sacrificial

---

5 In Exodus 12:5 B reads ἀρνῶν, while A reads ἀμνῶν and the Göttingen text follows A here. Wevers argues that כבש is consistently translated as ἀμνῶν in Exodus, and so is the preferred reading. Wevers, *Text History*, 263. Beyond the institution of the Passover, ἀμνός is only used in relation to Passover in 2 Chronicles 35:7–8, which refers to πρόβατα καὶ ἀμνοὺς καὶ ἐρίφους. This three-fold reference to the sacrificial animals does not suggest ὁ ἀμνός as the obvious word to indicate the Passover victim.

6 Passover is more closely linked to deliverance from death and release from captivity than dealing with sin, although Grigsby argues for understanding it as expiatory. Yet Nielsen observes that those who make such an argument rely on later evidence. For example, *Exodus Rabbah* which Grigsby relies upon is dated to the tenth-twelfth centuries. Grigsby, 'The Cross', 73–74; Nielsen, 'Lamb of God', 239.

7 While John 6 contains mention of the Passover (6:4) along with a discourse that could be linked to the Last Supper, it does not constitute a use of Passover to convey Jesus' identity. The mention of Passover is separated from the symbolic discourse by both the miraculous feeding and the walking on water, reducing the likelihood of a connection. In addition, the symbolic discourse is not primarily a reference to the Last Supper but conveys a metaphor for believing (see further §4 below).

8 This is usually understood to be the day before Passover, however Carson suggests that the reference to 'eating the Passover' (18:28) could refer to the rest of the week-long festival, allowing the Passover meal to have taken place the night before. He argues that παρασκευή can often mean Friday, and that if a symbolic reference to the timing of Jesus' death was intended, more dramatic effect would have been gained by inserting this statement after verse 16a. Carson, *John*, 589–90, 603–04.

9 Barrett, *John*, 48–51.

10 Meier and Matson argue for Johannine precedence in chronology, Carson argues that John follows the same chronology as the Synoptic accounts, and others such as Humphreys propose methods for harmonisation of the Gospel accounts. Meier, *Marginal Jew*, 399; Matson, 'Historical Plausibility'; Carson, *John*, 604; Humphreys, *The Mystery*.

connotations (18:28, 39; 19:14). The final reference, while relating Passover to Jesus' handing over for crucifixion, minimises the symbolism as the association is with Jesus being sentenced rather than with his actual crucifixion or death. The function of this reference may be more to prepare for the necessity of removing the bodies in 19:31–37.[11] At the point of Jesus' death, while it is repeated that it was the day of preparation, the next day is the Sabbath, not Passover (19:31). Finally, as it is likely the Gospel was written after the fall of Jerusalem and outside Judea, there is no basis for assuming an audience would be sufficiently familiar to make the connection between the sacrifices in the Temple and the time of Jesus death without the text making that connection clear.[12]

Alongside the timing of Jesus' death there are possible allusions to Passover in the use of hyssop in 19:29, and in the scriptural quotation in 19:36. The use of hyssop contrasts with the Synoptic accounts, and in view of the impracticality of hyssop, an intentional symbolic change is probable.[13] While it could reflect a Passover image (Exod. 12:12), hyssop is linked with other cleansing and atoning sacrifices (Lev. 14:1–7, Num. 19:17–19) and to forgiveness of sins in Psalm 51. The wider symbolism of hyssop suggests purification and forgiveness are in view rather than specifically evoking Passover.[14] The allusion in John

---

11 The reason being that it is a great Sabbath (that is a Sabbath falling during the Passover week). Carson, *John*, 604.
12 In terms of date and location of the writing of John: Barrett gives the boundaries of between AD 90–140, and favours Ephesus over Antioch and Alexandria. Barrett, *John*, 128–32. Brown also sees Ephesus most likely, between AD 90–110. Brown, *An Introduction*, 199–215. Bultmann, John, 11–12, favours Syria, AD 80–120. Carson, *John*, 82–87, suggests AD 80, and the traditional location of Ephesus as most plausible. Michaels, *John*, 37–38, like many, notes there is little evidence for place other than later tradition that links this Gospel with Ephesus, and notes that Alexandria and Antioch are plausible alternatives. He also states it was likely written after AD 70. John's Gospel also gives indications that it is written for an audience with limited familiarity with Jewish practices (2:6; 4:9; 18:28). This is suggested specifically with regard to Passover by terming it 'Passover, the feast of the Jews' (2:13, 6:4, 11:55).
13 Matthew and Mark both have 'reed' (κάλαμος, Matt. 27:48, Mark 15:36) while Luke omits this detail. Porter, 'Traditional Exegesis', 420; Barrett, *John*, 553.
14 It is even possible that this is an allusion to Isaiah. Outside of Passover, the hyssop is used to sprinkle the blood of the sacrifice. In Isa. 52:15 the servant 'will sprinkle many nations'. This phrase is textually difficult, for while the English here follows the MT, the LXX has instead θαυμάσονται. However, the Hebrew phrase which is initially unclear makes sense when we see the Servant is 'lifted up (52:13) after his appearance is 'marred beyond human semblance' (52:14). It is then those who 'see' and 'understand' (52:15) who are associated with this sprinkling. When combined with the following references to bearing sin, it evokes the image of sprinkling sacrificial blood upon the people. Gentry, 'Atonement', 29–31.

19:36, meanwhile, is ambiguous in its referent. There are similarities with Exodus 12:46, Numbers 9:12, and Psalm 34:20 (33:21 LXX), but none provide an exact match.[15] The identification of the source may depend on the degree to which Passover is seen as prominent in John 19.[16] If, as has been argued, the Passover connection has been overplayed, the Psalmic origin may be more likely. If Psalm 34 is the source, the quote may be used as an allusion to the Isaianic servant, as Psalm 34:22 states 'The LORD will rescue his servants'. The ambiguity leaves the interpreter vulnerable to circular reasoning, for we are likely to identify the origin of the quotation based on our overall position on the prominence of either Passover or Isaiah with regard to the identity of Jesus. While there may be connections between Passover and Jesus, it does not appear to be used with the clarity or frequency to argue that the Passover lamb is a primary image for Jesus' identity in John.[17]

2. Isaiah and John the Baptist

John the Baptist introduces the Isaianic connection within John's Gospel. In John 1:23 John the Baptist announces his mission using the words of Isaiah 40:3.[18] As John the Baptist presents his role in Isaianic terms, the reader is prepared for the Coming One to be presented in similarly Isaianic terms. John's initial acclamation of Jesus as ὁ ἀμνὸς τοῦ

---

15 The word order in John is closer to that in Exodus and Numbers (LXX), along with both the singular ὀστοῦν and singular possessive αὐτοῦ. However, each of those includes ἀπό, and it is only in Psalm 34:20 that the verb is in the same form. John and Psalm 34 use a singular future passive, while both Exodus and Numbers have a plural future active form.
16 Porter argues that the linguistic features are not decisive, and contextual issues, including the context of Passover in John 19, lead to the view that Exodus/Numbers is the source of the quote. Porter, 'Traditional Exegesis', 404. In contrast, Dodd, *Interpretation*, 233–34, argues based on the role of Psalms within John that the Psalm identification is more likely, following the other quotes from Psalms in 19:24 and 19:28.
17 Passover imagery in John may be interpreted through Isaiah and the new Exodus motif in Isaiah 40–55. This would further subordinate Passover imagery to an Isaianic background with regard to Jesus' identity in John's Gospel. Bauckham, *God Crucified*, 48, argues that allusions to Isaiah and the Servant in the New Testament should be read in the context of the new Exodus motif.
18 The Johannine version differs from the LXX, using 'make straight' rather than 'prepare', while in Isaiah 'make straight' is in following clause (in both LXX and MT). The mixing of the two clauses may be due to the author quoting from memory, although an alternative form of the LXX is possible. Williams identifies possible theological motivations for the alteration. Williams, 'Isaiah in John's Gospel', 103–04.

θεοῦ ὁ αἴρων τὴν ἁμαρτίαν τοῦ κόσμου (1:29) suggests a connection with Isaiah through the use of ὁ ἀμνός (Isa. 53:7). The Servant in Isaiah is described as 'like' a lamb, rather than directly called a lamb, but it is evident that John 1:29 is using 'lamb' as an analogy, given it is applied to Jesus. Isaiah 53:7 may not use the full expression 'Lamb of God', but that term appears in no biblical text outside John. The following statement about the removal of sin also corresponds with Isaiah.[19] It is said of the Servant that, 'the LORD has laid on him the iniquity of us all' (Isa. 53:6, cf. 53:11), that 'the LORD makes his life an offering for sin' (Isa. 53:10) and that 'he bore the sin of many' (Isa. 53:12). The Servant is the one who will deal with the sins, if not of the world, at least of many within it. Whilst Isaiah speaks in sacrificial language, he goes beyond the image of an animal sacrificed for sin in that he speaks of a person who will deal with sin. Therefore, the Isaianic Servant in Isa. 52:13–53:12 provides the most convincing background to John 1:29.

Having confessed Jesus as the Lamb of God, John the Baptist declares Jesus' messianic identity (John 1:34). There is a textual issue with this verse, which may read ὁ υἱὸς τοῦ θεοῦ or ὁ ἐκλεκτός τοῦ θεοῦ. Whilst 'Son of God' has greater external support, as standard Johannine terminology it is more likely this reading arose as harmonisation with the rest of the Gospel.[20] If 'the Chosen One of God' is taken as original, it would provide another Isaianic link, here to Isaiah 42:1, which refers to both 'my servant' and 'my chosen one'.[21] Following this is the declaration that God has placed his Spirit upon his servant, which parallels John 1:32 and Jesus receiving the Spirit. By this combination of the giving of the Spirit and acclamation as God's chosen one, John is evoking Isaiah 42:1–4 (the first of the Servant Songs) in a declaration of Jesus' identity. John the Baptist sets an initial picture of Jesus with his identity cast in Isaianic terms, following on from his own Isaianic mission.

---

19 Even Porter, 'Traditional Exegesis', 410–11, who argues that 'Lamb' in John 1:29 is a Passover reference, says that the second clause here is an intensification of Isaianic language.
20 According to UBS5, 𝔓⁶⁶, 𝔓⁷⁵, A and B all read ὁ υἱὸς, along with ℵ². However, ὁ ἐκλεκτός has early attestation in both 𝔓¹⁰⁶ and ℵ*. Flink, 'Son and Chosen', offers an alternative proposal, claiming 𝔓⁷⁵* reads ὁ υἱὸς ὁ ἐκλεκτός and this is the original reading. As Flink's reading includes ὁ ἐκλεκτός his assessment would still provide support for the view argued here.
21 Williams, 'Isaiah in John's Gospel', 105.

3. Isaiah and the Identity of Jesus in the Fourth Gospel

Following John the Baptist's Isaianic opening, the Gospel continues to use Isaianic titles to identify Jesus. The next example comes in John 4:42 when the Samaritans confess Jesus as 'Saviour of the World'.[22] As with the declarations that Jesus is 'the Lamb of God' and 'the chosen one', we find another expression unrepeated in the Gospel. Whilst it may have roots in an imperial acclamation, there are echoes of Isaiah 49:6, where God says of his servant 'I will also make you a light for the Gentiles, that my salvation may reach to the ends of the earth'.[23] As the confession is made by the Samaritans, following Jesus' comments on the harvest in 4:31–38, there is a parallel with Isaiah's context of mission to those who are not Jews in the second Servant Song (Isa. 49:1–6). Whilst this is an allusion rather than a quote, Isaiah provides a connection between the three confessions of Jesus in John 1–4 which do not use typical Johannine language (1:29, 34; 4:42). As each echoes Isaianic ideas, there is a consistent reason for John to include them, which is to convey the identity and mission of Jesus in Isaianic terms.

The Isaianic influence on the Johannine presentation of Jesus is seen in Jesus' self-description, notably in the 'I am' statements. The Isaianic origins of these statements has been established by both Williams and Ball.[24] The link is made in particular with Isaiah 43:10, which reads ἵνα γνῶτε καὶ πιστεύσητε καὶ συνῆτε ὅτι ἐγώ εἰμι. For Ball, the Isaianic origin of the term is particularly evident in the absolute statements (John 8:24, 28, 58; 18:5), but Old Testament backgrounds are evident in all of the predicate statements.[25] Unlike the previous connections to Isaiah, the connection here is not to the Servant but to God himself, thereby forming an allusion to Jesus' divine identity. Williams takes a broader view to include some 'I am' statements that have often been categorised as self-identification.[26] Thus, the appearance of Jesus in John 6:20 can be linked to the command not to fear in Isaiah 41:10 (cf. 43:1). This both

---

22 Koester draws parallels with Roman imperial titles rather than the Old Testament. Koester, '"The Saviour of the World" (John 4:42)'.
23 Brown, *John*, 1.175, notes that Old Testament passages including Isaiah 12:2 describe God as the salvation of Israel, but asserts that the Messiah is not called a saviour.
24 Ball, '*I Am*'; Williams, 'Self-Declaratory Pronouncements'. See also Lincoln, *Truth on Trial*, 44.
25 Ball, '*I Am*', 203–204.
26 Williams, 'Self-Declaratory Pronouncements', 346.

makes sense of John 6:19 which says the disciples saw Jesus rather than an unknown figure, and associates a revelation of Jesus' self-identity with the miraculous arrival of the boat at their destination. It also suggests a connection between the identity of Jesus and how one responds to him, for in light of the Isaianic allusion the disciples are not to fear because God is with them in the person of Jesus. The Isaianic connections in the 'I am' statements contribute to presenting Jesus as divine, as well as pointing to the response that such a figure requires.

Another confession connecting to Isaiah is found in John 6:69, where Peter calls Jesus the 'Holy One of God'. Brown suggests a background to this title in references to Samson (Judg. 13:7, 16:17) and Aaron (Ps. 106:16).[27] However, there is a significant textual issue with the Judges references.[28] These connections are also undermined by the lack of reference in the Gospel to Samson or Judges more generally, nor does John depict an Aaronic priestly Messiah. In light of the already observed connections to Isaiah, and specifically to Isaiah 41 and 43, a more likely origin for this title is the Isaianic 'Holy One of Israel', the title given to God in Isaiah 41:14,16,20 and in 43:14. As with the 'I am' statements, John uses Isaianic language to point towards Jesus' divine identity, in both cases drawing on the same sections of Isaiah. In both Isaiah 41:14 and 43:14 the title is connected to God as redeemer, and in 43:15 to God as king as well. In addition to alluding to Jesus' divine identity, the use of 'Holy One of God' points to the role of Jesus as both redeemer and king. This continues to build on the picture of Jesus' identity as drawn from Isaiah.

The influence of Isaiah upon John is evident in the explicit quotations from Isaiah. Aside from the quotation conveyed by John the Baptist (1:23), there are three other quotations from Isaiah. Particular attention is drawn to Isaiah as explaining the mission and identity of Jesus by introducing three of the quotations with the name of Isaiah (1:23; 12:38; 40), the only Scripture quotations in John whose origin is specified. Unlike the titles that have already been considered, the quotations from Isaiah do not explicitly state Jesus' identity. An implicit

---

27 Brown, *John*, 1.298.
28 LXX A and MT read 'Nazirite', while LXX B has ἅγιος θεοῦ.

indication of Jesus' identity is seen in John 6:45, where Jesus quotes Isaiah 54:13, saying 'They will all be taught by God'. Jesus not only sets the quotation in the centre of a discourse on his identity and mission but also he connects learning from God with coming to him (see further §4). By linking himself to the fulfilment of Isaiah's promises, and Jesus thereby closely aligns himself with God.

The other two quotations from Isaiah both occur in John 12:38–40, in response to the narrator's observation of unbelief.[29] The first quotation is the declaration in Isaiah 53:1, 'Lord, who has believed our message and to whom has the arm of the Lord been revealed?' By applying Isaiah's words to the lack of belief in Jesus, John equates the response Jesus experienced with that associated with the promised Servant. By aligning the rejection of Jesus with that of the servant, the Gospel draws a further connection between the Servant and the Messiah. The final quotation in 12:40 expresses a similar failure to respond rightly, although couched in terms of divine sovereignty (Isa. 6:10).[30] This is followed in John 12:41 by the assertion that Isaiah saw Jesus' glory and spoke of him. The author of this Gospel saw Jesus as both the motivation for and the fulfilment of the words of Isaiah, thereby making explicit the identification of Jesus with the Isaianic Servant.[31]

The trajectory of the Suffering Servant in Isaiah 52:13–53:12 is also reflected in John. A significant movement in this passage is the shift of the servant from humiliated to exalted. 'Lifted up' and 'glorified' (52:13 LXX) both refer to the future vindication of the Lord's servant and the realisation of his identity. This language is strikingly similar to that of the Fourth Gospel, where Jesus is presented as lifted up (John 3:14; 8:28; 12:32, 34) and glorified (7:39; 8:54; 11:4; 12:16,23,28; 13:31,32; 16:14; 17:1,5,10).[32] The Isaianic parallel is most evident in John 8:28, as Jesus declares it is his 'lifting up' that will reveal who he is. Later in that chapter when questioned about his identity he responds by referring to

---

29 On these quotations see Brendsel, 'Isaiah Saw His Glory'.
30 Painter, 'Eschatological Faith', 46, suggests that the devil is the agent of blindness here, but the devil is not mentioned here, nor is he given a role in bringing about unbelief.
31 Lett, 'Divine Identity', 170; Williams, 'Isaiah in John's Gospel', 114.
32 Lett, 'Divine Identity', 164–65.

his glorification by the Father (8:54).³³ Not only does Jesus' identity and mission align with what is presented in Isaiah, but so too some of John's characteristic language finds its origins in this Servant Song.³⁴ Jesus is the Servant who will be vindicated by being lifted up and glorified.

Finally, some of the images that form the base for extended metaphors in John's Gospel may originate with Isaiah.³⁵ Köstenberger, in his study on John 10, indicates that Isaiah 56 (along with Ezekiel and Zechariah) is part of background for the image of the shepherd.³⁶ This is evident particularly in Isaiah 56:8 with a reference to gathering others as in John 10:16. The parallel continues as Isaiah condemns false shepherds, matching the way Jesus condemns the Jewish leaders by speaking of thieves entering the sheep pen (10:8). There may be a similar connection between the vine image of John 15 and Isaiah 5:1–7 and 27:2–6. However, the vine is frequently used as a metaphor for Israel, so Isaianic origin cannot be asserted here, even if the already observed connections make it likely. These images also build on what was observed with regard to the 'I am' statements, that there is a link between the identity of Jesus and the required response to him. The sheep follow because he is the good shepherd, and the branches abide because he is the true vine. This connection leads us to ask, given Isaiah provides such a significant source regarding the identity of Jesus, whether it also provides a significant source regarding the required response to Jesus.

4. Isaiah and the Response to Jesus in the Fourth Gospel

The consideration of the influence of Isaiah on Johannine Christology has drawn particular attention to Isaiah 43, which may be the source not only for John's distinctive 'I am' language, but also the title 'Holy

---

33 John 8 provides numerous other parallels with Isaiah 53, as many do not perceive who Jesus is (8:22–27; cf. Isa. 52:14; 53:1–3), and therefore he is dishonoured (8:49; cf. Isa. 53:3) and even attacked (8:59; cf. Isa. 53:7). The identity of Jesus is seen as one who is from God (8:42; cf. Isa. 52:13), and one who speaks and acts rightly (8:45–46; cf. Isa. 53:9).
34 Williams, 'Isaiah in John's Gospel', 114–15.
35 There are further connections between John and Isaiah that might be drawn, however the focus here remains on those which are significant with regard to the identity of Jesus and the required response to him. For other connections, see Young, 'A Study'; Hamilton, 'Influence'.
36 Köstenberger, 'Jesus the Good Shepherd', 80–81.

One of God'. However, the LXX of Isaiah 43 contains another term which is prominent in the Gospel of John, which is πιστεύω.[37] The word πιστεύω appears 98 times in John, and its appearance in a passage in Isaiah that is already linked to Johannine thought is suggestive of a connection. Given that there are often connections between the identity of a person and the proper response to them, it may be that John has made use of an interconnected pattern in the Isaianic language of identity and response.

Beginning with the use of πιστεύω in Isaiah 43:10, the intended response to God is described as ἵνα γνῶτε καὶ πιστεύσητε καὶ συνῆτε ὅτι ἐγώ εἰμι. This can be compared to John 17:8 which says αὐτοὶ ἔλαβον καὶ ἔγνωσαν ἀληθῶς ὅτι παρὰ σοῦ ἐξῆλθον, καὶ ἐπίστευσαν ὅτι σύ με ἀπέστειλας. The two both use πιστεύω and γινώσκω to describe the response, as well as the use of ὅτι clauses to indicate that the knowing and believing relates to the identity of either God or Jesus (cf. 6:68–69). While the use of Isaiah in John 17:8 is not a direct quote, the connections already established with Isaiah 43 and specifically with verse ten regarding Jesus' identity, strongly support a link between the two. The verb πιστεύω appears fewer times in the entire LXX than in John, which suggests an initial significance as John picks up what is an uncommon term in the LXX for responding to God.[38]

One of the significant features of these two verses is the use of ὅτι with πιστεύω.[39] This expression, which is used to signify propositional belief, is rare in the Graeco-Roman context.[40] Πιστεύω and cognates are used primarily to indicate personal trust, and while there may be some propositional content entailed, the relational element is more

---

37 While Lincoln observes that the trial motif is intended to lead to belief, he makes no connection between Isaiah and John in terms of the language of belief. Lincoln, *Truth on Trial*, 47, 59, 177. The centrality of belief within the Gospel of John has been frequently observed and investigated. See Ueberschaer, 'Das Johannesevangelium'; Koester, 'Hearing, Seeing, and Believing'; Schlier, 'Glauben, Erkennen, Lieben'; Hawthorne, 'Concept of Faith'; Decourtray, 'La conception johannique de la foi'.
38 Morgan, *Roman Faith and Christian Faith*, 177.
39 While the ὅτι clause follows directly after συνῆτε rather than πιστεύσητε, it is connected to all three verbs, for while πιστεύω can be used absolutely to indicate trust, γινώσκω requires that something be known, and there is no implied object of knowledge supplied by the context. Given πιστεύω is the middle term of the three, it would be grammatically incongruous for the relative clause connect only to the first and third verbs.
40 Morgan, *Roman Faith and Christian Faith*, 123, 145.

prominent, even in the New Testament usage.⁴¹ The use of πιστεύω ὅτι is also uncommon in the LXX, appearing only 5 times.⁴² Similarly, πιστεύω ὅτι appears only on one occasion in each of the Synoptics, and each refers to believing that something can or will be done, rather than focusing on the identity of Jesus (Matt. 9:28; Mark 11:23–24; Luke 1:45). Outside the Johannine writings, there are only two instances which are used to convey identity, one about Jesus and the other about God (1 Thess. 4:14; Jas 2:19). Yet John uses the expression 13 times, suggesting that for John the propositional dimension of belief is significant and more so than for other New Testament writers. Isaiah seems to provide a basis for speaking of belief in propositional terms.

Johannine appropriation of the Isaianic language of belief is explicit in John 12:38. The quotations from Isaiah in John 12:38–40 are primarily an explanation of the response to Jesus, the failure of those who observed his signs to then believe in him. The quotation from Isaiah 53:1 uses the language of belief as it says τίς ἐπίστευσεν τῇ ἀκοῇ ἡμῶν; The quotation also presents the lack of belief as a failure to trust a 'report'—thus there is some propositional content that should be accepted but has instead been rejected. The framing of this verse in the LXX places the statement in the mouth of the Lord's servant. However, the plural ἡμῶν suggests that the message is not merely that of the servant, but the message of God as well. This aligns with the Johannine presentation of Jesus' message as both his message as the one sent by God, but also a message entirely derived from God himself (John 5:19–47). The use of this quotation from Isaiah strengthens the case that Isaiah is the source of the Johannine language of belief, and that Isaiah contributes to the Johannine concept of propositional belief.

Unlike John, Isaiah also uses the cognate πείθω. While this verb often means urge or persuade, in the perfect it has the sense of trust, and Isaiah uses it repeatedly to indicate trust in God (8:17; 12:2; 17:7). If Isaiah is the source of Johannine language of responding to Jesus, the question

---

41 Morgan, *Roman Faith and Christian Faith*, 30.
42 Three of the instances of πιστεύω ὅτι are in Job, which might raise the possibility that the influence of Job has contributed to the Johannine use of this expression. Such influence is unlikely given the lack of evidence for other connections, either in terms of language or concepts, between Job and John.

is raised as to why John does not also use πείθω. The most likely reason is stylistic, for John has evidently used πιστεύω as a key term throughout his Gospel, from the prologue (1:12–13) to the purpose statement (20:31).[43] Πιστεύω has a primary sense of trust, and this personal trust appears to be the main force of the πιστεύω εἰς construction in John. Thus, to use πείθω to indicate the same sort of trust would detract from the *leitmotif* of πιστεύω, without adding to what is conveyed in terms of responding to Jesus. That John made a deliberate choice not to use πείθω can be seen by considering the use of πείθω in Isaiah 50:10. There Isaiah indicates the idea of trusting in the name of the Lord, which echoes the Johannine idea of trusting in the name of Jesus (John 1:12, 2:23). John parallels the Isaianic idea but presents it with a characteristically Johannine use of πιστεύω.

Returning to the key passage of Isaiah 43, a further connection in terms of response is found in the language of witness. Isaiah 43:1–9 declares the redemptive work of God, in terms of gathering the exiles (43:5–7) and giving sight and hearing (43:8). The nations are to gather and hear the witnesses of the work that God has done (43:9). At the culmination of the account of what God has done comes a declaration from God regarding his unique identity (43:10–13). 43:10 begins with the call γένεσθέ μοι μάρτυρες, and it is this role of witness that is to lead people to know and believe that 'I am'. The same group is both the witnesses and those who know, believe, and understand, for Israel collectively is addressed (43:1). The nation has a role together to bear witness to what God has done for them, and thereby enabling the nation to know, believe, and understand (cf. 44:8; 45:23). The role of bearing witness, and specifically witness that leads to belief, is reflected in the Gospel of John. Witness is a central category for John, highlighting in the prologue that witness is to lead to belief (John 1:7–8). While this is initially presented in the context of the role of John the Baptist, it is echoed in the purpose of the written Gospel (20:30–31; 21:24–25). Throughout the Gospel, witness plays a key role, notably in the

---

43 Use of πείθω would also place a constraint upon tense-forms, as it only indicates trust in the perfect.

confrontation in 5:19–47.⁴⁴ The role of witness is also enacted in the characters who bear witness to their faith and tell others (4:28–30, 39; 6:68–9; 11:27). Jesus prays for a future generation of believers who will come to believe through the witness of the disciples (17:20). Both the idea of publicly confessing faith, as well as the language of μαρτυρία, connect the response to God in Isaiah with the response to Jesus in John.

The role of Isaiah 43 for John is reinforced by several further parallels which, although not indicating the response people are to make to God or Jesus, nevertheless reflect the status of people in line with their response. The first relates to the status of those who have responded rightly, those who are both the witnesses and those who believe from 43:10, of whom God says οὐκ ἔστιν ὁ ἐκ τῶν χειρῶν μου ἐξαιρούμενος (Isa. 43:13). The Lord asserts that he works and none can turn it back, and in light of the focus on his redemptive work in 43:1–9, the irreversibility of God's redemption is in view. A similar idea of security in God's hand for his people appears in the Johannine assurance that οὐδεὶς δύναται ἁρπάζειν ἐκ τῆς χειρὸς τοῦ πατρός (John 10:29). For those who have failed to respond rightly to God, Isaiah describes their condition as ἐν ταῖς ἁμαρτίαις σου καὶ ἐν ταῖς ἀδικίαις σου προέστην σου (Isa. 43:24).⁴⁵ While for John sin is not a prominent theme, he warns that those who fail to respond rightly to him ἀποθανεῖσθε ἐν ταῖς ἁμαρτίαις ὑμῶν (8:24). Isaiah provides John with the language for both the security of those who do respond to Jesus, and the dire fate of those who fail to do so.

There is one further connection to explore regarding the metaphorical language of response. In John 6 a distinctive Johannine metaphor occurs where the ideas of eating and drinking are used to flesh out the concept of believing in Jesus.⁴⁶ John 6 is linked to Isaiah through the

---

44 As well as highlighting the significance of witness and the trial motif in John, Lincoln sees the trial motif in Isaiah 40–55 as a key influence on the narrative of the Fourth Gospel. Lincoln, *Truth on Trial*, 12–13, 22, 38–51.

45 This condemnation, like the call to witness, is addressed to Jacob/Israel (Isa 43:22). The prophetic tradition juxtaposes the call for Israel to fulfil their purpose with condemnation for their failures. While Israel as a nation was called to be God's people, only some responded rightly to God, which does not include those described in 43:24.

46 Menken, 'John 6:51c–58: Eucharist or Christology?', 305; Webster, *Ingesting Jesus*, 3–4. Although there may be a secondary allusion to the Lord's Supper, to read the passage as primarily sacramental overlooks the Isaianic origins of the image, as well as importing later theological ideas. For the sacramental view see Brown, *John*, 1.287; Schnackenburg, *John*, 2.56.

quotation embedded in the middle of the discourse (6:45). The quotation refers to being taught by God (Isa. 54:13), rather than using images of eating or drinking, which suggests that the surrounding imagery is being used to depict a certain quality of relationship with God in the person of Jesus. Isaianic parallels are evident in the imagery, however, as the chapter following after the passage that is quoted begins with a call to come and eat and drink (Isa. 55:1; cf. 44:3). It includes a criticism of those who work for that which does not satisfy (Isa. 55:2), and in the same way Jesus criticises the crowd working for food which perishes (John 6:27). In Isaiah this food is metaphorical, since listening is coordinated with eating (Isa. 55:2). Similarly, in John hearing God is referred to alongside coming to him and so believing (John 6:45). The response conveyed through the imagery of eating and drinking in both instances is to lead to life (Isa. 55:3; John 6:51). Both Isaiah and John use the metaphor of eating and drinking to reflect the life-giving and essential nature of a right response to God or Jesus. Therefore, Isaiah provides a basis not only for the explicit language of response, in believing and witnessing, but also for the Johannine metaphors which illustrate such a response.

While the significance of Isaiah for John, particularly with regard to Christology, has been observed by previous scholars, what has been overlooked is this role of Isaiah in providing language and concepts that John uses to convey how one is to respond to Jesus. There is a nexus of connections in Isaiah 43, which is reflected in the Johannine presentation of Jesus' identity, how to respond to him, and one's status based upon that response. The way that several interrelated areas can all be linked back to Isaiah suggests that an understanding of the Isaianic use of these ideas is vital for a full understanding not only of Johannine Christology, but also of the response for which the Gospel calls. Indeed, the two are intertwined, for the Isaianic language of response which John appropriates is Isaiah's call for response to God, which contributes to the Johannine picture of Jesus as God.

5. The Isaianic Messiah in John

The preceding argument has demonstrated the significance of Isaiah for depicting of Jesus' identity in the Fourth Gospel, as well as for presenting the required response to him. While the argument began by considering which Old Testament image lies behind John 1:29, the significance of this argument centres on the question of what sort of Messiah Jesus is. The Messiah is a significant concept within John, and notably only John uses Μεσσίας alongside the usual Χριστός (1:41; 4:25). Whilst on both occasions the terms are equated, there must be a reason for including it. Most likely is that within the early church Χριστός rapidly became a proper name for Jesus.[47] Yet John wants to convey that Jesus is the promised Messiah, and not only that but a particular type of Messiah. This concept would potentially be missed if the reader simply saw Χριστός and took it as a name. The reference to Μεσσίας makes it clear that Χριστός is more than a name. For John intends the reader to believe that Jesus is the Χριστός, the Son of God (John 20:31), and he seeks to convey what sort of Messiah Jesus is through this Gospel. Conveying the nature of Jesus' messiahship was necessary as there was a range of messianic conceptions within Second Temple Judaism, as reflected in the Gospel itself.[48] In this context, John brackets Jesus' public ministry with Isaianic identifiers, beginning with the acclamations of John the Baptist (1:29,34) and closing with the Isaianic quotations in 12:38–40. The wealth and variety of connections between Isaiah and John's Gospel demonstrate the formative role played by Isaiah in John's presentation of Jesus the Messiah. From start to finish Jesus is to be understood in this Isaianic framework, while the nature of Jesus' messiahship shapes the way people are called to respond to him.

5.1 The Messiah as Servant

As John has used Isaiah as the primary framework for understanding and presenting Jesus as Messiah, we must observe what Isaiah contributes to Jesus' identity. While the Messiah in both the Old Testament and other literature is often victorious and reigning, in Isaiah 53 the Servant

---

47 Dunn, *Neither Jew Nor Greek*, 338.
48 de Jonge, 'Jewish Expectations'.

is not truly apprehended (52:14; 53:1). The Johannine Jesus is similarly misapprehended, and this Isaianic characteristic is linked directly as Isaiah 53:1 is applied to Jesus. The question of who Jesus is pervades this Gospel, yet many misunderstand him (3:1–10, 6:14–15), or reject his claims entirely (7:40–48, 8:59). Isaiah provides the background for a misunderstood Messiah, instead of one who is universally acclaimed.

In Isaiah this lack of recognition leads to suffering for the Servant. He is one who is pierced, crushed and wounded (53:5), oppressed and afflicted (53:7), and cut off from the land of the living (53:8). This final statement indicates the death of the Servant—Motyer points out the violence of the expression 'cut off', as well as the way 'land of the living' is elsewhere used literally to describe those who are alive (cf. Isa. 38:11).[49] In light of the cross, Isaiah provided the Gospel writer a theological basis upon which to understand Jesus as suffering and dying, yet vindicated as the Messiah.[50] John does not stress the suffering of Jesus, but by using figurative language that draws upon Isaiah (lifted up and glorified), the connotations of suffering could be conveyed to an audience familiar with Isaiah.

5.2 The Messiah as God in Person

While the Messianic identity of Jesus in John has been shaped by the figure of the Isaianic Servant, that is not the full extent of Isaianic influence with regard to Jesus' identity. For while some uses of Isaiah present Jesus as God's appointed representative, John also appropriates Isaianic language that refers to God himself. The adoption of the Isaianic 'I am' as a typical expression of Jesus' identity carries with it echoes of the God who calls himself 'I am'. Similarly, the adoption of the title 'Holy One of God' co-opts Isaiah's standard title for God and applies it now to

---

49 Motyer, *The Prophecy of Isaiah*, 434. While there are other interpretations of this passage, as potentially referring to corporate Israel, or being poetic language describing suffering that does not involve actual death, there are no indications that John understood Isaiah in these ways. Whybray, *Isaiah 40–66*, 171, 177.

50 Linked to the idea of vindication are the connections between the Servant and royal imagery, through the titles he is ascribed. On an identification of the Servant as a royal figure, see Morgenstern, 'The Suffering Servant', 411–13; Gentry, 'The Atonement': 24; Treat, *The Crucified King*, 70–71. Treat also connects the Servant to a royal figure foreshadowed in Isaiah 1–39. Similar royal imagery is connected with Jesus, notably in John 18–19, further evidence of the alignment of the Isaianic Servant with the Johannine Messiah.

Jesus. Alongside this, Isaianic language of being taught by God, and associated imagery of divine sustenance, attributes a divine role to Jesus. While none of these constitute an explicit claim to divinity, their divine connotations are coherent with Johannine assertions of Jesus' divinity (1:1; 20:28).

5.3 The Messiah in Whom One Must Believe

As more than merely God's appointed servant, but being God himself made flesh, Jesus demands a response. Just as Isaiah has provided the framework for conveying Jesus' identity, so too Isaiah provides the framework for the required response to Jesus. John makes use of Isaianic language that depicts the right response to God himself and applies it to responding to Jesus. In doing so, John confirms Jesus' divine identity, but if Jesus is divine then he also requires a response analogous to the response God requires. The Johannine Messiah seeks propositional belief, the acceptance of the message Jesus brings, which is primarily a declaration of his own identity. Accompanying this is a need for witness, for it is witness that leads to belief. The explicit aim of the Gospel is to evoke belief that Jesus is the Christ, the Son of God (John 20:31), and for this reason the Gospel itself bears witness. This central concern of John's Gospel is illuminated by understanding the Isaianic origin and significance of both the titles ascribed to Jesus, but also of the language of how one must respond to him.

Bibliography

Ball, D. M.	*'I Am' in John's Gospel* (JSNTSup 124; Sheffield: Sheffield Academic, 1996).
Barrett, C. K.	*The Gospel According to St. John* (Second ed.; London: SPCK, 1978).
Bauckham, R.	*God Crucified* (Carlisle: Paternoster, 1998).
Brendsel, D. J.	*'Isaiah Saw His Glory': The Use of Isaiah 52–53 in John 12* (Berlin: De Gruyter, 2014).
Brown, R. E.	*The Gospel According to John* (AB 29; 2 vols; Garden City: Doubleday, 1966–70).

———,	*An Introduction to the Gospel of John* (New Haven: Yale University Press, 2003).
Bultmann, R.	*The Gospel of John* (Oxford: Blackwell, 1971).
Carson, D.A.	*The Gospel According to John* (PNTC; Grand Rapids: Eerdmans, 1991).
Decourtray, A.	'La conception johannique de la foi', *Nouvelle Revue Théologique* 81.6 (1959), 562–76.
M. de Jonge,	'Jewish Expectations about the "Messiah" according to the Fourth Gospel', *NTS* 19 (1973), 246–70.
Dodd, C. H.	*The Interpretation of the Fourth Gospel* (Cambridge: University Press, 1968).
Dunn, J. D. G.	*Neither Jew Nor Greek* (Grand Rapids: Eerdmans, 2015).
Flink, T.	'Son and Chosen: A Text-critical Study of John 1,34', *Filologia Neotestamentaria* 18 (2005), 85–109.
Gentry, P. J.	'The Atonement In Isaiah's Fourth Servant Song (Isaiah 52:13–53:12)', *Southern Baptist Journal of Theology* 11.2 (2007), 20–43.
Grigsby, B. H.	'The Cross as an Expiatory Sacrifice in the Fourth Gospel', in *The Johannine Writings* (ed. S.E. Porter, et al.; Sheffield: Sheffield Academic, 1995), 69–94.
Hamilton, J.	'The Influence of Isaiah on the Gospel of John', *Perichoresis* 5 (2007), 139–62.
Hawthorne, G. F.	'The Concept of Faith in the Fourth Gospel', *Bibliotheca Sacra* 116.462 (1959), 117–26.
Hoskins, P. M.	'Deliverance from Death by the True Passover Lamb: A Significant Aspect of the Fulfillment of the Passover in the Gospel of John', *Journal of the Evangelical Theological Society* 52.2 (2009), 285–99.
Humphreys, C. J.	*The Mystery of the Last Supper: Reconstructing the Final Days of Jesus* (Cambridge: Cambridge University Press, 2011).
Koester, C. R.	'Hearing, Seeing, and Believing in the Gospel of John', *Biblica* 70.3 (1989), 327–48.
———,	'"The Saviour of the World" (John 4:42)', *Journal of Biblical Literature* 109.4 (1990), 665–80.

Köstenberger, A.   'Jesus the Good Shepherd Who Will Also Bring Other Sheep (10:16): The Old Testament Background of a Familiar Metaphor', *Bulletin of Bbilical Research* 12.1 (2002), 67–96.

Lee, D. A.   'Paschal Imagery in the Gospel of John: A Narrative and Symbolic Reading', *Pacifica* 24 (2011), 13–28.

Lett, J.   'The Divine Identity of Jesus as the Reason for Israel's Unbelief in John 12:36–43', *Journal of Biblical Literature* 135.1 (2016), 159–173.

Lincoln, A. T.   *Truth on Trial* (Peabody: Hendrickson, 2000).

Matson, M. A.   'The Historical Plausibility of John's Passion Dating', in *John, Jesus and History* (ed. P. N. Anderson, et al.; Atlanta: SBL, 2009), 291–312.

Meier, J. P.   *A Marginal Jew* (Garden City: Doubleday, 1991).

Menken, M. J. J.   'John 6:51c–58: Eucharist or Christology?' in *Studies in John's Gospel and Epistles* (ed. M. J. J. Menken. Leuven: Peeters, 2015), 285–308.

———,   'Observations on the Significance of the Old Testament in the Fourth Gospel,' in *Studies in John's Gospel and Epistles* (ed. M. J. J. Menken; Leuven: Peeters, 2015), 91–112.

Michaels, J. R.   *The Gospel of John* (NICNT; Grand Rapids: Eerdmans, 2010).

Morgan, T.   *Roman Faith and Christian Faith* (Oxford: Oxford University Press, 2015).

Morgenstern, J.   'The Suffering Servant: A New Solution', *Vetus Testamentum* 11.4 (1961) 292–320.

Morris, L. L.   *The Gospel According to John* (red ed.; NICNT; Grand Rapids: Eerdmans, 1995).

Motyer, J. A.   *The Prophecy of Isaiah* (Leicester: InterVarsity Press, 1999).

Nielsen, J. T.   'The Lamb of God: The Cognitive Structure of a Johannine Metaphor', in *Imagery in the Gospel of John* (ed. J. Frey, et al.; Tubingen: Mohr Siebeck, 2006), 217–56.

Painter, J.   'Eschatological Faith in the Gospel of John', in *Reconciliation and Hope* (ed. R. Banks; Grand Rapids: Eerdmans, 1974), 36–52.

Porter, S. E.	'Can Traditional Exegesis Enlighten Literary Analysis of the Fourth Gospel', in *The Gospels and the Scriptures of Israel* (ed. C. Evans, et al.; Sheffield: Sheffield Academic Press, 1994), 396–429.
Schnackenburg, R.	*The Gospel According to St. John* (3 vols.; New York: Herder & Herder, 1968–1982).
Schneiders, S. M.	'The Lamb of God and the Forgiveness of Sin(s) in the Fourth Gospel', *Catholic Biblical Quarterly* 73 (2011), 1–29.
Schlier, H.	'Glauben, Erkennen, Lieben nach dem Johannesevangelium', in idem, *Besinnung auf das neue Testament: Exegetische Aufsätze und Vorträge* (Freiberg: Herder, 1964), 279–93.
Skinner, C. W.	'Another Look at "the Lamb of God"', *Bibliotheca Sacra* 161.641 (2004), 89–104.
Treat, J. R.	*The Crucified King: Atonement and Kingdom in Biblical and Systematic Theology* (Grand Rapids: Zondervan, 2014).
Ueberschaer, N.	'Das Johannesevangelium als Medium der Glaubensvermittlung', in J. Frey, B. Schliesser, & N. Ueberschaer (eds.), *Glaube* (Tübingen: Mohr Siebeck, 2017), 451–71.
Webster, J. S.	*Ingesting Jesus* (Atlanta: SBL Press, 2003).
Wevers, J. W.	*Text History of the Greek Exodus* (Göttingen: Vandenhoeck & Ruprecht, 1992).
Whybray, R. N.	*Isaiah 40–66* (NCB; London: Oliphants, 1975).
Williams, C. H.	'Isaiah in John's Gospel', in *Isaiah in the New Testament* (ed. S. Moyise, et al.; London: T&T Clark, 2005), 101–16.
Williams, C. H.	'"I Am"; or "I Am He"? Self-Declaratory Pronouncements in the Fourth Gospel and Rabbinic Tradition', in *Jesus in Johannine Tradition* (ed. R.T. Fortna, et al.; Louisville: Westminster John Knox, 2001), 343–52.
Young, F.W.	'A Study of the Relation of Isaiah to the Fourth Gospel', *Zeitschrift für die neutestamentliche Wissenschaft und die Kunde der älteren Kirche* 46 (1955), 215–33.

CHAPTER 15

Unbelief in the Gospel of belief?

Bill Salier (Youthworks College) &
Benjamin Ho (St Lucia Evangelical Church, Brisbane)

'The grim reality of unbelief, which preoccupies the evangelist as much as faith, and torments him with its strange nature, motives and manifestations, also led him, no doubt to the profoundest view of faith, that it is grace.'

(R. Schnackenburg, *The Gospel According to John* Vol 1, p. 573)

Abstract

John's Gospel is concerned with encouraging belief that leads to life. In support of this purpose John also conducts an examination of unbelief as it occurs in the ministry of Jesus. Through an examination of key words and characters, especially the composite characters of 'the Jews' and 'the world', the theme of unbelief in the Fourth Gospel is explored. John presents the phenomenon of unbelief in response to Jesus' ministry, exploring its character, manner, motivation, and consequences. A number of suggestions are made to account for the presence and function of the motif of unbelief in his positive presentation of Jesus as the Christ, the Son of God so that belief in his name might lead to life.

1. Introduction

John's Gospel contains one of the clearest purpose statements of any book in the Bible (Jn 20:30–31). It is written in order that people might believe in the person of Jesus and affirm his identity as the Christ, the Son of God, the promised Messiah that God. The stakes are high because, according to John, life in the sense outlined in the Gospel hangs on this.

This makes the nature of belief, its content, mode, manner, and shape of fundamental importance as a theme in the Fourth Gospel. This is well recognised in Johannine scholarship and has been the subject of numerous treatments.[1]

Complementing the Johannine presentation of belief, as Schnackenburg suggests, is an exploration of unbelief and this has been relatively unexamined.[2] The theme is present in the Gospel via numerous explicit references, alongside narrative portrayals of unbelief in individual characters as well as two composite characters: the 'Jews' and 'the world'. This data provides ample opportunity to explore the theme of unbelief; its content, development, and contribution to the Gospel's larger concerns. An examination of the theme of unbelief will enable an appreciation of its contribution and significance in relation to the chief burden of the Gospel's presentation of the ministry of Jesus and its implications for its readers.

1.1 The Vocabulary of Unbelief/Identifying Unbelief

The noun 'unbelief' (ἀπίστια) occurs only once in John 20:27. The phrase 'not believe' can occur in three forms with the use of different negative particles (οὐ πιστεύω, μη πιστεύω, οὐ μη πιστεύω).

These constructions occur in 28 verses (John 2:24; 3:12; 3:18; 3:36; 4:48; 5:38; 5:44; 5:46; 5:47; 6:36; 6:64; 7:5; 7:48; 8:24; 8:45; 8:46; 9:18; 10:25; 10:26; 10:37; 10:38; 12:37; 12:39; 12:44; 14:10; 16:9; 20:25; 20:29).

---

1 For example, Schnackenburg, Excursus VII, 'The Notion of Faith in the Fourth Gospel'; Koester, 'Hearing, Seeing, and Believing'; Thompson, 'Signs and Faith'; Tenney, 'Topics'.
2 Culpepper, *Anatomy*, 89–98, is one writer who has attempted to at least outline the presence of the theme.

In terms of distribution, variations of these verbal constructions occur in five verses from John 1–4, in 19 verses in John 5–12, in two verses in John 13–17 and in two verses in John 18–21. The bulk of these occur during the account of Jesus' public ministry and indicate the negative response that is a prominent feature of that ministry.

To these items can be added expressions such as not receiving (οὐ παρέλαβον 1.11; 3.11; 5.43; 12.48; 14.17), 'reject' (ὁ ἀθετῶν 12.48), and hate when directed against Jesus and/or his disciples (μισέω 3:20; 7:7; 15:18, 19; 15:23, 24, 25; 17:14; noting the language of 'hate' occurs more frequently as the language of the world, κόσμος becomes more prominent in the second 'half' of the Gospel describing opposition to Jesus and his disciples).

Concepts can be expressed via more than lexemes and phrases and various narrative portrayals of unbelief occur through characters (singular or composite) who embody unbelief as a response and in a variety of ways. Some characters move in the narrative from unbelief to belief (e.g. the Samaritans in Jn 4:42; the formerly blind man in Jn 9:38); others appear to go the opposite way (the disciples in Jn 6:66; the Jews in Jn 8:31). Some characters appear to have no difficulty in believing (Jn 1:49–50) while others appear to have no difficulty in not believing (Jn 7:5) and find it impossible apparently to believe (Jn 12:39). A particular interest of this study will be the portrayal of the Jews and the world as they emerge in the narrative and are related to one another by the narrative. It is suggested that individually, and in relation to one another, these two characters are the main carriers of the theme of unbelief in the Gospel.

The proposed method will be to move through the Gospel section by section, observing how the theme of unbelief emerges, develops, and makes its contribution to the overall message of the Gospel.

2. Chapters 1–4: The Problem of Unbelief Established

John 1–4 is the first section of the Gospel.[3] With little or no opposition Jesus is presented to the reader by word and deed.[4] Following a lengthy introduction Jesus is introduced, gathers disciples, performs two signs and engages in a series of encounters with other characters. He is questioned but rarely opposed in the dramatic fashion that will characterise his interactions from chapter 5 forward.[5] In this presentation the context for Jesus' mission is established and, in this context, the primary elements of the Gospel's understanding of unbelief are introduced. These will be examined via discussions of material in chapters 1, 2, and 3.

2.1 The Prologue: A Foundational Story Established

We see this first in the prologue to the Gospel (1:1–18). In the first five verses of the prologue the identity and function of the word/light is laid out and a note of tension, even conflict between the darkness and the light is struck as the darkness is said to either not overcome or comprehend the light (παραλαμβάνω, 1:5).[6]

The narrative of light and darkness gives way to the narrative of the light and the κόσμος as the κόσμος is introduced into the narrative for the first time. The κόσμος does not know/recognise the true light (1:10) even though it clearly owes its existence to the λόγος/φώς (cf 1:3). As the narrative progresses the κόσμος in John's Gospel is predominantly the world of humankind and its affairs. The consistent picture of the κόσμος that emerges is that of an entity in rebellion against the Logos, although at this particular point it is simply ignorant. The concept of the κόσμος is narrowed when the prologue says that the word came to his own place and his own people did not receive him (1:11). There is a surprising use of both the neuter term τὰ ἴδια as well as the masculine term οἱ ἴδιοι. The neuter might mean 'his own property/possessions' or

---

3 The prologue is seen as a discreet section but the overall unit is delineated by the 'Cana to Cana' movement suggested by 2:1–11 and 4:46.
4 Culpepper, *Anatomy*, 91, refers to the powerful 'primacy effect' that firmly establishes the reader's first impression of Jesus' identity and mission'.
5 There is some discussion over the interaction between Jesus and the leaders in John 2. Culpepper, *Anatomy*, 90, suggests that opposition is 'at most implied'. Klink, *John*, 180–1, sees conflict in much starker terms in the light of the citation from Ps 69:9 in 2:17.
6 Carson, *John*, 138, notes the suggestion of BAGD that 'master' preserves the ambiguity.

'his own home/homeland'.⁷

The masculine more likely refers to 'his own people'.⁸ In the light of the rest of the Gospel, the author is probably thinking of 'the Jews'.⁹ The movement from verses 10–11 progresses from the culpability of humanity in general (the κόσμος) to that of 'his own people' in particular.¹⁰ A relationship is set up here between his 'own people' and the κόσμος.¹¹ The progression from verses 10–11 suggests that 'the primary historical referent of v. 11b, Israel (*sic*), is also representative of a much larger referent, the world'.¹² This relationship between the κόσμος and the Jews provides the broad structure for the variety of negative responses to Jesus in the rest of the gospel and so will be the focus of the following exploration of the theme of unbelief.

Unbelief here as exemplified by the κόσμος and Jesus' own, has a dual aspect. It does not know and it does not receive. These two aspects will continue to characterize the narrative portrayals of unbelief through the Gospel as characters display an inability to know Jesus as well as many rejecting him.

In verses 12–13 it is stated that all who receive the word are given the right or authority to become children of God. Receiving here is equated with believing in his name; not receiving is, by implication, equivalent to not believing. John is adamant that the move to belief is only possible through the exercise of the will of God himself and is therefore a movement of grace.¹³

---

7   Pryor, 'Jesus and Israel'; Klink, *John*, 102, suggests 'the world as "property" or "possession" ... of the Word'.
8   Pryor, *Evangelist*, 214.
9   Carson, *John*, 125. The precise referent of the controversial phrase οἱ Ἰουδαῖοι has attracted sustained scholarly attention. For the purposes of this discussion the phrase will be taken as referring to a composite character in the Gospel that regularly (though not always) opposes Jesus. A general consensus has emerged that sees the referent of the negative references as the Jewish leaders or authorities. See Von Wahlde's comprehensive survey of the issue in U. C. Von Wahlde, 'Survey', and the extensive discussion in Bieringer et al. Cf. Kierspel, *Jews*, 13–37.
10 Salier, 'World', 33, suggests a sharpening of thought between the two verses. Cf. Pryor, *Evangelist*, 218; Kierspel, *Jews*, 84.
11 Noted by Bultmann, *John*, 87, n1. Kierspel, *Jews*, 161–67, has a comprehensive discussion of those who have examined the relationship and attempted to articulate it. Kierspel, *Jews*, 76–154 also conducts a detailed examination of the parallelism between 'the Jews' and 'the world' in the Gospel.
12 Klink, *John*, 103. Salier, 'World', 34, suggests Israel's response 'typifies or exemplifies' the response of the world.
13 As arguably the 'good news' of verses 12–13 does for the variety of believing/positive responses to Jesus in the rest of the narrative.

The prologue's ultimate concern is the revelation of the true God by the unique Son (1:14, 18). Both belief and unbelief are to be seen therefore in terms of response to this revelation. Rejection and unbelief occurs within the context of this revelation.

Through the rest of chapter 1 the first week of Jesus' ministry is recounted as he is revealed to Israel by John (1:19–34). John's disciples transfer their allegiance to Jesus (1:35–42), and then Jesus becomes active in the narrative, gathering his own disciples (1:43–51). The sequence of encounters begin to build a picture of the constituent elements of belief as a positive response to Jesus (1:49): accepting the testimony of divine revelation (1:32); accepting the testimony of authorised representatives to that divine revelation (1:37); following that testimony to follow Jesus (1:38); responding to Jesus' own invitation to come and see (1:39, 43); confessing a response as a result of encountering Jesus (1:49). The response of unbelief will be seen in relation to these positive elements.

2.2 John 2: The Question of Unbelief

In John 2 an archetypal pattern of belief for the Gospel is established in the summary statement that concludes the first sign narrative (Jn 2:11). Signs will be recorded, and they will reveal the glory of the unique son. The appropriate response as attributed to the disciples is belief. However, this pattern is subverted at the end of the chapter when the first explicit reference to unbelief is recorded via the phrase οὐκ ἐπίστευεν (2:24).

The surprise is the first character said not to believe in in fact Jesus himself. This 'pun' is recorded in response to the observation that many believed in his name when they saw the signs he was doing at the festival (2.23). Jesus' knowledge of all people is emphasised and therefore he does not 'trust' (by not entrusting himself to) the faith he sees expressed. The tenor of the whole passage is broad and appears to encompass humanity (all men, v. 25), even though the Jews in Jerusalem are the focal point. There is an issue with the 'merely human' at this point reflected generally in the world. This reflection has the narrative effect of establishing a question in the Gospel concerning what it means to believe. Behind this lies a question of the (im)possibility of belief from a humanity that Jesus knows so well. Under what conditions will Jesus entrust himself to the belief of a respondent?[14]

2.3 John 3: The Background and Nature of Unbelief

In John 3 Jesus dialogues with Nicodemus. Nicodemus is an example of the Jews (and therefore 'the world') not knowing Jesus.[15] Their initial dialogue (3:1–15) and the narrator's extended reflection (3:16–21; 31–36) provide further information about the nature of unbelief, its characteristics, and its consequences.

The first point concerning the nature of unbelief is an implicit one. Unbelief can be explained by the failure to be born again or being born from above. This is the implicit teaching of 3:3–8. Jesus is forcefully articulating what must be experienced if one is to enter the kingdom of God, namely, that one must be given new birth/birth from above through the Spirit working. This can only occur according to the will of God (cf. 1:12–13). Unbelief can only be countered by the work of the Spirit in giving new birth, a birth that comes from above.

The second point is explicit: unbelief is the response of not accepting the testimony of Jesus. As dialogue becomes monologue from 3:1–9 into 3:10–15, Jesus points out the reason why Nicodemus (and others like him) are unable to understand this teaching about the new birth. They are by implication unbelievers. Unbelief is explained in 3:11 as the refusal to accept the testimony of Jesus. The vocabulary of unbelief becomes explicit in the commentary on the episode by Jesus and then the narrator: Nicodemus and those he represents have moved from not understanding what Jesus is talking about (v 10) to not receiving Jesus' testimony (v 11). Therefore, they do not believe and will not believe when Jesus speaks to them of heavenly matters (v 12).

The explanatory commentary by the narrator in 3:16–21 follows Jesus' monologue in 3:10–15 accounts for the reason and purpose of Jesus having to be 'lifted up'; the heavenly things Jesus has intimated.[16]

---

14 Cf. Culpepper, *Anatomy*, 90, who suggests the question of 'acceptable faith' is raised by this incident.
15 Klink, *John*, 194, describes Nicodemus as the 'representative Jew *par excellence*'.
16 The use of plurals in v. 11 and shift to the language of κόσμος from v. 16 echoes and confirms the relationship established between Jesus' own and the world in 1:9–11.

In doing the consequences of unbelief are laid out and an important characteristic of unbelief is mentioned.

In terms of the consequences of unbelief, the κόσμος (Jn 3:16) of which Nicodemus is a part stands in a position of condemnation and needs saving. This is confirmed when John observes that the one who does not believe ἤδη κέκριται, ὅτι μὴ πεπίστευκεν (3:18). The κόσμος as the world of humanity does not stand in a neutral position before God, but is sinful and in need of a Saviour (1:10, 29, 3:16–17). Therefore, to not believe in Jesus is to remain in a position of condemnation. In 3:36, this grave picture is further enhanced as God's wrath is said to remain on the unbeliever. An important characteristic of unbelief is outlined when the response of unbelief is described as the response of a people who love darkness and so reject the light that has come into the world (3:19; cf. 1:4–5, 9–10). They do this because their 'deeds were evil' and do not want to be exposed. Unbelief has a moral shape expressed in evil deeds and fear of exposure.

At the conclusion of the chapter the narrator combines shape and consequences as two alternatives are laid out (3:36). Unbelief 'does not obey' (ἀπειθῶν) rather than 'does not believe' (the antonym of belief in the previous clause) and is tantamount to disobedience. The consequence is wrath as opposed to eternal life.

2.4 Summary

The opening section of the Gospel presents a wide ranging and general portrayal of unbelief. Unbelief is presented as part of the broader cosmic story told of the relationship between God and his creation. It is characterised by ignorance and rejection. This general picture is localised in the specific story of Jesus coming to his own people. Ignorance and rejection will be focussed on his person and work. Unbelief will be characterised by evil deeds but these deeds will be focussed on the rejection of the Son and his claims. The consequences of unbelief are dire: the unbelieving one remains condemned; subject to the wrath of God.

3. Chapters 5–12: Unbelief Explored in the Response of the Jews

The nature, motivations, and manifestations of unbelief are best illustrated by the conflict between Jesus and the Jews in John 5–12. It is here that Jesus is presented as coming to his own and being rejected (cf. 1:11). The section is constructed around a series of conflict narratives where the clams made explicitly and implicitly about Jesus' person and work in chapters 1–4 are continually tested and adjudicated.[17] Comments on incidents from John 5–9 and 12 will fill out the picture of unbelief as it emerges in the portrait of the Jews in the Gospel.

3.1 John 5

Following the narrative of Jesus' healing of a crippled man on the Sabbath, a dispute occurs between Jesus and the Jews in response to his claim that his healing work on the Sabbath is continuing the work of the Father (5:17). This claim amounts to Jesus 'calling God his own Father, making himself equal with God' (5:18). The Jews' response of wanting to persecute and kill Jesus makes it clear that they reject the testimony and work of Jesus. A pattern of the Jews rejecting Jesus' works and accompanying testimony characterises the narrative through to chapter 12 and typifies unbelief as a response. This rejection will find its fulfilment in the passion narratives of John 18–20.

As the dispute between Jesus and the Jews ensues, it is clear that it is not the testimony of Jesus alone that is rejected by unbelief. Jesus presents four witnesses who testify to him: John the Baptist (5:33–35), his works (5:36), the Father (5:37–38), and the Scriptures (5:39). Ultimately behind these testimonies lies the testimony of the Father, who sent John, enables Jesus' works, and speaks through the Scriptures. The unbelief of the Jews is clearly evident in their response to these witnesses. This raises the stakes of unbelief in Jesus considerably. It is not only Jesus who is being rejected but the testimony of the Father has also clearly been rejected. This is expressed christologically in that 'they do not believe in the one whom he has sent' (5:38). It is the response of the

---

17 This is played out in a sequence of informal trials, that form the backbone of the important trial theme used in the Gospel. See Lincoln, *Truth,* for details.

Jews in unbelief towards Jesus that constitutes their not hearing, not seeing and not abiding in the *Father*. This is only possible, of course, only if the words of Jesus are the words of the Father and they exist in the closest possible relationship of identity which was the point made in the opening section of the Gospel (1:1, 18; 3:34).

The tragedy foreshadowed in the prologue (1:11) is played out as Jesus' own people fail to recognise his identity and fail to accept and believe his words.

The discussion of 5:31–47 includes an explicit explanation by Jesus accounting for the reason why the Jews do not believe. The Jews cannot believe in Jesus because they prefer the glory that they receive from other people rather than seek after the glory that comes from the only God (John 5:44). This is proof that they do not have love for God (τήν ἀγάπην τοῦ θεοῦ; objective genitive based on context) within them (5:42).[18]

What is the glory that the Jews receive from one another? Lincoln more broadly speaks of the 'human system of assessing reputation'.[19] Bauckham speaks of glory as honor and reputation, and points out how the Jews are judged negatively for doing what Jesus does not do: accepting glory from humans (5:41), accepting glory from one another (5:44), seeking their own glory (by implication, 7:18; 8:50), glorifying themselves (by implication 8:54) and loving the glory of humans (12:43).[20] Bauckham summarises by suggesting the essential difference between Jesus and the Jews is that while Jesus is God-centred (cf. 5:44; 7:18; 12:43); the Jews are self centred.[21] Unbelief looks for glory in the wrong place.

3.2 Unbelief in John 6

John 6 continues the portrayal of unbelief as being directed against the works and testimony of Jesus. A sign performed, and interpreted by Jesus as testifying to his identity. This is initially not recognised for what

---

18 Carson, *John*, 264.
19 Lincoln, *Truth*, 80.
20 Bauckham, *Glory*, 57.
21 Bauckham, *Glory*, 58.

it is, or to whom it points (John 6:30–34) and is eventually rejected by the Jews (John 6:41, 52) and many of his disciples (6:66).

The contribution of this chapter to the discussion of unbelief revolves around the relationship between God's sovereign electing activity and culpability of human choice to believe or not believe. This is part of a longer discussion prompted perhaps by the observation that Jesus' mission does not seem to be sweeping all before it.

John advances this discussion through statements of Jesus to the effect that believers are those whom the Father has given to Jesus who will come to Jesus (6:37) and those who come, will never be cast out or lost by Jesus (6:37, 39). The implication of this is that unbelievers have not been given by God to Jesus and so will not come to Jesus. John 6:44 makes this explicit when Jesus declares that people cannot come to Him unless they are drawn by the Father to do so. These hints at the discussion of sovereign will of God build on those already laid down in John 1:12–13 and 3:8. This discussion will culminate in an extended reflection in John 12:37–41.

John is suggesting that it is God's electing activity that explains why many have not come to faith.[22] However, it is also clear from this discourse that God's sovereign activity does not mitigate human responsibility. Interspersed between Jesus comments of election are his implicit warnings against unbelief (6:40, 47).[23] The metaphors of eating the bread/flesh and drinking the blood of the Son of Man are used by Jesus to further explicate the need for the appropriate human response (6:50–1, 53–8). Jesus speaks with equal ease of those who are elected to believe and the responsibility of personal belief.[24] The Jews have clearlyseen Jesus and yet have not believed (6:36). God's sovereign activity provides an extra perspective for their unbelief, but does not excuse it.

This same dynamic applies also to those who can be described as Jesus' disciples. To this group of disciples, Jesus similarly discusses

---

22 Culpepper, *Gospel and Letters*, 162. The question of election to unbelief is raised but it is not explicitly taught in the text, despite the temptation to draw the logical inference; cf. Carson, *Divine Sovereignty*, 196.
23 Carson, *John*, 294.
24 Carson, *John*, 291.

elements of both election and responsibility. 'It is the Spirit who gives life' and not the 'flesh' (6:63) echoes John 3:8 and 1:12–13 in particular. The response of unbelief amongst them is simply stated without explanation or qualification (6:64a). This short interaction with these disciples ends with another comment emphasising God's sovereign activity (6:65). Once again, the tension between sovereign election and human responsibility is upheld. Theology becomes reality when the narrator records many of Jesus' followers leaving his group of disciples (Jn 6:66). In the context of Jesus' prior discourse, the reader understands this turning away to be a result of both God's sovereign will and humanity's stubborn refusal to accept and believe in the word and works of Jesus.

3.3 Unbelief in John 7–8

In John 7 and 8 Jesus is presented at the Feast of Tabernacles and again the unbelief of the Jews is displayed in a series of encounters marked by both ignorance, expressed in their questions and misunderstandings (7:11–12, 15, 25–27, 31, 36, 41–42); and rejection expressed in their actions seeking to arrest and kill him (7: 19, 44; 8:59).

Not even a close family relationship can guarantee belief as the first in this section to express unbelief concerning Jesus and his mission are his own family (7:3–5). Jesus reinforces his observation that one reason the 'world' rejects him (hates, 7:7) is because he testifies that its works are evil (cf. 3:20). The use of κόσμος stands as a reminder of the relationship between the Jews and the κόσμος and anticipates the way that in John 13–17 the language of κόσμος will become prominent.

In John 8, Jesus' statements and responses to the Pharisees further the discussion as to why the Jews continue in their unbelief. It is a difficult dialogue. The Pharisees continue to display the ignorance and rejection of Jesus that is typical of the world's response (8:13, 19, 25). In one of the chapter's most controversial sections, even those amongst the Jews who are initially said to believe in Jesus (8:30–31) eventually demonstrate that they too do not believe. They reject Jesus' testimony that they are enslaved to sin and need freedom (8:33), resort to personal insult by calling Jesus a 'Samaritan' and demon-possessed (8:48, 52), and attempt to convict Jesus of sin (8:46). Finally, their unbelief climaxes in their attempt to kill Jesus (8:59). The content and the manner of the Jews' unbelief is again portrayed.

Jesus' response to the disbelieving Jews provides explicit commentary on this unbelief. The first issue is one of origin. The Jews reject the testimony of Jesus because they judge κατὰ τὴν σάρκα (8:15), being ἐκ τῶν κάτω and ἐκ τούτου τοῦ κόσμου (8:21–23). The judgement of the flesh corresponds to the judgement of fallen humanity and the fallen world. As Koester notes, 'a cleft separates the human from the divine' and provides one key explanation for the unbelief of the Jews.[25]

The second issue is one of recognition. The Jews simply fail to know Jesus and his words (8:19, 27–8, 43). This is best summed up in the question of 8:25—'who are you?' This theme is familiar already and is a function now of the Jews being 'from below' and being able to judge only according to the flesh.

The third issue is one of belonging.[26] The Jews do not believe in Jesus because they are not of God (8:47). The logic of Jesus' statement in 8:45–47 is clear: Jesus tells the truth in all that he says. Those who are of God hear and believe Jesus' words; and those not of God do not hear and believe. In the immediate context 'of God' refers to a kind of belonging with filial overtones.[27] The Jews claim to have Abraham as their Father is rejected by Jesus because Abraham's children would have done as Abraham: obey God's voice, follow his requirements, commandments, decrees and laws (8:39).[28] They have responded to Jesus' attempts to tell them the truth that comes from God by seeking to kill him. Jesus points to this as incontrovertible evidence that Abraham is not their father (8:40). The damning alternative is that they belong to the Devil as their actions and behaviour correspond to those of the Devil. Unbelief is therefore explained by the idea of belonging. The question of both origins and belonging is exposed by one's response to the truth.

---

25 Koester, 'Jesus the Way', 361.
26 Hoet, 'Abraham', 197.
27 Hoet, 'Abraham', 197–98. Hoet points out the context does not point to biological or ethnic descent, but a 'belonging' evidenced by a certain trait. Cf. the sense of filial/fatherhood relations in Mt 21:28–31 and Rom 4:11–12.
28 Carson, *John*, 351–2.

3.4 Unbelief in John 9

John 9 depicts a dialogue between the man healed of his blindness and his interlocutors who doubt the veracity and the implications of his healings. In this account we see some of the strategies of unbelief as the Jews deal not with Jesus directly but with a beneficiary of his ministry. It would also appear that the man's own journey to a full-blown confession of trust in Jesus is aided by his interaction with opposition.

After a long lead up in which the miracle is recounted, and some confusion noted amongst the formerly blind man's friends and neighbours, he is brought to the Pharisees/Jews for adjudication. In the face of an apparent miracle or sign the first impulse of unbelief presented is to deny its occurrence (9:18). There is a sense in which the whole discussion is pointless in any case as the circumspection of the man's parents is explained by the fact that anyone who confessed Jesus would be cast out of the synagogue (9:22). A verdict has already been reached on Jesus and anyone who would support him. There is a close-mindedness to the belief portrayed.

As the interrogation ensues 'the theme of knowing drenches the dialogue'.[29] Three times the man confesses his ignorance (12, 25, 36); three times the Pharisees confidently state what they do know (16, 24, 29), despite what appears to be the evidence before them, as the formerly blind man points out (9:25). The overall thrust of the Gospel thus far has been the ignorance of unbelief and these exchanges illustrate that as well as demonstrate the invincibility of that ignorance.

Unbelief moves to rejection as the man is reviled for his ignorance, comparative standing, and spiritual state (9:28, 34) and then, in a display of naked power, driven from their presence (9:34).

3.5 Unbelief in John 12

The final word on unbelief in John 5–12 comes at the end of chapter 12 in a summary spoken by the narrator. This is a reflection on Jesus' ministry and especially the response that has been recorded to his signs and works.

Unbelief dominates this discourse, as the narrator seeks to account

---

29 Klink, *John*, 448.

for the lack of response to Jesus despite him doing 'so many signs before them (12:37).[30] The summary is focussed on the response of the Jews, Jesus' own, seeking to account for it.

The response is explained in explicitly predestinarian terms (12:38–41), yet it is bracketed by remarks of distinctly human culpable terms (12:37, 43), maintaining the tension observed previously.

John turns to Isaiah to show that unbelief was predicted in Scripture and in a sense necessitated by it (12:38, 40).[31] John states that the Jews did not believe (v 37, οὐκ ἐπίστευον εἰς αὐτόν) because they could not believe (v 39, ἠδύναντο πιστεύειν). The statement concerning choice is qualified by a statement concerning ability. It is then made clear via a quote from Isaiah 6 that it is God who has actively and purposefully blinded and hardened eyes and hearts.

John draws deeply on Isaiah's theology via the dual citation of Isaiah 53 and Isaiah 6. He identifies Jesus with the servant king of Isaiah 53. He identifies the prophetic message of Isaiah and the words and works of Jesus. Finally he suggests that the unbelief in Jesus' ministry, the rejection of the message and the miraculous works ('the arm of the Lord') is a mirror of the rejection by Isaiah's contemporaries.[32] Jewish rejection of God's word and works is nothing new: they rejected Jesus just as they had rejected Isaiah. The metanarrative of the prologue describing the rejection of the world by the word played itself out in Isaiah's time and played itself out in Jesus' time.

The reason for the obduracy of both Isaiah's and Jesus' contemporaries is given in the Isaiah 6:10 quotation. The blinding and hardening of the Jews by God not only accounts for why they respond in unbelief, but also fulfils the purposes of God's prophetic message that salvation will come by a suffering servant.[33] This judicial hardening means that unbelief is woven into God's plans for the salvation of his people: he is not taken by surprise and it cannot ultimately thwart his plans.

In the face of this strong statement of sovereignty, John concludes

---

30 The referent of 'they' and 'them' are widely taken as the Jewish crowd. Given the summary nature of the passage, it could possibly have a wider referent to all who have responded with unbelief, which the Gospel has presented as the Jews up to this point.
31 Köstenberger, *John*, 391; Ridderbos, *Gospel*, 444
32 Beale and Carson, *Commentary*, 477–79.
33 Beale and Carson, *Commentary*, 481–82; Moloney, *Gospel*, 364.

the public ministry of Jesus with a general appeal to all who listen (12:44, 45, 46, 47, 48) to come to him, and therefore to the Father. This carries on the pattern observed in John 6 of the juxtaposition of the sovereignty of God with the assumption of human capacity for response, and therefore responsibility.

3.6 Summary

The section from 5–12 has been marked by escalating rejection of Jesus by the Jews. They show that they neither know or accept who he is and reject him in violent terms. Their actions show unbelief as characterised by ignorance and rejection of Jesus' testimony concerning himself and his mission and any testimony from others to the same. This in turn points to a rejection of the Father who sent him. Unbelief is explained in terms of origins and belonging. Those who originate from the 'world-below' do not and, in fact, cannot, judge properly the identity of the one from above and therefore receive him who originates from the 'heavenly-above'. The actions of unbelief demonstrate both origins and belonging. Unbelief is therefore characterised by a seeking of glory, honour, reputation from one another, from 'below'.

4. Chapters 13–17: The Universal Problem of Unbelief

The subject of unbelief shifts from the unbelieving Jews of the previous section to the hating world in this section. The specific rejection of the Jewish people which served as an example of the κόσμος' rejection of Jesus is now generalised to the κόσμος in Jesus' warnings to his disciples. Verbal constructions of 'not believe' occur only twice, once in reference to Phillip and once of the κόσμος. The verb μισέω occurs nine times, directed at God, Jesus and the disciples (on account of Jesus) eight times and once in fulfilment of an Old Testament quotation. The term κόσμος occurs 40 times. As such, the κόσμος comes to prominence as the main 'character' carrying the theme of unbelief. All of the features previously observed in the examination of chapters 1–12 relating to the theme of unbelief are reprised in this section, with a concentration of material in the section John 15:18–16:4.

4.1 John 15:18–16:4 The Hatred of the World

This section of Jesus' extended speech warns the disciples of the persecution that they will face at the hands of the world (15:18, 20). The world is said to hate, in turn, Jesus' disciples (15:18), Jesus (15:18, 23, 24) and the Father (15:23, 24). The unbelief of the Jews in the Jesus' public ministry is now recast as the hatred of the world.

Jesus provides explicit reasons for the world's hatred of the disciples, which draws upon the themes already developed in the unbelief of the Jews in the first part of the gospel.[34] The foundational reason is that the κόσμος has rejected the Father and the Son. This foundational reason is further elaborated in four ways.

The first reason is one of belonging (15:19; cf. 17:14, 16). The disciples ἐκ τοῦ κόσμος οὐκ ἐστε, not because they are ontologically alien to the world, but because Jesus asserts ἐγὼ ἐξελεξάμην ὑμᾶς ἐκ τοῦ κόσμου. They have been separated out of world to which they once belonged (cf. 6:70–71).[35] Just as Jesus was not of this world and so was not received by this world and rejected by it, so also the disciples who have been called out of this world will face the same rejection.

The second reason is one of knowledge (15:21; 17:25). At the root of it, the world does not οἶδα God, and in fact hates God (15:21, 23). In rejecting the Sender, they reject the One sent. This echoes the disputes in the previous sections between Jesus and the Jews, where Jesus had spoken about his identity and the various testimonies to himself which was wholly rejected by the unbelieving Jews (5:30ff; 7:28ff; 8:19, 51). Consequently, the world refuses to keep the words of the master and they will respond likewise to the servants of the master (15:20, 22; cf. 3:36, 12:48).

Third, Jesus' coming exposes the sin of the world and renders it without excuse (15:22). He inaugurates the judgement of the world.[36] This recalls Jesus' earlier explanation of the world's rejection of him because he testifies to its evil works (7:7; cf. 3:18–20). This will continue as Jesus speaks in 16:8 of the coming of the Helper to empower the disciples to continue to convict the world of sin.

---

34 de Jonge, 'Conflict', 348.
35 Salier, 'World', 81.
36 Klink, *John*, 666.

The final reason is a scriptural one (15:25). This quote sets the preceding comments on the κόσμος in the context of, and with respect to, Jesus' dealings with the Jews in the first part of the gospel.[37] The link between the Jews and the world is thereby reinforced. The response of the world to Jesus in hatred, exemplified by the Jews, is not something new and unexplainable (cf. 5:39, 45–47; 8:39ff; 12:46ff). This quotation comes from Psalm 35:19 or 69:4. Jesus is cast as a type of David and as the messianic David was hated, so also the true Messiah who is his descendant.[38] Not only is this hatred irrational, but the very source of Jewish claim to receive God's word condemns them in their unbelief. This same source condemns the world in its unbelief.[39]

4.2 Conclusions

The subject of unbelief shifts in focus from the Jews of 1–12 to the κόσμος in this section. At the same time we need to note that Jewish unbelief and rejection of Jesus has already been set in the context of the world's unbelief and rejection (cf. 1:9–11). As the Gospel shifts from recounting the public ministry of Jesus to the Jews to Jesus' preparation of the disciples for their ministry in his absence, the response of unbelief of the Jews towards Jesus becomes the type of the expected response of the κόσμος towards Jesus' disciples.

The response of unbelief is universal. While the Jews may have exemplified it in the previous section, it is the κόσμος in its sinful rebellion that stands in unbelief and hatred against the Father, Jesus His Son, and the disciples of Jesus. Questions of belonging and knowledge have been raised as drivers of the unbelief of the κόσμος. At the same time the clear correspondences between Jewish unbelief and the unbelief of the world suggest that other elements of Jewish unbelief, such as the seeking of glory in the wrong place will be elements of worldly unbelief.

---

37 Salier, 'World', 82; de Jonge, 'Conflict', 348.
38 Carson, *John*, 527.
39 Salier, 'World', 82.

5. Chapters 18–21: The Judgement of Unbelief

The final section of the Gospel recounts the playing out of the narrative as Jesus goes to the cross. In terms of the theme of unbelief there is little to be added other than to observe that the apparent triumph of unbelief takes place as the Jews and the world, represented by Pilate, collude to put Jesus to death.

6. Conclusions

While the aim of the Gospel suggests a positive presentation of Jesus aimed at belief it is clear that the theme of unbelief shadows the Gospel's presentation of belief throughout. The Gospel plainly asserts the response of *unbelief* on the part of the Jews and has framed this presentation within the presentation of the response of 'the world' to Jesus. It is now possible to suggest why this theme is prominent and how it contributes to the Gospel's message.

Unbelief in John's Gospel is presented as a rejection of the testimony of and to Jesus and ultimately a rejection of the revelation of the Father, which Jesus brings. Unbelief is a refusal to accept any and all of the witnesses to Jesus presented in the Gospel.

From the Fourth Gospel's point of view the theme reflects the reality of Jesus' ministry that it was met by unbelief. The public ministry to the Jews is outlined in chapters 5–12 under the rubric of John 1:11. The final section of the gospel (Jn 18–19) shows both the Jews and the World combining in their response of unbelief, rejection and hatred of Jesus. John has presented unbelief as a universal phenomenon and response to Jesus and his claims. The twin problems of not knowing, and rejecting, typify the response of the Jews and the world to Jesus. Doubtless, the historical reality of Jesus' ministry is played out in the experience of the early reader, as promised in John 15, and the faithful reader of the Gospel is prepared to live in the light of this response to their own efforts in living and testifying to Jesus in their own context.

The narrator does not simply tell the story, but seeks to provide both insight and explanation for the phenomenon of unbelief. This is particularly evident in the explicit commentary of the narrator and also the content of several of Jesus' discourses. It is this purpose that best explains the presence of unbelief so prominently through the narrative. The response of unbelief against Jesus, who has come as the saviour of his people and the world, raises questions as to why this happened, and what does it mean.

Ultimately unbelief is explained by two aspects of the human-divine divide. The first consists of origins and belonging as an explanation for unbelief. The second is the human responsibility-divine sovereignty antimony.

From an anthropological perspective, unbelief is tied to an understanding of humanity as being from below; of the flesh in the sense of weakness; and belonging to the world and the Devil. There is culpable element of unbelief that contains a strong moral component. Unbelievers have a preference for continuing in evil deeds and receiving the glory that comes from other human beings rather than from God. Unbelief is tied to the core of being sinful human beings.

From a theological perspective, unbelief is not a surprise. Unbelief is explained as a patterned response that marks God's dealing with his world and people; as the fulfilment of prophecy; and falling within the ambit of his saving plan and purposes.

The response of unbelief by the Jews in particular and the κόσμος as a whole is not unexpected and incredulous as it would first seem. As it has been in the distant past of the Old Testament, as it was in the life and ministry of Jesus and as it will be in the life of the disciples, the response of unbelief shows both the utter sinfulness and helplessness of humanity.

At the same time the theme of unbelief, as Schnackenburg hints, highlights the generous grace of God in his sovereign election of sinners who cannot save themselves. The reader who comes to recognise their plight, mired in unbelief, can be comforted by the message that trust in Jesus Christ, his person and work, and therefore life is possible on the sole basis of God's gracious and sovereign election (John 1:12–13).

Finally, for the believing reader of the Gospel, the exploration of unbelief provides a counterpoint to the broader presentation of the kind of belief that is the appropriate response to the person of Christ. The presentation of unbelief generates impetus in the challenge to the audience of the gospel to respond not with unbelief, but with belief and provides a mirror into which to look to assess their own response. As unbelief is described as the rejection of the testimony to and of Christ and a seeking after false glory; as it is explained through the various human and divine factors, the audience is left with no doubt as to what and how their response is to be while being comforted that it is the gracious and sovereign work of God to enable that response.

Bibliography

Bauckham, R. *Gospel of Glory: Major Themes in Johannine Theology* (Grand Rapids: Baker Academic, 2015).

Beale, G. K. & Carson, D.A. (eds) *Commentary on the New Testament Use of the Old Testament* (Grand Rapids: Baker, 2007).

Bieringer, R., Pollefeyt, D. & Vandecasteele-Vanneuville, F. (eds.) *Anti-Judaism and the Fourth Gospel* (Louisville: Westminster John Knox, 2001).

Bultmann, R. *The Gospel of John: a commentary* (Oxford: Blackwell, 1971 ET).

Carson, D.A. *The Gospel According to John* (Grand Rapids: Eerdmans, 1991).

Carson, D.A. *Divine Sovereignty and Human Responsibility* (Grand Rapids: Baker, 1994).

Culpepper, R.A. *The Anatomy of the Fourth Gospel: A Study in Literary Design* (Philadelphia: Fortress, 1983).

Culpepper, R.A. *The Gospel and Letters of John* (Nashville: Abingdon, 1998).

de Jonge, Marinus 'The Conflict between Jesus and the Jews and the Radical Christology of the Fourth Gospel', *Journal of Religious Studies* 20.4 (1993), 341–55.

Hoet, H. '"Abraham is our Father" (John 8:39). The Gospel of John and Jewish-Christian Dialogue', in R. Bierenger, D. Pollefeyt, F. Vandecasteele-Vanneuville (eds.), *Anti-Judaism and the Fourth Gospel* (Louisville: Westminster John Knox, 2001), 187–201.

Ho, Benjamin	'Unbelief in the Fourth Gospel: Literary and Theological Significance', (Unpublished Project, Moore College, Sydney, 2008).
Kierspel, L.	*The Jews in the Fourth Gospel: Parallelism, Function, and Context* (WUNT 2.220; Tubingen: Mohr Siebeck, 2006).
Klink, E.W. III.	*John* (ZECNT; Grand Rapids: Zondervan, 2016).
Koester, C.	'Hearing, Seeing, and Believing in the Gospel of John', *Biblica* 70.3 (1989), 327–48.
Koester, C.R.	'Jesus the Way, the Cross, and the World according to the Gospel of John', *Word & World* 21.4 (2001), 360–69.
Köstenberger, A.J.	*John* (BECNT; Grand Rapids: Baker Academic, 2004).
Lincoln, A.T.	*Truth on Trial: The Lawsuit Motif in the Fourth Gospel* (Peabody: Hendrickson, 2000).
Moloney, F.J.	The Gospel of John (Sacra Pagina; Collegeville: Liturgical Press, 1998).
Pryor, John	'Jesus and Israel in the Fourth Gospel: John 1:11', *Novum Testamentum* 32 (1990), 201–18.
———.	*Evangelist of the Covenant People: The Narrative and Themes of the Fourth Gospel* (London: Darton, Longman and Todd, 1992).
Ridderbos, H.	*The Gospel According to John: A Theological Commentary* (Grand Rapids: Eerdmans, 1997 ET).
Salier, W. H.	'The World of John's Gospel: The Function and Meaning of *kosmos* in the Gospel of John', (Unpublished Master's Thesis; Moore College, Sydney, 1999).
———.	*The Rhetorical Impact of the Semeia in the Gospel of John* (WUNT 2.186; Tubingen: Mohr Siebeck, 2004).
Thompson, M.M.	'Signs and Faith in the Fourth Gospel', *Bulletin of Biblical Research* 1 (1991), 89–108.
Tenney, M.C.	'Topics from the Gospel of John: Part IV: The Growth of Belief', *Bibliotheca Sacra* 132 (1975), 343–57.
Schnackenburg, R.	*The Gospel According to St. John*. Vol. 1 (London: Burns & Oates, 1982 ET).
Von Wahlde, U.C.	'The Johannine "Jews": A Critical Survey', *New Testament Studies* 28.1 (1982), 33–60.

www.ingramcontent.com/pod-product-compliance
Lightning Source LLC
Chambersburg PA
CBHW071725080526
44588CB00013B/1894